**CONSTRUCTION
DEPARTMENT
LIBRARY**

VALUE MANAGEMENT FOR CONSTRUCTION

CONSTRUCTION MANAGEMENT AND ENGINEERING
Edited by John F. Peel Brahtz

CONSTRUCTION PERFORMANCE CONTROL BY NETWORKS
H. N. Ahuja

CONSTRUCTION MANAGEMENT: Principles and Practices
Stanley Goldhaber, Chandra K. Jha,
and Manuel C. Macedo, Jr.

VALUE MANAGEMENT FOR CONSTRUCTION
Manuel C. Macedo, Jr., Paul V. Dobrow, and
Joseph J. O'Rourke

VALUE MANAGEMENT FOR CONSTRUCTION

MANUEL C. MACEDO, JR.
PAUL V. DOBROW
JOSEPH J. O'ROURKE

A Wiley-Interscience Publication
JOHN WILEY & SONS

New York • Chichester • Brisbane • Toronto • Singapore

Copyright © 1978 by John Wiley & Sons, Inc.

All rights reserved. Published simultaneously in Canada.

Reproduction or translation of any part of this work
beyond that permitted by Sections 107 or 108 of the
1976 United States Copyright Act without the permission
of the copyright owner is unlawful. Requests for
permission or further information should be addressed to
the Permissions Department, John Wiley & Sons, Inc.

Library of Congress Cataloging in Publication Data:

Macedo, Manuel C.   1942–
  Value management for construction.

  (Construction management and engineering series)
  "A Wiley-Interscience publication."
  Bibliography: p.
  Includes index:
    1. Construction industry—Management.
2. Value analysis (Cost control) I. Dobrow,
Paul V., joint author. II. O'Rourke, Joseph J.,
joint author. III. Title.
HD9715.A2M25   658'.92'4   78-6255
ISBN 0-471-03166-6

Printed in the United States of America
10 9 8 7 6 5

SERIES PREFACE

Industry observers agree that most construction practitioners do not fully exploit the state of the art. We concur in this general observation. Further, we have acted by directing this series of works on Construction Management and Engineering to the continuing education and reference needs of today's practitioners.

Our design is inspired by the burgeoning technologies of systems engineering, modern management, information systems, and industrial engineering. We believe that the latest developments in these areas will serve to close the state of the art gap if they are astutely considered by management and knowledgeably applied in operations with personnel, equipment, and materials.

When considering the pressures and constraints of the world economic environment, we recognize an increasing trend toward large-scale operations and greater complexity in the construction product. To improve productivity and maintain acceptable performance standards, today's construction practitioner must broaden his concept of innovation and seek to achieve excellence through knowledgeable utilization of the resources. Therefore our focus is on skills and disciplines that support productivity, quality, and optimization in all aspects of the total facility acquisition process and at all levels of the management hierarchy.

We distinctly believe our perspective to be aligned with current trends and changes that portend the future of the construction industry. The books in this series should serve particularly well as textbooks at the graduate and senior undergraduate levels in a university construction curriculum or continuing education program.

JOHN F. PEEL BRAHTZ

La Jolla, California
February 1977

PREFACE

Because of the rapid pace of changing technology, inflation, and the new problems of energy and environment, value management is a management tool the construction industry cannot afford to be without. With value management, life-cycle costs can be reduced without sacrificing quality, esthetics, maintainability, or other functions. It creates an atmosphere where creative thinking is encouraged and change is accepted. Value management is an organized, systematic approach to obtaining optimum value for every construction dollar spent.

In the traditional method of designing a facility, the designer develops plans and specifications that conform to the criteria of the owner. With these criteria, he must determine which equipment and methods are most suitable from the standpoint of economy, function, maintenance, and appearance. Generally, each selection is made by an engineer or architect working on a particular aspect of the design. For example, the electrical engineer selects the generators, conductors, panel boxes, and related equipment; the civil engineer selects the sewage and water systems; and so forth.

In some cases economic studies are conducted—for site selection, fuel selection, and structural system, for example. However, in most instances any selections or studies are made by an individual or by a group from within the same discipline. In some cases, a team is called together, but normally no formal job plan is followed, nor are any employees assigned full-time to organize and coordinate activities or to follow through on any new ideas generated.

Each discipline generates its own requirements, reviews these requirements, establishes and modifies its particular criteria, and even modifies the standards and criteria of the owner. This approach may not lead to decisions that are most economical for the end function of the facility. Instead, it encourages economical decisions within each area with maximum safety factors deemed necessary by each discipline. Although this system is not without merit, it tends to sacrifice overall system performance in maximizing subsystem performance. This is known as suboptimization.

The result is that total life-cycle costs are not adequately considered. The emphasis on first cost and the failure to consider the effect of related cost elements are probably the greatest shortcomings in today's planning, programming, and designing of facilities. These hidden costs have a considerable impact on cost of ownership. For example, the total cost of a hospital is about 10.5 times its initial costs. In addition to initial cost, life cycle costs include:

- Maintenance and operation costs.
- Money charges such as interest and insurance.
- Future income or needs, such as rentable or usable space, future expansion, and alterations.
- Fringe costs not subject to ready dollar analysis, such as esthetics and durability.
- Ownership logistic costs such as materials delivery, serviceability, and personnel access.
- Service and operating personnel costs, such as janitorial services and operating personnel (i.e., engineers, doctors in hospitals).
- Real estate and property taxes.

Each discipline's decision can affect costs in other areas. And it is these cumulative costs, which generally are the result of the A/E's decisions, that have the greatest impact on the total cost of the facility. It is in the overlapping area that value management has the greatest savings potential. It emphasizes the need for a system approach. For example, in an effort to optimize costs in his area, the architect can adversely affect the cost areas of all other disciplines. Therefore, a system approach is required for cost-effective decisions in major design areas.

With very few unique exceptions, cost is the predominant factor in construction, whether an owner is building to a budget, or a speculator or investor is building for a profit. During the past several years, the construction industry has been plagued by spiraling costs. Although the ruinous rate of inflation of the mid-1970s has abated somewhat, inflation will be a significant factor for the foreseeable future. Further, owners will have to cope with increasing costs of energy and environmentally related expenses. In addition, as technology advances, they will have to be prepared to alter their buildings to prevent them from becoming obsolete.

Now and in the future, cost control is and will be an absolute necessity. Since they usually do not have the talent or expertise, owners normally look to the architect or constructor to perform this function. Frequently, however, architects are not familiar enough with the building process to control costs as closely as the owner desires. Furthermore, during construction, there are no incentives for the constructor to reduce the cost of building, and often large incentives to increase it. For example, it is common practice in some sections of the industry to bid jobs low and make money on changes and "extras." In negotiations for changes and extras, the general contractor tends to side with subcontractors against the owner. The contractor, after all, will probably work with the same subcontractor on another job, while his commitments to the owner beyond the contract may be negligible.

The goal of this book is twofold: first, to introduce and define the value management concept; second, to discuss those principles and practices that make the value management concept work.

Value Management for Construction is innovative in several aspects. First, it truly deals with the management of value. It is concerned with the management of the life-cycle cost of a facility—from planning, to design, to procurement, to construction, to operation and maintenance. The reduction of construction and life-cycle costs in projects will ultimately benefit everyone—owners, designers, constructors, and industry. Second, it relates the value management concept to problem solving. Every major decision to be made can be treated as a problem to be solved. *Value Management for Construction* explains how the value management concept can be employed by management as a problem-solving tool. Third, procurement planning, project control, and fiscal/cost control usually are treated as independent and isolated functions. Quite often there is no procurement planning, especially for the procurement of long-lead items. Yet these items can have a significant impact on total project cost. *Value Management for Construction* deals with these items in depth and brings them within the value management concept. Finally, it relates the systems approach to value management. Projects are becoming much larger and more complicated, and taking longer to complete. Activity at the construction site is only part of the construction process. What is not observable is the office work of planning, designing, estimating, negotiating, purchasing, scheduling, expediting, review, control, and whatever else must be done to complete a quality project within budget and on schedule. These activities taken together represent the system that will produce the final product. It is as if value is flowing through the system from conception to occupancy, with each activity within the system adding to or modifying the value. Therefore, by applying the systems approach to the management of value, it is possible to optimize the benefits from the value management concept and maintain maximum control over total project cost.

Value Management for Construction brings together the current thinking on value management. It explains what is happening now in the industry and what we expect to see happening in the near future. Our hope is to start an industrywide dialogue on the value management concept. We have not attempted to develop an inflexible methodology. Nor do we consider this book the final word on value management. The experience of the recent past has proven the validity and usefulness of value management, but the next several years will see the concept revised and perfected into a classical management tool.

This is not a how-to-do-it book. Neither is it oriented toward ivory-tower academicians. *Value Management for Construction* is written primarily for managers and other decision-makers. Its contents are aimed at executives, construction managers, project managers, architect-engineers, general contractors, realtors, financiers, lawyers, and others involved with the planning, design, construction, operation, and financing of building projects.

Value Management for Construction can also be used for graduate, upper level undergraduate, and professional courses. We have tried to present a balanced compromise between theory and practice to serve both the practicing office and the college classroom.

MANUEL C. MACEDO, JR.
PAUL V. DOBROW
JOSEPH J. O'ROURKE

Washington, D.C.
Granada Hills, California
March 1978

CONTENTS

CHAPTER 1 HISTORY AND EVOLUTION OF VALUE
ANALYSIS AND VALUE ENGINEERING   1

1.1 Introduction, 1
1.2 Background, 1
1.3 Roadblocks, 5
1.4 Progress of VA/VE, 6
1.5 Armed Services Procurement Regulation, 8
1.6 Other Interests, 9
1.7 Summary, 12

CHAPTER 2 OVERCOMING RESISTANCE TO VALUE
MANAGEMENT   14

2.1 Introduction, 14
2.2 Benefits of Value Management, 16
2.3 Management Participation, 20
    2.3.1 Managing Innovation, 21
    2.3.2 When Is An Organization Ready for Value
           Management?, 22
    2.3.3 Implementing the Value Management Program, 24
    2.3.4 Management Control of Value Management, 26
2.4 Value Management Organization, 29
    2.4.1 Two Types of Value Management Functions, 30
    2.4.2 Key Variables Affecting Organization Structure, 31
    2.4.3 Value Management in the Producing Activity
           (Architect–Engineer, Construction Manager,
           Contractor), 34
    2.4.4 Value Management Organization in the Procuring
           Activity (Owner), 36

2.4.5   Determination of the Level of Effort, 37

2.5   Human Factors of Value Management Resistance and
       Acceptance, 38

2.5.1   Human Relations, 38

2.5.2   Why Unnecessary Costs Are Created, 40

2.5.3   Resisting Innovation, 43

2.5.4   Motivation and Incentives, 43

2.6   Training, 47

2.6.1   Techniques for Training Operating Personnel, 48

2.6.2   Selecting and Training Personnel, 54

2.6.3   Other Training Techniques, 55

2.6.4   Implementation of Training, 56

2.7   Summary, 57

CHAPTER 3   THE SYSTEMS APPROACH AND VALUE
            MANAGEMENT   59

3.1   Introduction to the Systems Approach, 59

3.2   Compatibility of the Systems Approach and Value
       Management, 61

3.3   Application of Value Management Through the Systems
       Approach, 63

3.3.1   Defining the Program, 65

3.4   Design to Cost/Life-cycle Cost, 74

3.4.1   How DTC/LCC Works, 75

3.5   The Bond-Energy Algorithm, 77

3.5.1   Developing Facility Requirements, 80

3.5.2   Adjacency Analysis, 87

3.5.3   Development Planning, 89

3.6   Systems/Value Management Philosophy, 91

CHAPTER 4   OPPORTUNITIES FOR VALUE MANAGEMENT   94

4.1   Introduction, 94

4.2   High Potential Value Management Areas, 95

4.3   Timing of Value Management Opportunities, 98

4.4   Design, 100

4.4.1   Present Method of Designing a Facility, 101

4.4.2   Performing Value Management During Design, 102

4.4.3   Designing for Value, 104

4.5   Construction, 107

4.6   Operations and Maintenance, 111

CONTENTS

4.7 Costing and Scheduling Techniques, 111
4.8 Procurement Planning, 114
4.9 Problem Solving, 115
4.10 Relationship to Other Cost Awareness Programs, 116
4.11 Circulating Valid Value Changes, 118
4.12 Realizing Value Management Opportunities, 119

CHAPTER 5   PROCUREMENT   122

5.1 Introduction, 122
5.2 The Procurement Organization, 122
5.3 Contract and Statement of Work Preparation, 123
5.4 Market Research, 124
5.5 Guidance Sources, 127
5.6 Procurement Activities, 129
      5.6.1 Two-Step Procurement, 131
5.7 Contract Management, 131
5.8 Contracting, 135
5.9 Indirect Advantages, 137
5.10 Other Procurement Activities, 138
      5.10.1 Purchasing, 138
      5.10.2 Vendor/Supplier Evaluations, 138

CHAPTER 6   FISCAL/COST CONTROL AND PROJECT
            CONTROL   140

6.1 Introduction, 140
6.2 C/SCSC Overview, 141
6.3 C/SCSC Implementation, 142
6.4 Project Management and Controls, 147
6.5 Configuration and Data Management, 148
      6.5.1 Configuration Management, 149
      6.5.2 Data Management, 203

CHAPTER 7   APPLICATION OF VALUE MANAGEMENT   207

7.1 Introduction, 207
7.2 Creating and Maintaining a Value Management Program, 207
7.3 The In-House Value Management Program, 208
      7.3.1 The Value Manager, 208

7.3.2 Responsibilities of the Value Manager, 209
7.3.3 Measuring the Effectiveness of the Value Management Program, 210
7.4 Contract Clauses, 215
7.4.1 Types of Value Clauses, 219
7.5 Consultants, 226
7.6 Value Management Workshops, 227
7.6.1 Information Required for a VM Workshop Study Project, 229
7.6.2 Composition of a VM Workshop Study Team, 230
7.7 Summary, 230

CHAPTER 8   VALUE MANAGEMENT METHODOLOGY   231

8.1 Introduction, 231
8.2 Functional Analysis System Technique (FAST), 231
8.3 The Job Plan, 240
8.4 Summary of the Job Plan, 252

CHAPTER 9   CREATIVITY—THE BACKBONE OF VALUE
               MANAGEMENT   254

9.1 Introduction, 254
9.2 Definition, 254
9.3 Hypotheses Concerning Creativity, 255
9.4 Attributes of Creative Individuals, 255
9.5 Negative Factors Affecting Creativity, 257
9.5.1 Internal, 258
9.5.2 External, 259
9.6 Positive Factors Affecting Creativity, 260
9.7 Creativity in Value Management, 261
9.8 The Creative Process, 263
9.9 Techniques for Creative Problem Solving, 264
9.10 Summary, 269
9.11 Generalized Creativity Checklist, 270

CHAPTER 10   MANAGING PROJECT VALUE THROUGH
                LIFE-CYCLE COSTING   273

10.1 Introduction, 273
10.2 Life-Cycle Costs, 278

10.3 Basic Concepts, 289
    10.3.1 Tradeoff Analysis, 290
    10.3.2 Design to Cost, 291
    10.3.3 Sunk Cost, 292
    10.3.4 Salvage Value, 292
    10.3.5 Present Value, Discount Rate, and Uniform Annuity, 292
    10.3.6 Price Level Changes, 296
    10.3.7 Equivalent Uniform Annual Cost, 297
    10.3.8 Uncertainty and Sensitivity Analysis, 299
10.4 Life-Cycle Cost Analysis, 300

CHAPTER 11   PROBLEM SOLVING AND PROJECT VALUE   306

11.1 Introduction, 306
11.2 Nature of a Problem, 308
11.3 Systems Approach to Problem Analysis, 311
11.4 Decision Making, 314
11.5 Potential Problem Analysis, 317

CHAPTER 12   CASE STUDIES   319

12.1 Life-Cycle Cost Analysis: Office Building Energy System, 319
12.2 Value Management Analysis: Site Selection, 327
    12.2.1 Evaluation of Site Organization Alternatives, 328
    12.2.2 Benefits and Economic Analyses, 335
12.3 Value Management Studies at the R. D. Bailey Lake Project, 341
    12.3.1 The Dam, 341
    12.3.2 The Access Road, Service Road, Recreation Area, and
        Operations Facilities, 344
    12.3.3 The Intake Structure, 348
12.4 A VM Study of the Southeastern Signal School (Phase III), Fort
    Gordon, Georgia, 350
    12.4.1 Site Layout, 350
    12.4.2 Tactical Equipment Shops and Facilities, 351

CHAPTER 13   OUTLOOK FOR VALUE MANAGEMENT   357

13.1 Background, 357
13.2 Incentives and Facilities Projects, 357
13.3 Incentive Systems, 361
    13.3.1 Nonfinancial Incentives, 361
    13.3.2 Financial Incentives, 362

13.4 Incentivization, 363
13.5 Value Management in an Operating Environment, 365
    13.5.1 Static and Time-phased Costs, 366
    13.5.2 Assets and Sunk Costs, 369
    13.5.3 Range versus Point Estimates, 369
    13.5.4 Estimating the Operating and Support Expense, 370
13.6 Life-Cycle Cost Management, 371
    13.6.1 Proposed Life-Cycle Cost System, 372
    13.6.2 Contracting Approach to Life-Cycle Cost
           Management, 374
    13.6.3 Warranties as a Life-Cycle Cost Management Tool, 375
13.7 Outlook, 376

BIBLIOGRAPHY, 379

INDEX, 383

VALUE MANAGEMENT FOR CONSTRUCTION

CHAPTER 1

HISTORY AND EVOLUTION OF VALUE ANALYSIS AND VALUE ENGINEERING

1.1 INTRODUCTION

Most witnesses to the evolution of value analysis (VA) and value engineering (VE) seem to agree that the World War II era opened the door to value analysis and was the beginning of a systematic, functional approach to cost reduction. This would explain why so many authors on the subject start their VA text with "back in 1947." It cannot be denied that the thrust of value analysis became quite evident during that period. However, as recent interviews have revealed,* the cost consciousness that led to Lawrence D. Miles being called "Father of Value Analysis" was evident much earlier.

1.2 BACKGROUND

In late 1938, Larry Miles, a design engineer for General Electric in Schenectady, New York, who was "divinely discontented" with the way things were going at the plant, went to see his supervisor, W. C. White, Manager of Vacuum Tube Engineering. Miles asked, "Doesn't anyone in GE care what things cost?" White immediately called Harry Erlicher, Vice President of Purchasing and Traffic and related the incident, which prompted Erlicher to confer with Miles and reassign him to Central Purchasing, directly under Erlicher.

When war broke out in Europe and the United States recognized its

*April and May, 1977.

1

obligations, U.S. industry was unprepared to meet the challenge. Transition from commercial goods to war materiel became a paramount objective throughout the nation. It was not long before every defense facility was scheduled to capacity, with priorities ever increasing. Steel of every description was totally committed, as was copper, bronze, tin, nickel, bearings, electrical resistors, capacitors, and a host of other vital products and materials.

Miles was assigned the task of "finding, negotiating for, and getting" a number of these vital materials: materials to expand production of turbo-superchargers from 50 per week to 1000 per week for B-24s, capacitors and resistors for skyrocketing military electronic needs, armament parts for expanding production of B-29s, and so on. In this environment, it was impossible to stop short of achieving the essential results.

Frequently, suppliers, already overextended, said No to increased schedules or new necessary products. In this desperate situation, Miles turned to basic considerations: "If I can't get the product, I've got to get the *function*. How can you provide the function by using some machine or labor or material that *is* obtainable?" Time and again there was another way to do the required task. Engineering tests and approvals were rushed and schedules were met. Thus, "function" grew in vitality, to mature later into the development of VA/VE techniques.

To assure the availability of materials for vital programs, Miles usually worked two days each week in vendors' plants, one to two days in GE plants, and one day in the Pentagon maintaining priorities, spending Saturdays and Sundays in his own office.

Because of Miles's successful application of the functional approach throughout the war years, Erlicher asked him in 1944 to become a GE Purchasing Agent. Now Miles faced another challenge—to maintain a competitive position in the marketplace for GE products. During the three years that followed, Miles applied the functional approach to all of his purchasing and achieved maximum results for that particular plant.

In 1947, Miles told Erlicher that he believed that much good could come to GE if he were relieved of line operating responsibilities and assigned full time to cost reduction work in the central purchasing office. Erlicher agreed, moving him later that year back to Schenectady, where his activity was named the Purchasing Department Cost Reduction Section (PDCRS).

Miles and his staff studied products and costs on a functional basis, associating costs with functions and thus beginning the formal functional approach of VA/VE methodology. They concentrated their efforts on reducing the cost of materials and products purchased from suppliers. The staff went considerably beyond this task by developing a systematic functional approach to cost reduction directed at the "identification of unnecessary cost, i.e., cost which provides neither quality nor use nor life nor appearance nor customer features." Miles named this new process value analysis because its scope went beyond analyzing merely cost and quality. It was clearly aimed at analyzing the overall value of an item.

After working out a general plan of procedure, Miles and his staff set to work on the first actual value analysis project and were able to reduce production costs by more than $200,000 annually on a low-sales item and turned it into a tremendous success.

Encouraged by such spectacular results, General Electric increased its VA staff, and other problems were attacked with equal success. Their fame and methodology spread throughout GE, and gradually, by word of mouth and articles in trade journals, their techniques were brought to the attention of American industry. Other industrial firms, faced with similar problems and situations, had also been exploring new methods of cutting costs. Thus, it was not long before virtually every large company—RCA, Westinghouse, IBM, and many others— had adopted value analysis. Whether they called it value analyzing, value engineering, or value specializing, the goals and principles were those of value analysis. Value analysis, conceived at GE, was proven at dozens of far-sighted, value-seeking organizations across the nation.

Miles noticed that every time he challenged the value of a product, it involved separate discussions with other departments. This tedious and time-consuming process was eventually replaced by the team approach, intended to ensure the maximum flow of creative ideas and the cooperation of the departments associated with the design, manufacture, and costing of a product. General Electric spent $800,000 developing these techniques, and in 17 years saved more than $200 million—a considerable return on their investment.

There are those who would hasten to point out that such pioneers in the field of management as Henry R. Towne, Frederic W. Taylor, Lillian and Frank Gilbreth, Eugene L. Grant, and a host of others were responsible for developing the techniques that were the basis for value engineering as we know it today. Although it cannot be denied that many individuals, knowingly or not, contributed to the development of the principles of value engineering, it was Miles who developed an organized approach to identifying the costs associated with the required function and then attacked those costs in a systematic manner without compromising quality or performance requirements.

Before value engineering, there had always been ways of cutting costs. Perhaps the most widespread technique used through the years was to concentrate on the reduction of material and labor costs, which often resulted in inferior products. This method, while reducing costs, also tends to reduce the number of satisfied users. Except for the most expendable of items, this approach has no place in our industrial or military systems. Value engineering never seeks such a solution; there is a vast difference between inexpensive materials and cheap materials, and between simple workmanship and poor workmanship.

It might be well to point out that value engineering had its share of critics and roadblocks. Roadblocks can be defined as negative generalizations that are intended to stop progress and keep things just as they are. Roadblocks are a natural hazard to value engineering, just as they are to about every constructive form of human activity. Certainly the history of science, like every other type of history, is studded with examples of resistance to change, even when the change brings benefits. A short seance with any of the great scientists of the past, from Aristotle to Einstein, would show the long history of human resistance to new ideas. We tend to blame such vague forces as bureaucracy, conformity, child-rearing techniques, or world tensions. But such resistance is inevitable.

As a rule, any change will meet resistance. As a psychologist might put it, people are naturally hostile or anxious when a change even remotely threatens their pattern of living.

Why is there such emotional resistance to change? Some of the reasons are:

1. If the nature and effect of a proposed change are not clearly explained, it may be considered a threat. Incomplete information produces insecurity; insecurity turns to hostility.

2. Different people interpret proposals in different ways, particularly if the suggestions are vague and not buttressed by adequate facts.

3. When there is great pressure both for and against change, resistance grows and ultimately immobilizes everyone.

4. The less opportunity people have to express themselves about a proposed change that affects them, the greater their resistance to it will be.

5. Proposals that are made on a personal basis, or that reflect on an individual's ability, produce hostility.

6. Strong resistance can be expected if a change will alter long-established institutions, habits, or customs.

1.3   ROADBLOCKS

Roadblocks can be easily recognized. Usually they take shape as verbal barriers. Occasionally, the verbal barriers are followed by a lack of cooperation. No matter how they are expressed, experienced value engineers can recall the variety of phrases that say No. For the serious collector, a list of 50 familiar roadblock quotations is provided below. Several of these were first discovered in Egyptian pyramids; others were uncovered in the ruins of Pompeii; one was taken from Napoleon's memoirs.

Familiar Roadblock Quotations
1. I agree, but . . . .
2. We've tried that too.
3. We did it this way.
4. Procedure won't permit.
5. It won't work.
6. There is no money budgeted for this.
7. Don't move too fast.
8. You can't do that.
9. It's never been done that way before.
10. Don't we have something just as good now?
11. It's not standard stock.
12. It costs too much.
13. Cost doesn't matter.
14. It's too big (or too small) for us.
15. We've tried that before and it didn't work.
16. We're not ready for that.
17. We can't do things that way.
18. We have the best system already.
19. Everybody does it this way.
20. We have too many new projects now.
21. It's policy.
22. It won't stand shock.
23. Not timely.
24. It's an untried gimmick.
25. Not for us.

26. It's difficult to maintain.
27. Not our responsibility.
28. Why should we change now?
29. We haven't tested it yet.
30. Impracticable.
31. Idea too radical.
32. Too complicated.
33. It isn't consistent.
34. Too theoretical.
35. I'm too busy to decide now.
36. That's unsound.
37. Not feasible.
38. Impossible.
39. The production department won't accept it.
40. The field will think we're long-haired.
41. Personnel aren't ready for this.
42. Engineering won't approve it.
43. The Army is different.
44. The men won't go for it.
45. You'd never be able to sell that to management.
46. We don't have enough facts.
47. Can't see it.
48. Too much trouble to get started.
49. Doesn't conform to policy.
50. We don't have the manpower.

The reader is cautioned against inferring that this is an exhaustive listing of roadblocks. Nor should it be concluded that these or any other roadblocks could stop VE progress. On the contrary, to the innovative and creative mind each challenge merely provides a greater opportunity to prove the merits of the VE technique. For many in the value engineering profession the motivating force can be found in the words of Thomas A. Edison, "There's a way to do it better. . . . find it."

1.4   PROGRESS OF VA/VE

Within the Department of Defense, the Navy, Bureau of Ships, was the first to initiate training and establish a formal VA/VE program. This was in 1954. The Navy called its program value engineering to reflect the Navy's emphasis and relation to engineering design application. During the first year, the Navy VE program was responsible for saving $35 million.

The Navy, Bureau of Yards and Docks, began to apply VE techniques to construction for the first time in 1963. Another success chapter was documented in an area heretofore believed by many not suitable for VE application.

In September 1955, Army personnel at the Watervliet Arsenal visited the Value Services Office at GE and discussed the possibility of starting a VA/VE program at Watervliet Arsenal. Within a year, the Army started its VA activity at the arsenal. Although it began on a limited scale, the results of first-year efforts were so convincing that the department's size rapidly increased. At the end of the first year's operation, a program report was made to the Chief of Ordnance. This report stirred considerable interest within Ordnance and the Department of the Army. Beginning in May 1958, briefings were scheduled throughout Ordnance; by September, all major Ordnance commands and arsenals had been covered and the Deputy Chief of Staff for Logistics and the Chiefs of the Technical Services had been briefed. Value analysis was in the Army to stay.

Official recognition of the program was announced by a letter (19 Sep 58) from Brigadier General F. J. McMorrow (Chief, Industrial Division, Office Chief of Ordnance) to all Ordnance installations, recommending that each Commander establish a value analysis program. Watervliet was commissioned to conduct an Ordnance-wide training seminar to assist in this program.

In April 1959, an Ordnance Corps Technical Instruction was issued requiring commanders of all installations with (a) national procurement and production, (b) national industrial engineering, (c) support industrial engineering, or (d) support manufacturing mission responsibilities, to implement VA programs and report progress at quarterly intervals.

In the months that followed, hundreds of specialists received VA/VE training and several hundred projects demonstrated worthwhile savings. It appeared that the Army was well on its way with a viable VE effort. These VE efforts had been largely in-house with little extension into the private contractors' efforts.

Recognizing that to find big savings one must go where the big money is, the Army began to investigate VE possibilities in the private contractor field. VE clauses had been developed but were not too well understood and required a concerted selling job with defense industry. Since a piecemeal attack by an individual Army command would not suffice, the Army began to organize and better equip itself to expand the function of value engineering on a broad front.

Progressive growth in VE savings encouraged the Army to increase its full-time VE staffs, but only modestly and only in the areas of procurement and production. In February 1965, Army savings resulting from VE efforts were approaching the $200 million mark and it became apparent to many in the Department of the Army that value engineering had proven itself as an effective management tool for combating costs and improving the value of Army materiel.

The Air Force did not provide for VA/VE in its contracts until late 1960, and then only at the discretion of the contracting officer. The discretionary situation changed in April 1962 and gave way to the present mandatory provision.

1.5   ARMED SERVICES PROCUREMENT REGULATION

Within the Department of Defense, probably the most significant action taken was the review undertaken in 1963 by the Armed Services Procurement Regulation (ASPR) review committee and the drafting of the first comprehensive treatment of value engineering. Earlier coverage in the ASPR had been more or less permissive insofar as whether value engineering was or was not included in the contract. The ASPR revision issued in November 1963 added an entirely new Part 17, Section I to the General Provisions, which made it mandatory that value engineering incentive provisions be included in all procurements exceeding $100,000 and that VE program requirements be included in all cost-plus-fixed-fee contracts exceeding $1 million. Almost immediately, questions arose concerning the duration of the sharing aspect (present versus future contracts), sharing in indirect savings (the operating costs), and changes developed at the subcontractor level. Provisions to cover these and thus expand incentives for contractor participation appeared first in Defense Procurement Circular Number 11, published in October 1964. These provisions were subsequently incorporated into Part 17, Section I by Revision 23 to the ASPR dated 1 June 1967.

Although Revision 23 was a rather thorough modification to previous guidance on the subject of value engineering, the Department of Defense found it necessary to refine it further. Defense Procurement Circular Number 65 was issued 20 December 1968, providing additional information on the sharing percentages when the incentive clause was incorporated into a contract. This was followed by a complete reissue of Part 17, Section I on 1 January 1969. Soon thereafter, construction agency representatives were studying the possibility of including VE provisions in ASPR specifically for construction contracts. This undertaking resulted in a comprehensive, yet uncomplicated, ASPR coverage in the 1974 revision. Since then, the language has not undergone any significant change.

1.6   OTHER INTERESTS

While the DOD was engaged in developing its own VA/VE goals and objectives, others outside the DOD who had heard of the VA/VE results began to implement their own programs.

In 1965, the Department of Interior, Bureau of Reclamation, began an intensive training program in value engineering for its entire engineering staff. In 1966, it began placing a VE incentive clause in its construction contracts.

In 1967, the Post Office Department (now the United States Postal Service), Bureau of Research and Engineering, instituted a formal program by creating a full-time VE staff.

In 1969, the National Aeronautics and Space Administration, Office of Facilities, began conducting formal VE studies and training.

In 1970, the *Federal Register,* Volume 34, Number 173, published the first VE incentive clause to be used by all agencies of the Department of Transportation.

In 1970, the General Services Administration, Public Buildings Service, published "Construction Contracting Systems," a report that recommended the establishment of a VE program. In September, the agency staffed its first full-time value engineer to implement a formal program.

In 1970, the Department of Health, Education and Welfare, Facilities Engineering and Construction Agency, held its first conference on value engineering to establish a program in that agency.

In addition, it might be well to point out that on August 1 and 2, 1967, the U.S. Senate Committee on Public Works held hearings concerning the use of value engineering in the government. Agencies testifying were:

Department of Interior, Water Pollution Control.
Department of the Army, Corps of Engineers.
Department of Transportation, Bureau of Public Roads.

General Services Administration, Public Buildings Service.
Department of Health, Education and Welfare, Public Health Service.

Again, on June 18 and 19, 1973, the U.S. Senate Committee on Public Works held hearings "to receive and have the benefit of testimony relating to the science of value engineering" and to learn about "efforts currently being made in that field." The committee heard testimony from Congressman Larry Winn (Kansas), well-known for urging widespread government use of VA/VE, and others representing Federal Highway Administration, American Institute of Architects, General Services Administration, General Accounting Office, Corps of Engineers, Associated General Contractors of America, National Society of Professional Engineers, Environmental Protection Agency, Society of American Value Engineers, Value Engineering media, the professional educational community, and private sectors of design and construction.

In 1969, the National Academy of Sciences, Federal Construction Council, Building Research Advisory Board, convened a conference to research the application of value engineering in construction. Symposium/Workshop Report No. 4, dated May 27, 1969, published its results. Agencies testifying were:

Department of the Army, Corps of Engineers.
Department of Interior, Bureau of Reclamation.
Department of the Navy, Naval Facilities Engineering Command.
Veterans Administration.
Post Office Department.
General Services Administration, Public Buildings Service.
Department of the Air Force, Civil Engineering.

On May 12, 1977, Senator Jennings Randolph (West Virginia), introduced Senate Resolution 172 relating to value engineering. Senator Randolph, Chairman of the Senate Committee on the Environment and Public Works, told his colleagues that value engineering is "the most effective technique available for identifying and eliminating unnecessary costs." He went on to explain that "a resolution has no force of law. But it does express the sense of the Senate. . . . sometimes resolutions have an even greater impact than a law."

The text of Senate Resolution 172 and the text of Senator Randolph's introductory remarks are quoted in full. The text of Senate Resolution 172 follows:

Whereas, it is recognized that value engineering is a proven method to conserve energy, improve services, save money, or otherwise generally control the expenditure of construction resources by means of budgeted, organized, multidisciplined and function-oriented team review, and

Whereas, the value engineering methodology is applicable wherever there is a function to be performed and a means to measure it, and

Whereas, the preponderance of testimony before committees of Congress has shown that value engineering saves at least five dollars for each value engineering dollar spent, and

Whereas, the General Accounting Office has recommended the use of value engineering be expanded in federal construction, and

Whereas, the Corps of Engineers in the past ten years has, by the use of value engineering, saved $200 million in construction costs for·an expenditure of $10 million, and

Whereas, the first four years of value engineering application in the General Services Administration has saved $12.84 for each dollar spent, and

Whereas, value engineering has been successfully applied in private industry to generate additional profits and better products and services,

Therefore, be it resolved that it is the sense of the Senate that all federal departments and agencies, in order to achieve maximum efficiency and economy, shall utilize, where possible, value engineering in carrying out their functions and administering their programs as part of their affirmative efforts for cost reduction.

The remarks of Senator Randolph follow:

I am today submitting a resolution stating the sense of the Senate on the importance of value engineering as a cost-reduction tool. Billions of dollars are expended by the Federal Government each year for construction of worthwhile projects for all Americans. Institution of value engineering practices will result in substantial cost reductions in those agencies employing this engineering cost-control procedure.

One of the strongest links of our past with our present is the American commitment to building. We have led the way not only in the amounts of our construction, but also in developing new techniques. In many respects, Americans had to be builders to survive.

Engineers contribute a necessary and important role in developing the projects which provide ultimate benefit to all Americans. Without this vital function, we could have no construction program which is so important for future growth.

With inflation forcing construction costs up at a rapid rate, we must undertake every opportunity to reduce the cost of each project. Value engineering is one technique which can have significant impact.

Like most other activities in our country, construction is a pluralistic endeavor with involvement by both the private and public sectors. The nature of our political system gives to the Federal Government a substantial involvement in construction, one which greatly influences activities throughout the economy.

With our construction dollars buying less, alternative engineering methods which reduce project costs must be encouraged. Congress should take every opportunity to reduce costs on federal and federally assisted construction projects. This technique has proven its effectiveness and should be implemented on all federal construction projects.

The facts prove that value engineering can successfully reduce costs when employed. One large federal-aid highway contract reduced cost $500,000 on the fencing through value engineering. This technique is currently being used by the Federal Highway Administration and the Army Corps of Engineers whose programs are under the Public Works Committee's jurisdiction. The interest of the Environmental Protection Agency in this tool is growing as evidenced by its cosponsorship of a conference on value engineering in St. Louis last November.

So long as we are a changing and developing nation committed to improved standards of living, I do not see how we can reduce our commitment to essential construction programs. There are many who say that the emphasis on growth during our two centuries as an independent nation has been harmful. I do not agree. I fully recognize that there have been undesirable side effects of our determination to build. Without that determination, however, our country and its benefits would not exist today.

I also believe that federal involvement is so well established that it must be a permanent feature of construction in our country. Federal programs will not be static in the years ahead. We must examine the needs of our country and respond to them. We must have reasoned involvement in the segments of our society.

Value engineering will not solve all the problems with construction costs; however, it is the most effective technique available for identifying and eliminating unnecessary costs. I strongly urge that my colleagues give careful consideration to this important tool which works effectively for our valuable construction program.

Senate Resolution 172 was referred to the Committee on Governmental Affairs. Because of the normal legislative process, it will not be passed until long after this book is in print. However, the fact that Senate Resolution 172 was introduced testifies to the importance and effectiveness of the value engineering concept.

1.7 SUMMARY

Having traced the origin of the concept from its formalized inception by Mr. Miles of the General Electric Company through its adoption and evolution to the present status within the Department of Defense and other government agencies, it might be well to define the subject. As a starting point, we quote the father of the child:

> Value analysis is a philosophy implemented by the use of a specific set of techniques, a body of knowledge, and a group of learned skills. It is an organized creative approach which has for its purpose the efficient identification of unnecessary cost, i.e., cost which provides neither quality, nor use, nor life, nor appearance, nor customer features.

Mr. Miles's definition leads to the conclusion that the process tends to relate product worth to product cost and implies an evaluation of the function performed by the product or its components. In terms of use, it is a measure of value to the user. In terms of cost, it is a measure of value to the producer.

Value Management for Construction presents an organized and acceptable approach to the all-encompassing job construction managers must recognize as their responsibility as they execute their best managerial skills to produce an economical, functional, attractive facility that meets the owner's criteria.

The terms value analysis and value engineering have of necessity been used in describing the evolution and history of the discipline. However, in recent years, value management has become more descriptive of the overall effort and will be used throughout the remainder of the book.

CHAPTER 2

OVERCOMING RESISTANCE TO VALUE MANAGEMENT

2.1 INTRODUCTION

No one can deny the need for more cost consciousness in the planning, design, construction, operation, and maintenance of complex building projects. This need has been recognized for many years, but the rapid pace of changing technology, inflation, and the new problems of energy and the environment have focused even more attention on the problem. The resurgent emphasis placed on the cost of a building and its maintenance makes it imperative that something be done to explore all avenues for producing the required facility at the lowest possible cost while maintaining the desired levels of performance and quality. Managers need a tool not only to control cost but to reduce initial costs and minimize the future costs of ownership. Yet in the process of doing this, the specified performance, quality, safety, utility and esthetics must be maintained or improved. Value management is just such a potentially powerful tool. The VM method as applied to construction is an objective, systematic means of obtaining optimum value for every construction dollar spent. Value management is a new tool the construction industry cannot afford to be without.

Value management is the present state of the art of a dynamic and continuously evolving science (or art) that is concerned with the systematic review and control of costs associated with acquiring and owning a facility. It has evolved through the years from the original concept that was created by the General Electric Company in the late 1930s and known then as value analysis. The details of its history are discussed in Chapter 1; we need not repeat them here. However, it should be noted that the pinnacle of this evolutionary process has not been reached. Value management is a dynamic concept. It is still

14

evolving. The next logical step in this evolution is life-cycle costing, which is discussed in detail in Chapter 10.

Although value management has been accepted and proven to be extremely successful in the manufacturing industries, it has been greeted with some apathy, and on occasion with outright resistance, in the construction industry. This resistance to value management can usually be classified into one of two categories. First, just as there tends to be a natural resistance to anything innovative, there is resistance to value management because it is a new concept to construction. Second, because it did evolve from value analysis and value engineering, to some it still has a stigma of engineering associated with it. As a consequence of this imaginary blemish, many potential practitioners are wary of participating in its use. Since engineering is a very technical and complicated profession, individuals who are not technically oriented hesitate to deal with any matter that smacks of engineering. Because of this combination of newness and historical association with value engineering, they have a natural resistance to the acceptance of value management. Although value management indeed did evolve from value analysis and value engineering, it is, in its present state of the art, an advanced cost control concept—a bona fide, innovative management tool.

This chapter will treat the subject of overcoming the resistance to value management by discussing the following topics:

- *Benefits*—The successes in cost control and reduction that can be achieved through the use of value management.
- *Management participation*—How management can provide the necessary leadership for inaugurating and using value management.
- *Organization*—Where in the overall organization does the VM staff best fit?
- *Human factors*—What are the human factors affecting the resistance to or acceptance of the VM concept, and how are people motivated to support a VM effort?
- *Training*—Individuals must be properly trained so they will clearly understand and efficiently execute VM techniques and procedures.

This chapter as well as the rest of this book is directed at the following two groups:

- The first group consists of the skeptics who must be convinced that value management is indeed an innovative and powerful tool for the construction industry. This chapter is required reading for any one in this group.

- The second group are advocates of value management who have the added task of initiating a VM program. This chapter aids them in developing an approach that will enhance the acceptance of a VM program.

This book is aimed at convincing the construction industry that value management is a valid concept that can be beneficially applied to construction.

2.2 BENEFITS OF VALUE MANAGEMENT

In June 1973, Congressman Larry Winn, Jr., from the state of Kansas, made the following statement to the Subcommittee on Buildings and Grounds in the United States Senate:

> Mr. Chairman, I submit to you and to the American people that the effective application of value analysis in the Federal Government should render tax dollar savings of $2 billion to $9 billion annually. Now, do these savings mean large-scale manpower layoffs? Certainly not. Do they mean an inferior or unsafe bridge or highway? Most assuredly not.
>
> But, could the reduction in cost possibly produce an even better end product? Experience by professional value engineers offers an unqualified "yes" to that question.
>
> Value analysis is relatively simple in its application. But, on the surface, many people might think they use the value technique when they do their jobs. As a matter of fact, one of the difficulties in gaining greater use of value analysis is that people have a tendency to be defensive if you even suggest there is a way to save money in the way they do their job.
>
> I think this is human nature. But value analysis is no more an indictment of current working procedures than flying in an airplane is an indictment against walking.
>
> Because of its almost legendary success in cutting costs—without impairing performance, quality, safety, or maintainability—value analysis has grown up these past almost three decades cloaked in a mystique; a mystique, I should point out, which is attributed to it by those who least understand it.
>
> Practitioners see nothing mysterious about it. They see value analysis as what it is: a simple method of identifying and eliminating unnecessary costs. And, it is that simple if you know how to use it.*

*Hearings before the Subcommittee on Buildings and Grounds of the Committee on Public Works, United States Senate, June 18 and 19, 1973.

Three comments are appropriate here. First, if it is possible to save $2 billion to $9 billion annually in the federal government, then think of the vast savings that can be realized in private industry, which is a far larger segment of our economy. Second, one of the major purposes of this book is to dispel the mystique that has grown around value management. Third, since the statement just quoted was made, the VM concept has undergone refinement to the point where it has outgrown its engineering and analysis restraints and has become truly a management tool. It is not just a matter of changing its name.

The systematic application of value management to the construction process can produce significant savings in the costs of the original project and subsequent projects. The three examples that follow demonstrate how these benefits can be derived by:

- Having a value management incentive program.
- Applying a proven value management proposal to future projects.
- Applying value management to standard designs.

Example 1

In August 1971, before the General Services Administration established its formal VM incentive program, it awarded a contract for constructing a federal office building in Chicago. At the suggestion of the contractor, GSA included an incentive clause in the contract providing for savings on the initial construction cost to be shared 70% by the government and 30% by the contractor. (The incentive clause GSA now uses under its formal program provides for the contractor and the government to share equally in savings in initial construction cost.)

By June 1972, less than one year later, the contractor had submitted 35 value proposals. GSA accepted 25 of these proposals, which resulted in savings to the government of about $1 million and an additional profit to the contractor of about $450,000.

Example 2

The Corps of Engineers' Fort Worth District, acting as the construction manager on a Randolph Air Force Base project, received a VM proposal from a contractor that involved a change in the material used for encasing underground electric cables. The proposal was initially rejected because Air Force specifications did not permit the use of the suggested material. The Corps' Fort Worth District, which was using the material on its own projects, estimated that its use would save the Air Force over $100,000 a year on contracts administered by the

District. The Corps convinced the Air Force to amend its specifications to permit the use of the new material.

Example 3

The Savannah District of the Corps of Engineers made an in-house VM study on the standard design for five administration and storage buildings. Several revisions to the standard design were subsequently adopted for Corps-wide use. In the Savannah District alone, these revisions saved an estimated $784,000 on nine projects over a two-year period.

The Savannah District also made an in-house VM study on its standard design for enlisted men's barracks. Resulting revisions were used to modify three existing contracts and were to be included in the designs of six other projects. Total estimated savings in the Savannah District on these nine projects was $65,000.

These are just three brief and simple examples of the benefits that resulted from the application of value management. This concept does produce tangible benefits.

Value management not only produces cost savings but also can contribute significantly to improving other important characteristics of the system under consideration. This fact was proven in a study conducted by the Department of Defense. The study results are based on a random sampling of 124 successful VM changes drawn from over 650. The eleven characteristics listed and defined in Figure 2.1 were reviewed to determine the following:

- Did the VM change have an advantageous effect?
- Did the VM change have no effect?
- Did the VM change have a disadvantageous effect?

Figure 2.2 illustrates that, in addition to cost savings, significant collateral gains such as improved performance, improved reliability, lower maintenance cost, and improved logistics support are derived from successful value management. The benefits discussed above are those that accrue to the owners or users of the facility, who, because of these obvious benefits, are usually very receptive to value management.

Benefits of value management can also accrue to other members of the building team, such as the architect-engineers, the construction manager, and the individual construction contractors. Architect-

1. **Reliability.** Ability to meet performance requirements for a determined number of times
2. **Maintainability.** Relative ease of repair or replacement
3. **Producibility.** Relative ease of repeatable manufacture
4. **Human factors.** Acceptability of change related to necessary education or dexterity
5. **Parts availability.** Relative ease in obtaining or manufacturing simplified or standard parts
6. **Production lead time.** Elimination, standardization, or simplification of operations or materials
7. **Quality.** Characteristics of parts to meet everything specified consistently
8. **Weight.** Lighter in weight
9. **Logistics.** Quantity and complexity of parts needed for field support of end items
10. **Performance.** Ability of the change to carry out the intended function at time of initial test or qualification
11. **Packaging.** Relative ease of protecting parts until ready for use

Figure 2.1 Definitions of collateral gains.

engineers and construction managers will find that value management enhances the capabilities of their firm to the benefit of present and future clients. By emphasizing cost as one of the essential design parameters, while retaining freedom of design expression and the value of the proposed facility, they are providing an additional valuable service to their clients. This in turn gives them a competitive edge over those architect-engineers and construction managers who do not offer VM services; the result shows up on the bottom line with more business and revenue.

Large and small contractors also find that value management gives them an opportunity to both build their profits and earn an enviable reputation as cost-conscious constructors. Contractors normally are compensated for VM services through an incentive clause in the building contract. They are encouraged to challenge unessential and high cost requirements of their contracts. Because of his expertise in construction material and methods, a contractor's innovativeness, ingenuity, and imagination can reduce costs without sacrificing necessary quality or function. Contractors can receive compensation from two sources. First, they share in the savings to current contracts that result from their proposals. Second, they share in life-cycle ownership

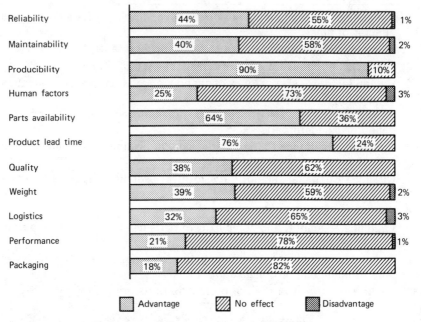

Figure 2.2   Collateral gains from VM changes.

savings that may accrue to the owner as a result of their proposals. Monetary benefits to the architect-engineer, construction manager, and individual contractors are discussed in more detail in Chapter 4.

Value management benefits also can accrue directly to individuals. Since cost is a major concern of every construction organization, individuals are rewarded in at least two ways. First, cost consciousness and innovativeness bring them to the attention of top management. This exposure is a definite aid to career advancement. Second, many organizations pass on to employees a percentage of the savings or profits resulting from their proposals. Moreover, all individuals benefit indirectly when their company increases its profitability and enhances its reputation as an advocate of construction cost control.

2.3   MANAGEMENT PARTICIPATION

Top management support is essential for the successful inauguration and continuation of an effective value management program. When a program is being initiated, top management support is needed for the selection and training of individuals in VM principles and methods. For programs in which funds are budgeted annually for value management activities or staff, continued top management support is mandatory. As a rule, continued support can be ensured only if savings can be demonstrated—for example, by tying the VM program to an audit system in which claimed savings are validated in accordance with established accounting principles.

Middle management support also is essential. A VM program will succeed only if the managers of the various functions such as finance, engineering, design, procurement, planning, estimating, and so forth understand and believe in value management. After all, it is the middle managers who are directly responsible for initiating and carrying out the VM activities and for implementing the resulting recommendations. Obtaining the support of middle management basically requires that many (preferably all) of the managers involved be fully trained in the principles of value management and be convinced that the concept is a powerful tool when used properly.

2.3.1 MANAGING INNOVATION

Value management is an innovative concept dealing with innovation, and the tendency to resist innovation, simply because it is change, is a natural characteristic of human behavior. In the case of value management, an additional factor enters into the picture. Value management is a relatively young endeavor; it is not as firmly entrenched and therefore not as accepted as finance, engineering, research and development, procurement, personnel, and other organizational functions. It is important for management to recognize that overcoming resistance to value management begins at the top—with top management itself.

Endorsement and support by top management is the prime ingredient necessary for the success of a value management program—the higher the level of endorsement, the greater the acceptance. Value management needs the backing of top management if it is to be accepted down the line and if it is to function effectively. This backing is vital because value management is not needed to develop a workable facility or to deliver it on time. Value management offers an objective appraisal that greatly contributes to the development of a facility that complies with specified performance requirements at lowest total cost. Value management may be looked upon as a luxury to be performed when time permits unless top management makes it known to everyone concerned that it seriously regards value management as a necessary and important part of the organization's operation.

The way innovation is managed is critical to its acceptance. For it to be controlled and directed, there must be an organized, deliberate, planned approach. An environment for accomplishing innovation must be developed, and a positive orientation toward innovation must be established in the organization. Once this positive climate exists, then the potential exists for the creation and acceptance of innovation. A respected senior executive should be assigned full-time to develop and implement a formal system for initiating innovative programs. This system identifies the strategies to be followed in managing innovation. At the same time the executive selects enthusiastic and aggressive individuals who are capable of executing the strategies.

Innovation can create competitive advantages and improve profits, but it doesn't happen automatically. In many organizations innovation is a way of life. Profit-motivated companies exist to create, build, and market products and services that satisfy the needs of their clients. If they are to survive and prosper, they must continuously improve the products and services they offer; they must be capable of recognizing problems, not symptoms, and develop new solutions for them. Construction-oriented firms will have to learn to develop and manage innovation if they are to remain competitive and profitable in the construction industry.

2.3.2   WHEN IS AN ORGANIZATION READY FOR VALUE MANAGEMENT?

Owners, architect-engineers, and constructors operate in an environment that is characterized by the following problems:

- Increased competition in all areas.
- Cost-price squeeze.
- Shrinking profits.
- High labor costs.
- Exponential increase in materials.
- Rapidly changing technology.
- High energy costs.
- Increasing environmental costs.
- Inflation.
- Need to complete projects quicker.

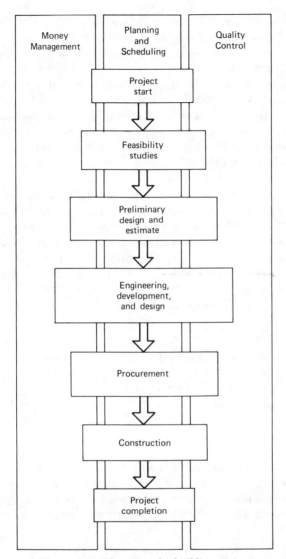

Figure 2.3   Elements of a building project.

In addition, the building process itself is very fragmented. Figure 2.3 illustrates the elements of a building project. Today, no one person is responsible for the complete development of a facility. Each function is executed by a different manager. Who is responsible for the total cost? Hundreds of people who may not even know one another and who usually do not care about costs contribute to the total cost. Those who do know what the project costs—the accountants—often do not know why it costs what it does. This fragmentation of project responsibility has so removed the decision maker from cost that very little incentive exists to minimize costs.

For these reasons, almost any construction-oriented company should be interested in value management. In fact, a good rule of thumb is that *any concern that does not have a staff and a systematic method to develop and implement value opportunities should consider value management.* Two factors have a heavy influence as to when a company is ready for value management:

- *Value problem*—There are an almost infinite number of ways in which a facility can be designed and erected. The combinations of configurations and materials are endless. By comparing any two alternatives, it is discovered that one is lower in cost than the other but meets all requirements. The difference in these costs can be defined as unnecessary costs. As more lower-cost alternatives are found, it is discovered that more and more costs are unnecessary. Does the present company climate provide an environment for identifying and reducing unnecessary costs?

- *Company size*—Value management is most urgently needed in large companies and on large, complex projects where the lines of communication are lengthened and responsibilities are fragmented. Unnecessary costs become greatly amplified. In these situations a VM program with a full-time staff and specialists is essential. Even in small companies the knowledge and use of value management may provide a competitive advantage.

Implementing a value management program incurs an investment cost, yet the program provides a return in the form of savings. The question of when to implement a program then becomes one of economics. Is the return (savings) on the investment (cost of implementation) satisfactory?

2.3.3 IMPLEMENTING THE VALUE MANAGEMENT PROGRAM

First, it is the responsibility of management to become familiar with these new concepts. Management should establish a full-time VM effort in the organization. This effort should start with a comprehensive training program for all personnel whose decisions affect costs. Training programs are discussed in more detail in Section 2.6.

The magnitude of the VM effort need not be large, but to succeed it must have top management support. The program should be established at a management level where it can effectively challenge design criteria, including established standards, and where it can have access to operational and maintenance costs. It should be concerned solely with identifying high-cost or poor-value areas and developing lower-cost alternatives. This VM program should supplement present methods and provide better information on which to base design decisions.

Admittedly, adopting such a program will require changes in organizational structure. But in view of all the other challenges (project management, environmental considerations, safety, technology, and so forth) that confront the construction industry, changes must be made anyway. Now is a good time to incorporate a value management program as part of these necessary changes.

Second, the principles of incentive contracting should be used wherever feasible. For example, consideration should be given to voluntary incentive provisions for competitively bid, fixed-price contracts. These provisions provide contractors with the means to share in any cost-saving proposals they submit after contract award. The obvious intent of these provisions is to encourage contractors to be alert for cost-saving ideas during construction.

Third, funded program requirements for large negotiated design and construction management contracts should be considered also. With funds available, designers and construction managers would be able to conduct additional studies outside of today's fee structure on any key design selection that has a significant impact on total costs. They also would have funds to challenge any owner's criteria or specifications that, in the designer or construction manager's judgment, represents poor value.

This program requirement provides a means by which the design or management costs can be increased by a small percentage to gain a large percentage reduction in total costs. To date, program requirements for hardware or systems design-oriented contracts have ranged from 0.3 to 0.5% of total costs. The savings (target goal) projected for this effort is a 1 to 5% reduction in total costs. For example, for a $10 million cost-plus-fixed-fee contract, a program requirement would range from $30,000 to $50,000, with a target savings of $100,000 to $500,000. To date, the results from limited efforts in the construction area have generally followed these parameters. For construction management contracts, the VM effort should range between 5 and 10% of total construction management fees. For these efforts, documented savings should approach the total fee of the construction manager.

The unprecedented challenge now confronting the construction industry requires new thinking to reduce unnecessary costs. The value management approach helps to achieve this new kind of thinking.

2.3.4 MANAGEMENT CONTROL OF VALUE MANAGEMENT

Any management program, if it is to be successful and attain its full potential, requires close control and monitorship by those responsible for achieving its objectives. This is particularly true of value management because of the critical need to allocate scarce talents in a manner that maximizes the return on their use.

Three basic devices are available to control a VM program: target savings, a reporting system, and an audit system. Collectively they provide a means to accurately measure the progress of the program and a method of directing management efforts toward a maximum contribution to product value.

Savings Targets

In order to motivate personnel and to obtain maximum savings from value management it is important to establish realistic savings goals to stimulate participation. These goals identify performance targets. They provide an added impetus to the value management staff to concentrate their efforts on projects promising the greatest dollar return per work hour of VM effort.

Since the basic objective of value management is to reduce costs, targets should always be expressed in terms of dollars. Wherever possible, target breakdowns should be established on individual projects and even on pieces of hardware and systems.

Targets should be set at reasonable levels; "reasonable" in this context means that the target should not be set so high as to be unattainable nor should it be so low as to require little effort to exceed it. The target level should be attainable only by a superior effort.

It is difficult to provide precise instructions on the setting of targets because several key variables affect the level of savings that can be achieved through value management. However, two rules of thumb can be stated.

First, although many examples of net savings-to-cost ratios of 15 to 1 and higher can be documented, a reasonable ratio of return is generally held to be 10 to 1. Therefore, one method of establishing a savings target is to compute the anticipated cost of the VM effort and multiply it by 10 to establish a savings target. A second method of computing a target figure is to assume an average level of cost reduction through value management over an entire project. To clarify this latter method, assume a project is composed of subsystems such as foundation, electrical, HVAC, and so forth. Since it normally will not be possible to subject all subsystems to a detailed VM analysis, the application of a priority selection system will indicate the three or four items that are to be analyzed in depth. Although 20%, 30%, or even 40% reduction in cost of a subsystem often is achieved through value management, the total cost of the end project obviously is not reduced this much. An across-the-board figure of 5% total cost reduction is reasonable, and targets can be established on this basis (refer to Section 2.3.3).

Targets should not be established and then forgotten. They must be given continued publicity. Progress toward the targets must be measured on a continuing basis. Measurement of progress is accomplished through another program control device, the reporting system.

Reporting System

The reporting system measures progress toward the targets and provides a quantitative measurement of the program. A well-designed reporting system will be concise, responsive, accurate, and timely. The concept of *reporting by exception* is used wherever appropriate.

Information that normally is included in a VM program reporting system is listed below. At higher reporting levels, not all items would appear and many would be summarized rather than reported in detail.

- Identification of the preparing unit/individual.
- Date the report was prepared.
- Time period covered by the report.
- Number of VM activities currently under study.
- Estimated potential dollar savings in items under study.
- Number of VM proposals currently under evaluation, either in house or by others.
- Estimated dollar savings on proposals under evaluation, if approved.
- Breakdown of "age" of proposals under evaluation: 0 to 90 days, 90 to 180 days, over 180 days.
- Number of VM actions approved and implemented—during the reporting period and year to date.
- Dollar savings of approved and implemented projects (only net savings should be reported), for the reporting period to date and also further broken down by the savings to be accomplished in the current year and in future years.
- Number of personnel engaged more than half time in VM work.

- Total cost of the VM program during the last 12 months.
- Ratio of savings to cost of program during the last 12 months.
- Individual listing of actions approved during current reporting period, including brief description, cost of the project, and net savings attained.

In addition to reporting the items listed above concerning its own in-house program, the owner, architect-engineer, or construction manager's procuring activities should report the following data on contractor VM programs.

- Number of active contracts containing VM provisions, broken down by type of provisions (required funded effort or savings sharing approaches).
- Dollar value of active contract containing VM provisions, broken down by type of provision (as above).
- Number of VM proposals approved for implementation this month and year to date.
- Dollar savings (owner's net portion only) on approved VM changes implemented this reporting period and year to date, and also further broken down by the savings to be accomplished in the current year and in future years.
- Number of VM change proposals currently under evaluation.
- Estimated dollar savings on proposals under evaluation if approved.
- Breakdown of "age" of proposals under evaluation: 0 to 90 days, 90 to 180 days, over 180 days.
- List of proposals approved during current reporting period, including brief description of proposal, owner's net savings anticipated, contractor share of savings (if any) and applicability of change elsewhere, if feasible.

For most activities, the above data can be arranged on a single sheet of standard size paper using the reverse side for the individual item listings. The reports must be read by the level of management responsible for making program decisions.

Audit System

The reporting system provides a quantitative measurement of the VM program, but adequate program control also requires a qualitative evaluation. This can be accomplished best by an on-site audit.

The audit includes an examination of the organization, staffing, procedures, and budgets of the VM function. In addition to evaluating the general effectiveness and technical competence of the VM staff, the audit team makes whatever inquiries are appropriate to determine the level of acceptance of the VM effort throughout the organization. Furthermore, the audit team performs a detailed analysis of reported VM savings to verify their validity.

To minimize their cost, VM audits can be integrated into already established audit functions. In addition to minimizing costs, this approach avoids the creation of an additional irritant to operating personnel.

The frequency of audits depends upon available human resources. Generally, throughout industry and government, a scarcity of qualified auditing personnel results in a longer auditing cycle than is desirable. Since VM audits normally are integrated into an established audit function, they probably are not carried out as often as they should be. Once a year is a reasonable cycle; however, it may be difficult to achieve this in actual practice.

Maintaining an effective VM program requires continuous monitoring and control. The use of these three control devices will help management obtain maximum return on its investment in value management. In addition, the savings produced by a VM program are tangible results with which individual participants can associate themselves, thereby motivating personnel to greater participation.

2.4   VALUE MANAGEMENT ORGANIZATION

A sound organizational structure is essential for an effective VM program. Therefore, methods of organizing the VM function are important. Full benefits of the program cannot be achieved without good planning.

An effective organization consists of more than a number of neat boxes and lines on a chart. It is a living organism made up of people whose efforts are directed toward a common objective. In the final analysis, its success or failure depends on the quality of people selected to staff it. The selection and training of qualified personnel and the motivational influences required to stimulate them are the subjects of Sections 2.5 and 2.6. However, the basic requirement for well-qualified people should be kept firmly in mind when considering the organizational aspects of a value management program.

2.4.1 TWO TYPES OF VALUE MANAGEMENT FUNCTIONS

Two functions must be considered in structuring an organization to carry out value management—the coordinating or planning function and the operating function. In smaller activities these two functions may be performed by the same group, yet they remain separate and distinct.

The coordinating function is principally characterized by its assistance to those who perform the VM analysis, while the operating function is concerned with the actual value management.

The Coordinating Function

The coordinating function is concerned with overall program control, the assignment of savings targets and the allocation of resources necessary to meet these targets, the determination of priorities, the measurement of progress both quantitatively and qualitatively, and the development of policy and procedures for the application of value management.

Responsibilities typically assigned to the coordinating function are:

- Program control throughout the organization. This includes selection of projects and systems to be studied, assignment of savings targets, allocation of resources necessary to meet these targets, development of reporting systems to measure progress toward these goals, and performance of periodic informal reviews to qualitatively evaluate the various elements of the program.
- Development and supervision of the VM training program in cooperation with the training department.
- Continuous review and followup on all VM changes in process, both within the organization and at the contractor level.
- Guidance of operating VM staff, including dissemination of information concerning any new technological advances that can possibly be of use in the VM effort.
- Management of a publicity program directed to top management and to all personnel who are or should be concerned with project value, informing them of the results of the VM effort.
- Accumulation of cost data, both internally and from outside sources, to support the development of valid value standards.

The Operating Function

The operating VM function is concerned with the actual performance of value management. The prime responsibility of this group is to conduct VM studies and generate VM change proposals. This function is carried out by personnel trained in the principles of value management.

Additionally, the operating function usually has the responsibility for ensuring that any value management proposal is carried through to completion—to either implementation or rejection. In other words, the operating function is responsible for "closing the loop" on the VM process, although in some organizations the coordinating function shares this responsibility.

2.4.2 KEY VARIABLES AFFECTING ORGANIZATION STRUCTURE

There is no one magic pattern that represents the optimum organizational structure for performing value management. However, a basic distinction must be made between producing activities and procuring activities, since their approach to value management is different, owing to their basic purposes. Even within these broad groupings, which are discussed separately below, organizational patterns vary from activity to activity depending on several key variables, such as the size of the operation, the activity mix involved, and the existing organizational structure of the activity.

The size of the activity will determine the number of levels in the VM organizational structure. For example, in a small company the VM function may be organized in only one unit or even in one person, embodying both the coordinating and operating functions. On the other hand, in a very large company there may be a corporate director of value management, division managers of value management, and project managers of value management, all performing only the coordinating function. In addition, there may be a number of operating VM staff members assigned to each major project.

The type of activity greatly affects the type of value management organization. For example, a company specializing in design will be heavily oriented toward engineering, and the principal focus for value management, therefore, will fall within the engineering department (Figure 2.4). On the other hand, a manufacturer of building systems will tend to concentrate the VM effort in the manufacturing depart-

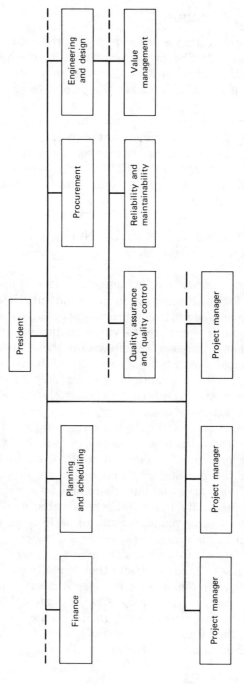

Figure 2.4 Value management organization—engineering and design oriented firm.

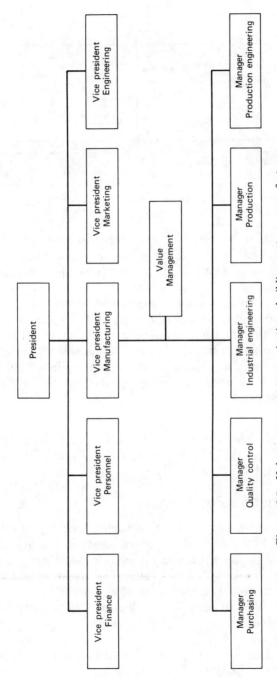

Figure 2.5 Value management organization—building systems manufacturer.

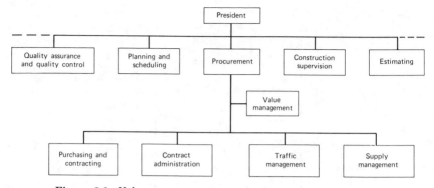

Figure 2.6 Value management organization—general contractor.

ment (Figure 2.5). A general contractor that subcontracts a great portion of the total dollar value of its contracts might well place primary emphasis on value management in the procurement department (Figure 2.6).

In order to introduce a new management tool into a going operation with the least possible confusion, it is desirable to make the greatest possible use of the existing organizational structure. There is an organizational similarity between value management and other disciplines such as reliability, quality control, and maintainability. Value management can be fitted into an organization in the same manner as these other disciplines.

2.4.3 VALUE MANAGEMENT IN THE PRODUCING ACTIVITY (ARCHITECT-ENGINEER, CONSTRUCTION MANAGER, CONTRACTOR)

The Coordinating Function

The specific location of this function varies from organization to organization due to the several variables mentioned above. Because of their natural tie-in, however, many companies have integrated the VM staff activity with quality control, reliability, and maintainability and have grouped these functions under the general heading of project assurance. This is a reasonable and logical way to organize the VM coordinating function, particularly in engineering and construction organizations.

The coordinating function is not limited to a particular level of an organization. For example, in a large company it may be required at two or more levels; in small operations, only a single level may be required. However, it is important in any size organization that the highest level coordinating function represent a clear focus of responsibility for the overall performance of the VM effort. It also is important that this function report to an executive with the power to cut across departmental or divisional lines, since there will normally be VM activities in two or more departments—engineering, purchasing, production, and so forth.

The Operating Function

The operating function of value management can be organized in a number of ways depending upon the size, project mix, and existing structure of the company. In practice, however, most of the patterns fall into three categories:

1. *Interfunctional project teams.* "Ad hoc" teams of specialists are assigned to value manage a specific subsystem or project. Normally the team comprises representatives from various departments: design, estimating, engineering, purchasing, construction, and so forth. The complexity of the project and its cost will determine the intensity of analysis undertaken by the project team. The team may work on a full-time or part-time basis and may be established for a short term (two weeks) or for a long period of time (six months). The team approach can be used in any stage of the project cycle. This method of organizing the operating function has the advantage of bringing together a number of diverse yet complementary talents, which provides a multidisciplined approach to the problem. The disadvantage of this approach is that it does not provide for the development of a continuing capability in depth, since project teams are normally disbanded when their task is completed.

2. *Project value specialist.* In this approach a value specialist is assigned to a particular project to do value management from design through production. In this case, the value specialist normally has a high technical capability in the project to which he or she is assigned. The specialist is responsible for ensuring that optimum value is built into the project at every stage in its development. This method of organizing the VM effort has the advantage of providing a continuity of value analysis through all design and construction decision points. Its disadvantage is that the number of projects that can be value analyzed is limited by the number of professionals who are trained in the VM concept.

3. *Procedural review points.* Under this method a value specialist participates in all committee decisions at the established review points: design reviews, make-or-buy reviews, systems integration, drawing release points, and so on. The specialist in this case is responsible for ensuring that value considerations are given proper weight at each decision point. This approach permits the value management staff to subject more projects to VM analysis. It usually is linked with widespread training programs that attempt to train all personnel concerned with product value to perform value management as part of their everyday job. The role of the value specialist at the review points is principally one of determining whether value has been properly considered in the product's development and production. The disadvantage of this system is that it does not encourage any intensive, in-depth VM studies.

There are many variations in these methods of organizing at the operating level. The three general patterns mentioned above obviously are not mutually exclusive. Many organizations use combinations of them; some even use all three at the same activity. The determination of the correct one to be applied to any given activity is a function of the variables referred to above (size, project mix, existing organizational structure).

The type of VM training program used by the activity can affect the type of organization selected. For example, as cited above, an activity that has put a large number of people through a seminar training program could decide to select alternative 3 and use a few value specialists only as monitors to ensure that value is built into the project.

2.4.4 VALUE MANAGEMENT ORGANIZATION IN THE PROCURING ACTIVITY (OWNER)

Many of the comments made in the preceding section about producing activities are pertinent also to a discussion of organizing value management in procuring activities. The basic difference, however, between producing and procuring activities is that the latter place primary emphasis on evaluation of proposals and on pre-procurement purification of specifications rather than on detailed VM studies. Generally, VM studies performed by a procuring activity are secondary in importance and are limited to a study of the specifications contained in procurement packages. The VM staff of the procuring activity also provides guidance to contracting officers concerning the type of VM incentive clause to be included in contracts.

As in producing activities, there is no one correct way to organize the VM effort in procuring activities. As a rule of thumb, however, it can be stated that value management has some close kinship with the disciplines of quality control, reliability, and maintainability and therefore could, wherever possible, be organized similarly to these functions.

2.4.5   DETERMINATION OF THE LEVEL OF EFFORT

Over a period of time, the level of value management to be applied will be determined by the ratio of net savings achieved to costs incurred. Generally this ratio should exceed 10 to 1; in other words, for every dollar spent for value management, the activity should recover $10 or more. This ratio of return may not be possible, however, where the total effort is applied to an extremely technical project such as a nuclear power plant. Returns as low as 2 to 1 may be worthwhile in such instances.

It is a more difficult matter, however, to determine how much to invest initially in a VM program. Experience to date indicates that a budget of from 0.3% to 0.5% of total project dollar volume is an appropriate level. These figures are presented only as guidelines and should not be taken as inflexible limitations (refer to Section 2.3.3).

The structure of the VM organization also is a determining factor in the level of effort to be applied. The overriding consideration is a reasonable return on the funds invested. Understaffing the VM function does not permit optimum application of the concept; overstaffing leads to a lowered savings-to-cost ratio and damages the program by subjecting it to charges of "empire building."

The management level to which value management reports is an important factor in the acceptance of the concept. The crucial question is not whether value management is attached to procurement, engineering, or manufacturing. The vital point is that, regardless of what functional area it is assigned to, the management level to which it reports must be extensive enough to cover all areas affecting the validity of a value study, high enough to communicate directly with decision makers responsible for implementation of a value proposal, and powerful enough to assume control and responsibility for the administration and assignments of the value management staff.

2.5 HUMAN FACTORS OF VALUE MANAGEMENT RESISTANCE AND ACCEPTANCE

Working with people is the most important aspect of most professional positions. No less is true for the VM staff. The way the staff interacts with others is a prime determinant in the success or failure of a VM program. People at all levels in an organization can become involved in some portion of the total VM effort. For the effort to be successful, all people involved must not only offer their cooperation but must become a part of the dynamic and creative spirit that is basic to value management. It is up to management to inseminate this spirit throughout the organization.

2.5.1 HUMAN RELATIONS

Favorable attitudes toward and acceptance of a new concept develop gradually and usually result from favorable individual experiences with the concept. Each member of the VM staff can make an important contribution toward gaining acceptance of value management by following the general principles described in the following paragraphs.

Empathy

In all dealings with other people, it is helpful to practice empathy—to imagine yourself in another's shoes. To successfully use empathy in dealings with people, ask yourself these questions:

- What do they say?
- What do their actions indicate?
- What do they really believe?
- Why do they believe this way, act as they do, and say what they do?

If you are able to answer these questions, you will overcome the hurdle of understanding others. If you maintain a state of relaxed objectivity, you will not be controlled by your emotions. This use of empathy paves the way for selecting the correct approach to whatever attitude is encountered. The wider your own interest, the better you can share the interests of others.

Honesty

If the staff member will remember that he or she is just one member of an organization involved in a total effort, the human relations part of the job should come easily. In most cases, those consulted contribute time and technical ability to the value management effort with no chance of praise or recognition for their contributions. For this reason, always give broad credit for contributions to a successful VM study. When asking for help and information, admit unfamiliarity with the subject and inform those asked that they are doing you a service, that their efforts are appreciated. Good manners and honesty help produce goodwill.

Individuality

It would be well to remember that every person is human, each with his or her own peculiar collection of frailities, ideas, habits, and ways of thinking. Individuals approach a problem in their own way, and each design is a product of the particular designer's sensitivities and pre-conceptions. The cooperation you receive from others depends to a large degree on your ability to convince them that their competence is recognized, and that as a result of the VM study you have the time for those "tough-nut" problems that were previously, probably through necessity, dealt with in a habitual manner.

Thoughtfulness

Regard for the feelings or circumstances of others is essential to establishing a climate where people will take an active interest in the performance of value management. Keep in mind that people have pride in their abilities and in the work they perform. It is the staff members' personal job to get people to relax and lose their apprehension of those who come to them asking questions and suggesting changes. People are committed to established ways of thinking and established ways of doing things, and they do not change easily. It is unreasonable to expect them to adopt new ideas and philosophies in a short time. Patience is a vital asset if constructive results are to be realized.

Positive Thinking

Positive thinking has been frequently touted as the best medicine for overcoming natural inertia. This is certainly true of value management. Positive thinking on the part of VM staff members leads to positive and dynamic actions. This is not to say that staff members must be completely extroverted. It is necessary that they be grounded well enough in the basic VM techniques that they are able to show confidence and firm resolve in its application. Such a positive approach must, however, be tempered by consideration of the human relations points made in previous paragraphs.

Flexibility

In this changing world, with its sophisticated electronics, journeys into space, computerized ships, tablet food, paper clothing, antibiotics, and a myriad of other "impossibilities," today's poison becomes tomorrow's food, today's dream is tomorrow's reality, and today's high cost problem yields to tomorrow's "value management" solution. Staff members must be aware of these new concepts and be flexible in their thinking so that a new idea injected into a proposal will be given full consideration from all angles and a prompt decision rendered. They must also accept the fact that circumstances do change with conditions and that an excellent VM proposal today might be outmoded tomorrow.

2.5.2 WHY UNNECESSARY COSTS ARE CREATED

Unnecessary costs are defined in Section 2.3.2. But what are some of the specific reasons for unnecessary costs? The most frequent reasons for unnecessary costs in a building or subsystem fall into one or more of the categories that follow.

Lack of an Idea

Unnecessary cost can be built into a service simply because of the failure to utilize creative ability in developing alternative solutions. In many cases the first workable solution that comes to mind is accepted. Unnecessary cost is eliminated by developing and analyzing alternative ideas, not only from a performance standpoint, but, equally as important, from an economic standpoint.

Lack of Information

Lack of information on exactly what function is to be performed, lack of information regarding what the owner actually wants or needs, lack of information on new processes, and lack of cost information are but a few of the "lack of's" that help create unnecessary costs.

Temporary Circumstances

Decisions that are forced, perhaps to meet an urgent delivery schedule, can result in a temporary condition to satisfy a requirement without regard to cost. Temporary measures often become a fixed part of the building, resulting in unnecessary costs year after year.

Honest Wrong Beliefs

Unnecessary costs are often caused by decisions based on false beliefs and not on the true facts. Someone may believe that there is good reason why something should not be done. "Honest wrong beliefs" can stop a good idea that could lead to more economical service.

Habits and Attitudes

Attitudes support habits. People must face the fact that some of their habits are in need of review. Old habits can be changed, new habits can be developed, and more important—if unnecessary costs are to be eliminated—decisions must be based on fact and not on habits and attitudes. Some people are reluctant to make a change of any kind regardless of the merits of the proposal. Some lack the positive attitude that a design or service can somehow be produced or done differently at a lower cost. Others feel that they perform value management every day on their job. This will usually prove to be only partially true since only a few of the VM techniques and procedures are normally used on anything but a formal program. Still others feel that their situation is unique and that value management is all right for everybody but them.

Reluctance to Seek Advice

Designers are often reluctant to seek advice from others; to admit that they do not know is regarded as a disgrace. That this feeling is not so prevalent in the medical profession is evidenced by general practitioners, who call in specialists when they need them. Architects and engineers must also seek the advice of experts outside their own areas if maximum value is to be achieved.

Shortage of Time

With the emphasis on reduction in lead time during the design phase, time is nearly always very limited. Frequently, the time pressure is so great that it is impossible to consider properly, if at all, the value of the item being developed. The people working on these projects usually find it necessary to accept the first workable solution to a problem in order to complete the job on time. Seldom is there time to sit back and contemplate ideas or to design for value. Items developed under such conditions are normally good candidates for VM study.

Changing Technology

Rapid strides in the development of processes, products, and materials present constantly changing, and often lower-cost, ways of performing the necessary functions. Every design or product can be thought of as advancing toward obsolescence.

Lack of a Yardstick for Measuring Value

Performance characteristics of an item can be rather accurately evaluated through various physical tests and measurements. No such test or measurement exists for determining the precise value content of an item. However, the value management procedure does compare present cost of performing a function with a best estimate of worth (or value) for that function. Lack of a precise yardstick complicates the problem of measuring value; nevertheless, value must be estimated in order to expose waste and permit management to put its resources to better use.

Old Specifications

Technology is advancing so fast, publications are never completely up to date. With increased emphasis on faster production, management is forcing the designer to use a specification unquestioningly. In today's environment, anything beyond five years old is almost sure to need value improvement.

Poor Human Relations

Poor communications, misunderstanding, and normal friction between human beings are frequent sources of unnecessary costs. This is true because such frictions impede the free flow of information that is needed if people are to be able to do their jobs completely and efficiently. On complex projects requiring the talents of many people, good human relations are especially critical. It is often difficult to get the various specialists on complex projects to work together; yet if they do not, they are likely to work at cross purposes, wasting a great deal of effort and yielding a final product whose value is not commensurate with its cost.

2.5.3 RESISTING INNOVATION

Innovation is a wonderful thing—as long as it involves somebody else! Doing things differently upsets comfortable habits of thought and action. It creates the need for thinking, planning, and making new decisions. Change always involves risk: the risk of failure, the risk that things will not turn out as planned! Who knows what problems will be created as a result of change? Because of this uncertainty many people automatically put up mental blocks to innovation. Figure 2.7 lists a few of the hundreds of possible mental blocks. To persons using them they are the best reasons in the world for doing things the old way. One way to overcome these mental blocks is to gain cooperation through good human relations.

Mental blocks to innovation existed for years before value management. Figure 2.8 illustrates a few lessons from history. Figure 2.9 includes a check list that can be used as a self-test for individuals to use to check their attitude toward innovation and progress.

2.5.4 MOTIVATION AND INCENTIVES

When dealing with the problem of motivation and incentives it is necessary to distinguish between those motivative and incentive forces aimed at personnel and those directed at organizations.

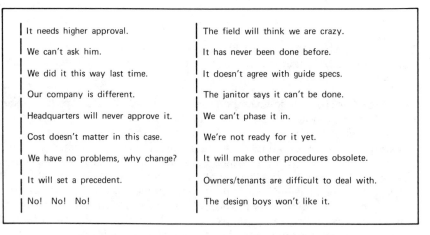

It needs higher approval.	The field will think we are crazy.
We can't ask him.	It has never been done before.
We did it this way last time.	It doesn't agree with guide specs.
Our company is different.	The janitor says it can't be done.
Headquarters will never approve it.	We can't phase it in.
Cost doesn't matter in this case.	We're not ready for it yet.
We have no problems, why change?	It will make other procedures obsolete.
It will set a precedent.	Owners/tenants are difficult to deal with.
No! No! No!	The design boys won't like it.

Figure 2.7 Mental blocks to value management.

THE LOCOMOTIVE / In 1781 George Stephenson, working in a colliery near Newcastle, England, developed a traveling machine for handling coal along the tramway from the pithead to the canal. By 1814, his locomotive was completed and could pull eight trucks loaded with 30 tons of coal up a slight grade at 4 miles per hour. After further development an engine was produced which would attain speeds up to 12 miles per hour. The cities of Manchester and Liverpool applied to Parliament for permission to build a railroad line. Stephenson went to Parliament to appear before the committee. His ideas, claims, and calculations were ridiculed. The scheme was called "the most absurd that ever entered the head of a man." It was claimed that the terrible spectacle of a locomotive rushing by would affect people and animals— ladies would have miscarriages, cows cease to give milk, and hens lay no more eggs; the poisoned air from the engine would kill all livestock in the district and the birds in the trees; houses along the line would be set on fire by sparks from the locomotive; there would be no more work for the horses, which would die out as a result, and coachmen and innkeepers along the deserted roads would become beggars while highwaymen would roam the countryside; the engine boilers would burst and scald the passengers to death—after they had gone mad because no human could stand a speed of more than ten miles per hour.

THE GASLIGHT / The invention of the gaslight was condemned because: according to divine order, night is appointed to be a darkness, broken only at certain times by the moon, and we should not try to turn night into day. Gaslights encouraged many illnesses by making it easier for people to stay out in the streets at night so that they caught colds, coughs, and sore throats. The brightness makes the drinker feel safe so he stays in the dens drinking until late at night. It makes the horse timid and the thief bold. These were considered reasons, in 1819, to discourage the use of gas street lights.

THE PENNSYLVANIA TURNPIKE / In 1938 the turnpike was termed "Governor Barle's folly" because cars and tires could not be built to withstand constant high speeds.

THE TELEPHONE / The following editorial appeared in a Boston Newspaper toward the end of the 19th century: "A man about 46 years of age, giving the name of Joshua Coppersmith, has been arrested in New York for attempting to extort funds from ignorant and superstitious people by exhibiting a device which he says will convey the human voice any distance over metallic wires, so that it will be heard to the listener at the other end. He calls the instrument a 'telephone', which is obviously intended to imitate the word 'telegraph' and win the confidence of those who know of the success of the latter instrument without understanding the principles on which it is based. Well informed people know that it is impossible to transmit a human voice over the wires."

Figure 2.8 Case histories—mental blocks to innovation.

THE AUTOMOBILE / People at one time were very stubbornly opposed to the automobile. After the turn of the century, motoring was said to be as injurious as excessive indulgence in alcohol or nicotine. Warnings were given against the inadequacy of the automobile, which was inferior to the horse and furthermore had no brains. The editor of the *Springfield Republican* refused an invitation to ride in an early automobile, claiming it was incompatible with the dignity of his position. Chauncey M. Depew warned his nephew not to invest $5000 in Ford stocks because "nothing has come along to beat the horse."

THE ELECTRIC LIGHT / Henry Morton, the president of Stevens Institute of Technology, protested against the trumpeting of results of Edison's experiments in electric lighting as a "wonderful success" when "everyone acquainted with the subject will recognize it as a conspicuous failure."

THE SKYSCRAPER / When Buffington took out patents for the steel-frame skyscraper in 1888, the *Architectural News* predicted that the expansion and contraction of iron would crack all the plaster, eventually leaving only the shell.

Figure 2.8   (Continued)

Personnel

There are two categories of personnel concerned with value management activities. One group consists of those people who do the actual value management work. The other group includes the peripheral staff who provide service or evaluation assistance to the value management staff, as well as managers who provide overall direction and policy for the VM effort. For both groups, the same motivating techniques can be used.

One of the strongest motivating influences on personnel is the knowledge that top management supports the program and is closely following its progress. Evidence of top management interest is shown in a number of ways, such as issuance of a management policy statement on the subject, appearance of top managers as guest speakers at VM training sessions, and participation by top managers in award ceremonies recognizing individual and group contributions to the program.

Financial incentives and accelerated career progression are excellent means of motivating superior support for value management. Financial awards, bonuses, and incentive plans can be based directly on the financial aspects of performance; that is, individuals would share in any savings resulting from their performance and participa-

Are you confident you don't resist progress? Well, just for fun, check the following list of expressions people use to avoid considering, or trying, new ideas.

IT ISN'T IN THE BUDGET / Well, maybe it isn't in the budget. But the budget represents yesterday's planning. If reasons are compelling enough, the budget can be—and should be—changed. The budget is not a strait jacket intended to freeze all thought and action.

WE DON'T HAVE THE TIME / This is the favorite comment of people who've planned something and don't want their plans changed. If they really want to change things, it's amazing what can be accomplished in a very brief period. How often is there time to delay contract award after bid opening but never time before bid opening to prevent the delay?

LET'S FORM A COMMITTEE / If you're opposed to action, this is a convenient way to put it off. A wise person once defined a committee as a group of the unwilling, chosen from the unfit, to do the unnecessary at an unsuitable time.

HAS ANYONE ELSE TRIED IT? / This is a good question—if it's asked for the purpose of obtaining information. The trouble is that it's so often asked by someone groping desperately for a reason to say no. And a "no" decision solely on this basis is just as wrong as a "yes" decision solely on the basis someone else has tried it.

WHY CHANGE IT? IT'S STILL WORKING O.K. / An organization which never changes anything as long as it works will never be known for progressiveness. Changes that are delayed until they HAVE to be made are often costly and more embarrassing.

WE TRIED THAT BEFORE / Did you? Precisely this idea or merely something like it? And how was it executed? Don't be too sure that ideas that were tried and didn't work are bad ideas. Many good ideas have failed simply because they were poorly executed.

THE BOSS WILL NEVER BUY IT / How do you know? Did you ask him? How did you ask him? Did you ask him in an off the cuff way over lunch or did you present him with a specific, well documented and completely staffed cost savings proposal?

LET'S SHELVE IT FOR THE TIME BEING / A convenient way to kill something without being charged with murder. Those making this remark aren't openly opposed to the idea; they just want to give it time to ripen. What they really want is time for it to die.

Figure 2.9 Checklist: Do you resist progress and innovation?

IT'S AGAINST OUR POLICY / Policies are a valuable guide to action. But there are also times when policy is a poor substitute for good judgment. When a policy blocks progress, it ought to be brought to the attention of people who have the authority to change it.

YOU'RE TWO YEARS AHEAD OF YOUR TIME / Spoken from the vantage point of superior experience, but seldom backed by good sound reasons. This is one of the favorite ways of turning something down without making the man who suggested it feel too badly. After all, who isn't flattered by the thought that he's ahead of his time? The organization, by failing to consider his idea, may find itself behind the times.

Under the proper circumstances, some of the above expressions make excellent sense. That's precisely what makes them so damaging. Wrongly used they sometimes stop a valuable idea dead in its tracks. When you catch yourself using one of these expressions—or one like it—stop and ask yourself a few questions: Do I really mean this? Do I have good reasons for what I am saying? Or am I merely looking for excuses to kill the idea and avoid action? You can't stop progress except in your own department. If an idea is a good one, someone somewhere is going to think of it and put it into use. Why shouldn't it be you? The man who kills progress is killing his own future.

Figure 2.9 (*Continued*)

tion in the VM effort. This performance and participation also can become a major element of career and promotion evaluation.

Organizations

For the organization, there are three major motivating forces prompting the use of value management, all related directly or indirectly to increased earnings and profits. The first of these forces is the part that value management plays in improving a company's future competitive position, ultimately leading to increased business and higher profits. The second is the company's desire to satisfy the client's cost consciousness by showing that active, fruitful efforts are being made to reduce costs and increase the value of the facility. The third is an important benefit: increased profit margins on existing and future contracts through financial incentives or additional fees for VM efforts. These contractual and financial opportunities are discussed in more detail in Chapter 4.

2.6 TRAINING

A planned program of training demonstrates an organization's interest in the subject and in the development of its personnel. Thus, training programs are an effective integration of the interests of both top management and employees. People are not born with the specific skills that society requires, but must develop them. Consequently, carefully formulated programs for training personnel are essential to any new program. Increased emphasis on value management is mandatory if its full potential is to be realized.

This section presents some of the techniques that have been used successfully in VM training. Workshop seminars and indoctrination lectures for training operating personnel are discussed in some detail. The contribution of formal institutional training, on-the-job training, and rotational work assignments to the development of full-time value specialists is outlined. Attention also is called to some other training techniques that have been found useful.

Obviously, these training techniques are not mutually exclusive, nor will every organization need to employ all types of VM training at one time. Decisions as to what types are appropriate and who is to be trained depend in part upon the size of the organization and the scope of its activities.

2.6.1 TECHNIQUES FOR TRAINING OPERATING PERSONNEL

The Workshop Seminar

PURPOSE. Workshop seminars are the main source of formal VM training for operating personnel. Because they identify individuals with special aptitude for value management, workshop seminars also can be considered one of the first steps in developing qualified full-time value specialists. Incorporation of the "learn-by-doing" technique in the form of project work demonstrates the feasibility of VM methodology.

The broad objectives of workshop seminars are to:

- Educate personnel in the methodology of value management.
- Demonstrate by personal participation that the methodology is effective as a routine discipline for cost reduction.
- Improve communication between all groups concerned with project value.
- Identify personnel who have talent for value management.
- Develop raw data for actual VM change proposals.

CHARACTERISTICS. The particular arrangement and curriculum for workshop seminars will vary according to the organization's major business, size, and structure. However, certain definable attributes of the workshop seminar are considered fundamental.

Priority of Attendance. Conflict between the pressures of daily task accomplishment and seminar attendance must be resolved prior to student selection. Stress should be placed on the need for regular attendance.

Duration and Session Schedule. A range of 40 to 80 hours is suggested for the full workshop. The time should be divided about 50-50 between lecture and project work. Half-day and full-day sessions have been found to work well; less than half-day sessions have been inadequate. In any event, the total calendar time between the first session and the last session should be between two and four weeks. Less than two weeks may not provide sufficient time for the attendees to obtain suitable cost data on their projects, especially if outside vendor quotations are required.

Number of Participants. Class size will vary according to the organizational needs and the availability of experienced personnel to serve as team project leaders. Past practice indicates that the optimum group is about 40 persons. However, satisfactory results have been obtained with groups of 100. The larger group obviously requires more careful planning of project work and vendor coordination.

Attendees for each seminar should be drawn from the various line and staff groups. The following groups should be represented at each seminar: engineering (design, project, specification, test), purchasing, manufacturing, reliability, finance, and quality control. One or more personnel from contracts, sales and marketing, industrial relations, and any other function that has interfaces with value considerations should be scheduled to attend the first seminar. They can then serve as the VM training contact within their respective areas.

The interfaces between owners, architect-engineers, construction managers, and contractors can be improved through the workshop seminar. Significant communication improvements have been achieved by inviting representatives of the various organizations to attend.

Team Organization and Responsibility. Seminar attendees are assigned to teams of from four to eight for the project portion. A team of six or seven permits more complete workshop coverage of advanced VM methodology such as the development of value standards or a cost target plan for the project.

Each team is held responsible for the preparation of a report that describes its application of the lecture theory to their workshop project. Upon completion of the seminar, these reports normally are submitted to the VM line organization for possible implementation.

Many workshop seminars devote their last few hours to oral presentations by a few or by all teams. Team members are called upon to present conclusions and recommendations resulting from their study project.

Workshop Projects. Projects are an essential element of the workshop seminars. The participants, working in teams, apply VM methodology to a building system. This exercise frequently results in significant cost reduction proposals, thereby proving to the individuals that they can improve product value and that VM methodology does work. Although seminar project work is an exercise, it must offer a real opportunity for the team's efforts to be realized. Every attempt should be made to select a "live" project, with actual savings potential.

The following features are desirable for workshop projects:

- Prejudged as susceptible to cost improvement.
- System sample or mockup is available.
- Drawings, specifications, and layouts are available.
- Total cost per program is large enough to achieve measurable reduction.
- Performs a distinct function by itself.
- Responsible designer or equivalent agrees to its use.

Seminar Leadership. Three types of leadership personnel are usually involved in a VM seminar: lecturers, guest speakers, and project leaders. The lecturers provide the theory and background of the VM methodology and creative problem solving. Guest speakers are called upon as needed to cover the areas of in-house disciplines that touch on value considerations. These include purchasing, cost accounting, contract administration, and estimating. Project leaders provide guidance and stimulation during the project work portion of the seminar. Ordinarily, project leaders work with one to three teams.

The lecturers must combine an understanding of their topic with the ability to communicate. They do not need to be actively working as full-time value specialists, but it is desirable that they have previously attended a seminar. At least one of the lecturers should be a value specialist. Guest speakers should be experts in their respective fields and from the ranks of top management. Project leaders must have previous value management experience. They should be able to keep the team energized toward the seminar goal. The value management staff is the best source of project leaders.

Curriculum. A seminar lecture schedule should be prepared in advance. The curriculum should cover all aspects of the VM methodology (discussed in Chapter 8). Lectures should be given on the details of internal procedures that bear upon the value program. This includes topics such as internal cost procedures, contractual aspects of value management, and the relationship of value management to reliability, quality control, and purchasing services. A typical workshop seminar curriculum used by a major government construction agency is presented in Figure 2.10.

Vendor Participation. To acquaint participants with the suppliers' role, a limited number of vendors may be invited to participate in the seminar. Vendors should be invited to send two representatives, one technical and one cost estimating, with a small display of their system or process. Invited vendors should be those appropriate to the workshop projects. A portion of the project time can be designated for team members to discuss their projects with vendors.

Indoctrination Lectures

This type of training encompasses one to eight hours of familiarization sessions, which introduce the fundamentals, goals, and operation of the VM program. Indoctrination lectures are appropriate for personnel whose primary responsibility does not warrant attendance at a full-scale workshop seminar, such as middle management executives, senior staff personnel, planning personnel, draftsmen, and newly hired personnel.

The specific content of indoctrination lectures must be tailored to the audience. However, certain basic features are common:

- Concepts of value.
- Principles of VM methodology.
- Criteria for application.
- Organization and operation of the VM program.
- Contractual aspects.
- Case histories.
- Relationship and contribution of the audience to the VM program.

Session I

10 minutes	Keynote
20 minutes	Value management's history, concepts, philosophy
20 minutes	General orientation of value management techniques
20 minutes	The importance of evaluating our habits and attitudes
10 minutes	Recognition of "roadblocks" and overcoming them
15 minutes	What value management can do for this division or operation
10 minutes	Break
15 minutes	Selection of product for study
15 minutes	Get all the facts
15 minutes	Determine costs
30 minutes	Determine the function
30 minutes	Functional workshop
1 hour, 15 minutes	Lunch
15 minutes	Put a $ on the specifications and requirements
30 minutes	Functional workshop
3 hours, 30 minutes	Project work (gather project information)

Session II

Project Work (gather project information), correlate project information, and determine project function

Session III

15 minutes	Developing alternatives
30 minutes	Creativity
30 minutes	Creative workshop
15 minutes	Blast and create
15 minutes	Break
2 hours	Creative workshop (on operation projects)
1 hour, 15 minutes	Lunch
1 hour, 45 minutes	Project work (creative session on project)
2 hours	Determine function and create

Figure 2.10 A typical VM workshop seminar curriculum.

Session IV

30 minutes	Recap on information gathering and development of alternative phases
3 hours, 15 minutes	Project work (Correlate information from functional and creative efforts)
1 hour, 15 minutes	Lunch

Session V

30 minutes	Every idea can be developed
15 minutes	The importance of testing and verification
15 minutes	How to refine ideas
15 minutes	Put a $ on each idea
15 minutes	Evaluate the function
15 minutes	Evaluate by comparison
15 minutes	Break
1 hour, 45 minutes	Project work—Evaluate ideas
1 hour, 15 minutes	Lunch
15 minutes	The use of specialty vendors
15 minutes	Consult vendors
15 minutes	Use specialty products, processes, and materials
15 minutes	Use company and industrial specialists
15 minutes	Use company and industrial standards
15 minutes	Break
2 hours, 15 minutes	Project work (Investigation of project ideas)

Session VI

60 minutes	Introduction of specialty suppliers
15 minutes	Vendor display time
15 minutes	Break
2 hours	Project work
1 hour, 15 minutes	Lunch
60 minutes	Introduction of specialty suppliers
15 minutes	Vendor display time
15 minutes	Break
2 hours, 15 minutes	Project work

Figure 2.10 (*Continued*)

Session VII

Project work

Session VIII

Project work

Session IX

3 hours, 45 minutes	Project work
1 hour, 15 minutes	Lunch
15 minutes	Developing the proposal
15 minutes	Motivate positive action
	Project work

Session X

3 hours, 45 minutes	Project work
1 hour, 15 minutes	Lunch
30 minutes	Value management—a new tool for everyone to use
1 hour, 45 minutes	Project work (wrap-up)
	Management presentation

Figure 2.10 (*Continued*)

The effort to plan and present indoctrination lectures should not interfere with or jeopardize the workshop seminar effort. However, they should be accomplished as soon as feasible after implementation of the workshop program. This type of training activity is normally performed by value management staff with top management participation as guest lecturers.

2.6.2 SELECTING AND TRAINING PERSONNEL

Selection Criteria

At present, no formal academic training exists for value management. Thus, value specialists must be developed by industry until academic institutions develop complete programs.

To be successful, value specialists must be respected for their professional competence, but equally as important, they must have the tact and diplomacy to sell themselves and their ideas. An effective VM program depends on the skill and persuasiveness of the value specialist in establishing close working relationships with all personnel concerned with project value. Thus, it is imperative that personality traits be strongly emphasized in the selection of VM trainees.

As previously discussed, the workshop seminar can serve as a screening device in the selection of VM trainees. The seminars provide an opportunity for individuals to display value talents and to be observed for evidence of desired personality traits. In addition, workshop seminars give potential value specialists an opportunity to get a taste of value work before they are committed to it. The interests of cost effectiveness are served by using the workshop seminar as a "test bed" before proceeding with on-the-job training.

On-the-Job Training

This is the practical school in which VM trainees learn approved methods of work. They deal with the tools of their trade under the tutelage of qualified value specialists. Trainees are given the opportunity to learn how to apply basic skills to specific and productive work assignments. Perhaps as important as the training received is the satisfaction gained from being productive while in a training status.

Rotational Job Assignments

Such training frequently is used in conjunction with on-the-job training. It requires each trainee value specialist to be assigned to various operational areas for limited periods of time. These areas may include purchasing, cost estimating, design engineering, construction, and so forth. Exposure to these other environments serves to broaden the individual's perspective and, in so doing, leads to an improved understanding of the complex nature of project value.

2.6.3 OTHER TRAINING TECHNIQUES

Many organizations choose to train personnel for value management through less formal methods than those previously discussed, and others with formal training programs supplement them with informal training devices. Some of these informal training approaches are discussed below.

Books and Manuals. Books and manuals are means of bringing about a climate of cost awareness throughout the organization. These documents can be oriented to value management in the sense that they define "how to do" value management or they can provide cost data relating to trade-off possibilities between materials, methods, or both.

Bulletins and Newsletters. A periodically distributed VM newsletter or bulletin could contain a section devoted to VM methodology.

Technical Meetings. Value management films or speakers from other facilities may be presented at in-house conferences.

Displays. Case histories annotated to indicate the VM method may be placed at strategic locations throughout the organization.

2.6.4 IMPLEMENTATION OF TRAINING

Value management training requires participation by many organization elements. Coordination by a central source is desirable to avoid conflict, duplication, and dilution of the primary effort. A VM training coordinator should be designated to act as the focal point for integration of the total effort. Each functional department should have one person responsible for coordinating its participation with the training coordinator.

Most large-scale organizations have training staffs, usually as a part of personnel or industrial relations departments. While the primary responsibility for VM training (as with all training) must rest with the line organization, the staff training personnel play a key role. Their assistance to line personnel includes coordinating individual specialty training such as value management with the activity's overall training program; developing training devices; providing and scheduling the use of training facilities; training instructors in the techniques of training, that is, "teaching the teachers how to teach"; and many other types of assistance that only professional trainers can provide.

A training plan is prepared as a portion of the overall VM program plan. In addition to those elements normally contained in program plans, it delineates the following:

- Annual training schedule for the overall organization and for each major functional division.
- Assessment procedure to evaluate training effectiveness.
- A method for developing an in-house training capability, if none exists and the size of the organization warrants one.

The establishment of in-house training capability must reflect the needs of the organization. Therefore, it is necessary that the personnel responsible for this task be familiar with value management and with the overall company operation. Where no VM program exists, the in-house training capability may be achieved by obtaining initial training outside the organization. Some sources of value management training are as follows:

- Consulting organizations with VM training capability.
- Professional societies such as the Society of Value Engineers (SAVE), Consulting Engineers Council (CEC), and the American Institute of Architects (AIA).
- Colleges and universities such as UCLA, Northeastern University, and Boston College.
- Large contractors, architect-engineers, and construction managers.
- The federal government.

Upon completion of this outside training, a VM training plan that incorporates the organization's specific requirements is formulated. The next step would be to schedule the first in-house workshop seminar, using the services of one or more of the sources listed above. In subsequent seminars, responsibility would gradually be shifted to in-house personnel, ultimately culminating in a complete in-house VM training capability.

Training is an important element of a comprehensive VM program and requires proper emphasis if value management is to reach its full potential. A planned training program develops the necessary skills to do the value management job.

2.7 SUMMARY

Value management is an organized approach to obtaining maximum value for every construction dollar spent. Its philosophy is to create an atmosphere where creative thinking is encouraged and change is accepted. An effort is made to bring out a person's latent creative ability and to get him or her to challenge a design in a creative atmosphere. Most professionals have this talent and need only the motivation and incentive to exercise it.

Top management can supply the worker with these ingredients by initiating an integrated VM program, making evident its full support of that program, and training personnel in VM methodology. Experience with a successful VM effort will convince even the skeptics that value management is indeed an innovative and powerful tool for the construction industry.

We have discussed the benefits that can result from a VM program; the need for top management participation; the relationship of the VM staff to the overall organization; the human factors involved in value management efforts, including motivation and incentives; and the training needed throughout the organization.

Value management benefits everyone. The owner obtains a structure of enhanced value and quality at a reduced cost. The architect-engineer, construction manager, and contractor have an opportunity to increase their profits while serving the best interests of their clients. The public and tenants see and use a pleasing building that incorporates the latest technology in line with energy conservation and other environmental considerations.

CHAPTER 3

THE SYSTEMS APPROACH AND VALUE MANAGEMENT

3.1 INTRODUCTION TO THE SYSTEMS APPROACH

During the past two decades the scope of technology has expanded at a great rate to meet the needs of the aerospace and nuclear energy programs. The concurrent impact of sociological, environmental, and energy requirements led to a serious reappraisal of government organizations and our national education systems. A corresponding evaluation of industry's management techniques indicated some rather serious shortcomings.

Previously, with a stable environment and local and unsophisticated operations, programs could be effectively accommodated by relatively straightforward managerial functions. The program goals were usually short range; activities to achieve the goals were linear rather than concurrent; and life-cycle cost considerations were seldom specified as functions of either planning or design.

The systems approach evolved from the need to incorporate the widely diversified efforts of a wealth of human talents to implement a complex technological program. The sophistication, however, no longer lies in the management techniques brought into being at the outset of the program and kept on line during the acquisition process. The evolution of concurrent program development of vehicle, personnel, equipment, and facilities is shown graphically for the transition from early aviation to deep space in Figure 3.1. The expanding scope of these concurrent elements resulted in the systems approach.

With the engineering effort associated with new space and subsea environments came a host of professional disciplines participating in what had been heretofore purely engineering. For example, the psychologist became a "human engineer." New specification series and

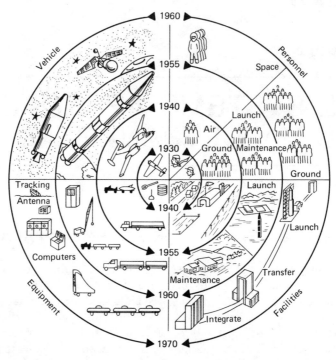

Figure 3.1 The expansion and evolution of space programs, 1930–1970.

design standards were generated to assure that human beings were fully considered not only from the standpoint of humanizing machines, but also with respect to reactions to colors, displays, and sounds. At the same time, concern that the safety of operational workers must be considered in design has resulted in laws governing occupational health and safety measures. Moreover, provisions must be made for handicapped personnel in every amenity that was previously treated as standard in facility designs.

Enactment of the federal, state, and local environmental protection regulations has had a most profound effect. Before a major program or project can be undertaken, a rigorous analysis of its potential impact on communities, land use, resources, flora, and fauna is required. Thus, ecological sciences become contributors to planning, design, and construction. The energy crisis, affecting both cost and conservation techniques in achieving effective savings, has further complicated the process of acquiring systems and facilities. Even the federal government must comply with the regulatory and conservation practices, whereas previously waivers were the watchword for all government programs and projects.

The planning activity prerequisite to design and engineering now requires that a number of trade-off studies be performed for concepts and siting to provide a careful balance between environmental impact, energy usage rates, and omnipresent costs. The trade-off studies are iterative, and, as will be seen later, they become more definitive when systems and hardware are specified. When components are identified, the normal function of value management rewards the program or project in the form of hard dollar savings.

3.2 COMPATIBILITY OF THE SYSTEMS APPROACH AND VALUE MANAGEMENT

The evolution of the systems approach was similar to the evolution of value management. Value management had its beginnings as value engineering (value analysis) when the General Electric Company launched an intensive effort in the late 1930s to identify the essential functions of their consumer and military products and to attain these functions at lowest cost. It has since emerged as an effective technique for achieving cost reduction in both governmental and industrial applications. Since value engineering was originally based on high-volume production, it was not initially acceptable for full-scale weapons and aerospace acquisition programs because of the one-of-a-kind and state-of-the-art characteristics of these programs. However, anticipation of substantial savings led the Department of Defense to adopt a more sophisticated approach to value engineering, and the resultant techniques and procedures are now accepted by defense industries in that most competitive environment.

The discipline of value engineering, now more adequately termed value management, is evident in formal program activities such as:

1. *Specification analysis.* Value management (VM) techniques are applied to identify and eliminate areas of "overspecification."

2. *Design reviews.* The opportunity to effect cost reductions is presented before the commitment is made to buy or build.

Both specification analysis and design reviews provide the "second look" that may have escaped the designer or engineer who has been seeking a physical solution to meet performance requirements. It may be that the designer/engineer is not aware of the target costs for the overall program and has not had the benefit of an overview from the standpoint of producibility, constructability, or even energy conservation.

The failure of the designer/engineer to recognize a candidate concept for cost reduction is no reflection on his or her capabilities. Traditionally, design/engineering disciplines function in a "line" organization and are supervised by the "staff" organization. The staff almost always comprises talented personnel who have progressed to staff from the line organizations and have their technical depth in the engineering discipline they started in. Basically, then, we have a twofold approach to cost reduction: line personnel charged with responsibility for design provide the focal point for the VM specialist, who has the full-time responsibility for seeking out more effective means to reduce costs without sacrificing functional integrity and design objectives.

On the other hand, a construction organization preparing bids makes its proposal based upon labor and material costs as well as its proposed plan of accomplishment. Because there is a limited response time between the time of the advertisement and the actual submittal of the proposal, there is little opportunity for the construction contractor to effect or implement cost reduction schemes. However, when there is a VM incentive clause within the contract, there will probably be proposals on either methods or materials of construction that provide shares of the savings for the contractor. For this reason, it is suggested that construction contractors have a professionally qualified value specialist in their organization as well as estimators, planners, and construction trade representatives.

It is recommended that a firm that specializes in construction management—that is, one that represents the owner contractually—have at least one value specialist.

For any program that involves the full range of acquisition activities, some part of the owner's organization should have a full-time, dedicated specialist to implement value management or assure that value management by others under contract is in force and in the proper perspective. If the owner, the owner's architect-engineer or designer, or the construction manager are not represented by qualified and dedicated VM specialists, the services of a value management firm should be solicited. In many cases the latter course will eliminate any bias that could be encountered when a cost reduction might result in a loss of fee to any of the participants.

One of the more important aspects of value management is its inherent potential for cost savings to the owner. Therefore, regardless of which segment of the program organization provides the service, the value analysis must not be a subordinate line function. As with the activities involved in quality assurance, the inspector/analyst must have the attention of the top managers in order to be effective. Only top-level responsibility can assure sufficient emphasis on value management.

Having awarded a degree of autonomy to the staff activities of value management personnel, we can foresee a similar situation for others such as quality assurance specialists, ecologists, and personnel who maintain control over target costs and schedules. In this environment the systems approach is most effective—particularly for any program or project that has over a half million dollars of anticipated acquisition expense. To a certain extent, autonomy has been attained for the value management activities by engaging the services of a firm that solely specializes in this service. This autonomous firm contributes to the activities of both the design and construction organizations for the client/owner by offering seminars, if value management is to be integral to the program, or it acts for the owner on a continuing basis by performing design and specifications reviews. It can be seen that in the management of the design or of the construction, whichever organization has the inherent capability to provide value management can probably render the service more economically for the owner, on a continuing basis, than can a consulting firm that provides only that service. The independent VM specialist who furnishes more than seminars and procedures is likely to end up in an adversary role, since much of his analysis would be judgmental and after the fact, rather than a considered value management judgment at the time of the initial design or as part of the specification.

The variations of a program organization shown in Figure 3.2 illustrate the relationships of an integral VM activity versus a consultant service. For major projects, Case 3 is the most effective, since the owner has retained a construction manager to look after his interests in quality, timing, and costs, each of which is a primary objective of the construction manager. Value management therefore fits well into the construction manager's role, provided he has the inherent capability.

3.3 APPLICATION OF VALUE MANAGEMENT THROUGH THE SYSTEMS APPROACH

Value management deals directly with design, procurement, and installation. Through the application of the systems approach, the same VM activities can be used on a preconceptual basis. The technique has

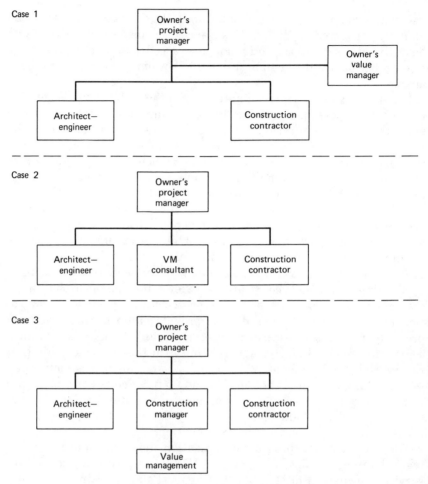

Figure 3.2 Program organizations.

been used for significant programs involving large and varied types of facilities with different costs. It has been used to establish the basis for "front-end" or programmatic cost estimates, which are presented to decision-making bodies such as the House of Representatives Appropriations Committee, for federal funds, and Department of Defense agencies for feasibility and cost studies. It provides the unique capability for preconcept trade-offs in consideration of both acquisition (nonrecurring) and operational (recurring) costs to ascertain a life-cycle or target cost. The step-by-step procedure is described below.

3.3.1   DEFINING THE PROGRAM

The essential tool for the initial planning/programming process is an analytical matrix. It is designed to bring together the three main ingredients of functions, characteristics (performance), and costs. The technique of matrix planning is best described by an illustrative case example. Assume a need has arisen for a manufacturing site of modest proportions. On a simplified matrix (Figure 3.3), the manufacturing site has been broken down into only five functions: (1) production/ assembly, (2) shops, (3) warehousing, (4) administration, and (5) security. Normally, using the systems approach, the functions would evolve from a formalized functional analysis, a flow diagram, and descriptive requirements that aggregate functions and requirements.

Functions and Characteristics

Functions are quantified horizontally under the facility characteristics, which are grouped by normal facility breakdown for units of measure. The first grouping, "Areas and Site work," could be expressed in separate columnar entries for total land, roads, parking, landscaping, and even rights of way and easements, when necessary. Under the simplified heading "Civil and Utilities," would be linear feet of water distribution, power lines, natural gas supply lines, and sewer lines; however, it must be kept in mind that these units of measure are outside the buildings. They include the linear distance that connects the onsite structures to the offsite utilities. It may even be necessary to include storm drains when this characteristic must be satisfied.

Under "Structural and Architectural," the breakout is again quantified by both functional and site-peculiar requirements. For instance, the ambient and geophysical constraints identified by the locale chosen (more than one locale may be under consideration at this point) are important. Thus, the definition of column entries for the structural and architectural group must take into consideration whether temporary, semipermanent, or permanent structures are to be characterized and priced. (Square feet is the normal unit of measure.)

A "Mechanical" grouping is next. This is likely to break down into tons for air conditioning, BTU for heating, tons for hoists, gallons per minute (or horsepower) for pumps.

Under "Electrical," such characteristics as KVA, KW for interior substations, or motor generating set values are important.

A final grouping under characteristics is "Occupancy," with an estimated proportion of male and female.

Facility Characteristics

Functions	Units of measure →	Areas and Site work / Civil and Utilities		Structural and Architectural	Mechanical	Electrical (Substations)	People (Occupancy)	
		Square yards	Linear feet	Square feet	Tons	KVA	Men	Women
Production/assembly		10,000 ($5)	10,000 ($15)	100,000 ($40)	50 ($200)	500 ($50)	200	100
Shops		1000 ($5)	500 ($15)	10,000 ($50)	10 ($200)	50 ($35)	20	5
Warehousing		5,000 ($3)	5,000 ($15)	50,000 ($30)	5 ($200)	50 ($35)	20	5
Administration		1000 ($5)	1000 ($10)	10,000 ($45)	10 ($200)	10 ($35)	30	20
Security		1000 ($5)	100 ($8)	1000 ($50)	1 ($300)	5 ($35)	10	2
Total	Units of measure	18,000	16,600	171,000	76	615	280	132
	Acquisition dollars	$80,000	244,300	6,500,000	15,300	29,025	⊠	⊠

$6,868,625

(For example only)

Figure 3.3 Simplified planning/program matrix.

The example in Figure 3.3 has been prepared on an extremely gross basis to illustrate how unit costs are applied to function. It is obvious that the columnar breakdown selected by the planner allows him the choice of the most definitive characteristics and units of measure that will lead to the most definitive unit costs. This is particularly important when good cost experience is available.

Unit Costs

The unit costs, placed in the matrix squares where quantified functions and characteristics/performance units of measure meet, have special meaning. It is generally accepted that the larger the quantity with respect to the facility, the lower the unit cost. The relationship, at least for the major consideration in the matrix, "Structural and Architectural," is shown in the special cost diagram provided as Figure 3.4. This will be particularly useful in conducting trade studies when the effort is made to define multiple functional structures (warehouse, shops, etc.) versus a megastructure in which all functions are incorporated. It is also very important that current-year costs, which will probably prove to be the most valid in any case, be used. The reason for using current-year costs, in addition to their validity, is that certain decisions may require study, such as the length of time to build the megastructure versus the incremental construction of the most needed buildings first. To amplify, the strategy of sequencing and packaging design and construction will offer benefits in the form of "cost avoidance"—the reduction of the inflationary effects of rising costs. Another feature of the unit cost is that when it is carefully defined a certain measure of visibility is afforded for the decision-making process in that the high-risk, long-lead items are segregated for procurement decisions. These are such items as large transformers, special air-conditioning systems, and heavy lift cranes. The unit cost for mechanical and electrical group characteristics is likely to include not only the labor and material costs for fit-up and installation, but also a subcontractor's overhead and markup as well as an allowance for the general contractor's fee for managing the subcontractors. In any case, a degree of visibility is also available for planning and strategy.

Acquisition Tabulations

It would seem that the planner need only calculate the quantities and unit costs to obtain the rough-order-of-magnitude costs for the initial estimate of the total site and facilities construction costs. However, several engineering checks are necessary to assure that the basis for

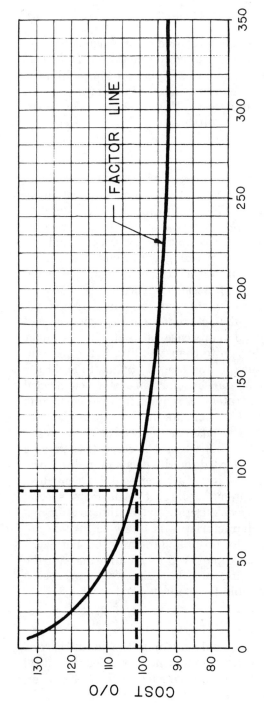

Figure 3.4 Unit cost adjustment table.

Example

1. To determine the square foot unit cost of a food service building (less special equipment costs) with a gross floor area of 17,700 S.F.

2. Experience is in hand for a similar facility that has a gross floor area of 19,800 S.F. and a unit cost of $28.40 per S.F.

3. Divide the area of the proposed building (17,700 S.F.) by the "experience" building size (19,800 S.F.) to obtain the percentage relationship (17,700 ÷ 19,800 = 0.89 or 89%)

4. From the percentage relationship of 89%, follow the broken line to the intersection with the factor line, then left to the percentage relationship line and obtain 101.0%.

5. Multiply the experience unit cost, $28.40 by 1.01 to produce the adjusted unit cost of $28.6840 (say $28.70 for planning purposes).

calculations is sound. An entry for water demand under "Civil and Utilities," for example, quantified in gallons per day, is compared with the production requirements and occupancy figures. Logic tells us that the linear feet for the water distribution piping must include pipe size, excavation, and backfill as well as the size of the buildings so that the fire demand is allowed for in establishing the unit cost. Following the same logical order of development, the sewerage is based on the occupancy, also apparent on the matrix, as well as on any effluent into the sewage from processes noted in the mechanical grouping. The matrix itself offers the best correlation of systems-to-cost and cost-to-function logic for the engineer to ensure that important elements are not overlooked at this stage of the planning as well as for cost trade-off.

Power is treated in the same way. For example, under the function of administration, if the only significant power requirement is for office services, it is fairly straightforward to estimate a power figure per square foot that takes care of lighting and utilities, not only for the cost of electrical installations, but also for operating costs. This will be seen in the second phase of the matrix planning technique. To find the total acquisition cost in current dollars, multiply the number of units in each matrix square by the unit costs in that square and add the products together as shown in Figure 3.3. Do not include the consumables, such as water and sewage in gallons per day, or power demand in KVA. Their total will be used to size the installation and to determine operating costs in the next step.

Tabulations—Operations and Maintenance

The upper half of the planning matrix (Figure 3.3) explained in the previous paragraphs led to an initial set of costs representing an engineering estimate for acquisition in current dollars. Bear in mind that if the facility characteristics quantities are varied, the unit costs for significant variations must also be adjusted. Not only will changes be reflected in the acquisition but we will now show how they cause variations in the operating and maintenance cost.

Following the same columns below the acquisition costs, the items for further analyses are shown on Figure 3.5. For illustrative purposes, the annual maintenance costs are summarized as percentages of the acquisition costs. While this is a valid planning method during the early stages of program definition, there are special factors to consider that will vary the general percentages used. Special considerations include, of course, the geophysical as well as climatological peculiarities of the site under consideration. Snow removal of parking areas

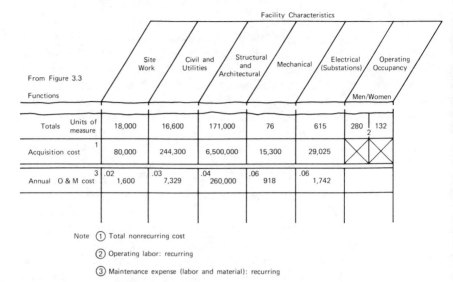

Facility Characteristics						
From Figure 3.3 Functions	Site Work	Civil and Utilities	Structural and Architectural	Mechanical	Electrical (Substations)	Operating Occupancy Men/Women
Totals Units of measure	18,000	16,600	171,000	76	615	280 ǀ 132
Acquisition cost 1	80,000	244,300	6,500,000	15,300	29,025	
Annual O & M cost 3	.02 1,600	.03 7,329	.04 260,000	.06 918	.06 1,742	

Note ① Total nonrecurring cost

② Operating labor: recurring

③ Maintenance expense (labor and material): recurring

Figure 3.5   Characteristics/functions matrix.

and access roads and landscaping of garden areas (breakouts in the matrix) cause a nominal 1% increase in acquisition cost of areas and site work. The nominal 2% shown in Figure 3.5 can be further defined to develop labor and material costs for maintenance if desired. Both government and industry have developed yardsticks for labor that correspond with facility characteristics. Thus the annual maintenance cost can be translated into both labor and material costs even at this early stage of program planning. Following the tabulations on Figure 3.5 across the page, the annual maintenance expenses for the facility characteristics group are:

Area and site work	2%
Civil and utilities	3%
Structural and architectural	4%
Mechanical	6%
Electrical	6%

Guidance is available for the planners from both sources, depending on the level of information needed. For example, if a decision must be made as to whether the proposed facility will use contract maintenance or hire maintenance workers, the relative costs can be ascertained.

Referring again to Figure 3.5, using an average annual base rate for the 412 employees results in a current-year dollar total of $4,120,000. The annual maintenance cost is $271,589. Since both are recurring costs, when a 10-year period of operation is established, the amount of $43,915,890 is determined. The nonrecurring cost of construction will be used first to determine the amount of money to be allocated for the preliminary engineering and conceptual design and then for the preparation of the construction documents. The formulas vary with scope and complexity, but the following general percentages are used to illustrate:

Planning, @ 2% of constructed value	$ 137,376
Construction documents @ 6% of const. value	$ 412,129
Construction management @ 5% of const. value	$ 343,441
Construction	$6,868,825
Total nonrecurring estimate	$7,761,771

To this we add a general contingency of 7% for this early stage of planning, which brings a rounded total of $8.3 million. Combining the nonrecurring and recurring costs, the program cost is estimated as approximately $52.2 million. When a product line is associated with the facility, the raw materials costs, shipping, and other expenses can be put into a cost model to determine profitability against the programmatic estimates. If loans are required, the rate of payback can also be studied. Use of "present value–present worth" economists' tools are also of value.

Energy as a Planning Parameter

In planning facilities today, two questions are asked that stem from the national concern over energy: How important is energy to the proposed project; that is, what role will energy consumption play? and How can the impact of energy use be assessed and evaluated as a function of value management?

A systematic approach to answering these questions in the early planning stages is essential. Several engineering and utilities organizations have devised an analytical methodology to estimate energy usage and the economics of design approaches that attempt to resolve consumption and conservation measures. One of the analytical tools developed by The Ralph M. Parsons Company provides a way to calculate and compare energy consumption for an existing locality, the ultimate consumption in a proposed facility, and, importantly, the energy to be used in the construction. Figure 3.6 is a simplified diagram of this activity.

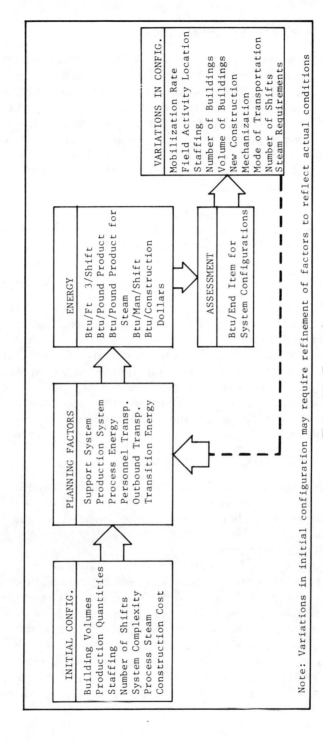

Figure 3.6 Energy planning.

Note: Variations in initial configuration may require refinement of factors to reflect actual conditions

This methodology is straightforward. All energy elements, lighting, heating, motive power for production machinery, and office aids are normalized to an "energy unit." The British thermal unit (Btu) was adopted for the normalization; standard conversion factors were used. Even inbound and outbound transportation of products and personnel were calculable.

What is important to value management is that the decisions related to cost and functionality can also be considered in the light of the energy baseline prepared at the programmatic stage in the program. It can be shown with this type of analysis that modernization of older facilities can amortize the construction energy when replacement of energy-deficient facilities is contemplated. Moreover, it is even practicable to refine the planning factors for value management into a format for planning and subsequent monitoring of design similar to the one shown below (derived from the Parsons file). The analysts isolated relationships to develop these specific energy planning factors:

Category	Planning Factor
Production system	100 or 530 Btu per lb of end product
Process energy	1,000 Btu per lb of end product
Support system	15 Btu/ft^3 per shift
Outbound transportation	300 Btu per lb of end product—rail
	960 Btu per lb of end product—truck
	200 Btu per lb of end product—water
Personnel transportation	162,000 Btu/man per shift
Transition energy	6,748 Btu per construction dollar

The average of the production end items that required steam was approximately 1,000 Btu per pound of end item weight.

The outbound transportation planning factor was derived for use only when no specific facility location(s) have been determined. Once potential locations have been determined, actual distances and quantities can be substituted. The planning factor is based on shipping equal quantities from one centrally located field activity to the East and West Coast outloading points by rail. Similar factors have been computed for truck and waterborne transportation.

The personnel planning factor was based on the following:

	Minimum	*Maximum*
Construction cost	$300 million	$11.3 million
Total estimated construction days	240	570
Btu per construction $	5,800	7,400
Mean Btu per construction $		6,478

The tabulation shows wide ranges in both construction costs and length of construction periods. However, when analyzing the data for each of the 14 modernized projects, the study team found a narrow range in energy units per construction dollar. The mean value of 6,748 Btu per construction dollar becomes the transition factor.

It is obvious that the planners must take into account the local characteristics of weather, distances, and many other factors peculiar to the project.

3.4   DESIGN TO COST/LIFE-CYCLE COST

The design to cost/life-cycle cost ratio (DTC/LCC) has received considerable emphasis and publicity. While we can discuss the environment that led the federal government to develop formal guidelines, we need to examine techniques that can be useful in value management. By way of background, U.S. Government agencies, most particularly the Department of Defense (DOD), have faced an immense task of modernizing systems and equipment. Concurrently, there is a myriad of programs dealing with environmental and energy issues as well as with improving the quality of life. With the shifting of national priorities, DOD has to compete for the purchasing power to develop or modernize.

About the same time as the Viet Nam conflict was winding down, DOD was faced with massive overruns. The General Accounting Office (GAO) reported a $21 billion cost growth in 38 DOD systems. Congress demanded remedial action, and the design-to-cost approach emerged. The need is shown dramatically on Figure 3.7.

The philosophy of DTC as a policy and practice is practically synonymous with value management. It is a goal-setting device that encourages dovetailing engineering creativity to price; it makes cost a primary variable in the design process. With this tool, the value manager's role and responsibility is reinforced from the earliest possible

Rank	Agency[a]	Percent Cost Growth
1	General Services Administration	13
2	Environmental Protection Agency	14
3	National Aeronautics and Space Administration	17
4	Department of Defense (Total)	33
	Department of the Army	28
	Department of the Navy	28
	Department of the Air Force	44
5	Tennessee Valley Authority	34
6	Department of Interior	46
7	Washington Metropolitan Area Transit Authority	86
8	Energy Research and Development Administration	88
9	Corps of Engineers (civil works)	96
10	Department of Transportation	159
11	Appalachian Regional Commission	321

[a]Agencies reporting over $1 billion acquisition.

Figure 3.7   Cost growth record. GAO report as of June 30, 1975, published February 27, 1976.

planning phase to the ultimate end; that is, for the complete life of a new program.

3.4.1   HOW DTC/LCC WORKS

As shown previously in this chapter, acquisition planning at an early stage of the program or project can provide cost parameters as a baseline for control and as a goal for value managers. These cost parameters consider the initial cost of acquisition (planning, design, construction, activation, etc.) and ownership. DOD Directive 5000.1 stated that discrete cost elements such as unit production, operating, and support costs shall be translated into "design to" requirements. The development of the program thereafter, including preparation of design criteria and design, shall be continuously evaluated against these requirements.

The factors that can affect "design to" acquisition costs and "design to" ownership costs include:

- Affordable cost.
- User needs.
- Standardization.
- Logistics concept.
- Environmental matters.
- Safety.
- Skills (manpower).
- Training (and trainers).
- Transportation (transportability).
- Regulatory practices.

The results of an interesting study, derived from DOD documentation, are depicted in Figure 3.8. The indications are that decisions having the most impact are made very early. Of course, in detailed design, trade studies can be made for cost control, but what is simply said is that the downstream impact of early decisions is quite large and that opportunities for cost savings pass quickly.

A checklist is provided as Figure 3.9. It is used by DOD for criteria to validate an acceptable contractor design to cost effort. What is suggested to value managers is that design to cost and life-cycle cost can be combined into a meaningful effort that should be identified as

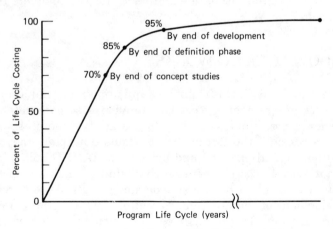

Figure 3.8   Life-cycle costing in DOD acquisition.

"design to life cycle cost." The adoption of DTC/LCC will have its effects on the procurement plan, as will be shown in subsequent chapters.

3.5 THE BOND-ENERGY ALGORITHM

Several years ago, a study published by the Institute for Defense Analyses presented methods for ordering and organizing technical, social, economic, and other data that can be presented in array form. The authors, members of the Systems Evaluation Division at IDA, developed algorithms for the ordering and organization of data that can be presented in a two-dimensional matrix form. The only restriction imposed on the analysis is that the rows and columns of the raw input data matrices can only be reordered. This prevents the creation of artificial coefficients or loss of essential input information. The purpose of their work was to develop methods to extract data patterns, groupings, and structural relationships that are not apparent from the raw data matrix. The bond-energy algorithm (B-E-A) method, one of three distinctive methodologies, was found to be applicable to a broader class of problems, and since it can be used to interrelate data of considerably more complex structure than the other methodologies, it was used for facilities and systems applications.

With the widespread use and availability of large digital computers, methods of multivariate analysis have been developed to maximize their computational resources and characteristics in detailed statistical techniques. What proves to be of value in B-E-A is that it is able to account for detailed individual relationships as well as macroscopic data structure—a technique that is classed as, and exemplified by, cluster-seeking—to identify groups of similar entities. B-E-A, operating directly on the non-negative raw input matrix data, reorganizes and reorders the matrix data by performing row and column permutations to reveal obscure and potentially informative data patterns. The output of all these algorithms is a new data matrix. In practice, B-E-A is capable of identifying and displaying natural groups and clusters that occur in complex data matrices. Moreover, the algorithm is able to uncover and display the associations and interrelationships of these groups with one another. This function is accomplished through the use of a numerical measure of how clustered or "clumpy" a matrix is. (A clumpy matrix is one whose large elements tie near other large elements, forming aggregates called clumps.)

Criteria	Yes	No
A qualified DTC management representative has been identified	___	___
The DTC cognizance has been located at an appropriate management level	___	___
A cost model has been constructed that distributes overall estimated production cost down to level that represents specific targets for individual design groups	___	___
Design groups are aware of their individual estimated production cost targets	___	___
The cost model was constructed in:	___	___
The first month or	___	___
The second month or	___	___
The third month of contract	___	___
Cost drivers have been identified for at least 80% of total estimated production cost	___	___
Special management emphasis is given to high-cost items	___	___
Progress toward DTC targets is provided to individual design groups in readily usable form	___	___
Variance from target is provided to design groups on a:	___	___
Weekly basis	___	___
Biweekly basis	___	___
Monthly basis	___	___
Other	___	___
Design groups review variance data for corrective action	___	___
Producibility estimating support to the design groups is available on a "same day" feedback basis	___	___
Preliminary production cost estimating results are fed back to design groups on less than one week basis	___	___
Production cost estimating results are fed back to design groups within 15 working days	___	___
Production cost estimate traceability is available at design location	___	___
Design to cost targets are incorporated into design sub-contracts	___	___
Prime contract exercises same control over sub-contract DTC efforts	___	___
DTC feedback from sub-contracts is available on a:	___	___
Weekly basis	___	___
Biweekly basis	___	___

Figure 3.9   Checklist to validate DTC effort.

Criteria	Yes	No
Monthly basis	_____	_____
Other	_____	_____
Provisions for validation audit of high-cost sub-contract items included in sub-contract	_____	_____
Progress in meeting DTC targets is reviewed by program management:	_____	_____
Weekly basis	_____	_____
Biweekly basis	_____	_____
Monthly basis	_____	_____
Other	_____	_____
Management planning/or action on program variances over targets are evident and available for review at the design location	_____	_____
Action has been taken to secure government program managers review and action on specification or requirement cost drivers	_____	_____
Reports generated internal to contractor are summarized for program managers and top management's use	_____	_____
Production cost feedback to designers is appropriate to their particular area of interest	_____	_____
Production cost estimates on all high-cost items (80% at least) can be validated by qualified government cost analyst/engineer	_____	_____
Production cost estimating methods used by contractor are sound and based upon his or her other prior experience for similar work	_____	_____
Tradeoff studies have been completed	_____	_____
Tradeoff studies are available at design location	_____	_____
DTC actions include consideration of LCC impact	_____	_____
There is a functional organizational segment accomplishing the task of reducing system costs	_____	_____
The escalation factors being utilized are representative of actual economic change	_____	_____
Experience curve projections are supported by historical patterns of yield improvements	_____	_____
Reliability and maintainability data is compatible with LCC goals	_____	_____
Government laboratory facilities in support of the program have been assigned a demand to design to cost which is a matter of official record	_____	_____

Figure 3.9 (*Continued*)

3.5.1 DEVELOPING FACILITY REQUIREMENTS

The general activities for developing facility requirements using the systems approach in conjunction with value management techniques are shown in Figure 3.10. An example of an analysis using the bond energy algorithm, performed by The Ralph M. Parsons Company for a government agency is presented in the following paragraphs.

The systematic activity analysis of the government organization was performed to obtain the optimum arrangement and location of various groups and divisions within a large building complex. There were

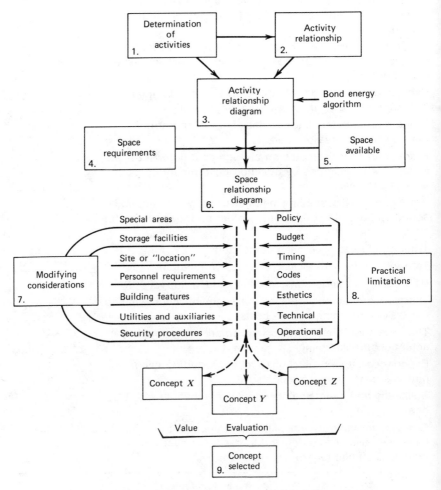

Figure 3.10 Simplified network for developing facility requirements.

many factors, considerations, physical features, and objectives to be integrated in establishing a plan to fit the organization into the physical structure. The number of variables dictated that a rigorous method be followed to establish a basis for the optimum result. The analysts recognized that there is no perfect system for solving this problem; all systems are subject to modification by judgment and intelligent consideration of the final result. However, the method chosen for this analysis was that developed by Richard Muther, an internationally recognized authority on plant layout. This method has been modified for the characteristics of the government organization.

The Adjacency Chart

An adjacency chart (Figure 3.11) formed the basis for the analysis of the activity relationship locations required in the proposed complex. This chart reveals the gradation in importance of the activity relationships, which are largely function-oriented and directed toward one large area of responsibility within each group or major line component (MLC). Each MLC, however, has activity relationships with the other MLCs at various levels within their respective organizations. It follows that the activities related to other MLCs should be located adjacent to each other for efficient coordination and work flow. This should be according to the degree of activity required in terms of the volume of work flow, as well as in terms of importance of work flow, even if the volume is small.

The adjacency chart is a cross-sectional form, where the relationship between each activity (or function or area) and all other activities can be recorded. The form of the chart is not new, although this method of using it is a recent development; the innovations were developed by The Ralph M. Parsons Company.

The adjacency chart shows which activities are related to each other. It also rates the importance of their proximity to one another and supports the rating with coded backup reasons. This gives a rated and reason-supported chart. These measures make the adjacency chart one of the most highly practical and effective tools available for layout planning. It is undoubtedly the best way to integrate support services with the operating or producing departments and to plan the arrangement of office or service areas with little or no materials flow but some amount of work flow. Figure 3.12 shows the basis of the adjacency chart used in this study. All activities (numbered divisions) within each MLC are listed; the functional description on the division activity* is

---

*Activity is a universal term used herein to designate people and process material being located as part of the layout planning. It will encompass, at different levels of planning

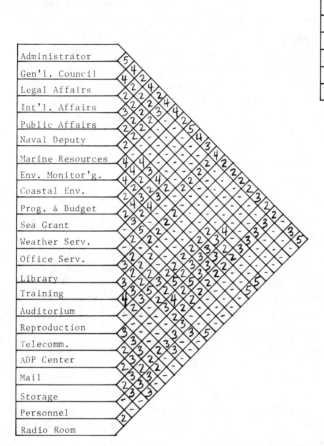

Figure 3.11   Adjacency chart.

included in the space to the right of the number designated. As indicated in part *b* of the diagram, the number rating is placed in each intersecting box.

The chart is almost self-explanatory. Where the activity on downsloping line 1 intersects the activity represented by up-sloping line 3, the relationship between activity 1 and activity 3 is recorded. In this way, there is an intersecting box for each pair of activities. The basic idea is to show which activities should be closely located and which

or in different situations: department, area, function, work center, building, building feature, machine group, operation, etc.

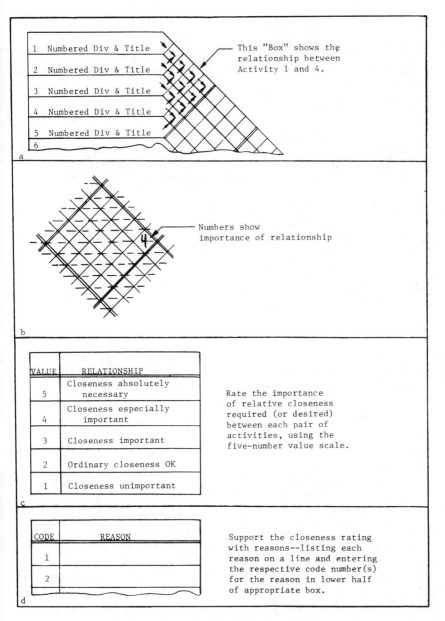

a

1	Numbered Div & Title
2	Numbered Div & Title
3	Numbered Div & Title
4	Numbered Div & Title
5	Numbered Div & Title
6	

— This "Box" shows the relationship between Activity 1 and 4.

b

— Numbers show importance of relationship

c

VALUE	RELATIONSHIP
5	Closeness absolutely necessary
4	Closeness especially important
3	Closeness important
2	Ordinary closeness OK
1	Closeness unimportant

Rate the importance of relative closeness required (or desired) between each pair of activities, using the five-number value scale.

d

CODE	REASON
1	
2	

Support the closeness rating with reasons—listing each reason on a line and entering the respective code number(s) for the reason in lower half of appropriate box.

Figure 3.12 Basis of adjacency chart.

should be far apart, with all in-between relationships also rated and recorded.

The chart can be likened to a from–to chart that has been folded diagonally so that the from–to and the to–from boxes fall on top of each other. The chart thus shows the total relationship—that is, both directions, when direction is involved.

Closeness was rated according to a value of 5, 4, 3, 2, or 1, where 5 indicates that closeness is absolutely necessary, and 1, that closeness is unimportant and the activities can be located with considerable latitude. The number was entered in its appropriate box(es). With this form, a great deal of information is gathered in one sheet.

Color Coding

Because the use of letters or symbols becomes confusing when so many boxes are involved, the boxes were originally color coded. Each box on the working charts was marked with the following color code (colors have been eliminated in printing this report): 5, red; 4, yellow; 3, green; 2, blue; 1, brown.

Chart Production Methods

The procedure for making a relationship chart varies. It depends, among other things, on whether or not the productive operations are included with service or support activities.

If the entire area is operations, there is little need for the relationship chart. A flow analysis will determine the relationships between operations. In most cases, however, it becomes practical to incorporate both the operating activities and the supporting services on the same chart.

The flow for operating activities can be produced by developing an activity relationship chart for the services and then including related operating activities on a combined relationship chart. Or the flow analysis can be translated directly onto a relationship chart when supporting services are first considered. The method actually followed will depend on the relative importance of the closeness of operations to each other, the closeness of services to each other, and the closeness of services to operations. When there is no significant flow or routing, as in many offices or service areas, there is no flow-of-material analysis, and all activities are related to each other through use of only the relationship chart.

The relationship chart is especially helpful when most of the relationships cannot be calculated. And when faced with only opinions, which frequently conflict, with false assumptions, and with personal desires for status or self-betterment, the chart is a great aid. Figure 3.13 shows how the type of work determines the right procedure. Flow of materials and activity relationships are the two basic procedures to establish the desired or required closeness of various areas, activities, or functions. When materials are large in size or quantity, flow of materials becomes the primary basis for determining the relationship of areas, with activity relationships used to tie in the service and supporting areas. When there is no problem of size or quantity and no difficulty of moving the product or material, determination of activity relationships becomes the chief procedure, with little flow-of-material study needed. Between these extremes, both procedures should be used, either integrated from the start or independently with subsequent tie-in. In the former method, flow of material becomes just one of the elements in the construction of the activity relationship chart.

There are several ways to establish the relationship ratings. The ways used in this study are:

- The analyst's own knowledge of the area being laid out.
- Solicited opinions of others involved with the operation or support of the area in question by face-to-face discussion.
- Recording by persons in charge of the activities involved.
- By personal survey, appraisal, and combination of the other methods, performed concurrently with gathering information on which to calculate space requirements.

Check and Endorsement

Regardless of the methods or combination of methods used to establish the rated relationships or to record the data, the chart should be checked by or with the people who will actually work in the final layout. The completed charts in this study were submitted to each major line component and to top management for review and validation.

Conclusion

The technique of the rated and reason-supported relationship chart is a systematic way of getting data into usable form. It results in a set of relationship requirements to which the layout planning can be keyed. Moreover, it provides a ready reason why departments are located near

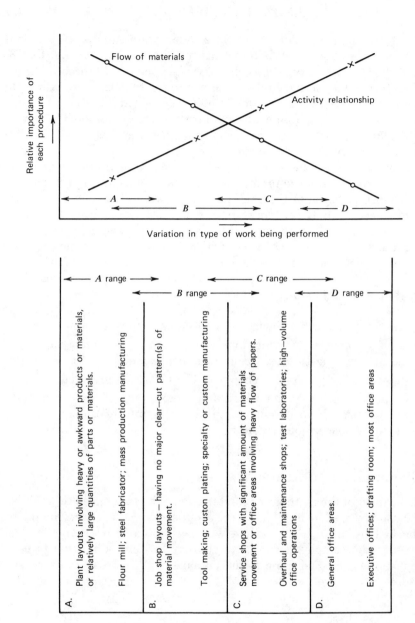

Figure 3.13 Flow of materials and activity relationships.

one another or far apart—sound backing for data and highly valuable when challenged. The chart serves as a check sheet, ensuring that a decision is made for the relation of each activity to each other activity.

3.5.2 ADJACENCY ANALYSIS

Following the activity analysis, the adjacency relationships between the divisions within an MLC, and with the other MLCs and various services, were determined in order to integrate the activity analysis to obtain the degree of adjacency desired between each function or numbered division in the building complex. The approach selected meets the following requirements:

- Speed and accuracy.
- Capable of handling an array of factors.
- Capable of handling a large number of probabilities.
- Capable of reordering the relationships according to a measure of effectiveness to show "clumpiness" of groups.

The technique selected, developed by Dr. William T. McCormick, Jr., of the Institute of Defense Analysis, is the bond energy algorithm.

The B-E-A is capable of identifying and displaying natural groups and clusters; it can also uncover and display the associations and interrelationships of these groups with one another. These tasks are accomplished through the use of a numerical measure of how clustered a matrix is. The proposed measure of effectiveness (ME) attains its maximum value when the matrix assumes a very clumpy or aggregated form. It was found that the structures and relationships existing in data matrices more clearly exhibit themselves when the matrices are presented in more aggregated forms corresponding to larger MEs.

The ME is defined as follows: Assume that the matrix of relationships has dimensions M by N with non-negative elements a_{ij}. The quantity is defined (with the convention $a_{0j} = a_i, 0 = a_i, N + 1 = a_{M+1}, j = 0$) as:

$$a_{ij} = \tfrac{1}{2} [a_{i+1,j} + a_{i-1,j} + a_{i,j+1} + a_{i,j-1}]$$

From the diagram on p. 88 it can be seen that a_{ij} is just one-half the sum of the horizontal and vertical nearest neighbors of a_{ij}. The unnormalized ME can now be defined as the product of the elements.

$$\mathrm{ME} = \sum_{\text{all } i,j} a_{ij} a_{ij}$$

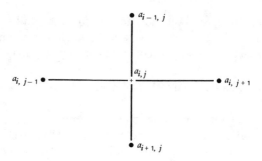

To obtain maximum clumpiness of the matrix, it is necessary to maximize the ME over all row permutations and column permutations of the matrix.

This problem can be formulated equivalently as two quadratic assignment problems, and its optimal solution determined. However, this rigorous solution is quite time-consuming, so a suboptimal algorithm has been developed. The suboptimal algorithm is a sequential selection procedure that has proven to be effective, efficient, and rapid.

A simple example will illustrate the sensitivity of the ME and the utility of a rearrangement of the matrix data. Suppose there is a symmetric matrix showing certain associations or relationships, entities $A, B, C,$ and D. The initial relationship matrix is shown in Figure 3.14, where the ones in the i, jth elements of the matrix represent the existence of relationships between entities i and $j,$ and the zeros indicate the absence of relationships. It is clear from the definition of the ME and the observation that there are no bonds, that ME = 0 for the matrix in Figure 3.14a. Figures 3.14$b, c, d,$ and e show progressively greater levels of clumpiness; their MEs are 2, 4, 6, and 8, respectively. Application of the B-E-A produces the ordering shown in Figure 3.14$e,$ where it is clear that two clusters have been uncovered, and in fact, the entities have been factored into two unrelated and distinct groups: AC and BD.

This simple example gives an indication of how the bond energy algorithm can produce clearer and deeper understanding of the matrix data by simple rearrangement.

Figure 3.15 shows a generalized result of the technique as applied to the total organization during this study. The control variables at the side and top of the matrix correspond to the numbered division in each organization and indicate clearly which groups must be located together. Together, all the factors resulted in layouts which were presented to an architect for the high-rise building complex concepts.

	A	B	C	D
A	1	0	1	0
B	0	1	0	1
C	1	0	1	0
D	0	1	0	1

(a) ME = 0

	A	B	C	D
A	1	0	1	0
B	0	1	0	1
C	0	1	0	1
D	1	0	1	0

(b) ME = 2

	A	B	C	D
A	1	0	1	0
C	1	0	1	0
B	0	1	0	1
D	0	1	0	1

(c) ME = 4

	A	B	C	D
A	1	1	0	0
B	0	0	1	1
D	0	0	1	1
C	1	1	0	0

(d) ME = 6

	A	C	B	D
A	1	1	0	0
C	1	1	0	0
B	0	0	1	1
D	0	0	1	1

(e) ME = 8

Figure 3.14 Illustration of the sensitivity of the bond energy ME.

3.5.3 DEVELOPMENT PLANNING

The use of various systems techniques for the value manager has been described for programmatic and facilities planning. Once they are known to the value manager, these methods can be used for various important cost-effective solutions. To illustrate, the same agency that retained The Ralph M. Parsons Company for a high-rise building complex was in receipt of a 100-acre land transfer from the U.S. Navy. The site, a former airfield, was irregular in shape, bordered by water to the east and south, and adjoining a city park and Naval property to the west and north, respectively.

Functional use of the site was required for a large number of organizations. The organizations, referred to as major line components (MLCs), each needed both specialized and common facilities. At the

CONTROL VARIABLES

	18	25	27	23	6	17	15	21	16	5	8	9	10	7	13	22	1	2	4	3	14	19	12	11	20	24	26
18	3	2	0	0	0	0	1	0	1	0	0	0	0	0	0	1	1	0	0	0	0	0	0	0	0	0	0
25	2	3	3	0	0	0	0	0	0	0	0	0	0	0	0	0	0	0	0	0	0	0	0	0	0	0	0
27	0	3	3	1	2	3	1	1	0	0	0	0	0	0	0	0	0	0	0	0	0	0	0	0	0	1	0
23	0	0	1	3	3	1	0	0	0	0	0	0	0	0	0	0	0	0	0	0	0	0	0	0	1	0	0
6	0	0	2	3	3	1	0	0	0	0	0	2	1	0	0	0	0	0	0	0	0	0	0	0	1	0	1
17	0	0	3	1	1	3	1	1	1	0	0	0	0	0	0	0	0	0	1	0	0	0	0	1	0	0	0
C 15	1	0	1	0	0	1	3	3	1	0	0	0	0	0	0	1	0	0	0	0	0	0	0	0	0	0	0
O 21	0	0	1	0	0	1	3	3	3	3	0	0	0	0	0	0	0	0	0	0	0	0	0	2	1	1	
N 16	1	0	0	0	0	1	1	3	3	3	1	0	0	1	2	0	1	0	1	1	1	0	0	0	0	0	
T 5	0	0	0	0	0	0	0	3	3	3	2	1	1	2	0	1	2	0	1	0	1	0	0	0	0	0	0
R 8	0	0	0	0	0	0	0	0	1	2	3	2	2	2	0	0	1	1	0	1	0	0	0	0	0	0	0
O 9	0	0	0	0	2	0	0	0	0	1	2	3	3	2	0	0	0	0	0	0	0	0	0	0	0	0	0
L 10	0	0	0	0	1	0	0	0	0	1	2	3	3	3	2	0	0	0	0	0	2	1	1	1	0	0	0
7	0	0	0	0	0	0	0	0	1	2	2	2	3	3	1	1	1	1	0	1	1	0	0	1	0	0	0
V 13	0	0	0	0	0	0	0	0	1	0	0	0	2	1	3	2	2	2	1	0	0	1	1	0	0	0	0
A 22	1	0	0	0	0	0	1	0	2	1	0	0	0	1	2	3	3	3	0	0	1	0	0	0	0	0	0
R 1	1	0	0	0	0	0	0	0	0	2	1	0	0	1	2	3	3	3	2	0	0	1	0	0	0	0	0
I 2	0	0	0	0	0	0	0	0	1	0	1	0	0	1	2	3	3	3	3	3	0	0	1	0	0	0	0
A 4	0	0	0	0	0	1	0	0	0	0	0	0	0	0	1	0	2	3	3	3	1	0	0	0	0	0	0
B 3	0	0	0	0	0	0	0	0	1	1	1	0	0	1	0	0	0	0	3	3	3	1	0	0	0	0	0
L 14	0	0	0	0	0	0	0	0	1	0	0	0	2	1	0	0	0	0	1	3	3	1	1	0	0	0	0
E 19	0	0	0	0	0	0	0	1	1	0	0	1	0	1	1	0	1	0	1	1	3	1	0	0	0	0	0
S 12	0	0	0	0	0	0	0	0	1	1	0	0	1	0	1	0	0	0	0	1	1	3	3	0	0	0	
11	0	1	0	0	0	0	0	0	0	0	0	0	1	1	0	0	0	0	0	0	0	0	3	3	1	0	0
20	0	0	0	0	1	1	0	2	0	0	0	0	0	0	0	0	0	0	0	0	0	0	0	1	3	3	1
24	0	0	1	0	0	0	0	1	0	0	0	0	0	0	0	0	0	0	0	0	0	0	0	3	3	2	
26	0	0	0	0	1	0	0	1	0	0	0	0	0	0	0	0	0	0	0	0	0	0	0	1	2	3	

Figure 3.15   Reordered dependency matrix for maximum clumpiness.

onset, it would have seemed advisable to put each organization into its own building; however, the preponderance of facility structures, by function, was in the area of commonality.

Providing a building for each MLC, with its mix of both common and specialized facilities within it, lent itself to autonomy. An alternative was to provide a megastructure for all MLCs and functions.

The Ralph M. Parsons Company used the bond energy algorithm to indicate the best site utilization. In addition to adjacencies, costs were an important factor, particularly when it is recognized that the unit costs are reduced when common facility functions are located together rather than segregated. The B-E-A clumps resulted in the following buildings and facilities, depicted in Figure 3.16, the optimum site layout:

Common Use

Operations	An office structure of 75,000 sq ft
Warehouse	Approximately 74,000 sq ft
Shops	24,000 sq ft
Biochemistry laboratories	75,000 sq ft
Electronics laboratories	22,000 sq ft
Food services	12,500 sq ft

Specialized Use

Piers	Four
Concrete apron (ship support)	80,000 sq ft
Education center	90,000 sq ft
Visitor center	Approximately 7550 sq ft

The centralized approach was clearly the cost winner over the individual building per MLC and megastructure. An incremental funding was prepared and submitted. An overview of the technique's application is provided in Figure 3.17.

3.6   SYSTEMS/VALUE MANAGEMENT PHILOSOPHY

As previously pointed out, each program starts out with programmatic goals for costs and schedules. It is the inherent responsibility of program management to stay within those goals. Its success depends on

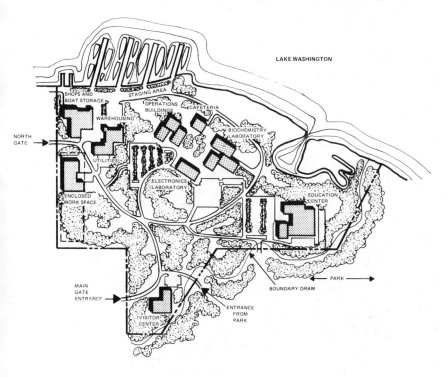

Figure 3.16   Optimum site layout.

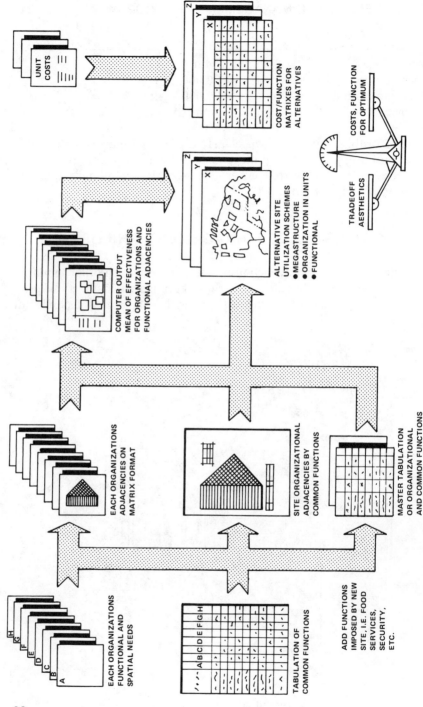

Figure 3.17 Adjacency analyses, individually by organization and for site utilization by consolidated functions.

92

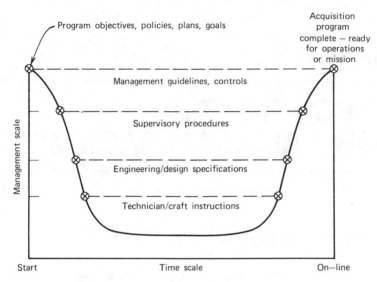

Figure 3.18   Management effort versus project time.

the effectiveness of controls and the corresponding degree of visibility. With rigorous VM activity within a program, the objectives can be more aptly stated as

1. Manage the program within the target cost goals for the risk elements.
2. Reduce the costs of variable elements wherever and whenever possible to enhance the probability of achieving those goals.

Recognizing that it is not the function of program management to evaluate every detail of the program for potential savings, its objectives can be achieved through value management. A graphic illustration of the philosophy as applied is provided in Figure 3.18. It shows that the program goals, from the highest on the management scale to the lowest are subject to a descending order of translation. Thus, a reliability goal, or a safety objective stated in probabilistic terms, is obscured when reduced in the secular sense by the construction worker who is implementing the results of analysis design criteria and design at the material level.

Value management activity initiated at the outset of a program and carried through to its completion provides the insights and continuity necessary to all levels.

CHAPTER 4

OPPORTUNITIES FOR VALUE MANAGEMENT

4.1 INTRODUCTION

With very few unique exceptions, cost is the predominant factor in building, whether an owner is building to a budget or a speculator or investor is building for a profit. For several years, the construction industry has been plagued by spiraling costs. Although the ruinous rate of inflation of the mid-1970s has abated somewhat, inflation will continue to have a significant effect on construction for the foreseeable future. Furthermore, owners will have to cope with increasing energy costs and environmentally related expenses. In addition, as technology advances, they will have to be prepared to alter their buildings to prevent them from becoming obsolete. Projects are becoming much larger and more complicated and taking longer to complete. Activity at the construction site is only part of the construction process. What is less visible is the office work of planning, designing, estimating, negotiating, purchasing, scheduling, expediting, review, control, and whatever else must be done to complete a quality project within budget and on schedule. These activities taken together represent the system that will produce the final product. It is as if value is flowing through the system from conception to occupancy, with each activity within the system adding to or modifying the value. (Refer to Figure 4.1.)

Now and in the future, cost control will be an absolute necessity. Since they usually do not have the talent or expertise, owners normally look to the architect or constructor to perform this function. Frequently, however, architects do not have enough knowledge of and familiarity with the building process to control costs as closely as the owner desires. Furthermore, during construction, there are no incentives for the constructor to reduce the cost of building, and often large

Figure 4.1 Each activity adds value to the system.

incentives to increase it. For example, it is common practice in some sections of the industry to bid jobs low and make money on changes and "extras." In negotiations for changes and extras, the general contractor tends to side with subcontractors against the owner. The contractor, after all, will probably work with the same subcontractor on another job, while commitments to the owner beyond the contract may be negligible.

Value management will reverse this trend as it provides a means of maintaining maximum control over total project cost. In addition, by using the proper mix of professional fees and contract incentives, the members of the project team are encouraged to support and actively participate in a value management effort. This chapter discusses the various opportunities for applying value management throughout the project cycle.

4.2 HIGH POTENTIAL VALUE MANAGEMENT AREAS

The Department of Defense conducted a study to determine the predominant sources of value management changes. The study was based on 415 successful changes categorized as follows:

- 116 instant savings changes resulted from contractor recommendations and provided a savings on the instant contract.

- 201 collateral changes resulted from contractor recommendations and provided savings on the ownership of the system (operation, maintenance, logistic support, and so forth).
- 98 changes resulted from DOD in-house value management activities.

These 415 changes provided a total savings of $106 million. The factors considered in the evaluation are defined in Figure 4.2. The results of the study are shown in Figures 4.3 to 4.5. Results indicate that rarely does any single factor cause a VM action to be successful. Significantly, "excessive costs of current design" was one of the two leading factors in all three portions of the study; the other related to the "updating" of the design or the design documentation.

ADVANCES IN TECHNOLOGY / Incorporation of new materials, components, techniques or processes (advances in the state-of-the-art) not available at the time of the previous design effort

ADDITIONAL DESIGN EFFORT / Application of additional skills, ideas, and information available but not utilized during previous design effort

CHANGE IN USER'S NEEDS / User's modification or redefinition of mission, function, or application of item (change in user's needs)

FEEDBACK FROM TESTS/USE / Design modification based on feedback from user tests or field experience suggesting that specified parameters governing previous design were unrealistic or exaggerated

QUESTIONING SPECIFICATIONS / User's specifications were examined, questioned, determined to be inappropriate, out of date, or overspecified

DESIGN DEFICIENCIES / Design in use prior to VM change proved inadequate in use (e.g., was characterized by inadequate performance, excessive failure rates, or technical deficiencies)

EXCESSIVE COST / Design in use prior to VM change proved technically adequate, but, through use of a cost model or comparative costing techniques, it was determined that the cost of that design was excessive

---

Figure 4.2 Factors leading to changes from VM efforts.

Factor	Total saving
Excessive cost	$ 5,736,000
Questioning specification	5,453,000
Advances in technology	4,938,000
Additional design effort	1,646,000
Change in user's need	860,000
Feedback from tests/use	832,000
Design deficiencies	421,000
	$19,886,000

Figure 4.3 Factors leading to VM changes—Contractor/instant savings (116 changes).

Factor	Total saving
Additional design effort	$ 7,786,000
Excessive cost	2,967,000
Questioning specifications	1,974,000
Advances in technology	1,668,000
Feedback from tests/use	911,000
Design deficiencies	123,000
Change in user's needs	86,000
Other	2,578,000
	$18,093,000

Figure 4.4 Factors leading to VM changes—Contractor/collateral savings (201 changes).

Factor	Total saving
Advances in technology	$18,268,000
Excessive cost	15,102,000
Change in user's need	11,698,000
Questioning specifications	11,497,000
Additional design effort	6,419,000
Design deficiencies	3,503,000
Feedback from tests/use	2,508,000
	$68,995,000

Figure 4.5 Factors leading to VM changes—DOD in-house activities (98 changes).

Keeping these factors in mind, it appears that the areas that have high value management potential include:

- Construction.
- Design.
- Equipment.
- Procurement and reprocurement.
- Publications and manuals.
- Quality assurance and reliability.
- Facilities, master plans, and concepts.
- Maintenance.
- Manufacturing processes.
- Material handling and transportation.
- Packaging, parking, and preservation.
- Procedures and reports.
- Salvage, rejected, or excess material.
- Site preparation and adaptation.
- Software (computer) programs and flowcharts.
- Specifications and drawings.
- Technical requirements.
- Testing, test equipment, and procedures.

4.3 TIMING OF VALUE MANAGEMENT OPPORTUNITIES

VM analysis should be applied at any place in the life cycle where it is profitable to do so. However, the greatest return on investment is realized when VM resources are allocated to the project early in the design process. This becomes obvious when Figures 4.6 through 4.8 are reviewed.

Figure 4.6 shows whose decisions have the most influence over the expenditure of funds during the life cycle of a facility. For example:

1. The using agency prescribes the quantity of lavatories per occupancy. The architect-engineer's influence on cost is reduced because he cannot determine quantity. However, he can influence layout, color choice, and so on.

2. The construction contractor's influence on cost is further re-

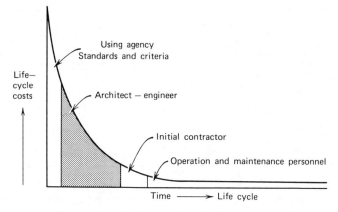

Figure 4.6 Decision-makers' influence on cost.

stricted. He can influence the cost of materials and installation by only a few percent.

3. Maintenance and operations personnel are left with the least influence because they must live with what is given to them.

Figure 4.7 represents the distribution of total costs as expended over the life cycle of a typical facility. The design effort represents the smallest expenditure, and all of the initial acquisition costs are less than 50% of the total costs.

Two of the most important factors influencing the selection of the most appropriate time for applying value management are (1) the magnitude of the savings from the effort and (2) the ease or difficulty of applying the VM change. Figure 4.8 portrays the typical life-cycle

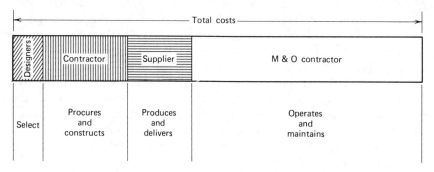

Figure 4.7 Average distribution of costs for a typical facility.

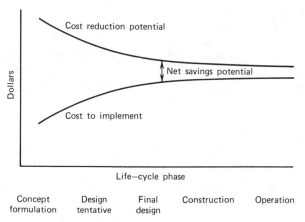

Figure 4.8   Life-cycle phases and savings potential.

phases of a facility and illustrates how the savings potential decreases as the project ages.

An examination of these figures reveals two significant facts. First, the smallest cost in the life cycle is expended during the design phase (Figure 4.7). Yet it is here that the decisions of the owner, designer, and construction manager make the greatest impact on total costs (Figure 4.6). Second, the greatest net savings potential of VM changes exists in the concept/design phase (Figure 4.8). Therefore, the greatest return on the VM investment can be expected when VM resources are allocated early in the design phase.

4.4   DESIGN

From the discussion in Section 4.3 it can be seen that VM techniques are applicable both before and after the point at which a project's design is released. Both types of value management are necessary if costs are to be minimized. It is still somewhat controversial, however, as to when, where, and how value management should be applied during design. Many factors enter into the decision—the competitive situation, time, technical complexity, testing requirements, and various unknown variables. However, there is general agreement that the time consumed during the design phase for value studies is more than recouped during procurement and construction, with the result that frequently the overall time cycle is reduced.

4.4.1 PRESENT METHOD OF DESIGNING A FACILITY

In the present method of designing a facility, the designer develops plans and specifications that conform to the criteria of the using agency. He or she must determine which equipment and methods are most suitable from the standpoint of economy, function, maintenance, and appearance, but within the standards and criteria set by the owner. Generally, each selection is done by an engineer or architect working on a particular aspect of the design. For example, the electrical engineer selects the generators, conductors, panel boxes, and so forth. The civil engineer selects such items as the sewage and water systems.

In some cases economic studies are conducted, such as for site selection, fuel selection, and structural system. However, in most instances any selections or studies are made by an individual or a group within the same discipline. In some cases a team is called together, but normally no formal job plan is followed, nor are any employees assigned full-time to organize and coordinate activities or follow through on any new ideas generated.

Each discipline thus generates requirements, reviews these requirements, establishes and modifies its particular criteria, and even modifies the standards and criteria of the owner. This approach may not lead to the most economical decisions for the end function of the facility. Instead, it encourages economical decisions within each area, with the maximum safety factors deemed necessary by each discipline. Although this system is not without merit, it tends to sacrifice overall system performance in maximizing subsystem performance. This is known as suboptimization.

The result is that total life-cycle costs are not adequately considered. The emphasis on first cost and the failure to consider the total effect of related cost elements are probably the greatest shortcomings in today's planning, programming, and designing of facilities. These hidden costs have a considerable impact on cost of ownership. For example, as Figure 4.9 shows, the total cost of a hospital is about 10.5 times its initial cost. In addition to initial cost, life-cycle costs include:

1. Maintenance and operation costs.
2. Money charges such as interest and insurance.
3. Future income or needs, such as rentable or usable space, future expansion, alterations.

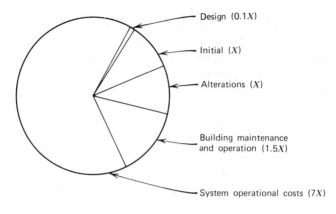

X = Initial construction costs

Figure 4.9   Hospital life-cycle costs (20 years).

4. Fringe costs not subject to ready dollar analysis, such as esthetics and durability.

5. Ownership logistic costs such as materials delivery, serviceability, and personnel access.

6. Service and operating personnel costs, such as the cost of janitorial services and operating personnel (e.g., engineers, doctors in hospitals).

7. Real estate and property taxes.

Each discipline's decision can affect costs in other areas, and it is these cumulative costs, generally resulting from the AE's decisions, that have the greatest impact on the total cost of the facility. It is in the overlapping area that value management has the greatest saving potential. Value management emphasizes the need for a team approach. For example, the architect, in an effort to optimize costs in his area, can adversely affect the cost areas of all other disciplines. Therefore, a team approach is required for cost-effective decisions in major design areas.

4.4.2   PERFORMING VALUE MANAGEMENT DURING DESIGN

Figure 4.10 portrays the typical life-cycle phases of a facility and the relative degree of project definition. Each phase of a project represents a known baseline that starts out broad in content and becomes more definitive as the project proceeds through its life cycle. Value manage-

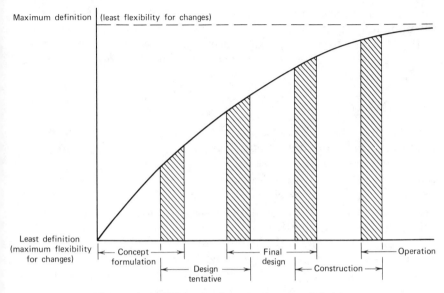

Figure 4.10 Life-cycle phases and project definition.

ment is applied repeatedly in any phase where it is profitable to do so. However, the discussion in this section is restricted to the concept and design phases.

Concept Formulation

The main effort in this phase is to translate the owner's requirements into feasible concepts that define future operational and support characteristics. Value improvement generated in this phase produces benefits that last throughout the life of the project; however, the savings generated are the most difficult to document. The competence of the VM staff is very important, since decisions and appraisals often must be made before the complete picture is available. The VM effort in this phase is directed to furnishing inputs that contribute to optimum, economical decision making.

Design Tentative

During this phase, approved concepts are defined, drawings and specifications are started, and sufficient detailed information is developed to substantiate all quantities and costs. This is the most opportune time to question and revise performance characteristics. Possible alternatives offering improved value at reduced cost are revealed by value studies that analyze essential requirements and characteristics. Value management efforts in this phase are directed toward creating value indexes of function, cost, and worth of the systems and subsystems. This highlights the costs that are directly related to specific requirements.

Final Design

During this phase, the specific design details are developed and schedules are formulated. At this point, VM efforts are normally limited to eliminating unnecessarily restrictive detail, ensuring standardization for details, minimizing the quantities of different types, and eliminating unnecessary requirements. Because of the costs involved, a project normally cannot be redesigned at this stage unless the life-cycle savings potential is large enough to justify the expense. However, when construction of a completely designed project is delayed for a year or more, then the latter portion of that delay time could be well spent on a value management effort aimed at updating project requirements and implementing VM changes.

4.4.3 DESIGNING FOR VALUE

Task Team

This is a multidiscipline team composed of members not responsible for the original design. The purpose is to bring an objective viewpoint to the design review. The objective of the team is to perform a design review to generate suggestions for value improvement of the design. The task team normally consists of an architect, structural engineer, mechanical engineer, and electrical engineer, with other support as necessary such as estimating, construction, purchasing, special consultant contacts, and clerical.

Operation of the team, as to duration and workloads, depends on the scope and complexity of the project or system under study. It need not be a full-time process, nor is it necessary that an equal amount of work be required from each member.

Ideally, the task team will be composed of employees who have had VM training. Their experience will be helpful in performing value studies of future projects. However, in the absence of qualified employees, outside VM consultants can be retained to perform the functions of the task team.

Workshop

This is a device that permits the study of selected design criteria or proposed design solutions to project requirements in a controlled environment using VM methodology. The workshop involves the employees who are working on the project design, representatives of all design consultants, and the VM task team. Effective value management requires the use of the best possible talent a company can provide. The objective is to develop recommendations for changes that will enhance project value.

The application of value management through the workshop is discussed in more detail in Chapter 7. In addition, the workshop is an excellent training tool for VM methodology. Its use for this purpose is discussed in Chapter 2. The following two examples illustrate the results that can be achieved by using the task team and workshop concepts.

Example 1

A restoration project for an historic Federal office building located in Washington, D.C., was studied by multidisciplined value teams during a workshop conducted in Washington. The application of the value process was particularly significant because it was probably the first time that a VM study identified a basic function as "restore heritage." The task teams had to keep in mind that the building is on the National Register of Historic Places. In addition, the required office facilities had to be provided within the available funding. Operating within these parameters, the teams generated several creative VM changes:

1. *Insulate the exterior walls.* Instead of insulating the interior surface, it was suggested that insulation be applied to the exterior surface. The insulation would then be covered with metal lath and stucco, which would be finished to simulate granite. This was the typical finishing method used at the time the building was under construction. The suggestion had the following advantages:

    a. The existing brick and mortar, which is deteriorating because it was not meant to be exposed to the weather, would be covered.

    b. The insulation would cover the entire wall area, instead of being interrupted on the interior by partitions.

    c. There would be no disruption of occupants while the work was performed.

2. *Use a raised floor.* A 6-inch raised flooring for electrical and mechanical distribution systems was proposed. This would eliminate the necessity of exterior wall chases and exposed wiring. This proposal had the following advantages:

a. With a raised floor, there is greater flexibility for locating floor outlets for telephone and electrical service.

b. It provides a new floor; the existing floor would have had to be removed and replaced anyway.

c. It eliminates exposed wiring.

d. Space lost because of wall chases is minimized.

Results of the weeklong workshop were impressive. The VM changes discussed above reduced the cost of this restoration project by $330,000, or better than 11% of the $2,941,400 estimate.

Example 2

A Federal office building and courthouse to be constructed in Florida were the subject of a weeklong workshop conducted near the construction site. The location of the workshop approached the ideal for a creative environment—a motel on a secluded Florida beach. It became both a temporary home and office for the workshop members. Problems and interruptions of their regular activities were minimized, and since the motel was close to the construction site, the members were able to walk the site and develop empathy for the community. By the end of the workshop, the task teams had developed VM design changes that resulted in reducing the project estimate by $1,224,000. A brief description of these ideas and the associated savings follow:

1. Change cost-in-place concrete superstructure from a "tree" system to flat slab, with interior coffers constructed with sheet rock and exterior coffers constructed with metal lath and stucco. The architectural appearance is maintained while reducing the mass and complex concrete form work. Reduction in estimate: $773,000.

2. Use split-face masonry units for exterior walls instead of textured concrete. This allows the architect a wider variety of materials with better control over finish uniformity. Reduction in estimate: $374,000.

3. Use linear diffusers in the ceiling for the HVAC system instead of casting openings in the original concrete "tree" design. Reduction in estimate: $62,500.

4. Eliminate the hot water system and related piping. Install only one water system, since the minimum water temperature in that area

of Florida is 70°F. This reduced energy consumption and maintenance as well as initial cost. Reduction in estimate: $14,500.

A significant factor in this example is that a construction manager had been hired for this project and attended the VM workshop. Of the four changes discussed above, three (those providing the greatest savings) are concerned with construction methods and materials. The combination of value management and construction expertise applied to the design phase furnished impressive results—a potential savings of $1,224,000.

Compensation

Architect-engineers and construction managers are normally compensated on a fee basis for VM services. The fee is negotiated as a professional service on a firm fixed price basis as part of the overall contract price. However, the portion of the total contract fee representing compensation for VM services is separately identified. Management then is able to determine the effectiveness of the VM design effort, to determine if there is a sufficient return on investment. Contract clauses and compensation are discussed in more detail in Chapter 7.

4.5 CONSTRUCTION

Value management is very important during the construction phase, almost as important as during design. Here is the last opportunity for reducing initial costs and making changes that will minimize life-cycle costs. The owner, user, and operation and maintenance personnel must live with the results of the construction phase. With few exceptions, future life-cycle costs are finally and firmly fixed by the systems and subsystems installed during construction. A final, major VM effort must be encouraged during the construction segment of the building process.

The construction manager, if there is one, and the contractors are important factors in the success or failure of value management during construction. The construction manager must constantly encourage contractors to submit VM proposals. He may even suggest specific ideas or areas that warrant value study. In addition, he provides guidance for preparing and processing proposals.

Competition among construction contractors is keen. As a result, a contractor generally prepares his bid by paring profit to the minimum.

Yet he is obligated to himself and to his firm to obtain maximum profits while maintaining his reputation of high quality and providing his client with a dollar's value of construction for every dollar paid to him. Therefore, the possibility of increasing profits after contract award through the value management process should be a welcomed opportunity.

Often the contractor is in a better position than the designer to keep up to date on advances in the state of construction art. Furthermore, he has the advantage of having much more personal contact with everyday problems and procedures in actual construction. Therefore, the contractor can scrutinize the design with a critical eye and propose changes that reduce cost without sacrificing quality.

Contractors normally are compensated for VM efforts on an incentive basis under an incentive clause included in the construction contract. They are awarded a portion of the savings realized from their proposals. Two types of sharings exist. The first type is an instant sharing, where the contractor is awarded a portion of the savings on the initial cost of the facility. On government contracts the sharing is on a 50/50 basis; on private industry contracts, it may be a matter for negotiation. The second type is a collateral sharing where the contractor is awarded a portion of life-cycle cost savings. On government contracts this amounts to a 20% share of an average one year's ownership savings. This also may be a matter for negotiation in private industry. Chapter 7 discusses the details of incentive contract clauses, including methods for calculating savings and sharing arrangements.

Subcontractors and suppliers may contribute significantly to a VM program. A subcontractor is motivated to participate when a contractor includes an incentive clause in the subcontract. In fact, many government incentive clauses require that similar clauses be included in the subcontracts. Usually incentive clauses provide for the contractor to also share in any savings proposed by his subcontractors. Suppliers may have some cost-effective new products that can be used. In most cases they will gladly provide technical data support of their products in return for a new market opportunity. The intent is to motivate those closest to and most knowledgeable of the product, method, material, subsystem, or system to suggest ways to provide the same or better quality of performance at a reduced cost.

To realize the benefits of an incentive VM program, an owner or his representative—whether he is an architect-engineer or construction manager—must promote contractor and subcontractor participation. This can be accomplished using the following:

- Letters encouraging participation by successful bidders and their subcontractors.
- Discussions at preconstruction conferences.
- Discussions by resident engineers at construction sites.
- Allowing contractor personnel to participate in owner (or owner's representative's) briefings, schools, workshops, and seminars on value management.

During construction, value management can be performed both internally and by the contractor. The internal effort is accomplished by the owner's VM staff, who review specific contract requirements and initiate change orders to save money. They also conduct value studies of potential change orders that tend to increase contract cost. These are reviewed to prevent adding nonessential functions and to create alternate solutions that lower the cost of or eliminate the necessity for the change.

The contractor can start the search for VM changes in his own company. He should involve the construction engineers, supervisors, foremen, purchasing agents, estimators, and others. All are potential sources for value proposals. The contractor should review his bid estimate, schedule of prices, and subcontractor and supplier quotations to see where his contract costs are and what he can do about them. There are many other areas where the contractor can reduce construction costs. For example, he can investigate construction procedures that reduce the amount of labor required at the job site, such as modular construction, prefabricated components, and building systems. He can study the latest construction methods being used abroad to see how he can adapt them to his own construction operations. The contractor should explore every possible avenue that might lead to construction savings. In general, any contract requirement that costs the contractor money to perform affords a potential opportunity for VM savings.

In submitting a value proposal, it is to the advantage of the contractor to include sufficient information that the owner and his representative can make a realistic review and determination of the proposal. As a minimum the proposal must contain the following:

- *Proposed idea.* Describe both the old way and the proposed idea. Give the advantages and disadvantages of each.
- *Supporting data.* Include subcontractor transmittals, manufacturers' literature, shop drawings, calculations, brochures, test data,

certification, samples, and any other data needed to completely understand and investigate the proposal.

- *Costs.* Provide separate cost estimates for the old way and the proposal. The difference between these estimates is what will be shared.
- *Collateral savings.* Give a best judgment of the effect the proposal will have on life-cycle costs. Savings on ownership costs are also shared.
- *Contract changes.* Identify each contract requirement that must be changed and recommend how to change it. Also comment on what effect the proposal will have on the rest of the unchanged contract work.
- *Time.* Describe the impact the proposal will have on the project completion time. Also state a deadline for the owner's decision that must be met if the savings are to be realized.
- *Previous submittals.* If the proposal previously has been approved for another contract, state so. This is precedent setting and thus enhances the chances of its being approved for the current contract.

By combining value management with other construction concepts in a systems approach, some very satisfactory reductions in construction time and cost can be achieved. For example, the combination of value management, construction management, and systemization resulted in a savings of $1 million on a school project. The project had previously been designed and bid using the traditional process. The low bid was $8.2 million, $700,000 over the budget of $7.5 million. The owner called in a construction management firm to determine if some of the new concepts would help bring the cost of the project within budget.

The construction manager suggested the use of value management and the building systems concept. A multidisciplinary team composed of value specialists, cost estimators, schedulers, purchasing personnel, and designers was organized to analyze the basic building design. The use of the multidisciplinary approach was the key to generating significant savings. This is because often there is a lack of integration among project personnel, with each seeking to optimize his or her own discipline rather than considering the whole building as a system.

The team broke down the project into 37 segments. After initial study, five segments were selected for in-depth analysis: structural; heating, ventilating, and air-conditioning; lighting/ceiling; demountable partitions; and roofing/insulation. Value management and building systems methodology were then applied to these segments.

As part of the effort there was considerable contact with the manufacturers before the performance specifications were made final. This was to assure that at least two or more manufacturers would bid and to give them a chance to review and analyze the specifications to identify restrictive or unnecessary requirements. As a result, rebids totaled $7.2 million, $1 million under the previous low bid and $300,000 under budget. The author's experience indicates that the sample cited here is not uncommon.

4.6 OPERATIONS AND MAINTENANCE

Operations, maintenance, and other support costs greatly affect the total life-cycle costs of owning a facility. For example, in Figure 4.9 it can be seen that the costs of maintenance, operations, alterations, and other system operational costs amount to 9.5 times the initial cost for a typical hospital project. Value studies during this phase offer an opportunity to make changes not made during design or construction due to a lack of time or other reasons.

As the building ages, its functions and use may be changed to something quite different from those for which it originally was designed and built. In addition, external factors such as energy and environmental considerations may require modifications to the building's systems. As a result, the existing systems become inadequate and inefficient. Value studies of these problem areas can result in the following advantages:

- Extension of the system's life and improved efficiency from application of new state-of-the-art designs, materials, and processes.
- Reduced repair costs by achieving the new functions with more economical and more appropriate building systems.
- Elimination of systems and hardware no longer needed.

A net reduction in operation, maintenance, and other support costs can significantly reduce the costs of ownership.

4.7 COSTING AND SCHEDULING TECHNIQUES

New developments affecting the value aspects of construction are design to cost (DTC); life-cycle cost (LCC); and cost/scheduling, planning, and control (C/SPC). Broadly, the DTC aspects involve initial setting of cost goals, dealing with inflation factors, and taking account of the influences of competition on program performance elements. Technical and cost performance are consistently measured. When certain elements of cost are predicted to exceed the "will cost" goal, actions are taken to keep the total cost down or to reduce the cost of the element that is going "out of excursion." The number of solutions and approaches to deal with what is affordable is constrained by time in the methods available in DTC implementation.

With respect to LCC, every investor, government, or commercial owner wants to know his operating cost. In life-cycle costing, operating costs are assessed in the preplanning phase to justify the program. The operating costs are expected to be updated in predesign activities as well as after the process, facilities, equipment, and personnel requirements are defined. It is obvious that the cost of operating and supporting new facilities over their useful life is generally greater than the acquisition cost (property, design, procurement, construction). Therefore, these future costs are an important part of decision criteria, not only in setting DTC goals but in justifying the acquisition to an investor (with respect to amortization, reduced production costs, etc.). Briefly, LCC analysis has three primary areas of activity:

1. Preparation of LCC estimates (development, acquisition, and ownership).

2. Use of contract incentive provisions to motivate contractors to design and produce equipment and subsystems that have low life-cycle costs and/or procurement benefits.

3. Designing to reduce life-cycle costs, which requires rigorous and sound management.

The LCC approach is not a bookkeeping effort. It does need a team approach to get inputs from operations and logistics specialists as well as from designers. Their collective approach is organized into sequential steps to formulate a model to determine the optimum performance, operational, and support characteristics. It deals with gross concepts, estimates, tradeoffs, and goals pertaining to reliability and maintainability stated in quantitative values. With descriptive and quantitative data derived empirically or historically, cost estimates in constant (base year) dollars are generated and compared with alternatives that have also been estimated in constant dollars. An assessment is then made of the feasibility of attaining the DTC goals, and a master schedule is prepared to identify the cost factor impacts of time.

Proper DTC/LCC analysis requires a "use cost" model. There are a number of cost models available, ranging from straightforward engineered cost estimates to more sophisticated modeling techniques that require computers. Without listing and discussing all the models, it can be said that what evolves is the need for an early LCC plan that provides for the specific tasks of controlling and reducing costs on an integrated and time-phased basis. In this plan a well-qualified and experienced construction management organization documents the project LCC objectives and the plans and procedures necessary to implement them in the best interests of the owner. The owner is then able to formulate and adhere to budgets that will carry through to operations.

The general capability of CPM scheduling systems verifies their applicability to the CM's activities. However, they alone will not meet the needs of a major program with respect to fiscal objectives and restraints, interfacing, and interactive program elements. Accordingly, a planning and control "module" must be added for budgetary and fiscal control. The module that appears best suited for this is called C/SPC (verbally referred to as "C-SPEC").

Use of CPM scheduling systems alone provides initially a clear picture of time and activities for the idealized situations. Given an ideal correlation with costs and work performed, management can compare not only actual accomplishments against schedules, but also costs against budgets. In practice, however, this has not proven easy to achieve on projects that have a functional mix of design, construction, and procurement with a combination of dispersed facilities and contractors controlled by a single CPM type system.

The primary difficulty stems from the single fact that actual costs invariably lag behind work performed, particularly in construction, where progress payments are the normal condition of business. It is not unusual to see delays of 30 or 60 days to payment. When there are changes and claims, even longer periods may elapse before the true costs, and often estimates to complete, are accounted for.

Another difficulty is getting engineering and construction personnel, who are in supervisory roles over technical progress of work packages, to utilize a CPM system for planning rather than simply accounting.

C/SPC is a proven and effective technique for relating costs and schedules in a meaningful way. It has been tested on a number of substantial facilities construction and modernizing programs lasting 5 years or longer. C/SPC provides these advantages:

1. It relates cost and schedule data in an *integrated* manner.
2. It presents a concise picture of project progress, uncluttered by the

operating details that are the day-to-day responsibility of the project team.

3. It enables top management to observe a large number of projects simultaneously in progress.

4. It structures reporting information so that top managers can make meaningful comparisons of projects on both a technical and fiscal basis and reallocate resources too when this action is necessary.

5. It reduces the amount of subjective estimating usually associated with other status reporting systems.

4.8 PROCUREMENT PLANNING

The entire building project from conception to occupancy can be viewed as a procurement process as follows:

- *Owner.* Procures the services of an architect-engineer, construction manager, general contractor, and perhaps individual specialty contractors. May procure long-lead-time items and furnish them to the contractors as owner-furnished equipment.
- *Architect-engineer and construction manager.* Procure the services of consultants.
- *General contractor and individual specialty contractors.* Procure the services of subcontractors and vendors. Procure material, supplies, hardware, and long-lead-time items.
- *Subcontractors.* Procure the services of vendors. Procure material, supplies, hardware, and long-lead-time items.

However, procurement planning, project control, and fiscal/cost control usually are treated as independent and isolated functions. Indeed, quite often there is no procurement planning, especially for the procurement of long-lead-time items. Yet these items normally have a significant impact on total project costs. The importance of these functions can be realized by recognizing that on complicated, multiyear projects the control systems can be expected to account for more than 10% of the total program costs. If not fully considered at the outset, bringing control systems on line during the course of a program can be more of a disaster, since the project team must play "catch up." Chapters 5 and 6 deal with these functions in depth and bring them within the value management concept.

4.9 PROBLEM SOLVING

Value management methodology provides a systematic approach to problem solving and decision making and can be applied to a wide variety of problem areas. All problems have certain characteristics. Figure 4.11 illustrates the essence of a problem. A problem has two essential characteristics. First, it is a deviation between what *should* be happening and what *actually* is happening. Second, the deviation is undesired and important enough that the responsible manager thinks it should be corrected. The second characteristic is what makes the deviation a problem. An example of an undesired deviation is a schedule slippage which, if large and important enough, could threaten the completion time of the project. In contrast, an overall acceleration of the project that could result in an early project completion date with the accompanying benefits of early occupancy and early generation of revenues or savings of rent payments is a desirable deviation.

A deviation is usually brought about by an unanticipated change or occurrence. Before the deviation the activity is proceeding as planned; afterwards it is off plan and possibly out of control. Proper problem-solving and decision-making techniques generate the necessary action to return the activity to the desired plan. Value management provides these proper techniques.

Perhaps even more valuable than problem solving, value management also is an effective instrument for preempting potential problems. Preventing or minimizing potential problems contributes the greatest return on the investment of a manager's time and effort. This fact is recognized in the axiom an ounce of prevention is worth a pound of cure. Yet the systematic analysis of potential problems is rare.

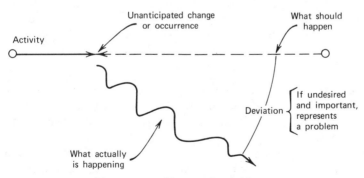

Figure 4.11 Nature of a problem.

Chapter 11 discusses in detail both problem solving and potential problem avoidance.

4.10   RELATIONSHIP TO OTHER COST AWARENESS PROGRAMS

There is an interface between other, more common, cost awareness programs and value management. While each has its own goals, uses, and techniques, each has the overall objective of supporting planning, design, construction, and maintenance activities. There is no conflict between value management and these other concepts; rather, there exists a complementary relationship that increases the probability of achieving top management's overall objectives. The relationship of value management to some of the more common cost awareness concepts is discussed below.

Cost Reduction

A cost reduction program usually is narrower in scope and objective than a VM program. It is often primarily an appeal to people to acquire a cost awareness and normally provides a system only for monitoring dollars saved. On the other hand, value management is a disciplined approach for examining costs and function from every conceivable aspect. It provides a methodology for reducing costs and a formal staff who actually participate in achieving the audited savings rather than just monitoring the program. Furthermore, cost reduction examines existing hardware to reduce its cost. Value management is a more fundamental approach that takes nothing for granted; it investigates everything about a subsystem or system, including the very existence of the item itself, subject only to the one restriction that the required function or performance must not be degraded.

Cost Effectiveness

Cost effectiveness and value management are somewhat similar in that both represent a systematic analysis of alternative ways of accomplishing required functions and the costs associated with each alternative. However, they are applied at different times. A cost effectiveness study is employed during the conceptual or early planning phases to compare the overall costs of broadly conceived alternative methods for satisfying major requirements. For example, a typical cost effectiveness study might compare alternative means of providing a facility such as leasing, constructing, or rehabilitating an existing structure. Value management complements a cost effectiveness study by verifying the value levels of the proposed alternatives and, if suitable, by proposing additional alternatives. Then, throughout the project's life cycle, value management is used to remain within budget and, very frequently, to even reduce the cost of the selected alternative.

Standardization

Contrary to the claim that standardization attempts to freeze the status quo while value management attempts to change it, value management and standardization are not opposing philosophies. Used properly, standardization can reduce total cost. In some cases, unnecessary costs occur because standards are not being used. In other cases, unnecessary costs occur because the standards are obsolete. Standardization efforts must include procedures for accommodating innovations in technology and changes in the owner's needs, and it is here that VM techniques can make a significant contribution to any standardization effort.

Zero Defects

A zero defects program is a motivational program aimed at employees. Its intention is to eliminate defects attributable to human error by inspiring employees at all levels to do their job right the first time. Value management can have a beneficial impact on this effort. For example, VM methodology and potential problem analysis will identify potential misinterpretations of specifications, uncoordinated elements of plans, and other potential defects. Correction of these discoveries can save both time and money by reducing the number of contract modifications and change orders.

Reliability, Quality Assurance, and Maintainability

These disciplines ensure that the final product and its operational capabilities meet the specified performance requirements. Value management techniques can make a significant input to the solution of a problem in any of these areas.

Often value management leads to a less complex solution that tends to further enhance quality, reliability, and maintainability characteristics. These programs and value management are complementary, and all proposed value changes must consider these programs.

Tradeoff Analysis

Tradeoffs by definition involve related changes. For example, reliability, quality, or maintainability is reduced to bring down cost; schedules are accelerated, so cost goes up; and so forth. However, in value management the necessary function and performance are constants rather than variables and may not be reduced to reduce cost. Although essential performance is never traded off for lower cost, the means of accomplishing the performance may be altered to reduce cost. For example, the required performance may be accomplished by components of another system rather than designing a special, separate system. In this restricted sense, value management may be thought to involve exchanges, but the necessary performance of the end product itself is not changed.

4.11 CIRCULATING VALID VALUE CHANGES

Proven value management changes should be circulated within the organization and among the various construction projects being carried out by the organization. The greater the exposure given a proven value change, the greater the opportunities for applying it to other projects. Circulating proven changes brings to the attention of those responsible for designing, approving, and constructing projects the latest cost-saving ideas, techniques, and materials.

Because of the lack of circulation, many organizations fail to realize potential savings. For example, on one project one department of an owner's firm approved a proposal to eliminate the painting of interior steel structures that resulted in a savings to the owner of $9,000. A short time later, on another project, another department of the same firm approved a similar proposal, resulting in a savings to the owner of $22,000 and an award to the contractor of $34,000. Circulating proven proposals might have enabled the owner to realize the total savings of $56,000 that resulted from the second proposal; the owner would have eliminated the requirement by modifying the contract documents via the regular change order procedures. This example illustrates how an owner could have benefited from circulating proven changes. A contractor also can reap such rewards. If he circulates to other jobs on which he is working a VM change that was approved on one job, the contractor may find that that proposal also is applicable to and accepted for one of the other jobs. Thus he gains an additional, substantial profit for a minimal amount of additional paperwork.

Potential benefits of circulation are maximized by designating a central point responsible for identifying and circulating proven VM proposals. The most logical central point in any organization for this activity is the VM staff. The central point will fulfill this task most efficiently if it develops and maintains a system that accomplishes the following:

- Receive from various organizational departments and projects all approved VM changes.
- Screen the changes to identify those having a potential for further application.
- Categorize the changes by discipline (such as mechanical, electrical, etc.) and by building system (such as foundation, heating, lighting, etc.).
- Circulate the changes regularly to responsible individuals in all the departments and on all the projects.

The last step of actually circulating the information can be accomplished by regularly publishing and distributing pamphlets. The format of the pamphlet should contain as a minimum the following information:

- Changes categorized by discipline and building system.
- A description of the change in concise and understandable terms.
- An individual (preferably) or office that can be contacted for more detailed information about the change.

4.12 REALIZING VALUE MANAGEMENT OPPORTUNITIES

To bring to fruition the greatest potential opportunities, the total VM effort must be coordinated into a comprehensive, organizational program. A major Federal construction agency accomplishes its total value management via a four-part program:

1. An internal program.
2. An architect-engineer and construction manager contract provision.
3. A construction contract incentive provision.
4. A leasing contract incentive provision.

Internal Program. The agency's internal program consists of value specialists located in each regional office and the headquarters office. These VM experts assist contractors and designers who participate in the three external programs. They also perform in-house value studies on VM ideas generated by agency personnel. In addition, the headquarters personnel provide instruction in value management at seminars conducted by various organizations throughout the United States and its possessions.

Architect-Engineer and Construction Manager Contract Provisions. Requirements for VM services are included in most agency contracts with architect-engineers and construction managers. The degree of services to be provided depends on the scope of the proposed project. The VM contract provision is a flexible, multisection clause. Sections are deleted or added depending on the level of VM service desired by the agency. Architect-engineers and construction managers are compensated for the VM services they provide on a negotiated, firm, fixed-price basis. That portion of the architect-engineer's fee representing payment for VM services may be excluded in determining whether the architect-engineer's fee is within the statutory 6% limit. Architect-engineers and construction managers do not share in any incentive payments, since the agency considers value management a professional service to be provided by the designer or construction manager for a negotiated fee. It is the responsibility of the architect-engineer and construction manager to acquire the trained personnel needed to provide the services required by the contract. However, employees of the architect-engineer or construction manager are eligible to participate in VM training courses held for government personnel provided that (1) space is available and (2) the architect-engineer or construction manager has a current contract with the agency.

Construction Contract Incentive Provision. All agency contracts in excess of $10,000 for procurement of construction, repair and improvement work, equipment maintenance service, and equipment purchases contain a value incentive clause. The clause applies to any cost reduction proposal initiated and developed by the contractor for the purpose of changing any requirement of the contract. To qualify as a value change proposal, two criteria must be met: (1) There must be a cost reduction, either on the current contract or in the cost of ownership of the work provided by the contract, and (2) there must be a change to some requirement of the contract. Contractors are eligible to share in two types of savings: The contractor shares in any savings to the current contract that result from his proposal and also in any resulting life-cycle ownership savings.

Leasing Contract Incentive Provision. The agency also is a major lessee of office and warehouse space. Many of its leases and lease-construction contracts contain a value incentive clause. This clause applies to any cost reduction proposal initiated and developed by the lessor for the purpose of changing any requirement of the lease or lease-construction contract. To be a valid cost reduction proposal, the proposed change must result in a net savings to the government by providing either (1) a decrease in the cost of the performance of the lease or (2) a reduction in the cost of the use of the leased space. Furthermore, the proposal must result in a savings without impairing any required functions and characteristics such as service life, reliability, economy of operation, ease of maintenance, standardized features, esthetics, fire protection features, and safety features originally required by the lease. However, if the lessor believes that certain functions and characteristics required by the lease are nonessential or excessive, he may submit a cost reduction proposal suggesting that they be combined, reduced, or eliminated. If a cost reduction proposal is accepted by the agency, the lessor shares in the savings.

CHAPTER 5

PROCUREMENT

5.1 INTRODUCTION

Value management, or rather its parent, value engineering, dealt with end items and specifications. The initial savings realized from VE techniques indicated that functional integrity need not be sacrificed for economies—economies that were not observable to the designer or specifier. In this chapter the importance of early procurement planning as a function of value management will be described. The savings, while not quantified, will be qualified to a sufficient level of information so that the planner can see the advantages and ultimate savings, in time or costs, to be achieved.

5.2 THE PROCUREMENT ORGANIZATION

At the outset of an acquisition program for a medium-sized to large facility ($1 million plus), the owner's organization should be carefully evaluated for its capability to perform the procurement function. As will be shown in subsequent paragraphs, procurement is a vital activity which, when performed effectively, can result in the achieving of optimums with respect to timing and purchases. Since this function is such an important part of a facility acquisition program, it is wise to apply the precepts of value management at an early stage. Acquisition activities and VM interrelationships are shown in Figure 5.1.

The owner organization will undoubtedly have the means to obtain services and materials even if this capability is achieved by consultant services on a continuing basis. However, if it is not an owner's business, the acquisition of facilities has certain specialized aspects with which the owner or developer should become familiar. These include:

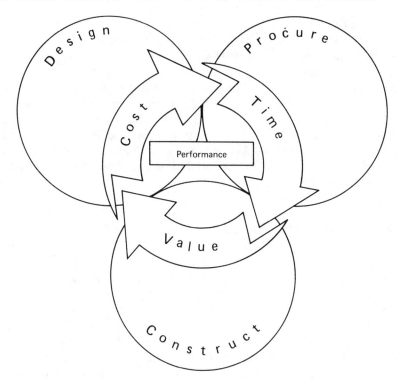

Figure 5.1 Elements of facilities acquisition and VM interrelationships.

- Contract and statement of work preparation.
- Market research.
- Guidance sources.
- Procurement activities (including two-step procurement).
- Contract management.
- Contracting.
- Indirect advantages.

These aspects are discussed in the remainder of this chapter.

5.3 CONTRACT AND STATEMENT OF WORK PREPARATION

The owner organization must have the capacity to define the scope and substance of the work to be performed and the services to be provided, and to realistically estimate performance or supply times and costs. Descriptions of work, services, and materials must be precise and specific because of both the technical and legalistic implications of contractual documents.

Once the scope of work is defined, experienced procurement specialists estimate the "level of effort" (man-hours or equivalent), materials, and other direct costs such as shipping, packing, storing, travel, printing, et cetera, and add the elements that will affect bidding. These elements include overhead, markup, fee or profit, payroll expenses, insurance, and other factors that will make the procurement organization's estimate effective for obtaining bids.

5.4 MARKET RESEARCH

Procurement personnel and value managers recognize the strategies of both wide and narrow competition. Based on the scope of work and the estimated total value of the materials or services under procurement, the strategy can be determined. Generally, the larger the value of the procurement, the greater the opportunity for savings through competition. At the outset of a major facilities acquisition program, thorough planning is essential to establish how the procurement process for services, materials, and construction will work to the advantage of the program.

The owner organization could allow consultants to accomplish the work for it. This has disadvantages, since procurement services themselves have expenses. Then, too, the owner must select the organization that will provide these services—a selection best not made from the Yellow Pages.

Assuming that the owner desires a range of services including design and construction management, it must be recognized that these constitute a major acquisition expense. It is advisable to "shop around."

The preparation of a listing of qualified architect-engineers for design services will require some research. The government maintains listings of architect-engineers at national, regional, and even local levels. Standard Forms 254 and 255 are used to record the experience of AEs as well as the qualifications of key personnel of the firm. When a design services contract is contemplated, government advertises for an expression of interest, or selects an AE based on the most current government listings. A commercial or industrial venture with the experience of various facilities design projects simply prepares letters to firms considered qualified. The uninitiated owner should investigate a firm before soliciting its interest in a new project. This investigation should include a check of the firm's Dunn and Bradstreet and Standard and Poor's ratings. A "short list" of from three to six well-qualified AEs is normal for a final selection process. More participants tend to draw out the selection process without increasing the owner's advantage through competition.

A construction management services listing requires essentially the same financial investigation—primarily to determine the maximum amount of construction that the contractor has managed in the past and can currently handle. "Track record" for on-time and at-cost performance are other particular considerations an owner faces in drafting a short list (which, like the AE selection, should comprise three to six firms).

Localization of the services, that is, the proximity of the design or construction management services contractor, has bearing. A design firm based in New York is not likely to be well versed in the Los Angeles building codes, nor will it be familiar with the regulatory requirements for occupational safety and health peculiar to the State of California (CALOSHA).

The "market" for both design and construction management services has its fluctuations. Large firms with large backlogs may not provide competitive bids on moderately sized projects ($1 million to $15 million). At other times, when construction money is tight, because of high interest rates or other related reasons, the design services will be most competitive, and construction contractors hungry for work will offer lower bids.

An assessment of the market could provide the basis for a tradeoff inviting a bid from a design services contractor in a relatively static area at savings over the cost of services that could be provided by an already busy local firm. The added insights to market research concerning materials (i.e., steel, high-performance machinery, decorative items) are also important to keep under initial and subsequent surveillance. The importance of utilities costs and cost projections is also well worth early investigation as adjuncts to the market research.

Associated with market research, to assist in determinants for procurements, some understanding of the why, what, and how is required. Keeping in mind that the procurements under discussion are associated with facility planning and acquisition, the value manager has two alternatives:

1. Allow the designer to specify end items in the construction specifications. The net result of this decision is that the owner pays the construction contractor for purchasing and, usually, for installing the

item(s). This also means that the owner will pay for the procurement as well as the fees for profit of both vendor and constructor. In some cases, where the constructor uses a subcontractor, all will receive overhead and profit in addition to costs.

2. Procure the items by purchase order; incorporate the configuration and interfaces associated with the item(s); and pay the construction contractor for installation.

Generally, the two approaches involve a treatment of costs, that is, either involuntary or discretionary. Government agencies make these decisions quite frequently because a great number of facility items have already been specified and are available through government channels. In these cases, both the designer and the constructor will have what is known as "government-furnished property or equipment" identified to them early in the program. Examples of government-furnished items include power generation plants and large electrical components such as transformers and switchgear. Government-furnished items provide a measure of standardization that tends to reduce maintenance and replacement costs of wear and breakage.

A value manager's input to procurement at the market research stage takes the following form: major functional items of procurement, either materials or equipment, are categorized for the research activity. A population of the items must also be established to obtain a cost analysis factor that will show the advantages of quantity buying.

Several approaches to the market research activity are available:

- *Historic method.* Involves gathering historical data so that comparisons and contrasts can be drawn and applications made.
- *Observational method.* The gathering of data by direct measurements of consumer and market phenomena as they occur.
- *Experimental method.* Setting up experiments with proper control procedures so that the effects of specific marketing actions can be determined.
- *Survey method.* The most widely used, it is the gathering of data by asking questions of knowledgeable vendors and suppliers to obtain information on probable cost advantages.

Some examples of what could be candidate quantity procurement items in a facilities acquisition program include:

- Amenity items, such as drinking fountains and water coolers.
- Production or shop equipment (when processes are involved).
- Furnishings (rugs, window blinds, drapes).
- Communications items (PBX, intercoms, security systems).

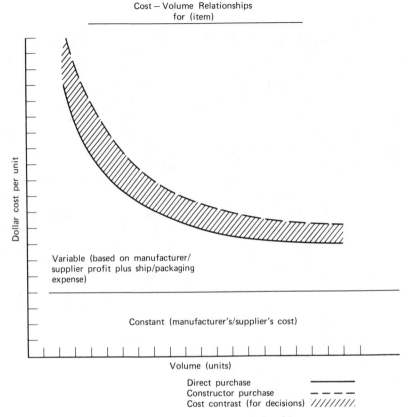

Figure 5.2 Cost–volume relationships.

As soon as quantities can be closely approximated using one of the marking approaches discussed on page 126, the value manager constructs a cost–volume relationship curve such as that shown on Figure 5.2.

An important adjunct to this analysis is addition of probable escalation factors. This item is discussed in subsequent paragraphs.

5.5 GUIDANCE SOURCES

It is wise for an organization setting out to construct a facility to seek and utilize selected guidance documents before soliciting bids for services. The government provides certain guidelines concerning predicted expenses of both architect-engineers and construction managers. In most cases, the guidelines are formulated on the basis of constructed value.

For the architect-engineer, Federal Procurement Regulations set forth a limit of 6% of constructed value for the design and engineering leading up to preparation of construction documents (e.g., drawings, specifications, and cost estimates). There may be other corollary services provided within the limitation, such as energy analyses, master equipment list work, and so forth. However, the 6% limit is a rigid ceiling. This becomes a stumbling block when an unusual or first-of-its-kind facility is planned, since there is likely to be a good deal of effort expended in detailed analysis and engineering to define the optimums for design. Often the government will provide funding for prerequisite studies to assure feasibility and/or establish a firm basis for estimates that require legislation and appropriations within government agency budgets. These studies are usually referred to as preliminary engineering reports (PER), or preliminary cost estimates (PCE). They are used for design criteria or the basis for design; the government can use them in negotiations with AEs after their selection as best-qualified. The PER or PCE cost of services has ranged from slightly less than 1% to 1½% of constructed value, depending on complexity and scope.

While a great number of techniques are used to perform the evaluations leading to a contract selection, one that has been proven is offered for consideration. The scenario for this evaluation and selection process is as follows.

Services of a geotechnical consultant are required for a major aerospace ground support system at a large Air Force base. Multiple structures such as airfield, launch pad, solid rocket motor, tank, vehicle checkout and maintenance, and marine facilities are involved. Consultant is to provide soil, geology, and seismic data incident to siting of structures.

Because the program is long and all the consultant's work could not be scoped at the outset for a single bid response, it was determined that the selection process would be made on a "best qualified" basis. Accordingly, the following list of factors was prepared.

- Response to direction and/or change.
- Quality of work and deliverables.
- Knowledge of terrain and local conditions.
- Prior satisfactory work for the evaluating organization.
- Prior satisfactory work for the government or other clients.

- Ability to meet precise schedules with promptness.
- Pricing rates of staff, services, equipment.
- Advantage of proximity to evaluating organization.
- Advantage of proximity to work site.
- Testing, geology, and seismic technology in-house.
- Adequacy and availability of professional and support staff.
- Use and management of subcontractors (surveyors, drillers).

The listing was circulated to 12 experts, who were requested to assign values to each of the factors on the following scale:

1 = least important
2 = moderately important
3 = most important

With the experts' input, weight points were aggregated against the number of inputs. Following this procedure, a slate of five reasonably proximate experienced and qualified firms was established; a generalized scope of services was prepared to determine comparative costs and rates; and interest and proposals were solicited.

The source selection team consisting of a nonvoting chairman, three technically qualified voting members, and a recorder was convened. The voting members were not aware of the weight values of the factors on the evaluation sheets (Figure 5.3). The chairman and the recorder did composites and calculations involved in translating the raw scores, adding the weights to obtain the adjusted scores.

Evaluation processes can include both sensitivity checks (shifting of weights to different factors), and normalization. To illustrate, if one of the candidates was unable to furnish pricing data, we can assume an average derived from those who did. It is likely that pricing, as in this example, was not a "most important" factor because the work involved a high degree of technology and professionalism.

5.6   PROCUREMENT ACTIVITIES

Whether procurement is inherently retained by the owner or is provided to the owner as a contractual service, procurement activities should be considered in planning. Moreover, surveillance over them, for cost reduction opportunities, should be a part of the value manager's responsibilities. With the programmatic decisions whether the owner will buy or furnish versus incorporation of requirements by the

Evaluation Sheet

Candidates	Evaluation Factors												Total
	A	B	C	D	E	F	G	H	I	J	K	L	Raw Scores
	1. Responses to direction and/or changes	2. Quality of work and deliverables	3. Knowledge of terrain and local conditions	4. Prior satisfactory work for the evaluating organization	5. Prior satisfactory work for the government or other clients	6. Ability to meet precise schedules, with promptness	7. Pricing rates of staff, services, and equipment	8. Advantage of proximity to evaluating organization	9. Advantage of proximity to the work site	10. Testing, geology and seismic technology in-house	11. Adequacy and availability of professional and support staff	12. Use and management of sub-contractors (surveyors, drillers, etc.)	

Assign scores:
3 = Highest
2 = Good
1 = Adequate
0 = Unknown
−1 = Potential problem

Figure 5.3 Evaluation sheet.

construction contractor, the procurement planning becomes more definitive.

It is a prerequisite that the acquisition activities be reasonably well identified with respect to time. Based on the schedules, the implications and advantages of two-step procurement should be exploited.

5.6.1   TWO-STEP PROCUREMENT

Two-step procurement requires the commitment of resources to purchase items at a later date. The first step is to obtain firm pricing for items that provide a cost advantage to the owner. A corollary requirement is that the offeror furnish specific information on configuration and interfacing on items he will physically deliver at the appropriate time on the acquisition schedule. The owner, or buyer, having selected the offer, provides the data (drawings and specifications) to the designer or architect-engineer. The architect-engineer designs the accommodations for the specified items, but indicates that provision of the item is "Not-in-Contract" (NIC) for the construction contractor. It can be seen that the installation of the owner-furnished item can be a specified (in construction document) activity for the construction contractor, or it can remain out of the construction documents for a subsequent and negotiated change or be provided for in a separate contract apart from the construction contract. The latter is a viable alternative, since many suppliers have the capability or like to supervise installations to protect the owner and themselves in meeting the warranty-guarantee provisions that dictate a proper installation.

The advantages of two-step procurement are enhanced by the timing of the cash outlay. Neither the owner nor the construction contractor is faced with the prospect of long-term storage and security that accompany early procurement and delivery. An added benefit is that more standardization can be incorporated in Operations and Maintenance (O&M) planning when the configuration of end items is established early in the acquisition process.

5.7   CONTRACT MANAGEMENT

In today's competitive environment, a large and complex facility acquisition program is subjected to rather sophisticated processes. The old procedure of advertising and award to the lowest bidder has proven to be ineffective when the life-cycle costs for ultimate operational expenses are considered. Moreover, the disadvantages that were incurred when a purely buying operation characterized the procurement included:

1. *Obsolescence.* The offerors bid low to rid themselves of products when they planned to upgrade a product line. The unknowing buyer was faced with an expensive reprocurement, since he bought a product that was "phased out."

2. *Poor quality.* Quality requirements are sacrificed when pricing is the sole determinant. Lot buying—that is, throwing a large number of items into an order that could be filled by a single supplier—is also a pitfall for equipment with a high performance requirement.

3. *Substitution.* An offspring of poor quality and lot buying. Lack of specified performance in a procurement invites suppliers to meet purchase orders with low-cost, low-quality substitutions.

Treating procurement as an activity that will reinforce the principles of value management requires the VM representative to look long and hard at the practices of buying, negotiating, and administration. A structured organization is a requisite for the owner unless he intends to delegate the procurement activity to his engineering design or construction contractor.

In almost every large facilities acquisition program, a large proportion of the effectiveness of the effort (on-time, at-cost) is attributable to successful contract management. This is true of both the design/engineering activities and those of the construction manager or construction contractor, depending on the acquisition approach most appropriate to the owner's needs. Therefore, it is well for the value manager, in providing alternatives, to have the awareness that comes with both experience and analytical capability. Some understanding of the function and fee structures of both is essential.

Architect-Engineering

There are three generally accepted pricing structures for the AE contract: a percentage of the (programmatic) construction cost; lump-sum, or firm fixed price; and time-and-material. Variations of these exist, such as the level-of-effort and "multiplier" schedules, with the multiplier being an aggregated factor of overhead, fee for profit, and payroll expenses applied to all direct hours charged. For the most part, the percentage fee basis is falling into disuse, particularly on government projects. Part of the reason is seen in the limitation imposed by Federal Procurement Regulations and other regulatory documents, which impose a 6% ceiling on design and engineering activities leading to preparation of construction documents. In certain cases, it has been shown that a percentage estimate of the AE effort is made early in the program. When the scope of the facility under design is well into the definitive stages, a lump sum contract can be negotiated.

Another important aspect to be considered is the structure of the AE organization. Should the design organization be primarily architectural, it will usually be supported by engineering firms or consultants. When the AE is primarily engineering, the architectural aspects are of lesser importance. The differences show up in the type of facilities; an industrial plant with production and processes is primarily allocated to an engineering firm, whereas high-rise or administrative office facilities are usually allocated to firms that are primarily architectural.

For a large, technically complex facilities acquisition program, the design and engineering activities are given special consideration. The usual competitors are large multidisciplinary organizations that can provide the wide range of planning and analytical services under a single management. For projects too large for a single firm to undertake, a joint venture or prime subcontractor organization can be put together, with the firm strongest in the required expertise taking the management lead.

The above discussion illustrates that potentially there are many combinations of AE services and organizations. However, the procurable mixture depends on many factors such as location of project, present supply and demand of AE services, and so forth. Ideally the most cost advantageous composition, consistent with the requirements of the proposed project, is selected prior to committing any resources. Therefore, the value manager must be aware of what is obtainable in order to make competent recommendations during the AE selection process.

Construction Management

There are three major approaches to providing for construction management. The first alternative is that the planned facilities acquisition may not require a construction manager. This alternative allocates management of construction to the owner or a general contractor. A variation is that the architect-engineer, if the capability exists in that organization, can assume responsibility for more activities than surveillance alone. A second approach is to hire a firm that specializes in construction management and provides a cadre of key personnel and the necessary cost and scheduling techniques to maintain management control over both design and construction activities. In the third approach, an interprofessional organization is contracted to provide cost and schedule control, with full responsibility for inspection, change processing, and other field activities, including safety, procurement, security, and monitoring of environmental conditions.

The methods of compensation vary with situations; however, the percentage of constructed value usually establishes a basis for the level of effort involved. In most cases, particularly for public projects, lump sum, firm fixed price contracts have been preferred.

It should be borne in mind that 80% of the construction dollars are usually spent on 20% of the building systems and activities. This indicates to the value manager the importance of spending a greater portion of his time and effort in identifying and analyzing these systems, which, as "swingers," offer the greatest return in the form of savings.

Activity reward for a given contract can be based on an estimated cost reduction that can be attributable to productivity gains. Below are listed some general principles and procedures that apply to estimating cost reductions and calculating productivity reward. These items are implemented at the time of selection and negotiation but are described here for the VM's consideration in preparing the overall procurement plan. The items are adaptable to design, construction, and equipment item supply.

1. The contractor will be expected to prepare and support cost reduction estimates.

2. The anticipated overall contract cost decrease is to be based on estimated decreases measured at the lowest, or unit, cost level.

3. The lowest average unit cost, exclusive of contractor's profit, for a preceding production run shall be used as the unit cost baseline.

4. A technique shall be employed to determine that portion of the cost decrease that is attributable to productivity gains as opposed to the effects of quantity differences between the base contract and the pending procurement action.

5. When the parties agree that the estimated overall contract cost decrease is materially affected by price level differences between the base period and the current point in time, an economic price adjustment may be applied to the estimate.

6. The productivity reward shall be calculated by multiplying the contract cost decrease due to productivity gains by the base profit objective rate.

7. The degree of review and validation of the data supporting the productivity reward calculation should be commensurate with the materiality of this profit element in relation to the overall price objective.

There are numerous methods available for measuring productivity gains, depending on whether the measurements are used for production and supply of hardware or equipment items, construction activities, or design. Any technique may be acceptable, provided it equitably takes into account the above-mentioned principles and procedures.

5.8 CONTRACTING

For a major facilities acquisition program, the value manager must have some knowledge of contracting processes to make advantageous procurement recommendations. Based on the phase and complexity of the work involved, a number of types of contract are available. The generally accepted progression in the procurement spectrum, ranging from basic research (first-of-a-kind, new processes, materials, etc.), through supply procurements and from cost to firm fixed price contracts, is shown on Figure 5.4. Note that emphasis is placed on incentive contracts; this emphasis should be a part of the VM strategy and recommendations, which set the description of contracting as an activity apart from a purely procurement discussion. Restated, the VM function in procurement planning is to influence contract strategy so that productivity and savings result in incorporating these objectives in procurement plans and contracts.

In making the determinations and recommendations, the value manager should consider the following:

1. The degree of cost responsibility the contractor is expected to assume.

2. The reliability of the programmatic estimates in relation to the contractor's proposed tasks and scope.

3. The complexity of tasks, scope, and schedules that will be assumed by the contractor.

The first and basic determination of the degree of cost responsibility assumed by the contractor is related to the sharing of total risk of contract cost by the government and the contractor through the selection of contract type. The extremes are a cost-plus-fixed-fee contract requiring only that the contractor use his best efforts to perform a task,

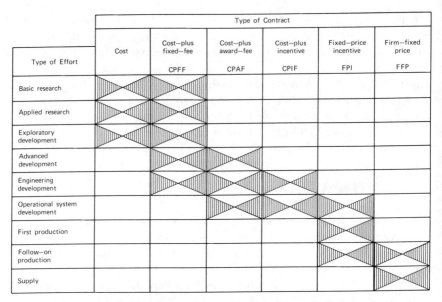

Figure 5.4   Types of contract versus types of effort.

and a firm fixed-price contract for a complex item. A cost-plus-fixed-fee contract would reflect a complete assumption of cost responsibility.

The second determination is that of the reliability of the cost estimates. Sound price negotiation requires well-defined contract objectives and reliable cost estimates. Prior production experience assists the contractor in preparing reliable cost estimates on new procurements for similar equipment. An excessive cost estimate reduces the possibility that the cost of performance will exceed the contract price, thereby reducing the contractor's assumption of contract cost risk.

The third determination is that of the difficulty of the contractor's task. The contractor's task can be difficult or easy, regardless of the type of contract.

Contractors are likely to assume greater cost risk only if contracting officers objectively analyze the risk incident to proposed contracts and are willing to compensate contractors for it. Generally, a cost-plus-fixed-fee contract would not justify a reward for risk in excess of 1%, nor would a firm fixed-price contract justify a reward of less than 6%. Where the proper contract type has been selected, the reward for risk would usually fall into the following percentage ranges:

Cost plus fixed fee	0 to 1%
Cost plus incentive fee	1 to 3%

| Fixed price incentive | 3 to 6% |
| Firm fixed price | 6 to 8% |

These ranges may not be appropriate for all procurement situations. For instance, a fixed-price incentive contract that is closely priced with a low ceiling price and high incentive share may be tantamount to a firm fixed-price contract. In this situation, the contracting officer might determine that a basis exists for high confidence in the reasonableness of the estimate, and that little opportunity exists for cost reduction without extraordinary efforts. On the other hand, a contract with a high ceiling and low incentive formula could be considered to contain cost-plus-incentive-fee contract features. In this situation, the contracting officer might determine that the owner is retaining much of the contract cost responsibility and that the risk assumed by the contractor is minimal. Similarly, if a cost-plus-incentive-fee contract includes an unlimited downward fee adjustment on cost control, it could be comparable to a fixed-price incentive contract. In such a pricing environment the contracting officer may determine that the owner has transferred a greater amount of cost responsibility to the contractor than is typical under a normal cost-plus-incentive-fee contract.

There are a great many facets to procurement and contracting strategies, the details of which are well-documented in current literature. The VM specialist will have to be knowledgeable in them to participate effectively in a plan that has cost advantages.

5.9 INDIRECT ADVANTAGES

The value manager, in support of the procurement planning, should have a general awareness of government policies and procedures that energetically support small business programs. If the owner is a government agency the consideration is almost mandatory; if the owner that the value manager is representing is a commercial or industrial enterprise, the advantages of small business transactions should be established and evaluated in procurement planning. It is quite likely that either a direct or indirect (subcontracting) activity engaging small business concerns could result in favorable pricing since small business may have lower overhead, labor, rates, and profit margins than larger concerns. Similar consideration should be given to doing business with firms that are located in labor surplus areas. Perhaps the work could be done in a high unemployment area and provide training for the handicapped and/or hardcore unemployed. Both the small busi-

ness and labor surplus considerations have to be evaluated in the light
of technological risk.

5.10 OTHER PROCUREMENT ACTIVITIES

Other procurement activities and the potential role of value management in identifying potential cost reductions are discussed in the
following paragraphs.

5.10.1 PURCHASING

Acquisition programs and, ultimately, operations are characterized by
purchasing, a basic function of any economy. The owner needs certain
goods and services and uses specialists to select suppliers and commit
resources. Additionally, the specialist must be able to be certain that
what he is buying will meet specifications and quality standards,
arrive on time to meet schedules, and be delivered in the quantities
specified.

Purchasing, traditionally an internal service function, has had management emphasis recently. Modern and skillful purchasing can reduce total cost of goods purchased by 5 to 10%. The purchasing agent's
goals are low prices, continuity of supply, consistency of quality, and
favorable relationships with suppliers.

It is a matter of history that value management and value engineering evolved from an activity known as value analysis, which was, at its
inception, an organized effort carried out by General Electric and the
Ford Motor Company to reduce costs on purchased parts and materials.
Since that time, purchasing has come to be considered during the
design phase because the new developments and techniques available
from suppliers can be advantageous in design solutions and cost control. Thus, purchasing can become involved in the design, supply, or
construction cycles long before drawings are made and handed over
with purchase requisitions.

5.10.2 VENDOR/SUPPLIER EVALUATIONS

One of the most important links in the purchasing process is the
supplier or vendor. Both new and established vendors/suppliers are
being subjected to more critical reviews with respect to plants,
capabilities, products, financial conditions, and performance. It is also

customary for purchasing personnel to conduct a physical inspection of potential suppliers or vendors accompanied by engineers and/or technicians. Even the use of statistical data for measuring vendor performance on price, delivery, and quality has become a standard purchasing practice.

These statistical techniques vary from a relatively rough approach of asking the buyers or engineers to rate suppliers and vendors on certain factors, to using index numbers of performance data taken from computer files (data banks are used by various government and public agencies). When a data bank is used, weights are assigned to each evaluation category (e.g., price, 40%; quality, 30%; delivery, 30%). Index numbers are calculated for each factor as well as for overall performance.

In large organizations with integrated data processing capability, purchasing can be tied together with inventory and other financial data. The computer stores purchase histories, price records, and inventory figures as well as the performance data on vendors and suppliers. In the more sophisticated installations, the machines produce purchase orders, expediting documents and vendor/supplier payments, and measure vendor/supplier performance during the procurement process.

Considering the tradeoff alternatives, and recognizing the myriad administrative and managerial tasks, the value manager determines and recommends how the purchasing process will be accomplished for the acquisitions associated with both in-house and contractual projects.

CHAPTER 6

FISCAL/COST CONTROL AND PROJECT CONTROL

6.1 INTRODUCTION

A dramatic change in the management approach for major acquisition programs was brought about by issuance of an important Department of Defense Instruction (DODI) regarding controls of costs and schedules.

The policies and procedures that flowed from this instruction led to implementation of the Cost/Schedule Control Systems Criteria (C/SCSC) now imposed by all military departments. The successes of the system have led other executive agencies to impose the C/SCSC on major contractors when their programs are large enough to require the contractors and the agency sponsoring the acquisition program to exercise intensive control and fiscal responsibility.

C/SCSC is not described here in detail since numerous documents have been issued for that purpose. The procedures it prescribes for implementation are summarized in this chapter because there are cost advantages that should be made known and that are within the province of VM personnel to deal with, at the planning stages as well as later in an acquisition program. Cost reductions, particularly with respect to the total spectrum of life-cycle costs, must be evaluated against a totally budgeted program. Moreover, since the cost of management control can be high, it is itself a candidate for value management.

A fundamental responsibility in every major acquisition program is to ensure that the owner has a continuing overview of the contractors' progress. Progress is defined in both fiscal and physical terms. To be absolutely meaningful, data must be collected on a regular basis during all acquisition phases. These data must:

1. Portray budgets allocated over the periods of time allotted for program activities and specific contract tasks.
2. Indicate work progress at meaningful milestones.
3. Properly relate costs, schedules, and technical accomplishments.
4. Be valid, timely, and auditable.
5. Supply management with a practical level of summarization.

It can be seen that there is no single or common set of management control systems that every organization and selected group of contractors can utilize. Individual organizations and contractors have different procedures, accounting systems, and controls. Therefore, as government agencies have learned, it is not reasonable to prescribe and enforce a universal system of cost and schedule controls. Accordingly, the federal government has adopted an approach that simplifies the criteria that contractors' management control systems must meet. By applying criteria rather than prescribed management control systems, contractors are given the latitude and flexibility to meet their unique needs—provided they can satisfy the criteria with systems and controls of their choice or customary usage.

An understanding of this system is useful to the value specialist at the outset of an acquisition program that has an estimated investment cost of $50 million. At present, the government does not impose the C/SCSC on firm-fixed-price or fixed-price-with-escalation contracts.

6.2   C/SCSC OVERVIEW

As a minimum, a contractor's management control system is expected to provide a framework for defining work, assigning work responsibility, establishing budgets, controlling costs, and summarizing with respect to planned versus actual accomplishments and related technical achievement information. Objectively, they must provide for:

1. Realistic budgets for increments of work scheduled within responsibility assignment.
2. Accurate accumulation of costs related to progress of work.
3. Comparison between actual resources applied and the estimated resources planned for specific work assignments.
4. Preparation of reliable estimates of costs to complete remaining work.

5. Support of an overall capability for managers to analyze available information to identify problem areas in sufficient time to take remedial action.

With these objectives, and a breakout of the program's identifiable work elements, a management control structure is formulated. The key to the orderly identification of these work elements is the work breakdown structure (WBS). The value specialist must recognize the WBS as the programmatic tool of management, and provide insights and alternatives in structuring assignments of work elements to his own organization or contractors. Once a work element in the WBS hierarchy is made contractual, the contractor uses that identity to formulate his own, which in turn becomes the contract work breakdown structure (CWBS).

Every owner, whether a private, commercial, or industrial organization, that faces a major acquisition program has to decide whether to manage and/or control the program or use one of the principal contractors' capabilities. It can be seen that a major facilities program could use the skills and services of an engineer-constructor or construction manager if his own organization cannot cope with the need for the management controls of acquisition.

The relationships and integration of CWBS elements and the functional organization with the prerequisite management control expertise and capabilities is graphically shown in Figure 6.1.

6.3 C/SCSC IMPLEMENTATION

To meet the requirements to satisfy the C/SCSC criteria, many major contractors had to drastically revise internal controls and accounting and reporting procedures. The system also meant that trained specialists had to train technical personnel in the overall system. The cost of the work in adapting internal systems to meet the criteria is not a reimbursible contract element; it is done at contractors' cost. However, once certified through a special audit agency, adaptations of internal systems are no longer required.

Important terms used in the system are summarized:

1. *Actual cost of work performed (ACWP).* The costs actually incurred and recorded in accomplishing the work performed within a given period.

2. *Budgeted cost for work performed (BCWP).* The sum of the budgets

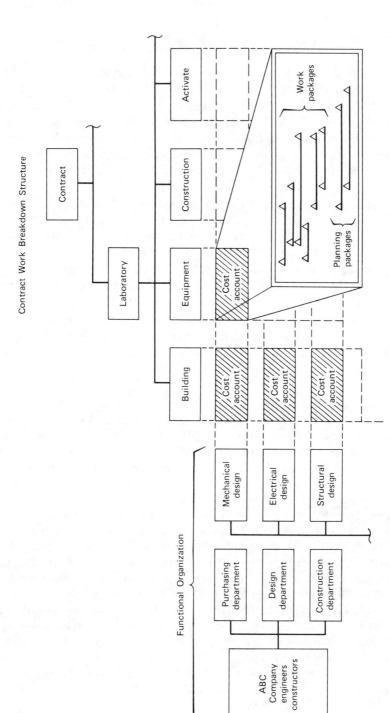

Figure 6.1 Integration of CWBS and organizational structure.

143

for completed work packages and completed portions of open work packages plus the appropriate portion of the budgets for level of effort and apportioned effort.

3. *Budgeted cost of work scheduled (BCWS).* The sum of the budgets for all work packages and planning packages scheduled to be accomplished (including in-process) plus the amount of level of effort and apportioned effort scheduled to be accomplished within a given time period.

4. *Cost account.* A management control point at which actual costs can be accumulated and compared to BCWP. A cost account is a natural control point since it represents the work assigned to one responsible organizational element on one CWBS element.

5. *Estimated cost at completion (ECC).* Actual direct costs, plus indirect costs allocable to the contract, plus the estimate of costs (direct and indirect) for authorized work remaining.

6. *Variances.* Those differences between planned and actual performance that require further review, analysis or corrective action. Appropriate thresholds must be established as to the magnitude of variance that will require special analysis and reports.

There are other terms that the value specialist should become familiar with in evaluating the need for, or implementation of, this type of system for a major acquisition program. Perhaps the most significant aspect of the system is that its intent and objectives are the same as for a minor program—it provides the overview for cost and performance measurement. It can be an integral system for a total program because it is not solely linear, such as the critical path method, with added cost modules; it has a hierarchy of indentured tasks and schedules with appropriate aggregations for ascending levels of management summarization. The need for multitiered controls has been recognized by several firms, which now produce the software programs adaptable to any technological effort and acquisition program—IBM has produced its PMS-4, McDonnell-Douglas has McAUTO. However, all the system needs is good accounting and intensive planning to implement its precepts without the exotic software. A procedure currently in use by The Ralph M. Parsons Company illustrates how a major subcontractor (Parsons) participates in a large and complex program using in-house accounting practices and reporting to the prime contractor's cost/schedule management system (C/SMS), an approved variant of the government's C/SCSC system.

It should be noted, however, that the actual scheduling of the activities of design, construction, and procurements for facilities are on critical path method schedules, since these activities involve other agencies or contractors. The external scheduling of these activities is shown in Figure 6.2.

The CPM methodology is a most useful tool to the value specialist. Illustrative of this is the example of the extended airfield.

The project, within a major acquisition program, involved extension of an existing asphaltic-paved runway 8000 feet long and 200 feet wide. The new requirement, based on landing performance characteristics of the Space Shuttle Orbiter, specified a 15,000-by-200-foot concrete runway for landing from either direction along the same axis of the original runway orientation.

Since the existing runway is sited at an active Air Force installation, the criteria required the design organization to retain use of the runway during the construction. This meant that the new extension of 7000 feet would be constructed first; temporary navigational aids would be emplaced; the extension would then be used while the existing runway was stripped and repaved.

Using the critical path method of analysis, the construction force labor, according to the network plan and cost estimates, yielded the dual peaks shown in Figure 6.3A. Given these data, a question was posed as to what the savings might be if the airfield were closed for the total construction period. The resulting analysis showed that the savings were primarily of time, but that some costs would be reduced. These costs essentially consisted of:

- Better utilization of equipment by the construction contractor.
- Reduction of expense in emplacement and shifting of airfield navigation aids.
- Reduced rate of insurance incurred by the construction contractor by not having to work on an operational runway.

The case is cited here as an example of how value analysis should utilize the management tools available and to illustrate that cost reduction proposals should be considered at the programmatic stage as well as during and after design. The point of using the labor force to determine the potential for savings of time and money is important even though the ultimate choice will rest on operation or shutdown of the airfield. If it were not for the use of an on-line CPM and cost estimates that separate labor from materials, the analysis would clearly be an engineering tradeoff study. Using the management tools, the value analysis was conducted within a day.

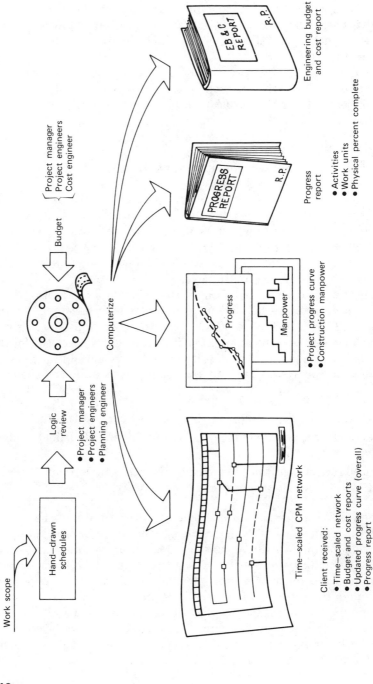

Work scope

Hand-drawn schedules

Logic review
• Project manager
• Project engineers
• Planning engineer

Budget
Project manager
Project engineers
Cost engineer

Computerize

Engineering budget and cost report

Progress report
• Activities
• Work units
• Physical percent complete

• Project progress curve
• Construction manpower

Progress

Manpower

Time-scaled CPM network

Client received:
• Time-scaled network
• Budget and cost reports
• Updated progress curve (overall)
• Progress report

Figure 6.2 CPM system overview.

146

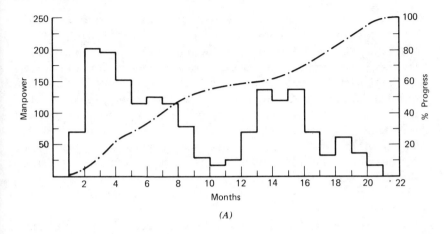

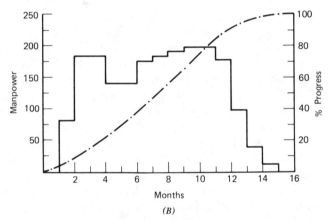

Figure 6.3   CPM analysis. (*A*) Two-phase airfield construction with continuous operations. (*B*) Single-phase, no airfield operations for total construction period.

6.4   PROJECT MANAGEMENT AND CONTROLS

Systems concepts and techniques are tools of the manager to help organize and administer resources. They are also of use in developing improved methods of operation. With an approved acquisition program, the organization must conceptualize the myriad interacting activities, the milestones, the growth and flow of documentation essential to get to the start of construction, and the data required to reflect the finished job.

At the outset of a program, the conceptualization may be only a series of bar charts spread over time for the major efforts of planning, design, and construction. Later, as the major efforts become defined as activities, events, and tasks, the quantities of information are staggeringly increased. The size and complexity of a large acquisition program require timely and useful information for management to be effective. The advent of electronic computers and various software packages met the need for the integration of massive input and selective output.

The planning, at the outset, is in effect an operational model of the activities and events that must take place to achieve the acquisition goals. As a model, the plan must reflect the tasks (or performance of them), the time it takes to do them (in series or in parallel), and, as a third ingredient, the costs.

Costs are identified as internal (planning, engineering, and management), or external (purchases, contracts for construction and other services). The planning and control system is not without its expense. It requires constant care and feeding; its output is only as effective as its input. Therefore, the basic estimates of time and cost for the activities that go into the plan should be based on experience. Even more important to the plan and control system is that it has the characteristic of being updated as new information or experience is gained.

Modern management information systems and/or project controls have had 20 years of shakedown and refinement. Where it was shown that cost/scheduling systems used up to 20% of the total cost for construction, that percentage has been dramatically reduced to less than 10%. The reason for a lower cost is that the management tools are more familiar, they are placed in use earlier than before, and most importantly, project control personnel are far more selective in data used for controls. This means savings in processing and analysis, and more effective data provide for better management decisions.

The value specialist must be aware of the techniques, the cost, and the use of the various project control systems, since they are not only useful tools for his activities, they also offer potential cost savings. Figure 6.4 illustrates a system in use and proven. It can be adapted for most facilities acquisition programs or projects.

6.5 CONFIGURATION AND DATA MANAGEMENT

Configuration and data management are two very important activities related to project controls that are of interest to the value manager or value specialist. Depending on the degrees of complexity and control, the activities are expenses to the acquisition, and to a certain extent to operations and maintenance after transition from construction and startup. They are discussed separately below.

6.5.1 CONFIGURATION MANAGEMENT

Configuration management has been familiar to designers and engineers for years. It became a formal process with the advent of the weapons/aerospace systems approach in the early 1960s. The formality consists of an evolutionary control over an end item from its first functional identification to its operating environment. In effect, as a system, its subsystems, assemblies, subassemblies, and components are defined; a specification hierarchy is created. As the preliminary drawings and specifications are aggregated into a feasible systems concept, a "baseline" is approved. For the concepts, a change in the requirements must be approved—usually by the owner as well as the anticipated user (if other than the owner). It is a common practice to prepare a programmatic cost estimate that reflects the baseline; thus, a change in baseline necessitates an evaluation of the impact on cost prior to approval. Often, a significant cost impact will lead to disapproval of the change.

Engineering and design solutions to the baseline undergo a review procedure to assure that the performance and cost goals are satisfied. While the engineering and design activities are in process, a number of changes and review comments are incorporated as a result, without formal change actions, as long as the design and engineering documents are under development, and as long as the baseline is firm. Once the drawings and specifications are complete and approved, no changes can be made without formal process.

It is important at this point to identify what an "end item" is. An end item is generally that specification level in the hierarchy at which the procurement and cost can most effectively be controlled within a single specification. An example of a "spec tree" is shown as Figure 6.5.

The exception, predictably, is the facility. The government, using public appropriated funds, will not permit name brand facility items to be used in the construction documents. Under this restriction, the design and specification for construction is, in its total form, an end item. Name brands of components, subassemblies, assemblies, or materials are not identifiable until the construction contractor obtains them by purchases, and these purchases must be approved by the owner or the agency authorized by the owner. It follows that each set of construction documents is reflective of a "build-to" configuration.

PURPOSE:

To define the procedure and responsibilities for implementing the Cost/Schedule Management System (C/SMS).

GENERAL:

A. This procedure defines and specifies responsibilities, and procedures applicable to the implementation of the RMP STS GSS Cost/Schedule Management System (C/SMS).

B. Cost/Schedule Management System - Elements

The Elements of the C/SMS are as follows:

. Objective of C/SMS

. Project Organization

. System Integration

.. Work Authorization

.. Budget System

.. Scheduling

. Accounting

. Work Package Planning

. Earned Value Methodology

. Variance Analysis

. EAC/ETC Procedures

. Baseline Maintenance/Change Incorporation

. Management Reserve and Undistributed Budget Use and Control

. Reporting

. Training Program

. Objective of C/SMS

To achieve an integrated planning and control system fulfilling RMPs cost and schedule management system requirements and to be compliant with MMCs cost/schedule control systems.

Program Organization

1. The program organization is task oriented with Task Managers permanently assigned to program. (Attachment A)

SYS 24

Figure 6.4 Cost/schedule management system and administration.

TITLE/SUBJECT: Cost/Schedule Management System and Administration

2. Key technical personnel (lead engineers) permanently assigned to program and function in engineering capacities on one or more CWBS Elements as required by Task Managers. (Attachment B)

3. The Task Managers function in the technical as well as the budget and scheduling responsibility directly related to the CWBS Elements.

4. Station Set Managers are also Task Managers and function in the technical as well as budget and scheduling responsibility related to individual Station Sets. Ultimate responsibility for the Station Set development rests with the Deputy Program Manager.

5. Technical personnel, (disciplines, e.g. civil, electrical, geophysical) upon request of Task Managers, are temporarily assigned from World Headquarters' technical divisions as necessary to meet requirements.

6. Upon the direction of the Task Managers temporary technical personnel are returned to their respective technical divisions for reassignment to other programs.

. System Integration

Work Authorization

Budgets

Scheduling

. Planning, scheduling budgeting, work authorization and cost accumulation will be integrated to the level which budgets are issued and responsibility is assigned to Task Managers. Basically, the SOW, correlated with the CWBS is broken down to functional groups. These groups then become the basic organization as well as the major work package.

. The Cost/Schedule Performance Management (C/SPM) is responsible to assure that integration occurs and is consistent with the program plan. (Attachment D)

. Work Authorization

. RMP Job Masters are the instruments that authorizes the start of contractual work.

. Job Masters - (Attachment E & F)

1. Identify specific CWBS Elements and SOW Tasks.

2. Establish subjob (account) numbers.

3. Contain brief description of specific task.

4. Provide for estimated budgets.

5. Coded to accept labor charges from approved departments.

SYS-24A

Figure 6.4 *(Continued)*

. Budget System

Program Manager and C/SPM are responsible for issuing the budgets by manhours. (Attachment G)

   . Manhour budget allocations and ODC's where appropriate, will not exceed the negotiated value of the contract including Target Fee which is the contract budget base.

   . Management reserve will be subtracted as determined by the Program Manager.

   . Undistributed budget will be identified separately.

   . The performance measurement baseline is the sum of the allocated budget plus the undistributed budget.

   . Original allocated budgets for each SOW Task were established from RMP Proposal R-3 (Modified) and manhour budgets were distributed to Task Managers by use of Project Memorandum. (Attachment G)

   . Baseline budget adjustments will be covered by issuing Budget Change Authorization (BCA) and RMP Change Order issued to Task Managers. (Attachments H & I)

   . Interoffice Correspondence is used to authorize labor charges and other direct cost items to a specific CWBS Element without budget changes. (Attachment J)

BASELINE BUDGET CONTROL SUMMARY (See Attachment K & K-2 for Data Flow)

   System provides for:

   . Current status and updated record of total budget transaction.

   . A top program master budget control log.

   . Four sub-tier budget control logs. (Attachments L, M, N N-2 & N-3)

      1. Management Reserve

      2. Undistributed Budget

      3. Allocated Budget

      4. Individual CWBS Budgets

   . Project Memorandum/Budget Change Authorization/RMP Change Order

      1. These are issued to Task Managers and used for input to the Manpower Forecast System.

   . Each budget transaction will carry the same program identifier throughout the system.

SYS 24A

Figure 6.4 (*Continued*)

TITLE/SUBJECT: Cost/Schedule Management System and Administration

- The total sum of Program Memorandum and all Budget Change Authorizations (BCAs) against a transaction must equal the total costs on the Allocated Budget Control Log.

- Once allocations are established, C/SPM will be responsible for maintaining the baseline.

SCHEDULING

- Program tasks are derived from the CWBS and broken down into manageable elements. This is accomplished by the integration of program scheduling to the Contract Work Breakdown Structure (CWBS).

- Work Package Plans and Planning Packages are initiated for discrete efforts consistent with detailed schedules of the CWBS Element. (Attachment O)

SCHEDULE HIERARCHY

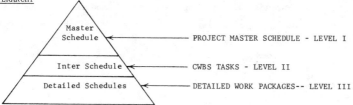

- Cost/Schedule Performance Management will assure the schedule hierarchy provides traceability from the highest level down to the lowest detail schedule for work package planning.

- Work package planning - Detailed schedules for discrete work packages will be prepared by the Task Managers and monitored by C/SPM.

- Detail work package scheduled milestone will be tracked using the Schedule Status Report (SSR).

- C/SPM will issue weekly schedule status reports to Task Managers to assess schedule performance, and recommend and initiate corrective actions.

- Weekly program meetings will then address the total project performance.

ACCOUNTING

- Parsons' World Headquarters accounting system is the single system used to provide actual cost data for all contracts.

- All program accounting and cost accumulations utilizes a standard account number system integrated to the CWBS Element.

SYS-24A

Figure 6.4 (*Continued*)

153

TITLE/SUBJECT: Cost/Schedule Management System and Administration

. Time card labor charges are reviewed and approved weekly by Task Managers prior to submittal to accounting. (Attachment P)

. Manual log of approved time charges segregated by CWBS Element maintained and updated weekly.

. Weekly labor manhours displayed in Program Control Display. (Attachment Q, R & S)

. Purchase orders for authorized subcontract work are identified to the appropriate subjob (account) number.

. Subjob (account) numbers will be opened and/or closed by C/SPM as tasks are added or completed. (Attachments T, U & V)

PROCUREMENT PROCESS

1. Requirement for material/supplies/services identified.

2. Request screened for possible available material/supply stock and actual necessity.

3. Process purchase requisition for proper approvals, charge number and budget considerations.

4. Purchasing (buyer) places order with vendor (send copy of purchase order to C/SPM).

5. Receive order for material/supplies, inspect and sign-off shipper (send signed-off shipper copy to Purchasing).

6. Committment of costs incurred during accounting period is posted on Project Control Display.

7. Booked costs occur when invoice received from vendor and payment made. Booked costs are posted on Project Control Display and committed costs reduced by booked amount.

WORK PACKAGE PLANNING

1. Work Package Preparation

a. The Task Manager has received an approved budget for each CWBS Element classified as either Discrete or Level of Effort (LOE).

b. A Discrete effort (which identifies a CWBS Element), further subdivides the work associated with the Element into several sequences of work with significant task milestones as technical performance goals, or other indicators that can be used to measure performance. As an example; CWBS 5164BA, SOW Task 3.6.3 would be divided into Station Sets as work package plans with milestones such as:

WP #1 FDS V86 Utilities

SYS-24A

Figure 6.4 *(Continued)*

TITLE/SUBJECT: Cost/Schedule Management System and Administration

Start	FDS Draft	Print Draft	Deliver Draft SDRL	Incorporate Review Comments	Print Final	Deliver Final SDRL

At the outset the following discrete CWBS Elements are broken down into Work Package Planning efforts:

5161AB	SOW Task	3.4.3
5161CG	SOW Task	3.6.1
5161D	SOW Task	3.4.1
5161FB	SOW Task	3.6.1
5161E	SOW Task	JB6 (Unidentified Trade Studies)
5164BA	SOW Task	3.6.3
5164BB	SOW Task	3.6.2
5164E	SOW Task	3.6.4

Others will be identified from time to time as a result of Client direction.

c. A Level of Effort (LOE) activity, (a continuing repetitive effort that cannot be subdivided into significant milestones), will be prepared as work packages, like discrete efforts. As an example: 516F, SOW Task 5.4 is comprised of secretarial, purchasing, accounting, etc., a continuing support effort with no meaningful milestones. Therefore, as budgeted, it can be spread over the life of contract.

d. The LOE/Work Package Planning Sheet (Attachment Y) will be used for detail planning of the discrete CWBS efforts and for time phasing of all budgets.
(1) The total contractual hour budget for each CWBS Element will be planned by RMP accounting periods. For most tasks this has already been done, the present spread must remain unchanged.
(2) For the tasks identified as discrete (paragraph 1b. above), Work packages will be established below the Intermediate CWBS Element Schedules level (see below) with specific start and end dates compatible with the schedule hierarchy shown. Completion dates, and interim milestones within each Work Package one interim milestone per accounting period are desirable and one at least every three accounting periods is mandatory. This is necessary to provide for measurement of earned value.

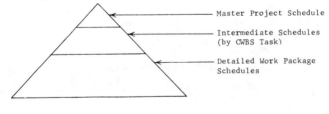

Master Project Schedule

Intermediate Schedules (by CWBS Task)

Detailed Work Package Schedules

SYS-24A

Figure 6.4 (*Continued*)

TITLE/SUBJECT:
Cost/Schedule Management System and Administration

(3) The total budget for each CWBS Element has been established, therefore a Planning Package consisting of that portion of the remaining CWBS budget which cannot be planned and budgeted to specific work Package(s) at this time will be identified and spread. The total for the planning package will still be in accordance with the original spread, minus the Work Package(s) that have been identified.

(4) Each Work Package milestone must be assigned percentages that relate to the degree of accomplishment of the total individual Work Package. Total credit of total milestone accomplished on a Work Package must equal 100% of the Budgeted Cost of Work Scheduled (BCWS) assigned to that Work Package.

(5) Detailed schedules of Work Packages and Planning Packages within individual CWBS Elements must show continuity to the CWBS Intermediate Schedule and must be worked closely with the Master Project Schedule, that has been adjusted for RMP submittals to the Client.

(6) Work Packages should be planned to range up to three RMP accounting periods, but not longer than six accounting periods.

(7) Changes will not be made to Work Packages scheduled to open within two accounting periods because of a two accounting period frozen baseline nor will changes be to opened or completed Work Packages.

(8) As previously described, level of effort activity, having no specific start and completion dates, are already time phased on the work sheets. No further breakdown is required.

e.   After the LOE/Work Planning Sheets are completed by the applicable Task Manager, the work sheets are sent to Administration Manager for input to the Cost-Schedule Management System. It is each Task Managers' responsibility to maintain traceability of work package credit below the Intermediate Schedule level. It is also his responsibility to notify the Administrative Manager of work package, scope and description. He will utilize the LOE/Work Planning Sheets to accomplish this.

2.   Detailed Instructions

Preparation and maintenance of the LOE/Work Package instruction for the Planning Sheet (Attachment Y) is referenced by bubble number.

1.   Program/Contract - Identify program name as DOD/STS/GSS and contract number as RMP

2.   Department - Identify RMP Subjob Number

3.   Element - Identify element of work and units of measure (i.e., labor-hours)

4.   CWBS/SOW -Identify the CWBS Element and SOW Task(s) to which the subjob number directly summarizes.

5.   LOE/Discrete - Indicate whether task is Level of Effort (LOE) or Discrete. If discrete add "Milestone/Estimate."

SYS-24A

Figure 6.4 (*Continued*)

6. Revision/Date - Identify latest revision number (if initial sheet identified as "Basic") and the date prepared or revised.

7. Title - Identify by brief description of work being performed.

8. Intermediate Schedule - Work area provided to show significant intervals of work and milestones, including start and completion date applicable to the CWBS Element at the Intermediate Schedule level. Each milestone must be identified.

9. Time Phasing (Basic-BCN Number) - Insert the original budget and any revisions to the budget. The labor hour budget has been spread in accordance with period of performance identified in the Intermediate Schedule, and loaded in accordance with the requirements as reflected in summary of Work Package identified in 11.

10. Project Total - Show total hour budget for CWBS Element

11. Work Package Planning - List and number each Work Package with a brief titled description of the task, a time phrased spread of budget requirements, milestones and interim dates of significant points of accomplishments where applicable. Milestones shown against each Work Package must be supportive of the values at the Intermediate Schedule level shown in 8. (Blank LOE/Work Package Planning Sheets are available from the Administration Manager.) Work Packages must:

   (1) Have discrete start and stop points indicated by a and connected by a solid line.

   (2) Be of short duration. Strive to plan the range for up to three (3) accounting periods, but not longer than (6) accounting periods.

   (3) Provide approximately one milestone per accounting period (a tangible output) but not less than one each three accounting periods.

   (4) Each milestone will be assigned a percentage figure that relates to the degree of accomplishment of the total work package through that point of the detailed schedule.

   (5) Show the names of persons to work the package and an hour spread for each by accounting period.

12. Total - Show total for each Work Package budget. The sum of all Work Packages and Planning Packages must equal the total budget shown in 10.

13. Totals - A summary of all Work Packages and Planning Package values will be shown. These totals will reflect the Budgeted Cost of Work Scheduled (BCWS for the total CWBS Element; same as totals shown in 9.

14. BCWP CUM% - Budget Cost of Work Performed (BCWP) can be calculated for each Work Package by period on this sheet. the BCWP measurement in hours should be annotated directly below the BCWS number for each work package for the period. All calculations will be summarized and noted as BCWP CUM percentage for the reporting accounting period by the Task Manager.

SYS-24A

Figure 6.4 *(Continued)*

157

TITLE/SUBJECT: Cost/Schedule Management and Administration

Earned value (BCWP) will be determined on the basis of completed milestones plus an estimated credit for incomplete milestones at the end of
each accounting period. The estimated credit of incomplete milestones
cannot exceed 85% of the milestone value until the milestone is actually
completed.

15. Prepared By - Once the total plan has been completed in accordance with
this procedure, it will represent the Performance Measurement Baseline
(PMB) for that CWBS Element. The Task Manager will sign the sheet.

16. Approval - The Task Manager of the CWBS Element into which this plan
summarizes will approve the plan if prepared by anyone, other than
himself.

EARNED VALUE METHODOLOGY

. Milestone/Estimate

1. Earned value may be taken for started but incomplete milestones at
end of each accounting month.

2. Earned value amount will be based on Task Manager's estimate of completion status of the milestone.

3. Earned value will never exceed 85% of the milestone value until the
milestone is completed.

. Level of Effort (LOE) - Effort which has no tangible outputs or discrete
milestones. BCWP is equal to BCWS schedules on LOE tasks.

VARIANCE ANALYSIS PROCEDURES

. Contract requirement for analysis in cost performance report.

1. 1st Quarter of Contract - = 10% and $5000 for reporting level CWBS
elements.

2. Remainder of Contract - = 5% and $5000 for reporting level CWBS elements.

. The reporting system will flag monthly those variances at the cost accounts
and summary levels which exceed the established tolerance limits.

. Task Manager completes the analysis on the RMP Variance Analysis Report
indicating:

1. Problem

2. Cause

3. Corrective Action Recommendations

4. At Completion Variance

. Task Manager signs report and forwards to C/SPM Manager.

SYS-24A

Figure 6.4 *(Continued)*

TITLE/SUBJECT   Cost/Schedule Management and Administration

. Cost/Schedule Performance Management

1. Summarize analyses for input into MMC cost performance reports.

2. Major variance items are added to the weekly Schedule Status Report.

    a. Provides basis for Program Managers weekly staff meetings and internal system for priority problems and proposed solutions as well as MMCs Open Item Status Reports.

    b. Remain on Schedule Status Reports as long as variance exists.

    c. Status is reported by Program Manager at Monthly Progress Meetings.

ESTIMATE AT COMPLETION/ESTIMATE TO COMPLETE (EAC/ETC) PROCEDURES

. EAC/ETC is updated at least quarterly or will be updated whenever a major problem or program perturbation occurs.

. ETCs will be "grass roots" estimates accomplished by each Task Manager for CWBS element.

1. Will assess performance to date (BCWP vs ACWP).

2. Based upon above, will scope remaining work to be accomplished and develop ETC for the CWBS element.

3. ACWP to date is added to the ETC to arrive at the EAC for each CWBS element.

. EAC is updated on all customer reports to MMC.

BASELINE MAINTENANCE/CHANGE INCORPORATION

. Baseline changes occur in two methods:

1. Internal changes in scope of work approved.

2. Receipt of authorized contract change from MMC via formal contract change request.

INTERNAL CHANGES IN SCOPE OF WORK

. No changes will be made to completed work packages or to open work packages.

. No changes will be made to work packages schedules to open within the next two accounting periods (frozen baseline).

. The frozen baseline will be extended each accounting period.

. Work packages outside of the two accounting periods frozen baseline may be replanned.

1. Effort and budget may be transferred between work packages/planning packages within a CWBS element.

SYS 24A

Figure 6.4 (*Continued*)

2. New work packages or planning of packages for internal increases in scope may be created and budgeted out of management reserve if approved by the Program Manager.

RECEIPT OF AUTHORIZED CONTRACT CHANGE FROM CUSTOMER

. All changes are authorized and budgeted via Program Memorandum/Budget Charge Authorizations and RMP Change Order previously described.

. For authorized/undefinitized changes:

1. Interim budgets issued to get work started.

2. Balance of funds placed in undistributed budget.

3. After negotiation:

    (a) Program Manager establishes management reserve.

    (b) Program Manager and C/SPM issues budgets to Task Managers.

4. Audit trail established.

5. CWBS, LOE/WP planning sheets either adjusted or new prepared.

MANAGEMENT RESERVE

. May be used for the following contingencies:

1. In-scope changes - adding or deleting scope in future time periods.

2. Economic escalation adjustments - unusual escalation projected only.

. Any budgeting from management reserve will be handled as follows:

1. Requires Program Manager's approval - he authorizes issuance of BCA for the specified amount.

2. BCA/RMP Change Order is issued to affected CWBS elements.

3. Allocated budget log is adjusted, increasing Performance Measurement Baseline (PMB).

4. Management reserve log is adjusted, decreasing management reserve amount.

5. CWBS, LOE/WP planning sheets are adjusted accordingly.

. MMC is notified via next Cost Performance Report (CPR).

SYS-24A

Figure 6.4 (*Continued*)

TITLE/SUBJECT: Cost/Schedule Management System and Administration

UNDISTRIBUTED BUDGET

. Occurs as a Contract Change where added effort may not be definitized.

. Budgets are separately identified in the Undistributed Budget Log.

. Budgets are reduced from Undistributed Budget Account by Program Memorandum/ BCA/RMP Change Order.

. Undistributed Budget, allocated budget and CWBS Budget logs are adjusted accordingly.

REPORTS - INTERNAL

. Time Cards

1. Subjob numbers are coded to identify and accumulate cost to CWBS elements. (Attachment P)

2. Time charges are verified and approved by Task Managers.

3. Manhours are posted in Manual Log to subjob (CWBS) element.

4. Manhours are posted on Project Control Display.

. Weekly Job Labor Reports (WJLR) - (Attachment W)

1. Computerized print-out of labor hours charged to each subjob (CWBS element).

2. Time charges are verified by Task Managers, reviewed by Program Manager and C/SPM.

3. Manhours are checked against Manual Log and adjustments, if any, are made.

4. Manhour adjustments are made on Program Control Display.

. Engineering Budget Cost Report (EBCR) - (Attachment X)

1. Bi-weekly computer print-out is available in Program Control Room.

2. The EBCR identifies current and cumulative hour expenditures, direct labor costs, and other direct costs on total project and each subjob (CWBS) element.

3. Establishes estimated bi-weekly and cumulative costs and average salary cost for period and project.

4. The EBCR is cross checked against the WJLRs.

SYS-24A

Figure 6.4 *(Continued)*

THE RALPH M. PARSONS COMPANY

TITLE/SUBJECT: Cost/Schedule Management System and Administration

.   Supplementary Payroll - (Attachment S)

1.   Establishes total actual billable labor hours and direct labor cost by subjob (CWBS) element.

2.   Functions as input of actual cost for SDRL PO24 (RMP Cost Progress Report).

.   Program Control Display

1.   In addition to the actual booked costs, committed costs for the period are added to provide overview of CWBS committed costs on a cumulative basis.

REPORTS - EXTERNAL

.   SDRL No. PO02/065

1.   Monthly Cost Schedule Summary - (Attachment Z)

2.   Billing Summary - (Attachment Z)

3.   Financial Status Summary - (Attachment AA)

4.   Actual Cost and Estimate to Complete - (Attachment BB)

5.   Project Manpower Utilization - (Attachment CC)

.   SDRL No. PO24

1.   Cost Performance Report - Work Breakdown Structure - (Attachment DD-1)

2.   Cost Performance Report - Functional Categories - (Attachment DD-2)

3.   Cost Performance Report Baseline - Attachment DD-3)

4.   Cost Performance Report - Manpower Loading - (Attachment DD-4)

5.   Cost Performance Report - Problem Analysis - (Attachment DD-5)

.   SDRL No. PO26

1.   Estimated Final Cost Report - (Attachment EE)

2.   Liability Plan - (Attachment FF)

TRAINING PROGRAM

Objective

.   To develop a level of understanding among all users of the C/SMS which will enhance its use as a viable management tool.

SYS-24A

Figure 6.4 *(Continued)*

162

. To maintain utility of system through periodic updates and insuring new personnel are properly trained.

Implementation

. Briefings to program management personnel.

. Conduct group briefings for task managers.

. Hold subsequent individual sessions with task managers to insure complete understanding.

. Conduct periodic retraining when required, and for new personnel.

SYS-24A

Figure 6.4 *(Continued)*

TITLE/SUBJECT:

CWBS ELEMENT	CWBS TITLE	TASK MANAGER
5161AA	System Engineering Management	Melton
5161AB	Environmental Impact Considerations	Fabrick
5161B	Level II Requirements Analysis	Melton
5161CA	Station Set Requirements	Melton
5161CB	Functional Analysis Data	Melton
5161CE	Interface Requirements	Melton
5161CG	Facility Requirements	Mitchell
5161D	System Analysis and Trade Offs	Fabrick
5161E	Trade Studies	Fabrick
5161FA	Integrated Program Acquisition	Harris
5161FB	Facility Acquisition Planning	Harris
5161G	Integrated Systems Activation	Harris
5161H	Verification Requirements Analysis and Planning	Melton
5161J	Project Interface	Brehany
5162A	Cost/Schedule/Performance Management	Thrasher
5162D	Meetings and Reviews	Thrasher
5162F	General Support Services	Thrasher
5163A	Integrated Logistics Support	Melton
5163B	Logistics Support Cost Analysis and Life Cycle Cost	Melton
5163C	Logistics Support Analysis and Optimum Repair Level Analysis	Melton
5164A	Station-Set Specification	Melton
5164BA	Facility Development Specification	Mitchell
5164BB	Geophysical Site Investigation	Mitchell
5164CA	Mechanical Unique Equipment Specifications	Melton
5164CB	Electrical Unique Equipment Specifications	Melton
5164D	Level III Interface Control Drawings	Melton
5164E	Facility Design Surveillance	Mitchell
5170	Data Attachment A	Woods

SYS-24A

Figure 6.4 (*Continued*)

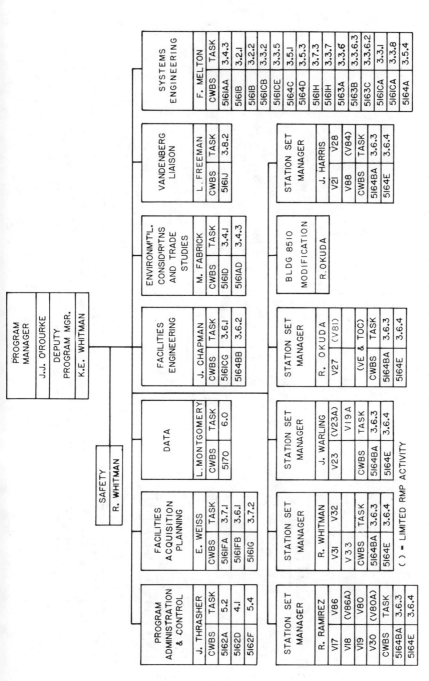

Figure 6.4 (*Continued*)

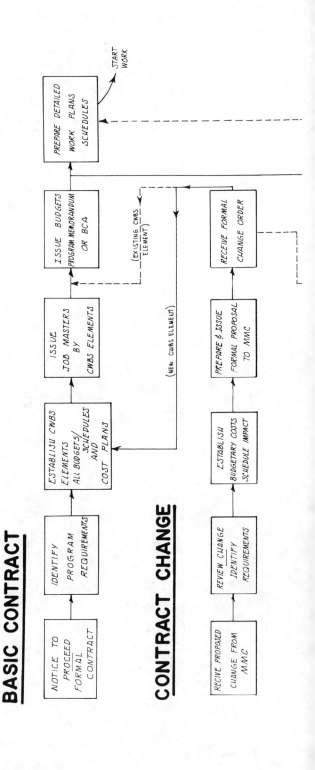

BASIC CONTRACT

| NOTICE TO PROCEED FORMAL CONTRACT | → | IDENTIFY PROGRAM REQUIREMENTS | → | ESTABLISH CWBS ELEMENTS ALL BUDGETS/ SCHEDULES AND COST PLANS | → | ISSUE JOB MASTERS BY CWBS ELEMENTS | → | ISSUE BUDGETS PROGRAM MEMORANDUM OR BCA | → | PREPARE DETAILED WORK PLANS SCHEDULES |

START WORK

(EXISTING CWBS ELEMENT)

(NEW CWBS ELEMENT)

CONTRACT CHANGE

| RECIVE PROPOSED CHANGE FROM MMC | → | REVIEW CHANGE IDENTIFY REQUIREMENTS | → | ESTABLISH BUDGETARY COSTS SCHEDULE IMPACT | → | PREPARE & ISSUE FORMAL PROPOSAL TO MMC | → | RECEIVE FORMAL CHANGE ORDER |

166

IN SCOPE CHANGE

OPERATIONAL PHASE

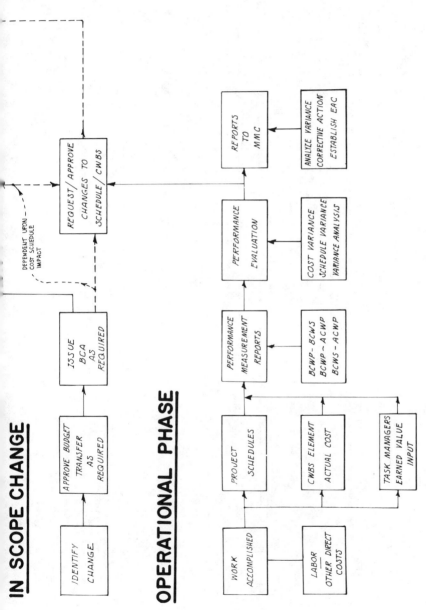

Figure 6.4 (Continued)

167

THE RALPH M. PARSONS COMPANY
JOB MASTER

CONTRACT TAKEN IN THE NAME OF:

MO DAY YR   JOB NUMBER   CLASS   SCHEDULE J

DIV. RESP

RENEGOTIABLE CODE LOCATION

OFFICE RESPONSIBLE

CONTRACT NUMBER   PRE—CONTRACT FILE NUMBER

CUSTOMER

PROJECT DESCRIPTION

PROJECT MANAGER

AUTHORIZATION

DATE WORK STARTED
MO DAY YR

ESTIMATED COMPLETION DATE
MO DAY YR

CONTRACT TYPE   GOV

JOB SITE

PROJECT SPONSOR

ALGERIA
MANILA
MID-EAST
MILITARY
NE CORRIDOR
NORTHEAST U.S.
PACIFIC
PASADENA
RDX-HMX
STS

CONTRACT ADMINISTRATOR

PROJECT MANAGER

W. P. JOHNSON, CONTRACTS MANAGER

REGIONAL MANAGER

PURCHASING (DEPT. 5) AUTHORIZED TO CHARGE: YES   NO

ESTIMATED VALUE (DOLLARS ONLY)

1. H. O. WAGES
2. WELFARE, PAYROLL
   TAXES AND
   INSURANCE _____ %
3. SUBTOTAL
4. OTHER DIRECT H. O. COSTS
5. H. O. OVERHEAD RATE _____ %
6. SUBTOTAL
7. FIELD COST OF PROJECT INCLUD-
   ING FIELD STAFF, LABOR,
   EQUIPMENT, MATERIALS AND
   SUBCONTRACTS
8. FIELD OVERHEAD
   RATE _____ %
9. SUBTOTAL
10. PROFIT
    TOTAL VALUE

TOTAL HOURS

Figure 6.4 (*Continued*)

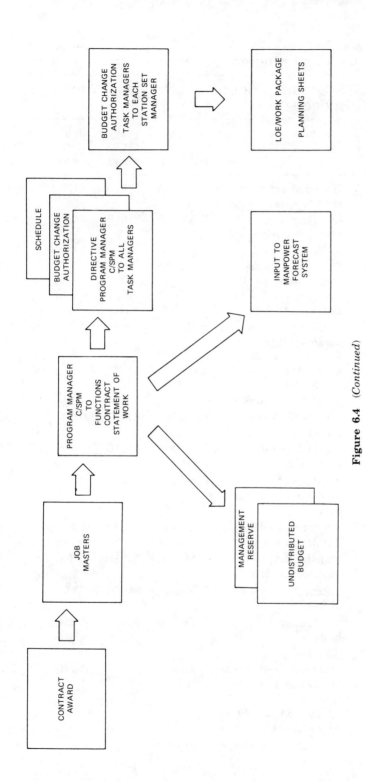

Figure 6.4 (*Continued*)

169

Program Memorandum

DOD/STS Ground Support Systems Job Number 5615 CWBS Budgets

Task		Manager	CWBS number	Job dash number	MH budget
3.2.1	Requirement assessment (Level II RA)	F. Melton	5161B	0102	859
3.2.2	Interface requirements analysis (Level II RA)	F. Melton	5161B	0102	1431
3.3.1	Requirements assessment (Level III RA) (Ground Operation Plan Update)	F. Melton	5161C	0103	416
3.3.1	Requirements assessment (Level III RA) (Station sets V-17, 18, 19, 19A, 21, 23, 23A, 28, 31, 32, 33, 80, 80A, 86 and 86A)	F. Melton		1601	1136
3.3.2	Functional analysis (Level III RA)	F. Melton	5161C	0103	859
3.3.4	Installation requirements (Level III RA)	F. Melton	5161C	0103	1719
3.3.5	Interface requirements analysis (Level III RA)	F. Melton	5161C	0103	1146
3.3.6	Integrated Logistic Support (Level III RA)	F. Melton	5163A	0301	1431
3.3.6.2	Logistic support analysis (Level III RA)	F. Melton	5163C	0303	2863
3.3.6.3	Life cycle cost (Level III RA)	F. Melton	5163B	0302	1431
3.3.7	Verification requirements analysis (Level III)	F. Melton	5161C	0103	3723
3.3.8	Station set requirements (Level III RA) (Station sets V-25, 27, 29, 30, 33A, 35, 70, 88, 95 and E&TOC)	F. Melton		1601	2426

Figure 6.4 *(Continued)*

Task		Manager	CWBS number	Job dash number	MH budget
3.4.1	Systems analysis and tradeoffs	M. Fabrick	5161E	0104	5801
	Trade studies		5161F		None
3.4.2	Systems engineering management	F. Melton	5161A	0101	10168
3.4.3	Environmental impact considerations	M. Fabrick	5161G	0105	9943
3.5.1	Support equipment prime item specification	F. Melton	5161H	0106	629
3.5.3	Interface control	F. Melton	5161J	0107	3315

BUDGET CHANGE AUTHORIZATION

To   :   BCA No.

From   :   Date

SUBJECT: Budget Change Authorization

Effect the following change to the subjob/CWBS Element noted:

	Subjob No.	CWBS No.	Hours	ODC	Start Date	Complete Date
Add						
Delete						

Revise affected Work Package Plan, if appropriate to incorporate the above change.

J. H. Thrasher
Administrative Manager

CC: J. J. O'Rourke
     K. E. Whitman
     J. H. Thrasher/BCN File

For C/SM Use

                                      Posted to Budget Control Logs
                                      Date _____
Transaction:

   From   :

   Title   :

   CWBS No.:

   To   :

   Title   :

   CWBS No.:

Figure 6.4   (*Continued*)

	THE RALPH M. PARSONS COMPANY		JOB NO.	
	ARCHITECT · ENGINEERING		CHANGE NO.	
	CHANGE ORDER		DATE CONCEIVED	
	ENGINEERING · DESIGN · DRAFTING CHANGES TO SCOPE OF WORK		REVISION NO.	
	CUSTOMER RESPONSIBILITY			

DESCRIPTION

AFFECTED	DEPARTMENT	MANHOURS	REMARKS & SPECIAL INSTRUCTIONS
	Project Manager and Project Engineer		
	Staff Engineers		
	Civil		
	Architectural		
	Structural		
	Piping		
	Heating and Ventilating		
	Mechanical Specialties		
	Electrical		
	Instrument		
	Nuclear		
	Scientific Study		
	Specifications		
	Special Drafting		
	Checking		
	Estimating		
	Technical Publications		
			NEW DRAWINGS REQUIRED
	TOTAL — ENG. & DRAFTING		
	Management and Administration		
	General Services Group		
	Clerical		APPROVAL
	Steno		
	Specification Typing		PROJECT MANAGER OR ENGINEER DATE
			DISTRIBUTION:
			Project Manager/Engineer Department Head. } As Required
			Production Administrator Job Engineers
			Contract Administrator Job Architect
	GRAND TOTAL		

RMP 224 (Rev. 1)

Figure 6.4 *(Continued)*

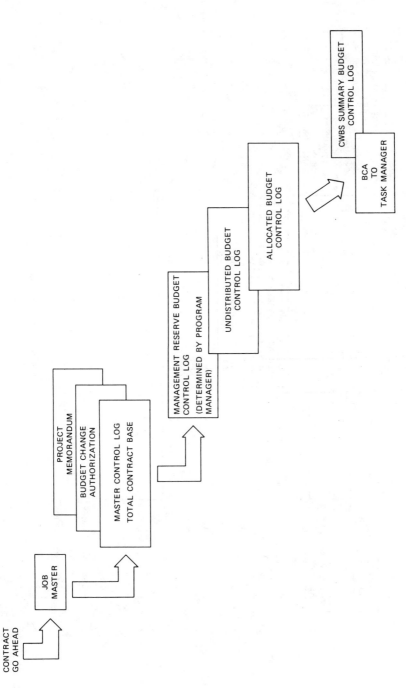

Figure 6.4 (*Continued*)

173

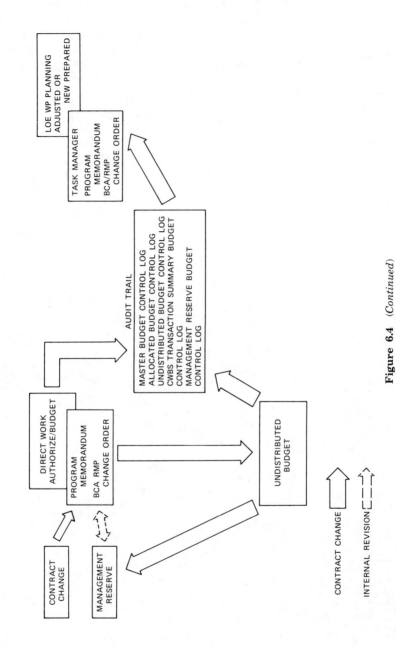

Figure 6.4 (*Continued*)

DESCRIPTION *TOTAL PROJECT*

CONTRACT NUMBER *VV6-940009*

MASTER CONTROL

TRANSACTION	DATE	IDENTIFICATION	HOURS	LABOR RATE APPLIED	LABOR DOLLARS	P. E.	O. H.	ODC'S	SUB-TOTAL DOLLARS	TARGET FEE	TOTAL DOLLARS
BASIC CONT.	23 JUL 76	DOO 573 G55	23+869	9.76	2,29,998	733,439	1,339,672	477,885	4,842,994	339,000	5,182,004

Figure 6.4 (Continued)

176

BUDGET CONTROL LOG

DESCRIPTION TOTAL PROJECT
CONTRACT NUMBER VVG-94009

MANAGEMENT RESERVE

TRANSACTION	DATE	IDENTIFICATION	HOURS	LABOR RATE APPLIED	LABOR DOLLARS	P. E.	O. H.	ODC'S	SUB-TOTAL DOLLARS	TARGET FEE	TOTAL DOLLARS
BASIC CONT.		FROM MASTER LOG	11,891	9.32	110,807	35,272	60,054	23,506	231,699	16,221	$247,920

Figure 6.4 (Continued)

BUDGET CONTROL LOG

ALLOCATED BUDGET

TRANSACTION	DATE	IDENTIFICATION	HOURS	LABOR RATE APPLIED	LABOR DOLLARS	P.E.	O.H.	ODC'S	SUB-TOTAL DOLLARS	TARGET FEE	TOTAL DOLLARS
BASIC CONT.	7.23.76	FROM: MASTER CONTROL	222,978	$9.78	2,181,131	698,167	1,277,618	454,379	4,611,295	322,789	$4,934,084

Figure 6.4 (Continued)

BUDGET CONTROL LOG

DESCRIPTION _TOTAL PROJECT_
CONTRACT NUMBER _VV6- 94009_

UNDISTRIBUTED BUDGET

TRANSACTION	DATE	IDENTIFICATION	HOURS	LABOR RATE APPLIED	LABOR DOLLARS	P. E.	O. H.	ODC'S	SUB-TOTAL DOLLARS	TARGET FEE	TOTAL DOLLARS

Figure 6.4 (*Continued*)

BUDGET CONTROL LOG

DESCRIPTION *SYSTEM ENGR. MGMT*

CONTRACT NUMBER *VVG-740009*

5161 AA 3.4.2 (INDIVIDUAL CWBS BUDGETS)

TRANSACTION	DATE	IDENTIFICATION	HOURS	LABOR RATE APPLIED	LABOR DOLLARS	P.E.	O.H.	ODC'S	SUB-TOTAL DOLLARS	TARGET FEE	TOTAL DOLLARS
BUDGET	11-11-76	FROM ALLOCATED BUDGET	10168	11.62	118140	37,805	70,175	0	226,120	15,828	$241,948

Figure 6.4 *(Continued)*

179

PROGRAM DOD/STS/GSS
CONTRACT RMP

JOB NO. 1800 HOURS
ELEMENT LABOR HOURS
CWBS/SOW TITLE: S/W DR/3.63
LOE ☐ DISCRETE ☒
REV. DATE 1-19-77

MITCHELL LOE/WORK PACKAGE PLANNING SHEET

	1976					1977												1978						TOTAL
	8	9	10	11	12	13	1	2	3	4	5	6	7	8	9	10	11	12	13	1	2	3	4	5	6	
SCHEDULE REV.																										
TIME PHASING:																										
BASIC–BCA NO.																										
WORK PACKAGE PLANNING:																										
WP / V-17 FDS Devel. to Final Sub	START	37%		81%		100% Final																			2035
WP / V-18 FDS Devel. to Final Sub	START	32%			89%		100% Final																			1000
WP / V-19			START #1			100% Status Review			100% #1				100% Internal Review												#1 500 #2 750
WP / V-19A				START #1					Status Review			100% #2				100% Internal Review										#1 365 #2 510
WP / V-21					START #1					100% Status Review			100% #2				100% Internal Review										#1 365 #2 510
WP / V-23			START #1								100% Prelim Submit			100% #2 Final Submit												#1 910 #2 896
WP / V-28					START #1										Prelim Submit											

180

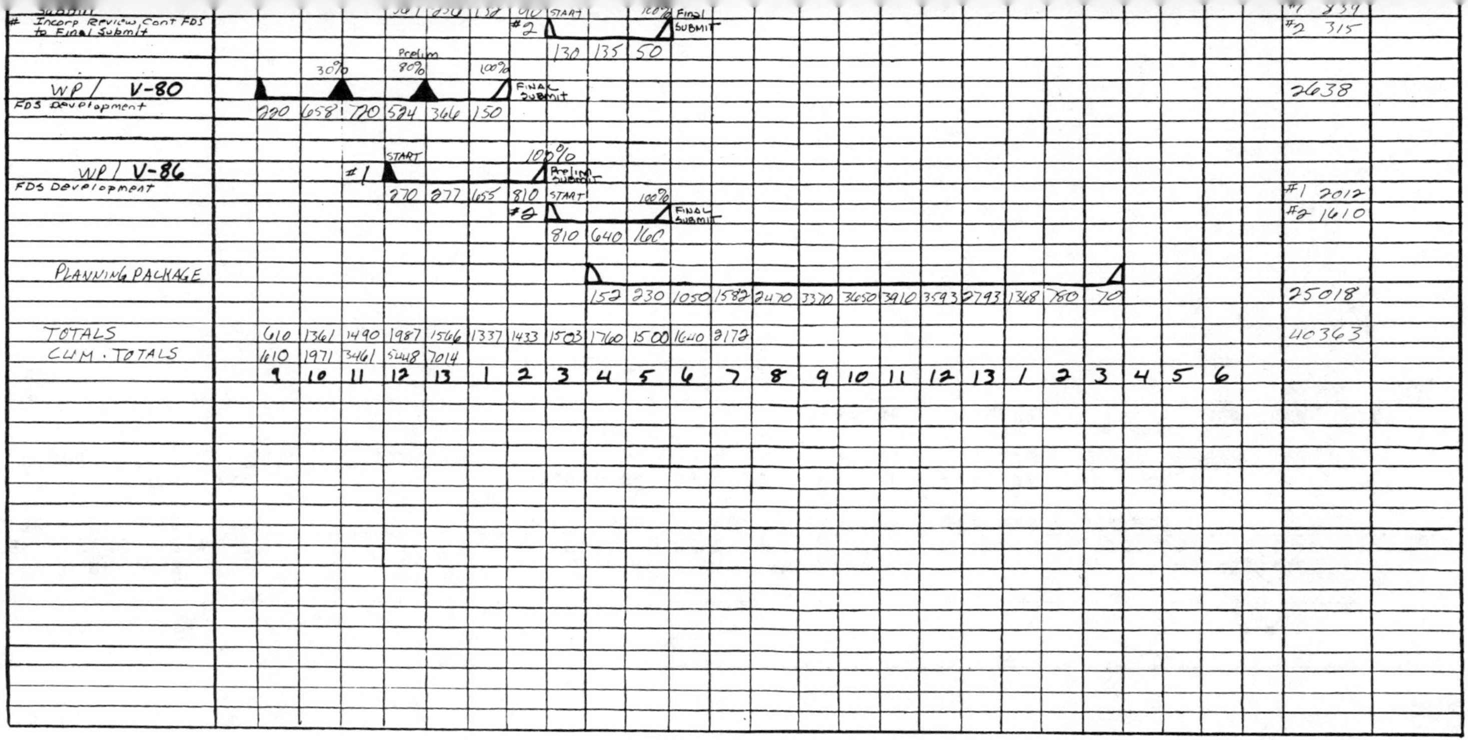

Figure 6.4 (Continued)

FABRICK

RALPH M PARSONS
WEEK ENDING 12 17 76

WEEKLY JOB LABOR REPORT
SYSTEMS DIVISION

PAGE NO. 1
R115B2.02

DATE	EMPLOYEE NAME		JOB	SUB	CC-NO.	TOT. HRS	ST. HRS	OT. HRS
12 17	J R EDWARDS		5615-0105	01	4320	40.00	40.00	
		PROCESS				40.00	40.00	
						40.00	40.00	JOB TOTAL

Figure 6.4 (*Continued*)

182

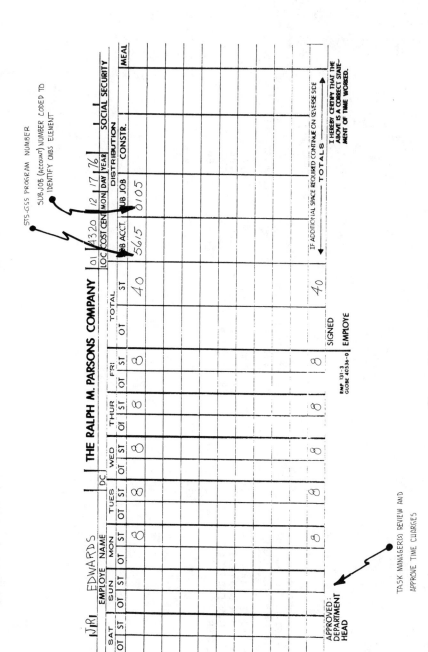

Figure 6.4 (*Continued*)

183

FABRICK

RALPH M PARSONS
WEEK ENDING 12 24 76
WEEKLY JOB LABOR REPORT
SYSTEMS DIVISION
R1158Z.02
PAGE NO. 1

DATE	EMPLOYEE NAME	JOB	SUB	CC-NO.	TOT. HRS	ST. HRS	OT. HRS
12 24	B I LORAN	5615-0105	01	4320	5.00	5.00	
12 24	J R EDWARDS	5615-0105	01	4320	29.00	29.00	
12 24	M N FABRICK	5615-0105	01	4320	40.00	40.00	
	PROCESS				74.00	74.00	
	PROCESS				74.00	74.00	JOB TOTAL

Figure 6.4 (Continued)

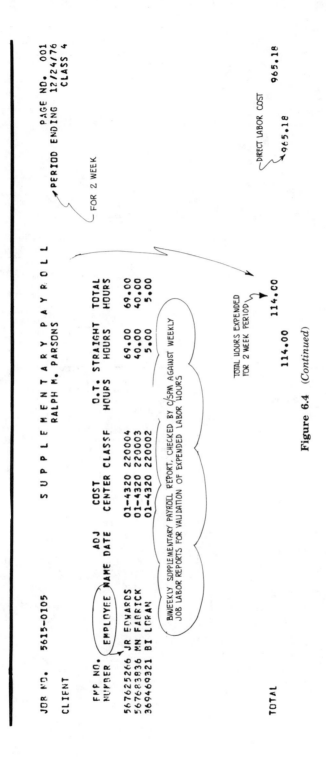

JOB NO. 5615-0105   S U P P L E M E N T A R Y   P A Y R O L L   PAGE NO. 001

CLIENT   RALPH M. PARSONS   PERIOD ENDING 12/24/76

                                                          CLASS 4

FOR 2 WEEK

EMP NO. NUMBER	EMPLOYEE NAME	ADJ DATE	COST CENTER	CLASSF	O.T. HOURS	STRAIGHT HOURS	TOTAL HOURS
567625266	JR EDWARDS		01-4320	220004		69.00	69.00
567683836	MN FABRICK		01-4320	220003		40.00	40.00
369469321	BI LORAN		01-4320	220002		5.00	5.00

BIWEEKLY SUPPLEMENTARY PAYROLL REPORT, CHECKED BY C/SPM AGAINST WEEKLY
JOB LABOR REPORTS FOR VALIDATION OF EXPENDED LABOR HOURS

                                         TOTAL HOURS EXPENDED
                                         FOR 2 WEEK PERIOD

                                         DIRECT LABOR COST

TOTAL   114.00   965.18

                                114.00   965.18

Figure 6.4 (*Continued*)

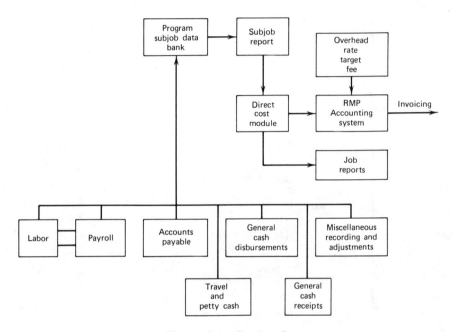

Figure 6.4 (*Continued*)

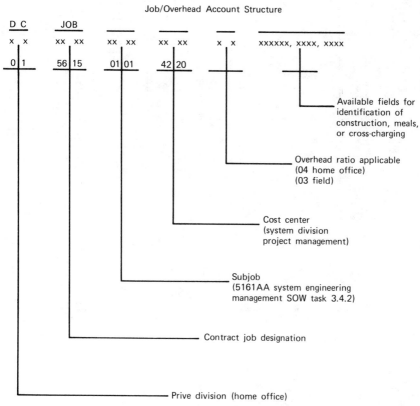

Job/Overhead Account Structure

Available fields for
identification of
construction, meals,
or cross-charging

Overhead ratio applicable
(04 home office)
(03 field)

Cost center
(system division
project management)

Subjob
(5161AA system engineering
management SOW task 3.4.2)

Contract job designation

Prive division (home office)

Figure 6.4 (*Continued*)

RMP CONTRACT WORK BREAKDOWN STRUCTURE

FIRST LEVEL	SECOND LEVEL	Code	THIRD LEVEL	Code
5161 SYSTEMS ENGINEERING MANAGEMENT	5161A SYSTEMS ENGINEERING MANAGEMENT		5161AA SYSTEMS ENGINEERING MGMT. 3.4.2	0101
			5151AB ENVIRONMENTAL IMPACT CONSIDERATIONS 3.4.3	0105
	5161B LEVEL II REQUIREMENTS ANALYSIS 3.2.1/3.2.3	0102		
	5161C LEVEL III REQUIREMENTS ANALYSIS		5161CA STATION SET REQUIREMENTS 3.3.1,3.3.8	0112
			5161CB FUNCTIONAL ANALYSIS DATA 3.3.2	0103
			5161CE INTERFACE REQUIREMENTS 3.3.5	0110
			5161CG FACILITY REQUIREMENTS 3.6.1	0108
	5161D SYSTEMS ANALYSIS AND TRADEOFFS 3.4.1	0104		
	5161E TRADE STUDIES			
	5161F ACQUISITION PLANNING/GFP BUDGET		5161FA INTEGRATED PROGRAM ACQUISITION 3.7.1	0114
			5161FB FACILITY ACQUISITION PLANNING 3.6.1	0115
	5161G INTEGRATED SYSTEMS ACTIVATION 3.7.2	0109		
	5161H VERIFICATION REQUIREMENTS ANALYSIS AND PLANNING 3.3.7/3.7.3	0111		
	5161J PROJECT INTERFACE 3.8.2	0113		

...SCHEDULE PERFORMANCE MGMT.
5.0

5162D MEETINGS AND REVIEWS 4.1 — 0202
5162F GENERAL SUPPORT SERVICES 5.4 — 0201

5163 INTEGRATED LOGISTICS AND SUPPORT MANAGEMENT

5163A INTEGRATED LOGISTICS SUPPORT 3.3.6 — 0301
5163B LOGISTICS SUPPORT COST ANALYSIS AND LIFE CYCLE COST 3.3.6.3 — 0302
5163C LOGISTICS SUPPORT ANALYSIS AND OPTIMUM REPAIR LEVEL ANALYSIS 3.3.6.2 — 0303

5164 STATION SET ENGINEERING

5164A STATION SET SPECIFICATIONS 3.5.4 — 1701
5164B FACILITY DESIGN CRITERIA AND GEOPHYSICAL INVESTIGATIONS
5164BA FACILITY DEVELOPMENT SPECIFICATIONS 3.6.3 — 1800
5164BB GEOPHYSICAL SITE INVESTIGATIONS 3.6.2 — 1901
5164C UNIQUE EQUIPMENT SPECIFICATIONS
5164CA MECHANICAL UNIQUE EQUIPMENT SPECS. 3.5.1 — 2001
5164CB ELECTRICAL UNIQUE EQUIPMENT SPECS. 3.5.1 — 2201
5164D LEVEL II INTERFACE CONTROL DWGS. 3.5.3 — 2101
5164E FACILITY DESIGN SURVEILLANCE 3.6.4 — 2300

5170 DATA (SDRL) — 0401
6.0

Figure 6.4 (Continued)

JOB NUMBER   5615-0401
CLIENT   ENGINEERING BUDGET AND COST REPORT - DETAIL
JOB DESCRIPTION
LOCATION

PAGE   98
REPORT NUMBER R2524A3.01
REPORT DATE   11 25 77
EFFECTIVE DATE   11 18 77

COST CENTER ACCT NUMBER	CURR. BUDGET HOURS	COST	TOTAL FORECAST HOURS	COST	JOB TO DATE HOURS	COST	CURRENT PERIOD HOURS	COST
01-7220 CIVIL/STRUCTURAL					58	435		
01-7310 INDUSTRIAL					2.444	20.426	82	840
01-7320 MECHANICAL					2	30		
** TOTAL DESIGN ENGINEERING					2.504	20.891	82	840
01-4220 PROJECT MANAGEMENT					502	6.855		
01-4300 PLANNING/PRECONTRACT					129	1.260	4	39
01-7130 PRODUCTION ADMINISTRATIO					20	72		
** TOTAL PROJECT STAFF					651	8.187	4	39
*** TOTAL PROJECT/DESIGN ENG					3.155	29.078	86	879
01-7180 STENO/CLERICAL					3.601	13.971	184	719
** TOTAL PROJECT STENO.					3.601	13.971	184	719
**** TOTAL DES/ADMIN/STENO					6.756	43.049	270	1.598
01-9000 OTHER SERVICES					190	1.058		
**** TOTAL OTHER DEPT					190	1.058		
***** TOTAL SALARY					6.946	44.107	270	1.598
***** FRINGE BENEFITS						13.813		
****** TOTAL PAYROLL COSTS					6.946	57.920	270	1.598
420 PROFESSIONAL SERVICES						9.554		
429 REPRODUCTIONS						9.805		
430 STATIONERY + OFFICE SUPP						369		369
433 FRT. EXP. CART + POST						133		
****** TOTAL OTHER COSTS						19.861		369
****** TOTAL HOME OFFICE DIRECT					6.946	77.781	270	1.967

JOB NUMBER   5615-0401
CLIENT   ENGINEERING BUDGET AND COST REPORT - DETAIL
JOB DESCRIPTION
LOCATION

PAGE   98
REPORT NUMBER R2524A3.01
REPORT DATE   11 25 77
EFFECTIVE DATE   11 18 77

Figure 6.4 (*Continued*)

MONTHLY COST SCHEDULE SUMMARY

ACTUAL COST 9/10 THRU 10/7	BUDGET FOR CURRENT PERIOD	ACTUAL CUMULATIVE COST TO DATE	COMULATIVE BUDGET COST TO DATE	VARIANCE
$ 305,219	$ 302,075	$ 3,499,433	$ 3512,939	− $ 13,506

TOTAL ALLOCATED BUDGET	ESTIMATED AT COMPLETION	MGMT. RES.	TOTAL CONTRACT
$ 4,918,173	$5,256,690	$ 116,805	**$5,373,495

INVOICES 5615-1 THRU 14	FOR PERIODS 7/23/76 THRU 10/7/77	AMOUNT BILLED $ 3,499,433	AMOUNT PAID $ 3,194,214

* INCLUDES ADJUSTMENTS DUE TO CHANGED PAYROLL AND OVERHEAD RATES AND THROUGH CONTRACT AMENDMENT NO. 12. DOES NOT INCLUDE CHANGE ORDERS NO. 3,4 AND 5

** INCLUDES CONTRACT AMOUNT NOTED IN AMENDMENT NO. 12 PLUS AWARD FEES I AND 2

Figure 6.4 (*Continued*)

FINANCIAL STATUS SUMMARY

23 JULY 1977 THRU 7 OCTOBER 1977	$ 161,134	$ 1,592,945	$ 277,841
ESTIMATE			
8 OCTOBER THRU 4 NOVEMBER	13,314	13 1,675 *$ 155,081	
TOTALS	$ 174,448	$ 1,724,620	$ 432,922
PAYROLL EXPENSES (33.76%)		582,232	
OVERHEAD (51.08 % PROJ. AVERAGE)		880,936	
SUBTOTAL		$ 3,187,788	
OTHER DIRECT COSTS		432,922	
SUBTOTAL		$ 3,6 20,710	
TARGET FEE (7 %)		253,450	
TOTAL		$ 3, 874, 1 60	

* INCLUDES 138K GEOTECH SUBCONTRACT AND OTHER COMMITMENTS

Figure 6.4 (*Continued*)

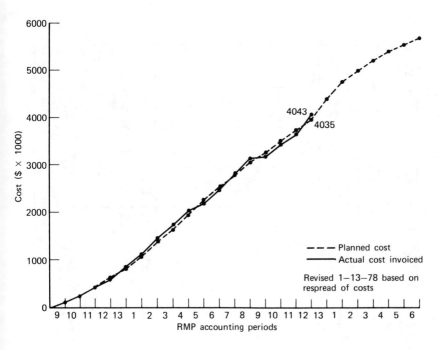

PROJECT MANPOWER UTILIZATION
PLANNED VERSUS ACTUAL

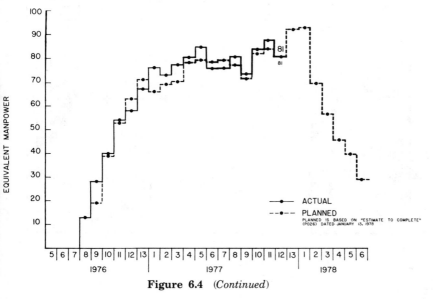

Figure 6.4 (*Continued*)

COST PERFORMANCE REPORT— WORK BREAKDOWN STRUCTURE

CONTRACTOR: THE RALPH M. PARSONS CO.
LOCATION 100 W. WALNUT STREET
PASADENA, CA 91124
RDT & E ☐   PRODUCTION ☒

CONTRACT TYPE/NO.:
CPIF VV6-940009

PROGRAM NAME/NUMBER
DOD/STS/GSS F04701-T6-C-0081

REPORT PERIOD:

QUANTITY	NEGOTIATED COST	EST COST AUTH. UNPRICED WORK	TGT PROFIT/FEE	TGT PRICE	EST PRICE	SHARE RATIO 80/20	CONTRACT CEILING	EST CEILING

ITEM	CURRENT PERIOD					CUMULATIVE TO DATE					AT COMPLETION		
	BUDGETED COST		ACTUAL COSTWORK PERFORMED	VARIANCE		BUDGETED COST		ACTUAL COSTWORK PERFORMED	VARIANCE		BUDGETED	LATEST REVISED ESTIMATED	VARIANCE
	WORK SCHEDULED	WORK PERFORMED		SCHEDULE	COST	WORK SCHEDULED	WORK PERFORMED		SCHEDULE	COST			
WORK BREAKDOWN STRUCTURE													
UNDISTRIBUTED BUDGET													
SUBTOTAL													
MANAGEMENT RESERVE													
TOTAL													

RECONCILIATION TO CONTRACT BUDGET BASELINE

VARIANCE ADJUSTMENT													
TOTAL CONTRACT VARIANCE													

(ALL ENTRIES IN THOUSANDS OF DOLLARS)

Figure 6.4 (Continued)

194

COST PERFORMANCE REPORT—FUNCTIONAL CATEGORIES

CONTRACTOR: THE RALPH M. PARSONS CO.,
100 W. WALNUT ST.
LOCATION: PASADENA, CA 91124
RDT & E ☒   PRODUCTION ☐

CONTRACT TYPE/NO.:
CPIF V76-940009

PROGRAM NAME/NUMBER
DOD/STS/GSS F04701-76-C-0081

REPORT PERIOD:

ORGANIZATIONAL OR FUNCTIONAL CATEGORY	CURRENT PERIOD					CUMULATIVE TO DATE					AT COMPLETION		
	BUDGETED COST		ACTUAL	VARIANCE		BUDGETED COST		ACTUAL	VARIANCE			LATEST	
	WORK SCHEDULED	WORK PERFORMED	COST WORK PERFORMED	SCHEDULE	COST	WORK SCHEDULED	WORK PERFORMED	COST WORK PERFORMED	SCHEDULE	COST	BUDGETED	REVISED ESTIMATE	VARIANCE
ENGINEERING AND SUPPORT													
OVERHEAD & G & A													
UNDISTRIBUTED BUDGET													
TOTAL													

(ALL ENTRIES IN THOUSANDS OF DOLLARS)

Figure 6.4 (*Continued*)

195

COST PERFORMANCE REPORT—BASELINE

CONTRACTOR: THE RALPH M. PARSONS CO.	CONTRACT TYPE/NO:	PROGRAM NAME/NUMBER:	REPORT PERIOD:
LOCATION: 100 W. WALNUT STREET PASADENA, CA 91124	CPIF VV6-940009	DOD/STS/GSS F04701-76-C-0081	
RDT & E [X] PRODUCTION [ ]			

(1) ORIGINAL CONTRACT TARGET COST	(2) NEGOTIATED CONTRACT CHANGES	(3) CURRENT TARGET COST (1) + (2)	(4) ESTIMATED COST OF AUTHORIZED UNPRICED WORK	(5) CONTRACT BUDGET BASELINE (3) + (4)	(6) TOTAL ALLOCATED BUDGET	(7) DIFFERENCE (5) − (6)

ITEM	BCWS CUM TO DATE	BUDGETED COST FOR WORK SCHEDULED (NON-CUMULATIVE)						(ENTER SPECIFIED PERIODS) TO COMPLETE	TOTAL BUDGET
		+1	+2	+3	+4	+5	+6		
PM BASELINE (BEGINNING OF PERIOD)									
UNDISTRIBUTED BUDGET									
PM BASELINE (END OF PERIOD)									
MANAGEMENT RESERVE									
TOTAL									

Figure 6.4 (*Continued*)

196

COST PERFORMANCE REPORT— MANPOWER LOADING

CONTRACTOR: THE RALPH M. PARSONS CO.				
LOCATION: 100 W. WALNUT STREET PASADENA, CA 91124	CONTRACT TYPE/NO. CPIF VV6-944009	PROGRAM NAME/NUMBER: DOD/STS/GSS F04701-76-C-0081	REPORT PERIOD:	
RDT & E (X) PRODUCTION ☐				

FORECAST (NON-CUMULATIVE)

ORGANIZATIONAL OR FUNCTIONAL CATEGORY	ACTUAL CURRENT PERIOD	ACTUAL END OF CURRENT PERIOD (CUM)	APPROXIMATE SIX MONTH FORECAST BY RMP ACCOUNTING PERIOD						TO COMPLETE	AT COMPLETION
ENGINEERING AND SUPPORT										
TOTAL DIRECT										

(ALL FIGURES IN WHOLE NUMBERS)

Figure 6.4 (*Continued*)

198

COST PERFORMANCE REPORT — PROBLEM ANALYSIS

CONTRACTOR: THE RALPH M. PARSONS CO. 100 W. WALNUT STREET PASADENA, CA 91124	CONTRACT TYPE/NO: CPIF VV6-940009	PROGRAM NAME/NUMBER: DOD/STS/GSS FO4701-76-C-0081	REPORT PERIOD:
LOCATION:			
RDT & E ☒ PRODUCTION ☐			

Figure 6.4 (Continued)

PROGRAM STS/GSS
CONTRACT RMP

Attachment 1

ETC/E/C Plan
(Including Target Fee @ 7%)
(Excluding Management Reserve)

CWBS Element		1976 8	1976 9	1976 10	1976 11	1976 12	1976 13	1977 1	1977 2	1977 3	1977 4	1977 5	1977 6	1977 7	1977 8	1977 9	1977 10	1977 11	1977 12	1977 13	1978 1	1978 2	1978 3	1978 4	1978 5	1978 6	Expended Thru 12-31-76	Estimated to Complete	Estimated at Completion
5161	AA							12500												12,500	13750				13750	6875	53,379	238,125	291,504
	AB							10218	10218	10559	11074								11074	10220	6836				6836	7326	29,999	182,387	212,386
	B							2996				2996	2781	2568	2568	2356	2142	1927	1715	1715	1670					1670	6,144	42,772	48,916
	CA							6702		6702	6617		6617	2772	3198	2985	2772	2666	2666	2344	2301	2260	2260	1918	1703	1744	13,427	71,546	84,973
	CB							1543	1543	1329	1329	1116	901	901	688	582	475	367	367	367	366	366	259		259	235	5,096	13,252	18,348
	CE							952												952	954	782	739	739	739	744	7,406	17,073	24,479
	CG							55383	56835	53718	56835	56835	53718	52137	47095	43272	36694	30199	23044	17832	17833	17833	17513	12044	11467	5042	218,843	665,329	884,172
	D							10253	8541	7900	2772		2772	1918	0											0	13,066	36,928	49,994
	FA							4210	3462	2735	2735	3145	3145	3590			3590	3419	2842	2842	2797		2797	2747	2797	2797	14,707	59,627	74,334
	FB							8883	7409	6001	6001	6725	6725	7621	7621	7664	7600	7301	6148	6148	5928					5928	23,696	127,415	151,111
	G							2618	3642	3770				3770	3642			3642	2618	3791					3791	3770	1,997	68,812	70,809
	H							7453		7453	9161	9161	8883	8733			8733	7453		7453	5741	5741	3605	3605	3180	1530	12,559	130,257	142,816
	J							12931	12931	13603		13603	12931	12931	13603	12931	13603	12931	12260	12931	7226	7226	7730	7730	5212	2927	62,966	208,843	271,809
5162	A							10912	10912	11198		11198	10912	10912	11198	10912	11198	10912	10629	10912	9651				9651	9671	39,436	200,929	240,365
	D							9763	11903	13187	12973	16397	18323	18323	18537	15327		15327	15113	12973	13185	12115	11045	9761	7621	5672	6,526	252,872	259,398
	F							11481	11481	11895	11895	9755	11481	11481	11895	11481	11895	11481	11063	11481	9379	9379	9793		9793	6835	61,014	203,737	264,751
5163	A							1773		1773	1347									1347	1346				1346	1323	3,724	26,842	30,566
	B							1911		1911	1699				1699	1528	1485			1485	1483				1483	1455	Ø	30,566	30,566
	C							3308					3308	3286	2880										2880	2049	4,291	56,863	61,154
5164	A							7145	9709	10008	9899	9922	9068	10349	10349	9494	8747	8747	8427	8427	7594	4174	3042	1591	1591	798	13,538	139,081	152,619
	BA							28198	30249	31744	37234	31680	34671	46034	52401	71625	77607	83159	76388	59300	28505	15944	781	0		0	156,652	705,520	862,172
	BB							11606	19981	21732	21943	14380	15512	15811	16388	16345	18951	19635	17286	17883	15100	15100	15635	12004	7624	6660	36,406	299,576	335,982
	CA							274											274	273	246				246	76	1,851	4,867	6,718
	CB							274											274	275	246				246	73	1,851	4,866	6,717
	D							3605			3605	4140		4140	3605					3605	3698		3698	3696	0	0	7,549	63,260	70,809
	E							2087	2059	2122	2487	10390	2271	5048	5901	21539	11885	8038	33109	17629	26441	5478	4623	9708	20942	19191	1,470	210,918	212,388
5170								3566	5103	5103	6638		6638	5102	5102	6637				6637	2286	2296	2286	2296	2286	2296	46,388	90,821	137,209
								232,545	247726	248352	255119	252668	246687	255547	257114	283549	275889	268232	272156	234202	191203	153016	133633	125718	113041	96687	843,981	4,153,084	4,997,065
																									Adjusted		Management Reserve		184,939
																									Contract		Target Cost		$5,182,004
																									(Including		Target Fee @ 7%		
																									and	Management Reserve)			

Figure 6.4 (Continued)

Liability Plan

At close of RMP accounting period	Cumulative (NTE) total liability
FY 1977	
1	$1,256,180
2	1,505,649
3	1,753,144
4	2,011,406
5	2,275,192
6	2,528,997
7	2,797,687
8	3,067,008
9	3,372,764
10	3,656,860
11	3,931,299
12	4,215,667
19	4,440,069
FY 1978	
1	4,618,523
2	4,762,790
3	4,895,673
4	5,025,978
5	5,155,834
6	5,182,004

Figure 6.4 (*Continued*)

When the construction begins, the formal change process continues, with each change evaluated to assure that performance (form, fit, and function) is not compromised. Costs associated with each change are also important since the estimates are no longer programmatic; like design, they reflect build-to configuration.

Completion of the specified construction work, to the build-to configuration, is reflected in the master equipment list, which identifies the name brand or name plate data for all equipment. To assure technical consistency between what is on the design drawings and construction specifications, the format for the master equipment list and all identification data is prescribed in the design criteria or development specification document. An example derived from a recent development specification is provided as Figure 6.6.

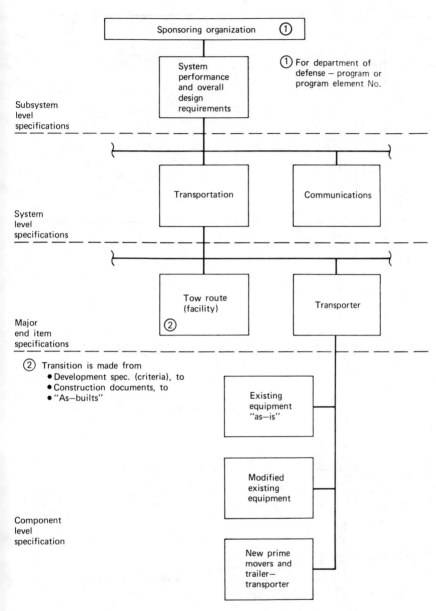

Figure 6.5 System specification tree section.

MASTER EQUIPMENT LIST

PAGE NO.

MAJOR SYSTEM	SUBSYSTEM	REVISION NO.	REVISION DATE		CONTRACT NO.
WATER	LAUNCH PAD FIREX WATER	BASIC			DACAXX-XXXX-XXXX

REFERENCE DESIGNATOR	ITEM OF EQUIPMENT	LOCATION	SPECIFICATION PARAGRAPH REFERENCE	MANUFACTURER (SUPPLIER)	MODEL, SERIAL NO., AND OTHER IDENTIFICATION	REMARKS
H1X001PFWF	FIRE HYDRANT, WET BARREL, 2 1/2-INCH HOSE CONNECTIONS.	LAUNCH PAD, NE CORNER	X.XX	RICH VALVE COMPANY 9217 SONGHELM AVENUE SANTA FE SPRINGS, CALIFORNIA 90670	MODEL 960, 2 - 2 1/2 - 4 INCH STREAMER, 36 INCH BURY	NO CHANGE

Figure 6.6 Master equipment list.

Following the same consistency in identification, the recommendation for spare parts for the master equipment list is prescribed as shown in Figure 6.7. A tabulation of interfaces is also incorporated in development specifications to track and control the match-up between items that are procured (support equipment) and items that are designed into facility to accommodate procured items. This format is shown in Figure 6.8.

The common denominator for the equipment and spare parts is, of course, the assigned designator and the specification source paragraph. To maintain an overview of configuration requires constant surveillance by personnel familiar with, and experienced in, the processes of configuration management.

The value specialist must recognize that a large acquisition will require this type of control, and that procedures have to be set forth for uniform identification and information processing. Depending on the size and complexity of the program itself, an apportionment of costs for labor and devices (some configuration management systems are computerized) has to be established for the function.

6.5.2 DATA MANAGEMENT

A corollary activity to configuration management is data management. On a large program, an index code system is established and often the listing is updated and printed by automated equipment.

Data management used to be a drawing control and library function. However, experience has shown that centralizing the activity gives management a better overview of costs and control. On a large design project, the costs for reproduction alone can range from 3 to 5% of the direct labor expense, exclusive of overhead and fringe. Again, the costs can vary with the facilitation—that is, in-house equipment or use of vendor services.

Startup of the program is the point at which the value specialist should make analysis and recommendations. The close relationships between project control (schedules), configuration management, and data offer opportunities for some consolidations and collocations that can provide savings of time and cost for the project.

An example of other types of savings that are possible is the use of standard forms for the submittal/transmittal and receipt of data. This saves labor and time. The publishing of status lists of drawings, specifications, and changes also requires attention to assure that all parties

RECOMMENDED SPARE PARTS LIST FOR 18-MONTH PERIOD

MAJOR SYSTEM	SUBSYSTEM	REVISION NO.	REVISION DATE	CONTRACT NO.	PAGE NO.
WATER	MOBILE SERVICE TOWER POTABLE WATER			DACAXX-XXXX-XXXX	

REFERENCE DESIGNATOR	COMPONENT/PART	SERVICE LIFE	SPARES QTY	SPARES UNIT	MANUFACTURER (SUPPLIER)	UNIT PRICE	PROCUREMENT LEAD TIME	PART NO.	REMARKS
STRO01MSTWP	STRAINER, 4 INCH, 250 PSI FLANGED, 20 MESH SCREEN	> 10 YEARS	1	EA.	CRANE CO. 4100 SO. KEDZIE AVENUE CHICAGO 32, ILLINOIS	$450	30 DAYS	991 1/2	

SAMPLE

Figure 6.7 Recommended spare parts list.

INTERFACE TABULATION SHEET

STATION SET

INTERFACE ID CODE	FACILITY INTERFACE DRAWING NUMBER	FUNCTION	LOCATION	INTERFACE HARDWARE		STATUS
				SUPPORT EQUIPMENT	FACILITY	

Figure 6.8 Interface tabulation sheet.

205

associated with the effort, who need to know, are using the latest information.

There is the problem of fixtures, furnishings, files, and space. Of concern to the value specialist are the total volume of data and the categoric handling required for storing, accessing, and processing data. Drawings that are current need "stick-files," where superseded or preliminary drawings can be rolled and more compactly shelved. On the other hand, master drawings—usually of more expensive materials such as mylar, vellum, or sepia—require flat storage, protected from potential damage from sunlight or rough handling.

Special consideration has to be given to distribution of received material as well as to providing the proper number of copies for output or transmittal. This is a high cost item, and the early planning of this requirement from a data management standpoint dictates a form that can be used to establish reproduction time as well as review time by cognizant managers who provide signature approvals.

Government is so concerned about data management that it requires contractors to supply proposals on the preparation, reproduction, and packaging costs of data separately from the technical effort. As a part of their formal requests for proposals (RFPs), a complete listing of all documentation is provided as the Contractor Data Requirements List (CDRL). The bidder notes the frequency of submittal and number of copies, and estimates the pages, binding, and other associated costs for CDRL items. Many of these items are typical, and wherever possible, agencies will specify content and format based on standards and experience. To illustrate, the U.S. Air Force not only has a manual of standard documentation, it also provides Data Item Descriptions (DIDs) to fully describe what is expected. Then the contractor's proposal is compared with Air Force cost experience to determine if the contractor understands what is required and what the required data should cost. The consistency of data costs has been fairly well established for design engineering efforts at between 3 and 5% of total cost. The percentage includes graphics (but not engineering drawings or design), typing, proofing, reproduction, collating, binding, and packaging.

On a $5 million program there are opportunities for value analysis and potential cost savings, assuming that the right alternatives are selected early. It will always be costlier downstream when an improvement on the data management operation is necessary to correct overrun conditions.

CHAPTER 7

APPLICATION OF VALUE MANAGEMENT

7.1 INTRODUCTION

Any industry, if it is to be competitive in the marketplace, must be cost conscious to some degree. The $100 billion plus construction industry recognizes the keen competition confronting it and is taking action to maintain its rightful place throughout the free world. Construction managers are becoming aware of value management techniques that focus attention on functional requirements and emphasize providing the essential functional requirements at the lowest total cost of effective ownership.

This chapter will discuss some of the managerial considerations that are necessary to ensure a successful VM program. In addition, this chapter will discuss the successful application of value management to in-house efforts, as well as governing clauses and VM workshops.

7.2 CREATING AND MAINTAINING A VALUE MANAGEMENT PROGRAM

Generally, a value management program is created for the purpose of obtaining maximum value or greatest benefit at the least cost to the customer. As a tool of management, value management, properly applied to projects, can be of immeasurable assistance to any organization in obtaining better value throughout the life cycle of the project, beginning at the concept phase and continuing through development, preliminary design, final design construction, operation and maintenance, and replacement.

Regardless of its size, an organization that establishes a VM pro-

207

gram must not become complacent in the belief that the mere creation of such an entity will ensure productive results. Maximum results are possible only with strong, active, and continuous top management support, not just lip service.

Managers at every level of organization must understand the logic and methodology of value management and support its objectives. Further, it must be made clear to all personnel within the organization that the VM program is everyone's responsibility and as such will require active participation by all.

7.3　THE IN-HOUSE VALUE MANAGEMENT PROGRAM

In establishing a value management program, it is prudent to centralize responsibility and direction near the top. There is no better way to obtain program visibility than to have the president or a vice-president require periodic reports of program performance.

Establishment of VM goals for major organizational components is essential to ensure continuous effort and middle management attention. Goals should be reasonable and attainable both in dollar savings and in generating VM studies.

Expeditious evaluation of VM studies must be emphasized to ensure prompt implementation of all approved studies; this will also give maximum results!

The full potential of the VM program cannot be realized unless all personnel are aware of the broad program objectives and understand what is required of them. To this end, top management must initiate action to train personnel responsible for the various facets of value management (training will be discussed later in this chapter).

7.3.1　THE VALUE MANAGER

Proper selection of the value manager cannot be overemphasized. The qualifications of the value manager should not be restricted to only education, technical training, experience, or specific knowledge of the value methodology. It should include an ability to skillfully and tactfully work with others and to gain full support and participation throughout the organization. One way to achieve complete and active support at every level of management is to establish a policy to the effect that value management is an integral part of the total organization. The VM effort is often thought of as an added requirement and consequently may or may not be applied to projects of high potential or to those experiencing difficulties. However, a properly selected value manager with responsibility for reporting to top management can be management's sentinel for accomplishing the necessary value studies, as well as achieving harmonious interface between organizational elements. As a special assistant to top management, the value manager has direct access to every operating level within the organization and as such emphasizes top management support of the program. In addition, the top management staff is kept informed of the progress, efforts, benefits, and difficulties on a routine basis. Difficulties or problems that arise are promptly resolved at the highest level of management. Should the value manager be assigned lower in the organization, then his effectiveness would naturally and proportionally be lower with each level of management placed over him.

7.3.2 RESPONSIBILITIES OF THE VALUE MANAGER

Within the framework of his charter, the value manager has general and specific responsibilities to ensure program effectiveness. General responsibilities include:

1. Establishing and maintaining an effective, continuing, productive value program.
2. Conducting or arranging for a value training effort to assure that appropriate personnel are familiar with the VM methodology.
3. Assurance of a continuous effort in the conduct of VM studies.
4. Assurance that maximum cost reductions through value management are accomplished on all projects selected for study.
5. Keep top management informed as to program effectiveness, especially as related to goals and objectiveness.

Specific responsibilities include:

1. Developing, planning, directing, coordinating, and executing the organization's VM program.
2. Recommending projects for VM studies.
3. Recommending specific personnel to serve on VM study teams.
4. Recommending personnel for VM training.
5. Monitoring all VM efforts.

6. Preparing periodic reports for submission to top management.

7. Coordinating all VM studies for submission to top management for approval and implementation.

8. Arranging for adequate funds and resources to maintain an ongoing VM program.

9. Assisting organizational elements in selecting projects and conducting value investigations.

10. Keeping abreast of new products, methods, and procedures in the construction industry.

11. Maintaining a file on the state of the art.

12. Promoting and publicizing the VM study results; this will promote interest and continued participation throughout the organization.

This list of responsibilities should not be construed as being complete but should serve as the basis for building or modifying, as required, responsibilities that will be tailored to the size and needs of the organization.

7.3.3 MEASURING THE EFFECTIVENESS OF THE VALUE MANAGEMENT PROGRAM

A meaningful method of measuring the effectiveness of the VM program should be instituted shortly after the decision is made to organize and staff such a program. In the past, most measures of effectiveness have been based upon dollar savings, either during or following the design phase. More recently, other criteria have been added; some of the usual ones are:

1. Target cost system.
2. Cost reduction goal.
3. Number of value management studies.

The target cost system method, normally applied during the development phase, evaluates performance against the target cost established for the system being developed. If the design organization, along with value management, is successful in meeting the target cost, then the VM program is apparently operating satisfactorily. The cost reduction goal method consists of comparing program savings with some pre-assigned savings goal. The number of studies in progress is often used for evaluating effectiveness of in-house and subcontractor programs.

Likewise, the criterion of the number of proposals received is similar, except that it is used in evaluating the effectiveness of motivating others to contribute.

There are certain dangers and shortcomings in measuring VM effectiveness solely in terms of dollar savings. Constant emphasis on dollar savings may eventually result in others in the organization feeling that value managers are willing to sacrifice anything to save a dollar. It must be realized that the actions that result in savings arise from the efforts by two distinct groups: those doing the VM work and those responsible for implementing the various changes. Efforts by the VM groups to gain recognition by reason of the dollar value of their proposals may eventually antagonize the very people that value management is designed to assist.

In an attempt to avoid these types of problems, the Society of American Value Engineers (SAVE) has proposed a system for evaluating value management programs that considers both monetary and a number of nonmonetary aspects. This system has two purposes: (1) to provide uniform guidelines on criteria for use in evaluating and comparing the VM efforts of various organizations; and (2) to provide guidelines on the elements that should be considered in developing and improving a VM program.

The system is divided into two sections: Section 1, Program Achievements; and Section II, Program Activities. Section 1 considers the following items:

1. Percent profit improvement from VM recommendations from subcontractors.
2. Percent profit improvement from in-house study changes.
3. Savings as a percent of sales.
4. Savings/expenditure ratio.
5. Percent of time devoted to value management.
6. Percent of salaried personnel trained.

Section II is somewhat more detailed than Section I and includes the following rather broad categories:

1. Management support.
2. Value management organization.
3. Use of cost targets.
4. Task team activity areas.

5. Distribution of cost information.
6. Value management review activities.
7. Value management activity by the purchasing group.
8. Contracts with value clauses.
9. Proposal activity.
10. Application of value management methodology.
11. Motivation and information services.
12. SAVE Society and state-of-the-art participation.

Using this system, weighting factors are assigned to the various elements. No provisions have been made for evaluating the quality of the value efforts; emphasis has been placed on the results achieved and whether or not certain activities of a well-balanced VM program are being conducted.

Some of the information required to calculate the rating points for some of the elements may be difficult to obtain in some organizations. It is assumed that the person making the evaluation will use discretion in deciding how much effort should be expended in obtaining hard-to-get information. A good estimate, or perhaps not bothering to calculate points, may be best if there happens to be relatively little activity in a certain area.

The information on the system as presented here is not sufficient to enable one to use it as intended by SAVE: to do this would require considerable additional space. It is suggested that the reader consult the SAVE publication "A System for Measuring Value Engineering Efforts"* before attempting to use the system.

A suggested list of questions compiled by the staff at the U.S. Army Management Engineering Training Agency, Rock Island, Illinois, is provided to assist any organization to appraise (1) organization and management support of the VM program, (2) activities of the VM program, and (3) achievements of the VM program.

Organization and Management Support of a Value Management Program

1. Does the organization have a strong and clear-cut policy statement regarding value management?
2. Are adequate implementation procedures provided?

*Inquiries should be directed to: The Society of American Value Engineers, 29551 Greenfield Road, Suite 210, Southfield, Michigan 48076.

3. What degree of interest exists at the policy-making level?

4. Is the value program manager performing a full- or part-time job?

5. Does the value program manager have access to sufficient personnel to adequately conduct business on a timely basis?

6. Are value proposals given proper attention by project supervision?

7. Are implementation policies, procedures, and other guidelines updated to reflect current thinking in the value management area?

8. Is there a satisfactory interrelationship between value management and the other managerial disciplines—reliability, quality control, purchasing, and so on?

9. To what degree does the VM office assist supervision in quickly implementing worthwhile training program proposals?

10. Is the value manager located sufficiently high in the line of command so as to be influential in providing emphasis to the program?

11. Has the VM program been allotted sufficient funds, office space, and equipment?

12. What is the relationship between the corporate VM office and the in-house resident?

13. Does the VM operation exercise sound value principles in its own operation?

14. Are services available to obtain rigorous evaluation of tradeoffs between reliability, performance, and cost?

15. Are value checklists included in all applicable Request for Proposals (RFPs)? With what results?

16. Does the subcontractor take specific actions to "close-the-loop" after value study proposals have been generated?

17. Does the organization select its value study projects on a systematic basis?

18. Is management setting realistic targets for the VM efforts?

19. Does the VM reporting system accurately report the progress of the program?

20. Are there periodic audits of the VM function?

21. Is management providing adequate incentives for the performance of value management?

22. Does management support a VM training program?

23. Do members of the top management hierarchy openly and actively support the VM program?

24. Are internal reviews of value study proposals sufficiently detailed

and analytical to ensure a high percentage of acceptance of proposals by customers?

25. Is the VM effort organized in an effective manner?

26. Is there a formal procedure for documenting and auditing savings resulting from value management efforts?

Activities of a Value Management Program

1. Are value studies conducted on a continuing basis rather than sporadically?

2. Are the VM publicity efforts of a continuing nature?

3. Are the VM publicity efforts broad in scope?

4. Is a formal training program for value specialists in effect?

5. Are orientation and progress report sessions conducted for top management personnel on a continuing basis?

6. Do the VM personnel work with personnel from other disciplines when performing studies and analysis?

7. Is the manner of selecting projects consistent with recommended practices?

8. How much leadership is being provided by value managers?

9. What action is taken by project supervision on value study proposals?

10. How well have accomplishments been summarized and documented as a result of systems review sessions?

11. What is the history regarding following up on worthwhile suggestions?

12. How often does a representative of value management participate in, or observe, another company, military, or university value management training course?

13. Do the VM personnel have available and make use of an adequate library and related educational material?

14. Do the VM personnel participate in value reviews?

15. What is the duration of formal training courses?

16. What is the general reaction, comment, and criticism elicited from participants at the conclusion of the course?

17. How suitable are the projects selected for training?

18. What is the spectrum of projects selected for courses?

19. Have accurate costs of parts, processes, materials, labor, and all other charges been obtained for projects recommended for formal value management study?

Achievements of the Value Management Program

1. Have cost savings goals been achieved?

2. What has been the record of locating potential VM projects and offering value study services?

3. Have cost reduction targets been met in "applied" VM projects?

4. When a cost target has been set on a design, how close does the value study usually come to the target when actual costs are tallied?

5. What is the average savings-to-cost ratio achieved by the VM program?

6. Have worthwhile training course proposals, as well as regular proposals, been implemented?

7. Are value studies processed expeditiously?

8. How many value studies have been initiated?

9. How many value studies have been accepted for implementation?

10. Are the value studies properly documented?

11. Are the VM reports submitted on schedule?

12. How many value studies have been completed?

13. Are the training programs productive?

14. On what basis are full-time value managers selected?

15. Are the trained personnel actively working in the VM area?

16. How many studies are in process?

17. Have value studies been conducted in all the different functional areas of the organization?

18. Are the goals of the present and future in excess of previous annual accomplishments?

7.4 CONTRACT CLAUSES

Generally, there are two methods of procurement used by the federal government; in the private sector there are more; however, only the federal provisions will be discussed here in the interest of brevity. The two methods of procurement employed by the federal government are: (1) those resulting from an advertised procurement, and (2) those resulting from a negotiated procurement.

Since advertised procurement affords the maximum opportunity for effective price competition, it is the preferred method of awarding contracts. Procurement by formal advertising is mandatory (10 U.S.C.

2304, a), and any circumstances permitting procurement by negotiation are stated as exceptions to that requirement.

The requirements for advertised procurement, as stated in Section II of the Armed Services Procurement Regulation (ASPR), are both detailed and strictly construed. Among the explicit instructions included in Section II are those governing the following requirements: (1) preparation of invitations for bids, (2) solicitation of bids, (3) submission of bids, (4) opening of bids, and (5) contract award.

As mentioned above, the authority for negotiated procurement exists by exception. In the negotiated procurement process, the procurement requirements are less rigid than under formal advertising, and the discretionary powers of the contracting officer are increased. As an example, proposals submitted by the contractor may be opened immediately upon receipt and late proposals or amendments may be considered if it appears to be in the best interest of the government. Either of these actions could void an entire procurement effort under the advertised procurement concept.

Section III of ASPR, which treats in detail the conduct of procurement by negotiation, includes instructions on the type of contract to be employed in negotiated procurements.

The term "contract type" as employed in this discussion is used in the context of the type of compensation arrangement between the government and the contractor, as opposed to the form and structure or end purpose of a contract.

Following the order of ASPR provisions dealing with contract types, fixed price contracts and cost reimbursement contracts are discussed in turn.

Several types of fixed price contracts are designed to facilitate proper pricing under varying circumstances. This flexibility allows maximum use of the fixed price concept in as many procurement situations as possible, with the possible result of an equitable contractual relationship to both the government and the contractor.

Under the firm fixed price contract, the most preferred for construction contracts, the maximum risk is placed on the contractor. At the same time, the maximum profit potential exists, since the contract price is not subject to either upward or downward adjustment solely by reason of cost experience of the contractor.

The firm fixed price contract is suitable for use in procurements where reasonably definite design or performance specifications are available and where fair and reasonable prices can be established at the outset. It is particularly suitable in the construction industry, for purchase of standard or modified commercial items or military items sufficiently described by specifications.

Other fixed price type contracts included in the ASPR are:

• Fixed price contract with escalation.
• Fixed price incentive.
• Prospective price redetermination.
• Retroactive price redetermination.

Cost reimbursement contracts differ from fixed price contracts in that a contractor may, in accordance with contract provisions, be reimbursed for allowable costs in excess of those costs originally estimated for contract performance. Risk to the contractor is minimized since he is generally under no obligation to continue with contract performance after such time as total estimated cost of the contract has been expended.

Contracts of the cost reimbursement type are not to be used except when they will probably be less costly to the government or when it is impractical, because of the nature of the supplies or services being procured, to utilize other contract types.

Under a cost contract, the contractor is reimbursed allowable cost of performance but receives no fee.

Some of the cost reimbursement types of contracts included in the ASPR are:

• Cost sharing
• Cost-plus-fixed fee
• Cost-plus-incentive fee

Since a value management change proposal may be incorporated into the contract through the use of the "changes" clause or article of the contract, the subject of modification of government contracts is briefly considered here. It is generally stated that the methods of modifying government contracts are: (1) by changes, (2) by supplemental agreements, and (3) by extras.

The first two of these, contract changes and supplemental agreements, are the most pertinent considerations here. Time alone would serve to rule out the third, since the exploration of extras would require a detailed study of case law on the subject.

The authority for a contract change stems from the contract instrument itself. The ASPR provides for "changes" clauses to be included in the various types of fixed and cost reimbursement contracts. The following clause in ASPR prescribes for changes in cost reimbursement supply contracts:

The Contracting Officer may at any time, by a written order, and without notice to the sureties, if any, make changes, within the general scope of this contract, in any one or more of the following: (i) drawings, designs, or specifications, where the supplies to be furnished are to be specially manufactured for the Government in accordance therewith; (ii) method of shipment or packing; (iii) place of delivery; and (iv) the amount of Government-furnished property. If any such changes cause an increase or decrease in the estimated cost of, or the time required for the performance of any part of the work under this contract, whether changed or not changed by any such order, or otherwise affects any other provision of this contract, an equitable adjustment shall be made (i) in the estimated cost or delivery schedule, or both, (ii) in the amount of any fixed fee to be paid to the Contractor, and (iii) in such other provisions of the contract as may be so affected, and the contract shall be modified in writing accordingly. Any claim by the Contractor for adjustment under this clause must be asserted within thirty (30) days from the date of receipt by the Contractor of the notification of change; provided, however, that the Contracting Officer, if he decides that the facts justify such action, may receive and act upon any such claim asserted at any time prior to final payment under this contract. Failure to agree to any adjustment shall be a dispute concerning a question of fact within the meaning of the clause of this contract entitled Disputes. However, nothing in this clause shall excuse the Contractor from proceeding with the contract as changed.

While the different types of fixed price and cost reimbursement contracts will require some variation in the language of the clause, the one quoted above is typical. The overall rights and obligations of the parties under the clause remain basically the same in all types of contracts.

The clause includes the following provisions:

1. The contracting officer can make changes, within the general scope of the contract, to designated areas of the existing contract agreement.

2. An equitable adjustment to cost, fee, and delivery schedule must be made by supplemental agreement to the extent that each of these elements is affected by the change.

3. The contractor must make a timely claim for any adjustment.

4. The contractor must continue with the contract work as changed pending resolution of any dispute that might arise over the terms of the contract adjustment.

Since the government is the contracting party with the right of initiating the change to the contract, and since the contractor is obligated to proceed with the work as changed, contract modification through the use of the "changes" clause is described as a unilateral right of the government.

As pointed out above, the right of a contract change is unilateral because the right to accomplish the change is vested in only one of the contracting parties. On the other hand, a supplemental agreement is bilateral in nature, requiring the formal assent of both parties to the contract. Actually, a supplemental agreement is a new agreement by the parties affecting their rights and obligations under the contract.

The distinction between a contract change and a supplemental agreement can best be drawn by referring again to the contract change provision. If a change initiated by the government has no effect on cost, fee, or schedule under the contract, the change is fully accomplished by the unilateral action of the government in issuing the change. If an adjustment to cost, fee, or delivery schedule is required by the change, this new agreement of the parties can be expressed only by the bilateral action of a new supplemental agreement.

In the consideration of the VM contract provisions, it should be noted that the "changes" clause of the contract may, and supplemental agreements will, be used to implement the value management changes.

7.4.1 TYPES OF VALUE CLAUSES

Although the ASPR contained provisions for contractor participation in the value program as early as November 1963, construction and supply contracts did not contain similar provisions until late 1964. At that time the ASPR provided for two types of value clauses: (1) the value incentive clause and (2) the program requirement clause. Both clauses have remained basically unchanged since then; both encourage maximum participation in the value program.

The Incentive Clause

The incentive clause provides for the contractor to share in any real savings that accrue to the government from a value management proposal initiated by him or his subcontractor or jointly developed. To be acceptable, the proposal must require some change in the contract specifications, purchase description, or statement of work. This may include the elimination or modification of any requirement found to be in excess of actual needs in such areas as design, components, materials, material processes, construction methods or materials, technical data requirements, or testing procedures and requirements.

It should be noted that while a value incentive clause seeks to encourage a contractor to engage in VM studies, he is not required to do so. The clause merely describes the sharing that will take place should he submit a proposal that the government accepts. Permissive in intent, it allows the contractor to ignore this provision and still otherwise perform under his contract. However, the wise contractor will not pass up the opportunity to gain a minimum of 50% of the net savings available to him through the incentive clause.

Though permissive in intent, the incentive clause has been successfully and widely used by the Army Corps of Engineers and other federal construction agencies since its inception. As a matter of policy the Army Corps of Engineers makes it mandatory for inclusion in all firm-fixed-price-construction contracts exceeding $10,000 in estimated cost. Many of the Corps district offices include the clause in their firm-fixed-price-construction contracts regardless of estimated cost.

The Program Requirement Clause

In contrast to the incentive clause discussed above, a program requirement clause obligates the contractor to engage in value studies to the level and scope required by the government as an item of work in his contract. The clause may contain provisions for incentive sharing, whether or not proposals submitted result directly from the program requirement. However, such sharing would be to a considerably lesser degree than in the case of the incentive clause.

One of the principal reasons for utilizing the program requirement clause is to obtain early results in the initial stages of the life cycle of a project. The program requirement clause was initially used in research and development contracts, especially in major weapon system development contracts. However, in recent years the Army Corps of Engineers and the General Services Administration have added modified program requirement provisions to architect-engineer and construction manager contracts for major facilities. This is a major step toward reducing initial construction costs, improving designs, reducing operation and maintenance costs, and achieving maximum cost benefits on a life-cycle basis.

Value incentive clauses currently prescribed by the Armed Services Procurement Regulation and by the General Services Administration, Public Buildings Service are shown in Figures 7.1 and 7.2.

Value Engineering (VE). Insert the following clause in
all Fixed Price type construction contracts:

VALUE ENGINEERING INCENTIVE

    (a) Application. This clause applies to a contractor developed
and documented Value Engineering Change Proposal (VECP) which:

        (i) requires a change to this contract to implement
        the VECP, and

       (ii) reduces the contract price without impairing essential
        function or characteristics, provided that it is not
        based solely on a change in deliverable end item
        quantities.

    (b) Documentation. As a minimum, the following information
shall be submitted by the contractor with each VECP:

        (i) a description of the difference between the existing
        contract requirement and the proposed change, and the
        comparative advantages and disadvantages of each;
        justification where function or characteristic of a
        work item is being altered; and the effect of the
        change on the performance of the end item;

       (ii) an analysis and itemization of the requirements of
        the contract which must be changed if the VECP is
        accepted and a recommendation as to how to make each
        such change (e.g., a suggested specification revision);

      (iii) a separate detailed cost estimate for both the existing
        contract requirement and the proposed change to provide
        an estimate of the reduction in costs, if any, that will
        result from acceptance of the VECP, taking into account
        the costs of development and implementation by the Con-
        tractor (including any amount attributable to subcon-
        tracts in accordance with paragraph (f) below);

      (iv) a prediction of any effects the proposed change would
        have on related costs to the Military Department such
        as Government furnished property costs, and costs of
        maintenance and operation;

       (v) a statement of the time by which a change order adopting
        the VECP must be issued so as to obtain the maximum cost
        reduction during the remainder of this contract, noting
        any effect on the contract completion time or delivery
        schedule; and

Figure 7.1 Value engineering incentive clause (ASPR).

        (vi)   identification of any previous submission of the VECP,
including the dates submitted, the agencies involved,
the numbers of the Government contracts involved, and
the previous actions by the Government, if known.

    (c) Submission. To expedite a determination, VECPs shall be
submitted to the Resident Engineer at the worksite with a copy to the
Contracting Officer. Proposals shall be processed expeditiously; however, the Government shall not be liable for any delay in acting upon
any proposal submitted pursuant to this clause. The Contractor has the
right to withdraw, in whole or in part, any VECP at any time prior to
acceptance by the Government.

    (d) Acceptance. The Contracting Officer may accept, in whole
or in part, by contract modification any VECP submitted pursuant to
this clause. The Contracting Officer may accept the VECP even though
an agreement on price reduction has not been reached, by issuing the
Contractor a notice to proceed with the change. Until a notice to
proceed is issued or a contract modification applies a VECP to this
contract, the Contractor shall remain obligated to perform in accordance with this contract. Contract modifications made pursuant to this
clause will so state. The decision of the Contracting Officer as to
the acceptance of any VECP under this contract shall be final and shall
not be subject to the "Disputes" clause of this contract.

    (e) Sharing. If a VECP submitted by the contractor pursuant to
this clause is accepted, the contract price shall be adjusted without
regard to profit in accordance with the following provisions:

        (i) Definitions.

             (A) Instant contract savings to the contractor (ICS)
are the estimated reduction in the contractor's
cost of performance resulting from the acceptance
of the VECP. The proposed cost reduction includes
estimated allowable contractor development and
implementation costs (CC). The contractor development and implementation costs include any subcontractor
development and implementation costs and any subcontractor incentive payments. (See (f) below.) For
purposes of this clause, contractor development costs
are those costs incurred after the contractor has
identified a specific VE project and prior to
acceptance and implementation by the Government.

             (B) Government Costs (GC) are those DOD costs which
directly result from development and implementation
of the VECP, such as test and evaluation of the VECP.

        (ii) Calculations and Actions. Multiply ICS by 45% and GC
by 55%. Add these two results, e.g., (.45 ICS + .55 GC)
and subtract from the contract price.

2

Figure 7.1 (*Continued*)

(f) Subcontracts. The Contractor shall include appropriate VE arrangements in any subcontract of $50,000 or greater, and may include such arrangements in contracts of lesser value. To compute any adjustment in the contract price under paragraph (e) above, contractor's cost of development and implementation of a VECP which is accepted under this contract shall include any development and implementation costs of a subcontractor, and any VE incentive payments to a subcontractor, which clearly pertain to such VECP. However, no such payment or accrual to a subcontractor will be permitted, either as a part of the contractor's development or implementation costs or otherwise to reduce the Government's share.

(g) Data. The Contractor may restrict the Government's right to use any sheet of a VECP or of the supporting data submitted pursuant to this clause, in accordance with the terms of the following legend if it is marked on such sheet:

> "This data furnished pursuant to the Value Engineering Incentive
> clause of contract _____ shall not be disclosed outside
> the Government, or duplicated, used, or disclosed, in whole or
> in part, for any purpose other than to evaluate a VECP submitted
> under said clause. This restriction does not limit the Govern-
> ment's right to use information contained in this data if it is
> or has been obtained, or is otherwise available, from the Con-
> tractor or from another source, without limitations. If such a
> VECP is accepted by the Government under said contract after the
> use of this data in such an evaluation, the Government shall have
> the right to duplicate, use, and disclose any data reasonably
> necessary to the full utilization of such VECP as accepted, in
> any manner and for any purpose whatsoever, and have others so do."

In the event of acceptance of a VECP, the Contractor hereby grants to the Government all rights to use, duplicate or disclose, in whole or in part, in any manner and for any purpose whatsoever, and to have or permit others to do so, any data reasonably necessary to fully utilize such VECP.

END OF CLAUSE

Figure 7.1 (*Continued*)

VALUE INCENTIVE CLAUSE

(CONSTRUCTION CONTRACT)

1. *OBJECTIVES*—This clause applies to any cost reduction proposal (hereinafter referred to as a Value Change Proposal or VCP) initiated and developed by the Contractor for the purpose of changing any requirement of this contract. This clause does not, however, apply to any such proposal unless it is identified by the Contractor, at the time of its submission to the Government, as a proposal submitted pursuant to this clause.

1.1 VCP's contemplated are those that would result in net savings to the Government by providing either: (1) a decrease in the cost of performance of this contract, or: (2) a reduction in the cost of ownership (hereinafter referred to as collateral costs) of the work provided by this contract, regardless of acquisition costs. VCP's must result in savings without impairing any required functions and characteristics such as service life, reliability, economy of operation, ease of maintenance, standardized features, esthetics, fire protection features and safety features presently required by this contract. However, nothing herein precludes the submittal of VCPs where the Contractor considers that the required functions and characteristics could be combined, reduced or eliminated as being nonessential or excessive to the satisfactory function served by the work involved.

1.2 A VCP identical to one submitted under any other contract with the Contractor or another Contractor may also be submitted under this contract.

1.3 A proposal to decrease the cost of performing the contract solely or principally by substituting another Subcontractor for one listed by the Contractor in his bid is not a VCP. In considering a VCP which, as an incident thereof, would entail substitution for a listed Subcontractor, maintaining the objective of the Subcontractor listing will be taken into account along with factors cited in paragraph 1.1 above.

2. *SUBCONTRACTOR INCLUSION*—The Contractor shall include the provisions of this clause, with a provision for sharing arrangements that meet or exceed the minimum percentage contained herein, in all first-tier subcontracts in excess of $25,000, and in any other subcontract which, in the judgment of the Contractor, is of such nature as to offer reasonable likelihood of value change proposals. At the option of the first-tier Subcontractor, this clause may be included in lower tier subcontracts. The Contractor shall encourage submission of VCPs from Subcontractors; however, it is not mandatory that the Contractor accept and/or transmit to the Government VCPs proposed by his Subcontractors.

3. *DATA REQUIREMENTS*—As a minimum, the following information shall be submitted by the Contractor with each VCP:

3.1 A description of the difference between the existing contract requirement and the proposed change, and the comparative advantages and disadvantages of each; including justification where function or characteristic of a work item is being reduced;

3.2 Separate detailed cost estimates for both the existing contract requirement and the proposed change, and an estimate of the change in contract price including consideration of the costs of development and implementation of the VCP and the sharing arrangement set forth in this clause;

3.3 An estimate of the effects the VCP would have on collateral costs to the Government, including an estimate of the sharing that

the Contractor requests be paid by the Government upon approval of the VCP;

3.4 Architectural, engineering or other analysis, in sufficient detail to identify and describe each requirement of the contract which must be changed if the VCP is accepted, with recommendation as to how to accomplish each such change and its effect on unchanged work;

3.5 A statement of the time by which approval of the VCP must be issued by the Government to obtain the maximum cost reduction during the remainder of this contract, noting any effect on the contract completion time or delivery schedule; and,

3.6 Identification of any previous submission of the VCP including the dates submitted, the agencies involved, the numbers of the Government contracts involved, and the previous actions by the Government, if known.

4. *PROCESSING PROCEDURES*—Six copies of each VCP shall be submitted to the Contracting Officer, or his duly authorized representative. VCPs will be processed expeditiously; however, the Government will not be liable for any delay in acting upon a VCP submitted pursuant to this clause. The Contractor may withdraw, in whole or in part, a VCP not accepted by the Government within the period specified in the VCP. The Government shall not be liable for VCP development cost in the case where a VCP is rejected or withdrawn. The decision of the Contracting Officer as to the acceptance of a VCP under this contract shall be final and shall not be subject to the "Disputes" clause of this contract.

4.1 The Contracting Officer may modify a VCP, with the concurrence of the Contractor, to make it acceptable, and the Contractor's fair share will be based on the VCP as modified.

4.2 Pending written acceptance of a VCP in whole or in part, the Contractor shall remain obligated to perform in accordance with the terms of the existing contract.

4.3 An approved VCP shall be finalized through an equitable adjustment in the contract price and time of performance by the execution of a contract modification pursuant to the provisions of this clause bearing a notation so stating.

4.4 When the necessity to proceed with a VCP (in whole or in part) does not allow sufficient time for execution of a contract modification, the Government may issue a letter accepting the VCP (in whole or in part), authorizing the Contractor to proceed with the work, as changed, on the basis of contract price adjustment to be determined at the earliest practicable date but not to be less than the decrease nor more than the increase, as the case may be, than the decrease or increase set forth in the VCP submitted and accepted.

5. *COMPUTATIONS FOR CHANGE IN CONTRACT COST OF PERFORMANCE*—Separate estimates shall be prepared for both the existing (instant) contract requirement and the proposed change. Each estimate shall consist of an itemized breakdown of all costs of the Contractor and all Subcontractors' work in sufficient detail to show unit quantities and costs of labor, material, and equipment.

GENERAL SERVICES ADMINISTRATION

GSA FORM 2653 (REV. 11-77)

Figure 7.2 Value incentive clause (construction contract) (GSA).

5.1 Contractor development and implementation costs for the VCP shall be included in the estimate for the proposed change. However, these costs will not be allowable if they are otherwise reimbursable as a direct charge under this contract.

5.2 Government costs of processing or implementation of a VCP shall not be included in the estimate.

5.3 If the difference in the estimates indicate a net reduction in contract price, no allowance will be made for overhead, profit and bond. The resultant net reduction in contract cost of performance shall be shared as provided hereinafter.

5.4 If the difference in the estimates indicate a net increase in contract price, the price shall be adjusted pursuant to an equitable adjustment that will include Contractor's overhead and profit on his additional work or the additional work of one of his subcontractors.

6. COMPUTATIONS FOR COLLATERAL COSTS—Separate estimates shall be prepared for collateral costs of both the existing contract requirement and the proposed change. Each estimate shall consist of an itemized breakdown of all costs and the basis for the data used in the estimate. Cost benefits to the Government include, but are not limited to: reduced costs of operation, maintenance or repair, extended useful service life, increases in usable floor space, and reduction in the requirements for Government furnished property. Increased collateral costs include the converse of such factors. Computation shall be as follows:

6.1 Costs shall be calculated over a 20-year period on a uniform basis for each estimate and shall include Government costs of processing or implementing the VCP.

6.2 If the difference in the estimates as approved by the Government indicate a savings, the Contractor shall divide the resultant amount by 20 to arrive at the average annual net collateral savings. The resultant savings shall be shared as provided hereinafter.

6.3 In the event that agreement cannot be reached on the amount of estimated collateral costs, the Contracting Officer shall determine the amount. His decision is final and is not subject to the provisions of the "Disputes" clause of this contract.

7. SHARING ARRANGEMENTS—If a VCP is accepted by the Government, the Contractor is entitled to share in instant contract savings and collateral savings not as alternatives, but rather to the full extent provided for in this clause. For the purposes of sharing under this clause, the term "instant contract" will include any

changes to or other modifications of this contract, executed subsequent to acceptance of the particular VCP, by which the Government increases the quantity of any item of work or adds any item of work. It will also include any extension of the instant contract through exercise of an option (if any) provided under this contract after acceptance of the VCP. The Contractor shall be entitled to a contract modification for instant or collateral savings shares on changes or options only at such time as a change order has been issued or an option has been exercised.

7.1 When only the prime Contractor is involved, he shall receive 50% and the Government 50% of the net reduction in the cost of performance of this contract.

7.2 When a first-tier Subcontractor is involved, he shall receive a minimum of 30%, the prime Contractor a maximum of 30%, and the Government a fixed 40% of the net reduction in the cost of performance of this contract. Other Subcontractors shall receive a portion of the first-tier Subcontractor savings in accordance with the terms of their contracts with the first-tier Subcontractor.

7.3 When collateral savings occur the Contractor shall receive 20% of the average one years net collateral savings.

8. ADJUSTMENTS TO CONTRACT PRICE—

8.1 The method for payment of instant savings shares shall be accomplished by reducing the contract price by an amount equal to the Government's share of the savings.

8.2 Collateral savings shares and costs of increased work shall be paid by increasing the contract price.

9. DATA RESTRICTION RIGHTS—The contractor may restrict the Government's right to use any sheet of a VCP or the supporting data, submitted pursuant to this clause, in accordance with the terms of the following legend if it is marked on each such sheet:

The data furnished pursuant to the Value Incentive Clause of contract No._____ shall not be disclosed outside the Government for any purpose other than to evaluate a VCP submitted under said clause. This restriction does not limit the Government's right to use information otherwise available, from the contractor or from another source without limitations, or if release of the data is required under the Freedom of Information Act.

In the event of acceptance of a VCP, the Government shall have the right fully to utilize such proposal on this and any other Government contract.

Figure 7.2 (*Continued*)

7.5 CONSULTANTS

Regardless of the size of the organization, a qualified value consultant can provide an invaluable service. Given an opportunity and with top management support, a value consultant can return many times over the cost of his professional services in a relatively short interval of time. There must be a strong determination exhibited by top management and a commitment of resources before considering the services of a consultant. In addition, top management must determine the scope of the undertaking and expect commensurate results.

The value consultant services can include a myriad of areas or may be restricted to the resolution of a specific area of concern.

Many of the recognized value consultants can and do provide professional services in the following areas of value management.

- In-depth investigation of organizational need for a VM program.
- Assist in the establishment of a VM program where none exists.
- Reorganize an existing VM program to increase effectiveness.
- Select a value manager.
- Identify areas for the application of VM studies.
- Identify VM training needs.
- Conduct VM training.
- Organize and conduct VM studies.
- Prepare contract clauses.
- Assist in contract administration.
- Publicize progress of value studies.
- Establish audit procedures for validating value study results.
- Establish reporting procedures to keep top management informed.
- Establish awards procedures to recognize individual contributions.
- Establish a crossfeed procedure by which all organizational elements can obtain prompt and detailed information on implemented value studies.

This list is not all-inclusive nor is there any attempt to make it so; nor is there any valid reason for listing all known value specialists and consultants since the list grows periodically. Such information may be obtained from The Society of American Value Engineers, 29551 Greenfield Road, Suite 210, Southfield, Michigan 48076, or from Commissioner, Public Buildings Service, General Services Administration, Washington, D.C. 20405.

7.6   VALUE MANAGEMENT WORKSHOPS

The primary purpose of a VM workshop is to provide the needed training. Chapter 2 contains an additional discussion on workshops. All personnel who are designated to work in value management should participate in a 40-hour VM workshop as a minimum. Included in this training effort are:

- Value managers/specialists.
- Persons designated as team leaders of VM study teams.
- Persons designated as team members of VM study teams.
- Persons working in areas where VM methodology should be practiced (design, development, construction, operation and maintenance, etc.)

A properly organized and conducted VM workshop will not only provide each participant with a thorough understanding of the value methodology, but will result in savings on those projects studied during the workshop that will far exceed the cost of conducting the training.

An important consideration for ensuring the success of a VM workshop lies in the proper selection of projects to be investigated. This responsibility is generally vested in the value project selection board assisted by the value manager. However, it is entirely within the realm of reason that the value manager would make the selection with the approval of the board.

In considering a project for a VM workshop, strong emphasis must be placed on:

- Potential return on investment (10:1 minimum).
- Priority.
- Timely implementation.
- Apparent poor value.
- Functionality.
- Availability of drawings, specifications, cost estimates, and other related information.
- Security classification.
- Sufficient cost of total project.
- Complexity.
- Multiplicity.

- Constructability.
- Obsolete materials, methods, or procedures.
- Operation and maintenance costs.
- Over the budget condition.
- Status of completion.
- Ability to complete the study on time.

To maximize the results of any VM study, projects must be selected at the proper time. The proper time for selecting a project for value study may be influenced by at least two factors: (1) the potential for obtaining the greatest savings, if implemented, and (2) the ease or difficulty of applying the VM methodology. Experience has shown that the greatest benefits have resulted when VM studies were undertaken after the preliminary submittal phase or just prior to start of the working drawings. This determination will vary from organization to organization and will depend on the timing of major design decisions. In any event, an examination of Figure 7.3 should be of assistance in the selection of a project for a VM study.

Figure 7.4 illustrates rather clearly that on a repetitive project the timing in the selection of such a project for VM study is not as accurate as in the prior instance unless, of course, it happens to be the last of a series of projects and is nearing completion.

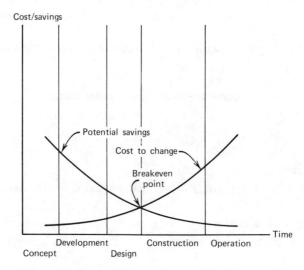

Figure 7.3 Potential for savings and breakeven point.

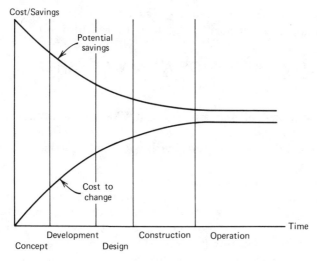

Figure 7.4   Potential for savings vs. cost to change.

7.6.1   INFORMATION REQUIRED FOR A VM WORKSHOP STUDY PROJECT

It is important to the success of any VM workshop to have available all necessary data prior to the start of the workshop. This will conserve valuable time and effort, as well as ensure unimpeded progress throughout the duration of this effort. Generally, the value manager is responsible for the conduct of the workshop and should be present from start to finish.

As a minimum, data required for the workshop should include:

- Complete and current graphic data including drawings, sketches, standards, supplier specifications, functional characteristics, and so on.
- Project specifications, pertinent guides, user requirements, technical manuals and references.
- Complete and detailed cost data.
- Special information relevant to historical data, design or construction status, schedules for design or construction.
- Anticipated volume or repetition of use for the present as well as the future.

- Names of information sources (responsible engineer or architect, design approval authority, and user representative).

7.6.2 COMPOSITION OF A VM WORKSHOP STUDY TEAM

The total number of participants in a VM workshop may vary for a variety of reasons. However, most value manager/instructors agree that the ideal size is 30 persons with varying expertise or background and experience.

The 30 participants should be grouped into teams of five, with special attention paid to the team mix. A typical team might consist of an engineer, architect, procurement specialist, and cost analyst. The mix can vary in some instances depending upon the type of organization. If an engineering consulting firm desired to train their engineers, then it would be proper to structure the teams so that one might consist of a civil engineer (soil mechanics as a specialty), structural engineer, electrical engineer, mechanical engineer, and chemical engineer. Once the teams have been organized and assigned their study projects they would be instructed in VM methodology and would follow the job plan step by step to completion in the form of a written VM proposal. The proposal should be in the format described in Chapter 8 to facilitate a prompt evaluation and decision by management.

7.7 SUMMARY

Value management workshops provide valuable training for those who actively participate; people learn by doing. That VM methodology has proven itself is evidenced by the many successful results throughout the federal, state, and local governments, as well as in the private sector. Properly planned, organized, and conducted, the VM workshop offers a twofold benefit for the organization that enthusiastically utilizes it—valuable training for personnel and a high return on investment. Actual VM studies are included in Chapter 12 for the reader's consideration.

Any organization desiring to establish a VM program or further develop its in-house capability would do well to invest in the professional services of a qualified, certified value consultant.

CHAPTER 8

VALUE MANAGEMENT METHODOLOGY

8.1 INTRODUCTION

The fundamentals of any VM study are identified as the concepts and evaluations of function, cost, and worth. An organized, systematic approach, commonly referred to as a job plan, must be employed to achieve maximum results. Various writers on the subject have depicted a variety of steps ranging from five to eight phases. The number of phases into which the VM study is divided is not as important here as the application of the methodology. This chapter will address the six-phase job plan approach shown in Figure 8.1.

8.2 FUNCTIONAL ANALYSIS SYSTEM TECHNIQUE (FAST)

Before discussing the job plan it is beneficial to first discuss the Functional Analysis System Technique (FAST). In 1964, Charles W. Bytheway, Value Engineering and Cost Reduction Administrator for UNIVAC, Salt Lake City, developed a technique that would show specific relationships of all functions with respect to others, test the validity of the functions, and thus enhance the functional analysis effort of the value management study or job plan. He named this technique Functional Analysis System Technique (FAST). This effective technique for logically identifying, developing, and analyzing the functions used in a VM study has been successfully applied by numerous large corporations, management consultants, and local, state, and federal governments, and is taught in some universities. This tech-

231

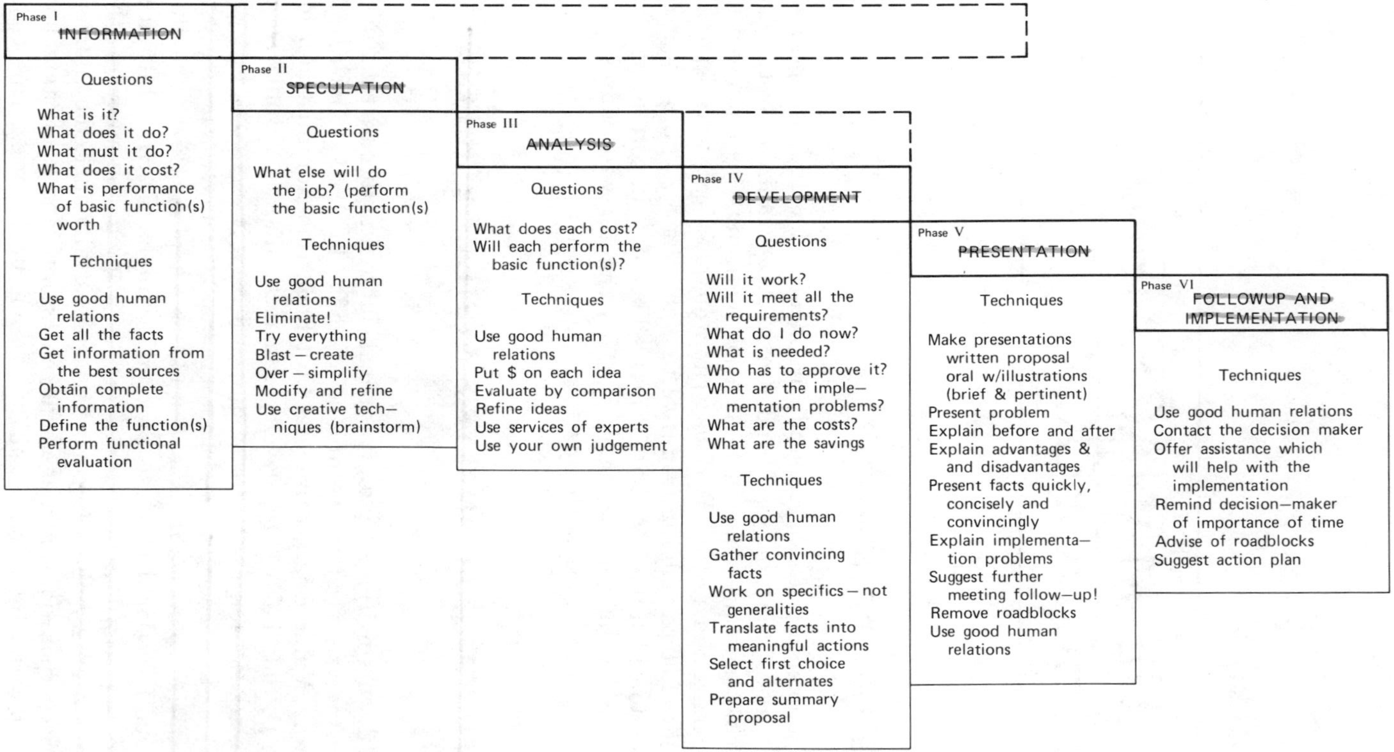

Figure 8.1 The job plan.

Phase I **INFORMATION**

Questions

What is it?
What does it do?
What must it do?
What does it cost?
What is performance
of basic function(s)
worth

Techniques

Use good human
relations
Get all the facts
Get information from
the best sources
Obtain complete
information
Define the function(s)
Perform functional
evaluation

Phase II **SPECULATION**

Questions

What else will do
the job? (perform
the basic function(s)

Techniques

Use good human
relations
Eliminate!
Try everything
Blast — create
Over — simplify
Modify and refine
Use creative tech—
niques (brainstorm)

Phase III **ANALYSIS**

Questions

What does each cost?
Will each perform the
basic function(s)?

Techniques

Use good human
relations
Put $ on each idea
Evaluate by comparison
Refine ideas
Use services of experts
Use your own judgement

Phase IV **DEVELOPMENT**

Questions

Will it work?
Will it meet all the
requirements?
What is needed?
What do I do now?
Who has to approve it?
What are the imple—
mentation problems?
What are the costs?
What are the savings

Techniques

Use good human
relations
Gather convincing
facts
Work on specifics — not
generalities
Translate facts into
meaningful actions
Select first choice
and alternates
Prepare summary
proposal

Phase V **PRESENTATION**

Techniques

Make presentations
written proposal
oral w/illustrations
(brief & pertinent)
Present problem
Explain before and after
Explain advantages &
and disadvantages
Present facts quickly,
concisely and
convincingly
Explain implementa—
tion problems
Suggest further
meeting follow—up!
Remove roadblocks
Use good human
relations

Phase VI **FOLLOWUP AND
IMPLEMENTATION**

Techniques

Use good human relations
Contact the decision maker
Offer assistance which
will help with the
implementation
Remind decision—maker
of importance of time
Advise of roadblocks
Suggest action plan

nique is important since functional analysis is recognized as the fulcrum of every VM study.

In essence, FAST is a method of stimulating organized thinking about any subject by asking thought-provoking questions. In these questions, the subject is expressed by a verb and a noun, together with an occasional modifier. In VM terms, this verb and noun combination is called a function. As the answers are agreed upon, they are arranged in a unique manner relative to each other on a diagram. The diagram thus formed is called a FAST diagram. *FAST diagrams,* then, are graphic representations of functional logic developed by in-depth functional investigation of the topic undergoing study.

FAST diagrams are used to communicate with subject matter experts; to understand the problems of users and of specialists in their own profession; to define, simplify, and clarify problems; to bound the scope of a problem; and to iterate the interrelated string of functions needed to provide a facility, product, or service.

However, it should be noted that the value of a completed FAST diagram is somewhat insignificant contrasted to the value of the thinking and creativity performed in developing the diagram. The important thing about a FAST diagram is that it demonstrates that the VM study group or committee has completely analyzed the subject or problem. Obviously, many different FAST diagrams may be charted on a given subject, depending on the method selected for performing each function. Usually only two diagrams are of interest—the diagram that represents an existing plan, program, or design, if any, and the diagram that represents the proposed concept.

FAST diagrams, since they show the relative importance of functions involved, may also be used as visual aids to orient people after the methods of performing the various functions have been agreed upon. They're handy; they're understandable; they're succinct. Before proceeding with examples of FAST diagramming, it is essential to examine definitions of the terms as they are used in this context.

FAST is a method of analyzing, organizing, and recording the functions of systems, products, plans, processes, procedures, facilities, supplies, and so on, to stimulate thinking and creativity.

A FAST diagram displays in an organized manner the functions of a project and their relationships to each other. It is created by applying the Functional Analysis System Technique.

A *function,* as it relates to FAST, is a required performance action described by a verb and a noun without identifying a specific method of performing the action. The method of performing the action is frequently found within the description of a subsequent action or function; therefore, a subsequent function often describes a method of performing a preceding function.

A *dependent function* is a function that depends on another higher order function for its existence. When a method is selected for performing one function, a dependent function may be brought into existence. These are also called secondary functions. A secondary function may be further classified as "esthetic," "wanted," or "unwanted."

An *independent function* is a function whose existence does not depend upon one or more other functions or the methods selected to perform those functions. It may be basic or secondary.

A *critical path function* is any function that sequentially describes how or why another function is performed. When searching for the critical path function to the right of a given function on a FAST diagram, ask "*How* is this function performed?" When searching for the critical path function to the left of a given function, ask "*Why* is this function performed?" Critical path functions usually refer to the sequence of functions that concludes in a basic function by asking "Why?" Those functions do not necessarily guarantee reliable performance or provide for all of the acceptability features, but they are considered to be essential if the basic function is to be performed, either momentarily or continuously, in the manner conceived. Supporting functions frequently are needed to achieve the required level of reliability and acceptability.

The *critical path logic* is the logic or reasoning process employed by an analyst in searching for critical path functions.

A *supporting function* is a function that assists a critical path function in doing its job in a reliable and acceptable manner. It is a function that exists because of the method selected for performing a critical path function.

A *higher level function* is a function that appears to the left of another function in a FAST diagram. The basic function, or highest level function, is located to the extreme left of the diagram.

A *lower level function* is a function that appears to the right of another function in a FAST diagram.

Creative hitchhiking is the process by which new ideas are generated by use of someone else's idea to stimulate creativity.

A *functional family tree* is a set of FAST diagrams for all basic functions of a product or service arranged in their order of sequential importance. A complete functional family tree is a compact method of FAST diagramming a complete system.

The *scope* or *limit* of a study includes everything up to and beyond that which is under study in order to focus attention on the chosen subject.

The *cost-function technique* is a technique of establishing a cost-function relationship. This technique:

Is a marriage of the cost visibility worksheet and the FAST diagram.
Identifies the amount of cost of doing basic function work.
Identifies functional areas that represent "poor value."
Points direction as to what work to do first, second, etc.

A skeletonized outline establishing ground rules for one type of FAST diagram is shown in Figure 8.2. Figure 8.3 is a FAST diagram prepared for an existing product—a light bulb. The reader will find it helpful to keep these two diagrams in mind while reading the following description of how to construct a FAST diagram.

1. *Use of the "How" question.* Determine the highest level function, write it on a small card about 2 inches by 3 inches, and place the card in front of you and to the left on a table or desk. Then insert the words describing this function into the question:

How is —————— actually accomplished or *how* is it proposed to be accomplished?

Now answer the question as specifically as you can, being as creative as possible. Record the results in functional form and keep track of each method conceived or considered while you record the results. If you are developing a FAST diagram for an existing system, determine the function that best describes the action performed in that system. If you are developing a FAST diagram for a proposed system, base the function on the method you consider to be the most promising. Write this function on another small card and place it on the table to the right of the card containing your basic function.

Observe that the skeletonized chart (Figure 8.2) indicates that all critical path functions answering "How" questions fall to the right of the function questioned. In the case of the light bulb (Figure 8.3), when we ask "How is providing luminous energy accomplished?," the team selected the answer "By producing light." (Note that the method a person is thinking of to perform a given critical path function would usually appear in the second succeeding function block. The object is for a team member to record in the first succeeding function block a function that does not disclose the method he is thinking of. His answer, of course, will be a method also, but it will be nonrestrictive and thus have the potential of stimulating many different methods.)

2. *Establishing critical path functions.* Repeat the procedure outlined

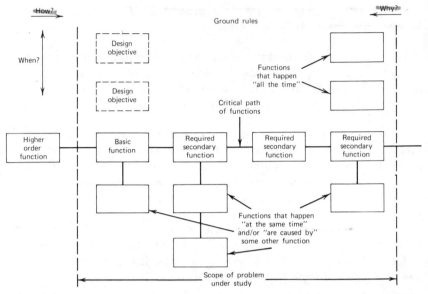

Figure 8.2   Ground Rules—Functional Analysis System Technique (FAST) diagram.

in step 1 for the function written on the second card. Repeat this for the third, fourth, etc., cards, each time placing the new function card to the right of the last card, until you feel you have adequately analyzed the subject under consideration. This row of functions is called the "critical path."

3. *Use of the "Why" question.* Check your row of critical path functions to see if they are correct by inserting the words describing the function at the far right into the question:

Why is it necessary to _____?

The answer to this question should be the same as the function located on the card at its left. As each answer is verified, it, in turn, is inserted into the question:

Why is it necessary to _____?

This is repeated again and again until all critical path functions have been verified. If any critical path function is wrong, repeat the first two steps. If the function that created your basic function is desired, you can obtain it by inserting the words that describe the basic

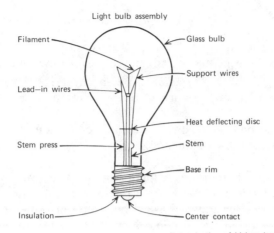

Light bulb assembly

Filament

Glass bulb

Support wires

Lead—in wires

Heat deflecting disc

Stem press

Stem

Base rim

Insulation

Center contact

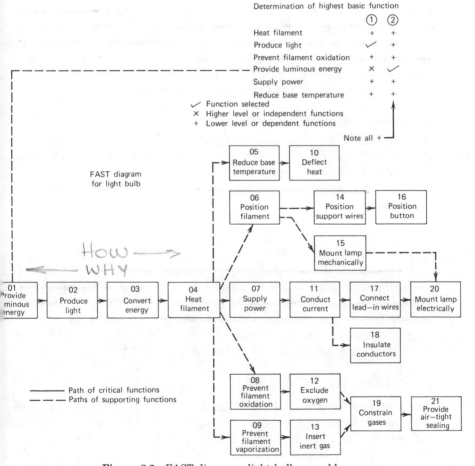

Determination of highest basic function

	①	②
Heat filament	+	+
Produce light	✓	+
Prevent filament oxidation	+	+
Provide luminous energy	✗	✓
Supply power	+	+
Reduce base temperature	+	+

✓ Function selected
✗ Higher level or independent functions
+ Lower level or dependent functions

Note all +

FAST diagram
for light bulb

HOW →
← WHY

Path of critical functions
Paths of supporting functions

05 Reduce base temperature
10 Deflect heat

06 Position filament
14 Position support wires
16 Position button

15 Mount lamp mechanically

01 Provide luminous energy
02 Produce light
03 Convert energy
04 Heat filament
07 Supply power
11 Conduct current
17 Connect lead—in wires
20 Mount lamp electrically

18 Insulate conductors

08 Prevent filament oxidation
12 Exclude oxygen

09 Prevent filament vaporization
13 Insert inert gas

19 Constrain gases
21 Provide air—tight sealing

Figure 8.3 FAST diagram—light bulb assembly.

237

function into the question, "Why is it necessary to _____?" This question may be repeated if still higher level functions are desired.

4. *Finding supporting functions.* When the critical path functions have been verified, insert each of these functions into the question:

Does the method selected to _____ cause any supporting functions to come into existence?

and determine whether any supporting functions are required and what the supporting functions are. List these on cards also. Supporting functions guarantee that the basic function is performed momentarily, repeatedly, or continuously, depending on the requirements. [Observe that the skeletonized chart (Figure 8.2) indicates that functions that happen "all the time" are placed above the critical path and functions that happen "at the same time" and/or "are caused by" some other function are usually placed below the critical path.] The method selected for performing a critical path function frequently creates problems that cannot be solved merely by performing a critical path analysis. Supporting functions solve these problems, thus permitting the system to be as reliable as possible.

5. *Critical path for supporting functions.* Next, generate a row of critical path functions for each supporting function listed and locate these on your FAST diagram.

6. *Use of the "What" or "Who" question.* Now insert each function into the question:

What or who actually _____?

and determine who or what performs that function. Write your answers immediately below each appropriate function. The cost of performing each function can then be determined by estimating the time, material, labor, overhead, etc., involved for each entry. These costs may be assigned to each function so that in the future you may apply your greatest effort to the areas that are the most costly.

Brainstorming the Diagram

As a final creativity stimulator, determine by the use of the techniques described in Chapter 9 whether a given part can be modified so that it can perform several functions. The method is also covered in considerable detail in Bytheway's paper entitled "Simplifying Complex Mechanisms During Research and Development," presented at the 1968

SAVE National Conference in Atlanta, Georgia, and published in the Conference Proceedings. This paper demonstrates how 16 of the 17 parts identified were eliminated from a timing mechanism.

The preceding paragraphs point up the fact that FAST diagrams are as varied as the persons creating them; hence, the rules for their preparation and the techniques used are flexible. However, they all parallel the general ground rules and as you become more familiar with constructing FAST diagrams, you will learn to tailor them to your specific needs. Typical uses of FAST diagrams are illustrated in the references cited at the end of this chapter.

Functional analysis is the fulcrum of every value management study. The skill and creativity with which functions are explored determine, to a large degree, the results achieved and consequently the success or failure of any VM study.

FAST is a structured method of function analysis that results in defining the basic function and establishing the critical path functions, supporting functions, and unnecessary functions.

FAST diagrams should be constructed at a level low enough to be useful but high enough to be advantageous to your purpose of creatively seeking alternative methods.

FAST diagrams are excellent tools for controlling or managing a system.

The FAST procedure will be useful only if the thinking outlined in the steps is performed. The value of this technique is found not in recording the obvious but in the extension of thinking beyond the usual habits as the study proceeds. FAST diagrams, as first constructed, may not completely comply with How and Why logic. This is because it takes additional thinking to get everything to agree. However, if you are persistent and insist that the logic be adhered to, you will discover that understanding has expanded and creativity has led you into avenues that would otherwise have been left unpursued. When the How and Why logic is not satisfied, it suggests that either a function is missing or that the function under investigation is a supporting function and not in the critical path.

The basic reason for extensive functional analysis is to visualize the project more clearly in its true light. Once you perform an extensive functional analysis on a given project, you can quickly see that the only reason a lower level function has to be performed is that a higher level function caused it to come into being. Essentially, whenever we establish one of these functional relationships that is visually presented by a FAST diagram, we correct our ignorance factor and open the door to greater creativity.

8.3 THE JOB PLAN

The job plan contains a systematic procedure for accomplishing all the necessary tasks associated with a value management study. Adherence to a definite plan is essential to obtaining the best value alternatives. The key features separating the job plan from other cost reduction techniques are functional analysis, use of creativity to develop multiple alternatives, and the principle of maintaining the necessary quality to meet the user's needs. As in any other problem-solving situation, a systematic approach will produce better results than undisciplined ingenuity. Use of the job plan will provide:

A vehicle to carry the study from inception to conclusion.
A convenient basis for maintaining a written record of the effort as it progresses.
Assurance that consideration has been given to facts that may have been neglected in the creation of the original design.
A logical separation of the study into units that can be planned, scheduled, budgeted, and assessed.

Although the job plan is described as six precise and distinct phases, these six phases tend to overlap or merge as shown by Figure 8.1. Some studies may require recycling through several phases of the job plan. The six phases are as follows:

1. The information phase (for information gathering).
2. The speculation phase (for the generation of alternatives).
3. The analysis phase (for the evaluation of alternatives).
4. The development phase (for development of firm proposals).
5. The presentation phase (for presentation to a decision-making authority).
6. The followup and implementation phase (for obtaining a management commitment of resources to implement).

The Information Phase
(Gathering of Information—Phase I)

The first phase of the job plan has two basic objectives:

1. To obtain a thorough understanding of the system, structure, or item under study, by a rigorous review of all pertinent factual data.

(The complexity of the system, structure, or item under study, the amount of information available, and the study schedule will all bear upon the level of effort devoted to the information phase in a particular study.)

2. To ~~define the value problem~~ by means of functional description(s) accompanied by an estimate of the worth of accomplishing the basic function(s).

KEY QUESTIONS TO ANSWER.

1. ~~What is it?~~
2. ~~What does it do?~~
3. ~~What must it do?~~
4. ~~What does it cost?~~
5. ~~What is performance of the basic function(s) worth?~~

TECHNIQUES USED. The matter of ~~human relations~~ is of utmost importance to the success of any VM study. "People problems" are usually more difficult to resolve than technical problems. The effectiveness of a value manager's efforts depends on the amount of cooperation he is able to obtain from engineers, designers, estimators, managers, and others. A value manager who has an adroit approach, is diplomatic when resolving opposing viewpoints and tactful in questioning a design requirement or specification, will minimize the problems of obtaining the cooperation needed to do his or her job effectively.

All pertinent facts concerning the system, structure, or item must be drawn together. These include information regarding (1) ~~the item~~, (2) ~~item performance~~, (3) ~~present cost~~, (4) ~~quality and reliability requirements~~, and (5) ~~development and user history~~. All aspects of the item must be questioned: how it is constructed, or how it is made, shipped, fabricated, and installed, and how it is repaired, operated, and replaced. Data must be collected from a variety of sources, such as drawings, specifications, planning documents, criteria, engineering manuals, fabrication and test data, material lists, estimates, and maintenance manuals. It is often helpful if the items can be observed in field use. The ~~paramount considerations~~ are (1) ~~getting all the facts~~, (2) ~~getting them from the best sources~~, and (3) ~~separating facts from assumptions~~.

OBTAIN COMPLETE INFORMATION. The VM team should gather complete information consistent with the study schedule. All relevant information is important, regardless of how disorganized or unrelated it may seem when gathered. Wait until all facts have been gathered before organizing them. The data gathered should be supported by tangible evidence in the form of copies of all appropriate documents. Where supported facts are not obtainable, the opinions of knowledgeable personnel will have to act as a substitute. Some of the types of data that are required during a VM study are:

1. Complete and up-to-date graphic data, including any drawings, sketches, and standards pertinent to the study. However, drawings should be kept to the minimum number actually necessary for the study.

2. Complete and up-to-date specifications, and any pertinent local guides/codes as well as technical manuals.

3. Complete and detailed cost figures—the best available.

4. Special information, including relevant historical data; status of design or construction; schedules for design and construction; and any pertinent customer or user requirements.

5. Persons to be consulted including responsible engineer(s); design approval authority; and customer/user.

6. The anticipated volume or repetition of use for the present and future.

In addition to specific knowledge of the item, it is essential to have all available information concerning the technologies involved and to be aware of the latest technical developments pertinent to the item being reviewed. Knowledge of the various manufacturing, fabrication, or construction processes that may be employed in production of the item is essential. The more information that is brought to bear on the problem, the more likely is the possibility of a substantial cost reduction. Having all the above information would be the ideal situation, but if all of this information is not available, it should not preclude the performance of a successful VM study effort.

Determine the Function(s)

The determination of function(s) is a requisite for all value studies. Emphasis should be placed on the use and esthetic functions being performed by the item. The decision to pursue the project through the remaining phases of the job plan can only be made by determining function(s), classifying the function, and evaluating its worth against actual or estimated cost. The determination of function(s) should take place as soon as sufficient information is available to permit determination of true requirements. All members of the VM study team should participate in this exercise, since the determination of required function(s) is vital to the subsequent phases of the job plan.

Evaluate the Function(s)

After the functional description has been developed, the next step is to estimate the worth of performing the basic function(s). Remember, we are seeking to determine the approximate appropriate costs of each basic function. The worth determined should be compared against the estimate of the item's cost. The comparison indicates whether the study should be terminated because worth and cost are approximately equal, or pursued because cost greatly exceeds worth.

THE INFORMATION PHASE CHECKLIST. The following is an excellent checklist to assure that all needed information has been collected and recorded during the information phase:

1. Do you have all relevant background historical information?
2. Have you checked future use requirements?
3. What is the status of design?
4. What items are used on other designs?
5. Who has design approval authority?
6. Have you reviewed all specification and criteria requirements?
7. Did you double check for multiple-use items?
8. Have you listed high-cost items?
9. Have you checked for unnecessary requirements and features?
10. Are there unnecessarily tight tolerances?
11. Have you checked for high-cost materials, labor, and construction methods?
12. Did you check for costly operation and maintenance?
13. Have you secured the best, up-to-date cost information available?

The Speculation Phase
(Generation of Alternatives—Phase II)

OBJECTIVE. The objective of this phase of the job plan is to generate by creative techniques numerous alternative means for accomplishing the basic function(s). Consideration of alternative solutions should *not* formally begin until the problem is thoroughly understood. As soon as required functions have been identified, speculation upon alternatives can start. All members of the VM study team should participate, for the greater the number of ideas conceived the more likely that equally effective, less costly alternatives will be among them. Be alert to the fact that it is a normal tendency to defend the current design rather than speculate on a possible new design. A proper frame of mind is important at this stage of the study; creative thinking should replace the conventional. It should be a unique flight of the imagination undertaken to generate numerous alternative methods of providing the necessary function(s). Judicial thinking does not belong in this phase and should be strenuously precluded. As an aid to speculative thought, the techniques of creative thinking, such as brainstorming, should be employed along with the technique of "blast, create, and refine." Every attempt should be made during this phase to depart from ordinary patterns, typical solutions, and habitual methods. Experience indicates that it is often the new, fresh, and radically different approach that uncovers the best value solution(s). The individual or group members may supplement their ideas with those of others—everyone is expected to contribute. However, it is only in the individual brain that new ideas are developed. The best solution may be complete elimination of the present function or item. This possibility should *not* be overlooked during the initial phases of this step. Perhaps some aspect can be modified to permit elimination of the function under study. Only after determining that the function must remain should the study group look for alternative ways to perform the same function at the lowest conceivable cost. Free use of imagination is encouraged so that all possible solutions are considered.

KEY QUESTION. The speculation phase answers the question, "What else will do the job (perform the basic function(s))?" The completeness and comprehensiveness of the answer to this question determines, to a very high degree, the effectiveness and caliber of value work. The greater the number and quality of alternatives uncovered, the greater the likelihood of developing an outstanding solution. Additional alternatives that have not been considered will usually exist regardless of the skill and proficiency of the study team.

TECHNIQUES USED. Blast, Create, and Refine. Blast—tear apart the present design to its most elementary form. Create—really reach for unusual ideas; build a new design in place of the original. Refine—strengthen or add to develop an idea to perform the basic function(s) in a new and unique manner.

Functional Comparison—What Are Other Means of Performing the Basic Function(s)? Conduct a creative problem-solving session (brainstorming) in which new and unusual contributions of known things or processes are combined and/or rearranged to provide different ways of performing the basic function(s).

Simple Comparison (With the Study Item). Conduct a thorough search for other items that are similar in at least one significant characteristic to the study item. Determine if they can be modified to satisfy the basic function(s).

Scientific Factors (Application of New Disciplines). Conduct a search for other scientific disciplines capable of performing the same basic function(s). This involves interviewing specialists in disciplines that did not previously contribute to solving the problem. An industry (or its representatives) that specializes in some highly skilled technique(s) often can make a substantial contribution when they are called upon for technical assistance.

GOOD HUMAN RELATIONS. As in the information phase, the use of good human relations is of considerable importance to the success of the speculation phase. Ideas will flow in on environment where team members are encouraged to think imaginatively without fear of immediate ridicule or rejection.

THE SPECULATION PHASE CHECKLIST. The following listed items are suggested for use to stimulate and trigger ideas.

- Can it be eliminated?
- Can a change in design reduce operation and/or maintenance costs?
- Can construction methods or procedures be simplified?
- Can specification requirements be eliminated or modified?
- Can a standard part or commercial product be used?
- Can we improve the sequence of construction?
- Is there a less costly part, product, or method that will satisfy the function?
- Can two or more parts be combined into one?
- Do we need the present shape, size, or weight?
- Are features that improve appearance justified?
- Can less expensive materials be used?

- Can we reduce the energy consumption?
- Can less costly surface coatings or surface preparation be used?
- Can soldering or welding be eliminated?
- Can connectors or connections be standardized?
- Would a coarser finish be adequate?
- Can tolerances be relaxed?
- Can a fastener be used to eliminate tapping?
- Have you considered newly developed materials?

The Analysis Phase
(Evaluation of Alternatives—Phase III)

The objective of this phase is to evaluate, criticize, and test the alternatives generated during the speculation phase, with the ultimate objective of determining which alternatives offer the greatest potential for cost savings and the lowest risk to the decision maker. During speculation there is a conscious effort to prohibit any judicial thinking so as to not inhibit the creative process. Now the alternatives must be critically evaluated.

KEY QUESTIONS. What does each alternative cost? Will each perform the basic function(s)?

TECHNIQUES USED. Put a Dollar Sign on Each Alternative. The first step in the analysis phase is to assign a gross dollar cost to each alternative generated during the speculation phase. Alternatives are then ranked according to cost savings potential.

Evaluate by Comparison. The second step in the evaluation process is to judge as objectively as possible the advantages and disadvantages of each alternative. No alternative should be discarded without preliminary evaluation. This initial analysis will produce a shorter list of alternatives, each of which has passed the evaluation standards set by the team. Areas that require further investigation should be determined at this time and recorded.

Refine Alternatives. The alternatives that survive are refined further to obtain more detailed cost estimates from sketches, etc. The cost estimating for each alternative proceeds only if the preceding step indicates that the alternative is still a good candidate. Although evaluation is the responsibility of the VE study team, others should be consulted for help in estimating the potential of these alternatives. Cost estimates must be as complete, accurate, and consistent as possible to minimize the possibility of errors during the assessment of the relative economic potential of the alternatives. Specifically, the method which is used to cost the original or present method also should be used to cost the alternatives.

Select Alternatives for Further Development. After the detailed cost estimates have been developed for the remaining alternatives, one or more are selected for further study, refinement, testing, information gathering, and evaluation in the Development Phase. Normally, the alternatives with the greatest cost reduction potential will be selected. However, if differences among several alternatives are not decisive at this point, they should all be developed further.

THE ANALYSIS PHASE CHECKLIST.

- Does the alternative conserve manpower, energy, or material?
- Does it improve construction methods, maintenance, or operation of the facility?
- Can you combine the best two or more of the feasible alternatives?
- Did you develop and compare costs for all feasible alternatives?
- Have you double-checked the requirements and your computations?
- Can you further simplify or combine the feasible alternatives?
- Have you reviewed the feasible alternatives with specialists?
- Does the alternative reduce risk to the decision-maker?

The Development Phase
(Development of Firm Proposals—Phase IV)

OBJECTIVE. The objective of this phase is to develop final written recommendations for the surviving alternative(s). The process involves not only detailed technical and economic evaluation but also consideration of the probability of successful implementation. The alternative(s) are investigated in sufficient depth to enable the development of specific recommendations for implementation.

KEY QUESTION. Will the alternative(s) meet all necessary requirements?

TECHNIQUES USED. General. In order to satisfy the key question above, the alternative(s) must be subjected to the following:

Careful analysis to insure that the user's needs are satisfied.
A determination of technical adequacy.
The development of accurate estimates of costs, implementation expenses, and schedules, including schedules and costs of conducting all necessary tests and evaluation.

Develop Accurate and Complete Data. All pertinent cost figures and technical information should be obtained. Any technical problems must be determined with cognizant personnel concerning what the item must do, within what constraints it must perform, how dependable it must be, and under what environmental conditions it must operate. In addition, any problems related to design, fabrication, construction, implementation, or operation and maintenance must be determined.

Develop Actions Required. The VM study team may arrange the necessary testing and evaluation, although normally this will be done by personnel in the appropriate organization. Library searching may be needed; detailed computer operations may be involved. Pilot tests, or even full-scale field tests, may be required. Normally, full-scale testing is not a part of this process, but if tests are necessary to demonstrate technical feasibility, they are performed before the alternatives are recommended for implementation. Since the new design will usually have to be fabricated or constructed, an important part of this phase is to draw up sketches of the proposed redesign. The sketch is also useful when obtaining additional information concerning the alternative(s) to be recommended when the technical aspects of particular alternatives are well established, detailed, and accurate. Problems relative to implementation should be anticipated and answers secured to as many such problems as possible. Conferences with specialists in areas such as the following are most helpful:

Engineering personnel.
Legal counsel.
Materials specialists.
Cost estimating personnel.
Construction/operations/supply/safety.
Procurement personnel.

Select First Choice. Finally, one alternative is selected for implementation as the best value alternative, and one or more other alternatives are selected for presentation in the event the first choice is rejected by the approval authority. The implementation schedule that will yield the greatest cost reduction should also be specified.

Prepare Written Recommendations. The formal written report is prepared in a summary book and covers the study results and recommendations. The report summarizes the results of the investigation, recommends specific action, and requests implementation approval from those responsible for making the decision. It should include: (1) the identity of the project; (2) a brief summary of the problem, before-and-after descriptions, and cost of the original design; (3) the estimated cost of the alternatives; (4) technical data supporting the alternatives; (5) quantity requirements; (6) the cost of implementing the changes; (7) a summary of the potential savings; (8) a list of actions necessary for implementation; (9) acknowledgment of contributions; and (10) a suggested implementation schedule.

THE DEVELOPMENT PHASE CHECKLIST.

- Does each alternative provide the necessary performance requirements?
- Are quality requirements met by each alternative?
- Are reliability, maintainability, and operational requirements met by each alternative?
- Will each alternative prevent waste of labor, material, or time?
- Is each alternative compatible with the overall design?
- Are safety requirements met by each alternative?
- Have accurate cost comparisons been developed for alternative(s) and the original design?
- Does each alternative improve construction methods, operation, or maintenance?
- Has someone double-checked the quantities and costs used in the calculations?
- Have all supporting data been documented?
- Are the estimated net savings correct?
- Has the proposal been reviewed to ensure that diminishing returns have not drastically reduced the potential savings?

- Has the first choice been selected?
- Are there additional alternatives to be proposed?
- Does the proposal present all the facts clearly, concisely, and convincingly?
- Do the alternatives have an environmental effect?

The Presentation Phase
(Presentation of VM Proposal—Phase V)

OBJECTIVE. The objective of this phase is to ~~present the VM study report to the decision makers~~. The report includes a statement of the followup necessary to ensure implementation. The presentation may be in written form as in the summary book or both written and oral.

TECHNIQUES USED. ~~Human Relations (Gaining Cooperation)~~. The best value management proposal ever written is a wasted effort if the proposal is rejected by management. The effective value manager must be able to see the "big picture"; must be able to see the problem through the eyes of management; must be a salesman, a psychologist, an engineer, an opportunist, and a student of human nature; and, above all, must be sincere in the belief that the proposal will result in real savings. There may be a number of excellent technical reasons for not implementing a change proposal, or the reason may be purely personal and emotional. It is up to the value manager to determine the real reasons, and if the reasons are based on personal beliefs, he should take the necessary actions to overcome individual biases and established work patterns. Generally speaking, cooperation problems are caused by insecurity, habitual or negative thinking, fear, wrong beliefs, ignorance, laziness, self-defense, pressure of time schedules, reluctance to seek outside advice, and undesirable habits. The decision maker assumes the responsibility and the risk if a poor decision is made. Fear of change is very real. ~~It is the job of the value manager to identify the problem and gain cooperation through tactful advice, a diplomatic approach, and logical reasoning, thus reducing the probability of failure.~~

　~~Use Specifics, Not Generalities~~. The danger inherent in a generalized statement is that if one exception can be found, the statement is proven wrong. If the proposal depends upon a generalized statement, the validity of the entire study may be doubted. ~~Be brief and pertinent. Present the facts clearly, concisely, and convincingly.~~ If assumptions must be used, they should be clearly labeled as such.

The Oral Presentation. An oral presentation is most helpful for presenting the report to the individuals making the decision or those responsible for implementation. The oral presentation should include, but not necessarily be limited to, the following:

Identification of the project studied.
Brief summary of the problem.
Description of original design.
Cost of original design.
Results of the functional analysis.
Technical data supporting selection of the alternative(s).
Cost data supporting the alternative(s).
Explanation of advantages and disadvantages and reasons for accepting the alternative(s).
Sketches of before-and-after design, clearly depicting proposed changes. (Drawings marked to show proposed changes are acceptable.)
Problems and cost of implementation.
Estimated net savings.
Acknowledgment of contribution by others.
A summary statement, which may suggest a meeting to discuss the proposal further.

THE PRESENTATION PHASE CHECKLIST.

• Is the summary book complete and accurate?
• Has someone double-checked the recommendations, costs, and savings?
• Is all the information complete?
• Has someone prepared backup material for questions that may be asked?
• Can the use of mockups or models help sell the proposal?
• Can the use of visual equipment be of assistance?

The Followup and Implementation Phase (Obtain a Commitment of Resources to Implement— Phase VI)

Even after formal presentation, the objectives of a VM study have not been fully attained. The recommendations must be converted into actions; hence, those who performed the study must maintain an active interest until the proposal is fully operational. The continued interest or followup has three major objectives:

1. To provide assistance, clear up misconceptions, and resolve problems that may develop in the implementation process.

2. To minimize delays encountered by the proposal in the implementation process.

3. To audit actual results for comparison with what originally had been expected.

Where unexplained delays are encountered, a polite followup note or telephone call may serve as a reminder to the responsible authority that those who made the study are available for assistance and that savings are being lost because of the delay in implementing the proposal. A VM proposal should not die because of inaction in the implementation process. Instead, implementation should be monitored until it is complete. If management approves the VM study, then it should simultaneously commit resources to ensure its timely implementation.

8.4 SUMMARY OF THE JOB PLAN

Purpose

The job plan can be applied to any subject suitable for study. It provides a logical plan to carry the study from inception to conclusion. By avoiding excessive informality, it assures that proper consideration has been given to all necessary facets of the study. The job plan divides the study into sets of work elements or phases. Judgment is required in determining the depth to which each phase is performed. All plans must be made in light of the resources available and the results expected. The job plan requires those making the study to clearly define the function(s) performed by the item under study. It provides the study team with a plan for securing all of the information needed to successfully accomplish the study. Following the job plan assures that time is made available to create the maximum number of alternatives to thoroughly analyze the creative work so that superior choices can be made for further development. It leads those making the study to establish an effective program for selecting recommendations, data supporting these recommendations, the identification of actions necessary to implement these recommendations, a proposed implementation schedule, and a summary of the benefits.

Sequence

The job plan will normally be followed in sequence, phase by phase. However, in actual practice, it is frequently necessary to return to a previously completed phase for additional work before reaching a decision. A team may be working on two or more phases at the same time. Thus, in practice, the phases may overlap broadly, and the early steps such as information gathering may continue throughout most of the study effort.

CHAPTER 9

CREATIVITY—
THE BACKBONE
OF VALUE MANAGEMENT

9.1 INTRODUCTION

Much has been written about creativity, and yet it remains a subject of much discussion among educators and other professionals concerned with innovation, the creative process, and the development of more creative people. Value management requires the use of creative problem-solving techniques. Creativity is necessary to discover alternative designs, construction methods, systems, or processes that will accomplish the required function at the lowest overall cost. Creative thinking should be used in all phases of construction management, from the formulation of the basic user requirements and criteria through design, development, and execution of the project. Creativity in value management relates primarily to the speculation phase of the VM job plan discussed in Chapter 8. Creative thinking techniques are designed to be used as aids in seeking solutions to existing problems. They are designed not to replace but to supplement traditional methods of problem solving.

9.2 DEFINITION

Creativity is one of those divine attributes that all people possess to some degree. It is the single characteristic that has made humans unique and superior to all other forms of life on earth. It has contributed immeasurably to our accomplishments in harnessing the forces

254

and resources of nature to the benefit of humanity throughout the world.

The dictionary definition of create is simply "to bring into being; make; originate." It therefore follows that creativity is the development of new ideas that will satisfy an expressed or implied requirement.

9.3 HYPOTHESES CONCERNING CREATIVITY

John E. Arnold, in an article in *The Creative Engineer,* cited four hypotheses concerning man's creative potential. They are:

1. All men are born with a very definite, though limited potential for creative work.

2. This creative potential is at least partially independent of any other mental potential we have. (The three basic mental potentials are: (1) analytical or deductive, as measured by IQ tests; (2) creative or synthetic; and (3) judicial, the ability to judge and evaluate.)

3. The creative process is itself unique; that is, it is the same whether it expresses itself in art, music, literature, engineering, or another form.

4. Individual creative potential can be realized through training and exercise.

In value management, assistance in achieving increased realization of each individual's creative potential is predicated on the assumption that Arnold's fourth hypothesis is valid.

9.4 ATTRIBUTES OF CREATIVE INDIVIDUALS

Many studies by different researchers have identified numerous attributes of creative individuals. One such author, Eugene Raudsepp, identified 30 attributes of the creative engineer. He divided them into mental and emotional categories. The more important attributes are listed as follows:

A. *Mental Attributes*
   1. High Sensitivity to Needs or Problem Demonstrated
      a. Keen observation
      b. Inquisitiveness

   c. Constructive discontent

   d. Healthy skepticism

   e. States questions and problems so they do not limit or confine his thinking.

2. Fluency of Thought. A measure of output of ideas per unit of time; closely coupled with the ability to restrain judicial thinking.

3. Flexibility

   a. Effects quick and frequent reorientation of approaches.

   b. Can toy with elements and concepts.

   c. Can juggle elements into seemingly impossible juxtapositions.

   d. Can formulate wild hypotheses, express the ridiculous.

4. Originality. Ability to associate unrelated ideas and things and synthesize them into new, unique combinations.

5. Imagination. "Imagination is more important than knowledge"—A. Einstein.
Imagination can be divided into two general categories—controllable and uncontrollable. Only the controllable contributes to creative ability. The uncontrollable leads to extreme neurosis and psychosis. The controllable types can be further subdivided into three categories:

   a. Visual imagery. Includes structural visualization, ability to reproduce or recall images, etc.

   b. Hypothetical ideation. The ability to formulate hypotheses from observed conditions or data.

   c. Ability to think in analogies. Aristotle felt no other ability could better convey an individual's creative stature. In the technical field, analogical constructs have been indispensable tools for discovery and invention. They form the bridge that unites novel ideas with old conceptual frameworks.

6. Fundamental Knowledge. It is necessary to understand basic laws, concepts, and relationships. It enables one to search through widely scattered fields, taking basic information from one and applying it to a problem in another.

7. Curiosity. The creative individual not only maintains an active curiosity in how things work; he has an insatiable appetite for discovery, which forces him to delve into the reason-why of phenomena, into the cause/effect relationships. He also has a wide spectrum of interests that embraces many diverse fields and areas.

B. *Emotional Attributes*
1. Openness to Experience (Existential Orientation). Each stimulus is freely related through the nervous system without being distorted by any process of psychological defensiveness.
2. Internal Locus of Evaluation. The value of his output is, for the creative person, established not by the praise or criticism of others but by himself.
3. Self-Confidence. He has confidence in his own ability to find a new and better solution and the willingness to take a chance. He must overcome the fear of making mistakes.
4. Motivation. A strong desire or need to create is considered basic to creative performance. An individual must be interested in attacking a problem. Highly creative individuals are not only interested in work, but obtain relief from tension by engaging in it. They are characterized by strong inner drive or compulsiveness.
5. Tolerance for Ambiguity. Engineers and scientists have strong preferences for order. The vagueness, the seemingly irresponsible, uncertain groping that is characteristic of the creative process is a frightening, uncomfortable feeling to him. But, at the right time in the process, a certain amount of temporary ambiguity and disorder is desirable in order to perceive all the implications and possibilities inherent in the situation.

A common fallacy is the belief that highly creative people are, in general, either extremely neurotic or just emotionally unstable. To support such a belief, the emotional problems and eccentricities of a few artists, composers, scientists, and educators in history are usually cited. However, if one is rational and considers again the attributes of a creative individual, which have been identified heretofore, one must conclude that these attributes are not only highly desirable, but that they contribute to one's psychological well-being.

9.5 NEGATIVE FACTORS AFFECTING CREATIVITY

It has been said that the lack of creative problem-solving ability in most people is not so much due to the absence of creative potential as it is to the negative factors affecting creativity. These factors can be broadly categorized as internal and external.

9.5.1 INTERNAL

Internal factors can be classified into three main types: perceptual, cultural, and emotional. Perceptual factors relate to the methods by which we obtain, or fail to obtain, pertinent information regarding the outside world. These factors can be barriers to obtaining true, reliable, adequate, and relevant information. It may simply be a case of failing to use all the senses of observation or to investigate the obvious. When a familiar problem or item is presented, the usual reaction is that it does not present a challenge, since everyone knows or should know that the task in question has always been done or accomplished in a particular manner. Another form of perceptual barrier may be in the form of failure to distinguish between cause and effect or in visualizing remote relationships or simply in defining the problem and its terms succinctly enough that isolation of the real problem becomes unmistakably clear.

Cultural factors are usually those that have their roots in our environment and heritage. They are the result of education, morals, and customs of our society. They are influenced by prevailing religious, political, and sociological beliefs and values; they are closely tied in one way or another to emotional influences.

Emotional factors may vary between individuals, but most research in this area appears to have some commonality worthy of mention. If an idea is unique or original, it is vulnerable to criticism and the one who proposes it may be called foolish. If the proposer is overly sensitive to this type of treatment by colleagues, it will inhibit his free-thinking and end further creative accomplishment.

The most common cause of poor motivation in an organization is the failure of top management to provide a proper climate for creativity. Most organizations are profit motivated; this by itself cannot be criticized. However, when the organization fails to establish reasonable creativity goals and environmental conditions and concentrates solely on profit-making, it restricts the scientist or engineer to a rather narrow field of consideration. In such a situation, many avenues leading to more novel and better solutions will be ignored for the sake of finding a more expedient and obviously relevant solution to introduce into the market.

Most of us become victims of habit, and with the passage of time we become stagnant. Familiar patterns, approaches, and procedures become the acceptable and easy way of performing our work. We gain a false sense of security, a belief that the established method is foolproof and that there is no better way. Such a belief, if not corrected in time, is a straight path to eventual failure and extinction of creativity.

Not to be overlooked as a deterrent to creativity is the ability to challenge and even reject decisions that appear to possess authoritative validity but less than optimum value. Dependence on authoritative judgment and approaches frequently stifles potential creativity.

9.5.2   EXTERNAL

External factors tending to inhibit creativity are many. Some will never be known; however, some are frequently recognized by researchers in this field of interest. To be different from someone else or to conduct outselves differently, although within the realm of reason and the law, singles one out as an "oddball." Our society forces all toward conformity. Such a condition stifles creativity and forces a "no-change" condition.

In most organizations, control procedures are established to ensure stability and a smooth operation. Such controls, if rigidly enforced, will also inhibit innovation toward improvement.

Many business managers do not understand creativity or creative people and therefore are very apprehensive about entertaining any recommendations that may provide a more creative atmosphere and improve operations in the long run. Such managers may deny that they are not interested in change for the better; they may even cite occasions where they supported such programs as the "suggestion program." In reality, these managers are more concerned with the immediate situation and the marketability of products or services that reflect an immediate return. Excessive management emphasis on the immediate market situation and profit tends to narrow the creative problem-solver's sphere, thus curtailing motivation and productivity.

Other considerations that influence creative potential are reflected in management's failure to recognize and reward any creative endeavor that results in increased benefits. Fragmentation of work, particularly in large organizations, cuts one off from the end result and precludes creative effort because identification with the "big picture" is lost. Finally, incentives must be made available by management for those who produce good ideas; they must be protected from those supervisors or managers who are willing to accept credit that is not theirs.

9.6 POSITIVE FACTORS AFFECTING CREATIVITY

Perhaps the most important factor necessary for the development of creative effort is provision and maintenance of a conducive atmosphere for the creative endeavor. In value management, supervisors and managers at every level of organization must constantly be aware of the creative environment in their respective areas of responsibility. They must encourage subordinates to engage in creativity.

Some helpful hints toward a more creative atmosphere in an organization follow:

- Seek out the individual who has constructive ideas toward improvement even though those ideas may be radically opposed to organization policy.
- Evaluate *objectively* all recommendations.
- Modify those controls that tend to force conformity and restrict individual initiative.
- Encourage informal discussion groups that identify areas for improvement.
- Vary the degree of control over individuals and functional offices of the organization commensurate with assigned missions.
- Allow highly creative individuals freedom to manage their own task assignments.
- Allow individuals freedom to perform to their own professional standards and do not expect them to compromise those standards for the sake of short-range objectives.
- Permit individuals to complete tasks assigned without unnecessary changing of those assignments.
- Allow individuals to discuss decisions involving their work and voice their opinions regarding the selection of task assignments.
- Recognize that an environment that severely penalizes failure will encourage few or no attempts to innovate; for with innovation there is as much of an inherent risk of failure as there is chance of success.
- For creativity to flourish, one must also allow for flexibility in working hours, occasional relaxation without an attendant feeling of guilt, and freedom to communicate with colleagues both within and outside of the organization.
- Encourage and assist the creative individual in self-development through advanced education, participation in related symposiums, orientations, and group discussions.

- Promote self-control and direction in the individual by establishing mutually agreed upon goals that coincide with or are compatible with those of the organization.
- Organize special teams where free-thinking, constructive nonconformity and originality are pursued without organizational restriction.
- Endeavor to develop a high degree of group loyalty and mutual confidence and respect between management and employees.

The reason for the emphasis on the creative potential of people and organizations and why this potential is seldom realized is to encourage you as employees and managers to think in terms of creativity. The following paragraph by Dr. Carl Rogers in his paper "Toward a Theory of Creativity," which appears in Parnes and Harding's *A Source Book for Creative Thinking*, stresses the need for creativity.

Why be concerned over this? If, as a people, we enjoy conformity rather than creativity, shall we not be permitted this choice? In my estimation, such a choice would be entirely reasonable were it not for one great shadow which hangs over all of us. In a time when knowledge, constructive and destructive, is advancing by the most incredible leaps and bounds into a fantastic atomic age, genuinely creative adaptation seems to represent the only possibility that man can keep abreast of the kaleidoscopic change in his world. With scientific discovery and invention proceeding, we are told, at the rate of geometric progression, a generally passive and culture-bound people cannot cope with the multiplying issues and problems. Unless individuals, groups, and nations can imagine, construct, and creatively devise new ways of relating to these complex changes, the lights will go out. Unless man can make new and original adaptations to his environment as rapidly as his science can change the environment, our culture will perish. Not only individual maladjustment and group tensions, but international annihilation will be the price we pay for a lack of creativity.

9.7 CREATIVITY IN VALUE MANAGEMENT

Creativity in value management provides the key to highly successful results when vigorously pursued and properly applied. It identifies and recommends possible alternatives that management can adopt in solving specific problems.

Approaches to Problem Solving

There are at least two approaches to problem solving, analytical and creative. A discussion of both follows, with some helpful suggestions for applying them.

The strictly analytical approach is substantially singular in purpose. The problem is stated exactly. A direct approach to the solution is taken, proceeding through a step-by-step progression of experiments, evaluations, and mathematical manipulations to arrive at a single answer. An analytical problem is one that frequently has only one successful solution. For example, excessive sweating had been observed on the interior of windows and window frames in the wards of a large hospital. In addition, the plaster adjacent to the windows had started to powder and cause paint to chip and peel, resulting in costly maintenance and inconvenience. "Find the cause of the failures" is an analytical problem. One pursues the problem through a progression of suppositions to be proved or disproved by experimentation, tests, calculations, and so on, until the problem is successfully narrowed to a single cause for each failure. Once the cause is ascertained, that problem is solved.

The creative approach is used whether or not there appears to be one or more solutions to a particular problem. The creative approach is an idea-producing process intended specifically to generate a number of solutions, each of which will solve the problem at hand. All solutions will work, but one is better than the others; it is the optimum solution among those available. The best solution to the problem may not even have been generated.

In the hospital example just cited, the situation posed by "excessive sweating on windows and frames, plaster powdering and paint peeling" may be resolved into two problems:

1. Determine the cause of trouble (analytical problem).
2. Prevent recurrence of this problem for future construction (creative problem).

The cause was determined to be a buildup of humidity in the space coupled with the low temperature of the glass, metal frames, and frame supporting system. Plaster powdered and paint peeled when moisture formed on the metal frame and supporting system. What is the solution to this portion of the problem? A number of ideas may be proposed:

1. Use wood-frame windows.
2. Use thermopane glazing.

3. Reduce the source of humidity buildup.

4. Change the frame support system.

5. Use Keene's cement plaster.

6. Install thermal insulation between the frames and supporting systems.

Any of these ideas may provide a solution to the problem, but one of them is better than the rest. Its selection is an analytical problem. However, the best solution that could be found may not even be on the list.

Up to a point, the human mind is greater than the most elaborate computer. It can store an almost infinite number of data, but unfortunately it can only process and integrate up to about seven bits of these data simultaneously. Recognizing the mind's limitation, we find the following rules helpful in applying either the analytical or creative approach to problem solving (the first three are preventive and the last three are remedial):

1. Review the elements of the problem several times.

2. Suspend judgment. Don't jump to or be led into false conclusions.

3. Rearrange the elements of the problem; get a new viewpoint.

4. If still getting nowhere, try various new approaches.

5. Take a break when you are stuck.

6. Discuss your problem with others.

9.8 THE CREATIVE PROCESS

Steps in the Creative Process

To gain a greater understanding of the nature of creativity, you must study the creative process. The process follows a step-by-step sequence in the solving of problems. You must not conclude from this approach that innovation or creation is always the result of conscious or even logical effort. The creative process is the process the mind normally follows in seeking the solution to a problem. It follows these steps:

1. *Orientation*. Defining the problem to be solved and selecting the approach that should be taken to solve it.

2. *Preparation*. Information gathering and fact finding.

3. *Analysis*. Evaluation and analysis of the data gathered.

4. *Ideation*. Production of alternative solutions to the problems.

5. ~~Incubation~~. Sorting and combining the information (slowing the pace to invite illumination).

6. ~~Synthesis~~. Bringing all the ideas together into a complete whole.

7. ~~Verification (evaluation)~~. Evaluation of the proposed solution or resultant ideas.

9.9 TECHNIQUES FOR CREATIVE PROBLEM SOLVING

There are a number of ~~creativity techniques~~ available for solving problem situations. These techniques stimulate the generation of creative solutions. It is necessary, during their use, to conscientiously think creatively. The ~~ground rules for creative idea generation~~ may be summarized as follows:

1. Do not attempt to generate new ideas and to judge them at the same time. Reserve all judgment and evaluation.

2. Generate a large quantity of possible solutions. Brainstorming develops 70% more good ideas than individuals can develop alone. Deferred judgment produces 90% more useful ideas than immediate judgment.

3. Seek a wide variety of solutions that represent a broad spectrum of attacks upon the problem.

4. Watch for opportunities to combine or impose ideas as they are generated.

5. Do not discard any idea, even if it may appear most impractical.

6. Do not ridicule any ideas.

7. Before closing the book on possible solutions, allow time for subconscious thought on the problem while consciously performing other tasks. Techniques most often used in creative problem solving are free association techniques and organized techniques.

Free Association Techniques

These techniques are used to seek a large number of ideas. They are primarily based on the premise that one idea suggests others, these suggest others, and so on.

BRAINSTORMING. By definition, ~~brainstorming is a conference technique by which a group attempts to find a solution for a specific problem by spontaneously contributing and amassing ideas~~. Brainstorming is a problem-solving conference method used to great advantage by many organizations in VM studies as well as in other problem-solving sessions. The principal advantage of brainstorming is that it can produce a large volume of good ideas in a short time. This method is based upon the stimulation of one person's mind by another's idea. An average brainstorming session consists of a group of four to six people spontaneously producing ideas designed to solve a particular problem. During this session, no attempt whatsoever is made to judge or evaluate the ideas. Evaluation takes place after the brainstorming session has ended. Brainstorming does not always directly provide final solutions or ideas ready for immediate implementation. However, it is always capable of suggesting the final solution. Brainstorming can be accomplished by an individual, but past experience has shown that a group effort can generate 70% more ideas collectively than the same number of persons thinking individually. Prior to any brainstorming session, the group leader sets the stage by appointing a secretary (or by using a tape recorder) and reviewing the following rules:

1. *Criticism is ruled out.* Adverse judgment of ideas must be withheld. A perfectionist complex will inhibit the free flow of ideas.

2. *Free-wheeling is welcomed.* The wilder the idea, the better; it is easier to tame down than think up.

3. *Quantity is wanted.* The greater the number of ideas, the more likelihood of a winner.

4. *Combination and improvement are sought.* In addition to contributing ideas of their own, participants should suggest how ideas of others can be turned into better ideas, or how two or more ideas can be joined into still another idea.

During brainstorming sessions it is essential *not* to exercise critical judgment of any offered idea. Critical judgment will tend to inhibit thinking and will stifle the generation of additional ideas. With practice, people can adjust to the brainstorming method. This means one should follow the rules and control the natural tendency to instantaneously evaluate ideas. It should be emphasized that brainstorming does not always give the final problem solutions or ideas for immediate implementation. Brainstorming produces leads that direct decision making toward the final solution.

GORDON TECHNIQUE. The Gordon technique (developed by William J. J. Gordon, Cambridge, Massachusetts) is closely related to brainstorming in that it is a group conference method in which an unevaluated free-flowing discussion is encouraged. However, no one except the group leader knows the exact nature of the problem under consideration. The reasons for this requirement are to avoid arriving at a hasty solution and to permit the broadest level of disassociation from specifics. It has been found that a participant may become convinced that one of the ideas he has proposed is the best solution to the problem. Then he may cease to produce additional ideas and may devote his energies to defending and selling his own idea. It is more difficult to select a topic for such a session than for a brainstorming session. The subject must be closely related to the problem at hand, but its exact nature must not be revealed until the discussion is concluded. The following problem situations are examples of how this technique works:

1. The problem is to design a new roofing system, so the group leader might have the group discuss "enclosures" or "ways things are enclosed."
2. The problem is to design a new well-point system, so the group leader might have the group discuss "removing." By this process, some unusual approaches are likely to be found—approaches that otherwise may not have been associated with the problem at hand.

Organized Techniques

In the use of these techniques, a logical step-by-step approach is followed to generate ideas, one or more of which may provide the solution to the problem at hand.

CHECKLISTS. A checklist is an accumulation of points, areas, or possibilities that serve to provide idea clues, or leads, when the items on a prepared list are compared with the problem or subject under consideration. The objective is to obtain a number of ideas for further followup and development. The checklist is one of the most commonly used aids in the search for new ideas. Checklists range in type from the specialized to the extremely generalized. Examples of specialized checklists used in value management may be found in numerous works on the subject. A generalized creativity checklist (developed by the Massachusetts Institute of Technology) is included at the end of this chapter.

MORPHOLOGICAL ANALYSIS. Morphological analysis is a structured comprehensive way to list and examine all of the possible combinations that might be useful in solving a problem. The steps in morphological analysis are: First, define the problem in terms of its dimensions or parameters; second, develop a model that makes it possible to visualize every possible solution. If a problem has only two parameters, or variables, the model takes the form of a large rectangle divided into a series of small squares. The horizontal axis represents one variable and is subdivided into the different forms of this variable. The vertical axis represents the other variable and is similarly subdivided. Each small square represents a combination of one version of each variable. If the problem had three variables, the model would take the form of a cube or a parallelepiped. More than three variables can be used, but the technique then becomes unmanageable by usual paper-and-pencil techniques.

The technique can be illustrated by approaching the problem of analyzing the possible combinations of windows for a new building. The three variables might be type, material, and glazing material. One axis of the cube lists all the different sizes (shapes) that might be considered. Another axis is subdivided into the different types that the windows might be. The third axis lists the various materials with which the windows might be glazed. Figure 9.1 illustrates the resulting structure, which offers up to 125 possible combinations. Each of these possible combinations could be considered in turn.

ATTRIBUTE LISTING. This method of idea stimulation was developed by R. P. Crawford, Lincoln, Nebraska. The first step in attri-

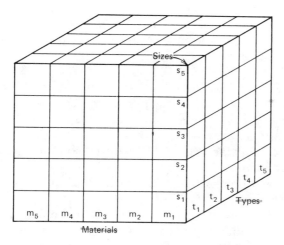

Figure 9.1 Morphological analysis model.

bute listing is to ~~list all of the various attributes of an object~~, and the second step is to ~~change or modify each of the characteristics~~. Using this technique, new combinations of characteristics (attributes) may be brought together that will better fulfill some existing need. As an example, consider one type of cast-iron radiator that was common a few years ago. Its characteristics are multiple iron tubes, four legs to allow free standing, high inlet and low outlet, valve for control, 22 to 26 inches high by 4 to 8 inches deep, and installed 1 to 2 inches from walls. The attributes could be changed as follows:

- Multiple tubes changed to single tube with fins to increase heat transfer.
- Legs eliminated to allow attachment to wall brackets.
- Inlet and outlet at same low level.
- Dampers and attractive cover for control and beauty.
- Height decreased to 10 inches and width to 2½ inches.
- Installed flush with wall.

FORCED RELATIONSHIPS. This technique was developed by Charles S. Whiting for the purpose of inducing original ideas based on a forced relationship between two or more unrelated objects or ideas. An example of a forced relationship would be to take the initial list of ideas developed during the brainstorming and combine these ideas to generate a new list. This device is quite useful when the major objective is to produce new construction methods or building components by initiating a chain of associating one component with another seemingly unrelated component. We may, for example, combine an interior load bearing wall with the exterior brick facing of a building to form a precast wall panel.

INPUT-OUTPUT TECHNIQUE. The input-output technique considers the use of energy of one form or another. The three steps in the use of this technique are: (1) Establish output; (2) establish the input as the starting point; and (3) determine the various forms of energy or reactions that are available to provide the initial stimulus to set in motion a dynamic system.

As an example, consider the following problem:

Required: Warning of fire one mile away from building within matter of seconds after fire starts, must work seven days a week, 24 hours a day, must be trouble free and cost under $5000.

The input-output technique could generate the listing:

Input: Fire.
Output: Heat, light, smoke, gaseous products.
Reactions caused by output: Expansion of metals, gases, and liquids, melting of metals, changes in chemical composition.

The same problem might be approached differently, expressing input as a power or force, output as the corresponding action or reaction, and solution specifications in terms of limiting requirements:

Problem: Design smoke alarm system
Input: Smoke
Output: Audible and/or visible alarm
Specs: (1) Sensitive enough to detect potential fire. (2) Will ignore cigarette and pipe smoke, etc.

9.10 SUMMARY

Creative thinking, particularly in the area of generation of ideas, should be used in all phases of construction. Brainstorming, as a problem solver, is used extensively by many organizations in VM studies and other problem areas. In value management, a number of techniques are used to assist in the identification of value problems, the generation of ideas that suggest solutions, the analysis of these for feasibility, and finally, the development of practical solutions. No specific combination of these techniques is prescribed for all VM efforts, nor is there a predetermined degree to which they should be utilized. The selection of specific techniques and the depth to which they are utilized is primarily a matter of judgment and varies according to the complexity of the subject under study.

This chapter, obviously, could not possibly address the entire subject of creativity, but it has attempted to touch on those areas directly related to value management. An attempt was made to indicate some theories about highly creative people and how they respond to circumstances and the environments in which they work or live. Many of the traits found in creative people exist, to a degree, in everyone and can be developed through training and exercise of the brain to the maximum potential.

It is hoped that this chapter might stimulate the reader to further explore the area of creativity and its uses.

9.11 GENERALIZED CREATIVITY CHECKLIST

Put to Other Uses?
New way to use as is?   Like using helicopters to patrol high-tension wires over mountains.
Other ways if modified?   Like fishing rods made from fiberglass embedded in plastic.
What could be made from this?   Like the wallboard manufacturer who added a line of jigsaw puzzles.
How about salvaging?   Like the rubber maker who found that wasted strips of surgical tubing could be sold as rubber bands.
What other use could be added?   Like telephone companies installing transcribed records to furnish correct time and latest weather report.
Greater width?   Like the center strip on new thruways.
Include "plus" ingredient?   Like chlorophyll in toothpaste.

Minify or Less So?
What if lower?   Like the trend in motor cars a few years ago.
Narrower?   Like brims of men's hats.
Lighter?   Like new Taigo railroad cars that weigh no more than trailers.
Streamline?   Like tank-type vacuum cleaners.
Condense?   Like full-size umbrellas that fit into purse.
Eliminate?   Like tires without tubes.

Substitute?
Other parts?   Like fluid drive instead of gears on cars.
Materials?   Like argon instead of vacuum in electric light bulbs.
Other process?   Like stamping instead of casting.
Other power?   Like using electricity instead of vacuum to run windshield wipers.
Other way?   Like the airlift that saved Berlin.

Rearrange?
Change pattern?   Like one-way streets.
Revise layout?   Like new wrinkles in supermarkets.
Alter sequence?   Like flashbacks in movies.
Transpose cause and effect?   Like doctors do in diagnosis.
Repackage?   Like popcorn that comes in its own popping pan.
Regroup?   Like new defensive systems in football.

Reverse?

Transpose?   Like putting engine in rear of bus.

Borrow or Adapt?

What else is like this?   Like the studies of birds made by the aircraft pioneers.

What parallels do the past provide?   Like what modern dress designers do in devising new creations from ancient art.

Could other processes be copied?   Like the Japanese copying nature by sticking a grain of sand into oysters to produce cultured pearls.

What other ideas might be adaptable?   Like Diesel, who got his engine ideas from a cigar lighter.

Modify or Give a New Twist?

What other shape?   Like the buggy maker who tapered the roller bearing that Leonardo de Vinci had invented 400 years before.

What other form?   Like detergent powders instead of bars of soap; like liquid soap instead of either.

How to create a new look?   Like higher (or lower) skirts.

What could color do?   Like what the automobile industry did to make 1955 the biggest new-car year in history.

How about motion?   Like Christmas tree lights that bubble.

Magnify or More So?

Longer time?   Like the baker who featured slow-baked bread.

Greater frequency?   Like the doctor who originated the idea of lighter but more frequent meals for ulcer victims.

Increased strength?   Like reinforced heels and toes in hosiery.

Height?   Like circus clowns on clear plastic stilts.

Down instead of up?   Like furrier who attaches his label upside down so it can be read when the coat is over a chair.

Switch roles?   Like female executives with male secretaries.

Up instead of down?   Like dining room light that throws beam upward from floor to reflector on ceiling.

Do the opposite?   Like Howe, who perfected his sewing machine by designing a needle with a hole at the bottom instead of the top.

Combine?

How about alloys?   Like the new mixtures of synthetic fibers.

What old ideas could be merged?   Like window washers that combine a brush with a built-in hose.

Ensembles?   Like shirts with neckties and handkerchiefs to match.

Hook appeals together?   Like drugstores selling blades to those who ask for shaving cream and vice versa.

Combine purposes?   Like Benjamin Franklin, who, to avoid changing from one pair of glasses to another, cut the lenses in two and stuck them together with the reading halves below, thus inventing bifocals.

CHAPTER 10

MANAGING PROJECT VALUE THROUGH LIFE-CYCLE COSTING

10.1 INTRODUCTION

Escalating costs and recurring energy shortages are increasing the need for the design and construction of buildings with low operating and energy costs. Laws and regulations aimed at abating pollution and improving the environment have further complicated the planning and design of both new construction and rehabilitation. The impact of these and other economic and social phenomena on the construction industry is attracting attention to the technique of life-cycle costing.

In essence, life-cycle costing is the systematic evaluation of alternative building designs and the comparison of their projected total owning, operating, and maintenance costs over the economic life of the proposed building. The intent is to identify that design which would be the most economical over the useful life of the proposed building. Application of the life-cycle costing technique holds a promise of improving decision making while stimulating competition. Although its use by both the public and private sector is rapidly increasing, life-cycle costing is in the early stages of application in the construction industry.

Life-cycle costs are the total acquisition and ownership costs of an item throughout its life. This is shown graphically in Figure 10.1. The most economical building is one that is designed for the lowest life-cycle cost, not just the lowest initial cost. Such an effort requires the analysis of the effects that alternative component systems, materials, and other features have on construction and ownership costs throughout the expected economic life of the proposed facility. Analyses of this

273

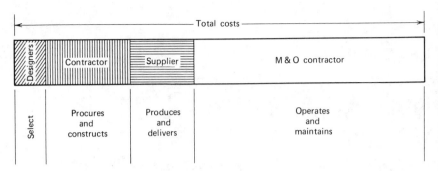

Figure 10.1 Average distribution of costs for a typical facility.

type require information on current acquisition costs, as well as on current and estimated future ownership costs.

One proposed design may have a high initial construction cost because it specifies more durable building systems that minimize future ownership costs. Another proposed design may have a low construction cost by specifying less costly building systems that will require large future expenditures for maintenance, repair, operation, alterations, and utilities. In between are many alternative designs representing a variety of current acquisition costs and future ownership costs. This balance of present costs versus future costs is affected by the interest cost of money. Figure 10.2 illustrates that for a typical office building the cost of capital could represent about 33% of total ownership costs.

The cost of capital includes interest, inflation losses, and opportunity costs and is a significant portion of total ownership costs. Before life-cycle costing there was no feasible method of including the impact of the cost of capital in the evaluation of total ownership costs. At best it was treated as an isolated subject in dealing with the return on investment, and even then only the initial acquisition costs commonly were evaluated. Present value techniques and the equivalent uniform annual costs concept employed in life-cycle costing brings cost of capital into the decision making process in a meaningful way.

In the past, owners, designers, and constructors were concerned mainly, if not exclusively, with the initial cost of the structure. The effect of the basic design on life-cycle costs was not adequately considered. Each design discipline generated requirements, reviewed these requirements, established and modified its particular criteria, and even modified the standards and criteria of the owner. This approach did not lead to the most economical decisions for the end function of the facility. Instead, it encouraged economical decisions within each area,

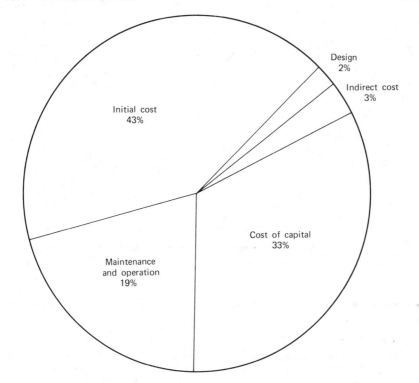

Figure 10.2 Total cost of ownership—typical office building.

with maximum safety factors deemed necessary by each discipline. Although this system was not totally without merit, it tended to sacrifice lifetime system performance in maximizing the initial performance of subsystems. The emphasis on first cost and the failure to consider the total effect of related cost elements were probably the greatest shortcomings in planning, designing, and constructing facilities. These hidden costs have a considerable impact on the cost of ownership. For example, as Figure 10.3 shows, the total cost of a hospital is about 10.5 times its initial cost.

The difficulty with implementing life-cycle costing as a standard approach to cost analysis centers around two problem areas.

1. *Acceptance of the concept.* Because of the visibility of initial costs versus the lack of visibility of future operating costs, it is difficult for owners and designers to accept the concept that initial acquisition

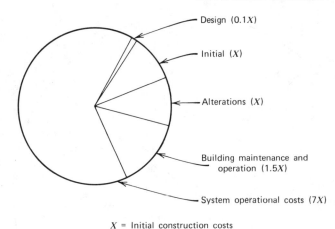

Design (0.1X)

Initial (X)

Alterations (X)

Building maintenance and operation (1.5X)

System operational costs (7X)

X = Initial construction costs

Figure 10.3 Hospital life-cycle costs (20 years).

costs are only a small fraction of the total ownership costs over the life of a building.

2. *Accuracy.* Prior to the recent advances in life cycle costing, it was difficult to generate reasonable numbers for use in developing estimates of future costs.

The value of life-cycle costing is illustrated by comparing the acquisition and operating costs of an automobile to that of a building. A consumer can purchase an inexpensive automobile that runs perfectly well for a period of time. Then he discovers that design and manufacturing deficiencies begin to exert pressure on his pocketbook, and accelerating maintenance costs soon offset the initial low purchase price. The low-cost automobile soon becomes a liability, draining his resources throughout its life span. An owner is faced with the same problem in the acquisition of buildings or building systems. Unless future operating, maintenance, repair, and alterations costs are given more than casual consideration, apparent savings generated by low initial procurement costs soon disappear because of abnormal future ownership costs.

Life-cycle costing provides cost information that is valuable in choosing from among those alternative building designs and systems that meet established baseline performance requirements. It improves the budget estimation process by providing more accurate, complete, and detailed information than was previously available. The necessity for life-cycle costing has been made even more apparent with the occurrence of the energy crisis; it makes available to the decision makers information as to the life-cycle cost impact of energy conservation measures. Further, life-cycle costing is a valuable management tool for the comparison and analysis of alternative means of satisfying space requirements—should the owner lease, build, or rehabilitate existing space? Life-cycle costing shifts attention from initial acquisition costs to total life-cycle costs, and if this is accomplished during the development and design plases the owner achieves even greater performance and cost efficiencies than previously realized.

Life-cycle costing as an economic tool has existed for a number of years in one form or another. Everyday decisions made by the layman involve life-cycle costing; an example of an automobile purchase was previously cited. The use of life-cycle costing as a standard tool for economic analysis was developed by the Department of Defense in the early 1960s for the planning and procurement of weapons and weapon support systems. In the ensuing years the concept became a highly formalized methodology to which computer technology was applied. Experience has proven the concept to be extremely useful as an aid in the decision-making process. It was found to be of special assistance in choosing among a range of complex alternatives, each with an equivalent performance baseline. In particular, it proved to be extremely valuable in choosing among alternatives with different life spans and varying annual cash flows. The Department of Defense has found life-cycle costing to be very important during the development and design phases. During these first two phases, commitments for the life of the system are made, and a life cycle cost estimate is essential during these periods if the decision-making process is to be meaningful.

Although in use in the Department of Defense for many years, life-cycle costing is just now beginning to receive recognition in the construction industry. The application of life-cycle costing to the building process will show decision makers the realistic total cost consequences of their decisions. In addition, it will expand the designer's planning horizon so he will no longer concentrate on just the initial acquisition costs of a facility but will also take into account the effect of design on the recurring costs of operations, maintenance, repair, and alterations. Further, this approach will allow the owner to analyze his requirements in light of the total cost constraints imposed by his budget. Although in its infancy in the construction industry, life-cycle costing already is a meaningful management tool that is used to obtain the best building for the dollars expended.

10.2 LIFE-CYCLE COSTS

The life cycle of a facility is that time period that begins when the owner establishes the need for the facility and ends when the facility passes out of the original owner's hands. This definition includes the replacement of one tenant by another and the associated space alterations necessary to meet the requirements of the new tenant. The actual length of the life cycle will vary from facility to facility and even among building elements. At present, the Public Buildings Service uses a 40-year building life for the typical federal office building. The life expectancy of the building must be specified by the decision maker concerned with the life-cycle cost analysis. Figure 10.4 illustrates life-cycle estimates of individual building elements. In lieu of actual data on the length of the life of building elements, the owner must use manufacturers' data, industry estimates, or personal experience.

The life cycle of a building can be divided into the following phases:

- Development
- Design
- Construction
- Operation and Maintenance *occupancy*

Development Phase. During this period the need for a facility is identified and defined. Then alternatives to satisfy the need are generated, defined and analyzed, and the appropriate course of action is determined. If the decision is to build, site requirements are defined, and action is initiated to acquire the site. Project management and implementation plans are prepared and approved. Preliminary estimates are prepared. Approval is granted and sufficient funds are provided to proceed with the next phase.

Design Phase. The defined need is translated into plans, specifications, and other contract documents. More definite estimates are prepared. Funds are allocated for the next phase.

Construction Phase. The plans and specifications are converted into a finished product that satisfies the defined need. Frequently, by the use of the phased construction concept, the design and construction phases are overlapped. At the end of this phase the owner occupies the facility.

Operations and Maintenance Phase. This is the predominant and normally the longest phase of the building's life cycle. It is the phase during which the owner uses the building. This phase begins at beneficial occupance and ends when the building passes out of the hands of the owner.

Economic life and life cycle are different and important concepts. The life cycle of a facility has been defined as that time period that begins when the owner establishes the need for the facility and ends when the facility passes out of the original owner's hands. The economic life is the period of time during which the building or system provides benefits. The two are not necessarily of equal duration. Differences arise when:

- The building passes out of the hands of the original owner yet still provides benefits to the new owner. Here the economic life exceeds the life cycle of the building as it relates to the original owner. By acquiring the building, the new owner has established a new building life cycle. In essence, in this type of situation, the economic life spans two or more building life cycles.
- Individual systems or components have completed their economic life and are replaced while the facility is still within a life cycle.
- The building has reached the end of its economic life but is still retained in the owner's inventory because of a lack of marketability or due to some intangible factor such as historical value.

Essentially, economic life relates time period and benefits, whereas life cycle relates time period and ownership.

Economic life is limited ultimately by the physical life of the building or its systems. When it is more economical to replace than renovate and operate or repair and operate the building, the end of the true economic life has been reached. In reality, however, structures are traditionally designed and built with materials and systems whose actual physical life far exceeds its economic life. Consideration should be given to buildings and systems that have a shortened physical life corresponding to the projected economic life.

Technology has a tremendous impact on economic life. Rapidly changing technology can quickly make a building or its systems obsolete and thereby greatly reduce its economic life. For example, it was more economical to demolish a 10-year old Miami, Florida apartment building and build a new structure because the outdated air-conditioning system of the original building hurt its rentability. Recurring

Element	Item	Estimated life (years)
Foundation	General	75
	Wood piles	Indefinite
	Concrete	Indefinite
	Steel piles	Indefinite
Structural Frame	Wood	30
		Almost indefinite
		75
		66
		50
		40
	Wood floor joists	40
	(various kinds)	30
		25
	Concrete	Indefinite
	Steel	75
		Indefinite
		(40–50) +
		30 +
Exterior Walls	Wood (untreated)	1–10
	Wood (creosote)	20
	(various kinds)	15–20
	Brick (various kinds)	75
		75
		66
	Concrete (various kinds)	75
		40 +
		Indefinite
	Terra cotta (various kinds)	120 +
		100 +
		60 +
		50 +
	Rock	75
	Metal	75
	Shingles	16
Heating	Boilers (various kinds)	30
		20

Figure 10.4 Building element/item life-cycle estimates. Data extracted from J. G. Kirley, et al., *Estimating the Life Expectancy of Facilities,* Army Construction Engineering Research Laboratory, Champaign, Illinois. Distributed by the National Technical Information Service, U.S. Department of Commerce, April 1974. These data represent the range of estimated lives of various building elements/items.

Element	Item	Estimated life (years)
	Stokers and burners	20
	Furnaces	15
	Concealed radiation	25
	Direct radiation	25
	Pipes, general	20
	Pipes, copper	Life of building
	Pipes, iron	20
Air Conditioning	Units	10
	Refrigeration units	7
	Centrifugal refrigeration	20
	Reciprocating refrigeration	20
	Evaporative coolers (small)	5–8
	Evaporative coolers (large)	12–20
	Pipes, copper	20
	Pipes, steel	20
Ventilation	Ductwork	Indefinite
		Indefinite
Wiring	General	20
	Sheathed	20
	THWN	50
	RH	30
Conduit	Rigid	Indefinite
Cables	Plastic vinyl clad	Indefinite
Pipes	General	500
		40 +
	Brass (various kinds)	Indefinite
		Indefinite
	Copper (various kinds)	Indefinite
		Indefinite
	Iron (cold water)	25
	Iron (hot water)	20
	Cast iron (sewer)	Indefinite
	Galvanized iron	50
	Vitrified clay (sewer)	Indefinite
	Plastics	Almost indefinite
	Steel	14 +
	Asbestos cement	Indefinite

Figure 10.4 (*Continued*)

energy crises and increasing energy prices are accelerating the development of new building systems, and this, in turn, will render the current systems obsolete.

Locational factors also affect the economic life of a building. For example, when the character of an area shifts from low- and medium-use buildings to high-use buildings, land values increase. The market value of land on which a low- or medium-use building rests may have increased to the point where it is economically advantageous to release the land for high rise development—the proceeds from the sale would exceed the cost of acquiring another site and building that would meet the owner's current needs. In such a situation, the decision to demolish the building and release the land for further development is an economic one.

Changes in user locational preferences, business activities, and space requirements can reduce the economic life of a facility to less than its physical life. A multitude of virtually indestructible, but obsolete, multistory New England factories is illustrative of this condition.

Life-cycle estimates of HVAC equipment are in a state of flux. This is the result of two major factors.

1. Life-cycle costing is relatively new to the construction industry. At this stage it is more of an art than a science, and the fundamental concepts are just beginning to be definitized.

2. The recurring energy crises and the constantly increasing energy prices are forcing designers to specify more energy-efficient HVAC systems. These new systems have different life cycles. In addition, manufacturers of the various systems and components vary in their life-cycle estimates, depending on the type of equipment in which they specialize.

The life-cycle estimates shown in Figure 10.5 can be used as a guide. A word of caution is in order here. An analyst making a life-cycle cost analysis very possibly could arrive at different HVAC "best selections," depending on whether he is using, for example, a 25-year life cycle or a 10-year life cycle. It is imperative, then, that all life-cycle alternative comparisons use the same life-cycle values.

Life-cycle costs are all costs incurred from the time that a space requirement is identified and defined until that facility passes out of the owner's hands. Figures 10.6 and 10.7 illustrate the relationship among costs incurred during the life cycle of a typical office building. It can be seen that over a typical life expectancy of 40 years the cumula-

Equipment	Years
Centrifugal fans	25
Centrifugal refrigeration machines	25
Absorption machines	20
Reciprocating water chillers	15
Central air handlers	20
Ducts	[a]
Chilled-water piping	[a]
Steam or condenser water	25
Electric motors, starters	20
Pumps	25
Control systems	20
Steam turbines	25
Gas turbines	20
Air terminals	20
Boilers	20
Residential furnaces (gas, oil, electric)	15
Window units (appliance type)	10
PTAC's (through-wall or water-cooled packages)	15
Reciprocating condensing units—2 to 50 tons (including rooftop multizones)	15
Screw compressors	20

[a]Life of building.

Figure 10.5 HVAC life-cycle estimates.

tive operation and maintenance costs greatly exceed the initial costs of development, design, and construction. Yet it is during the early phases of a project that the magnitude of the total operation and maintenance costs is determined. During the development phase, before the first brick is put in place, the owner makes decisions that affect not only the construction cost of the facility but also the total life-cycle costs. In the design phase, the architect-engineer defines the building configuration and associated systems to a level of detail that further influences total life-cycle costs. Finally, during the construction phase, contractors use materials and systems that determine operation and maintenance costs for many years into the future.

The magnitude of life-cycle costs is illustrated by Figures 10.8 and 10.9. Figure 10.8 graphically portrays the cost elements involved. However, applicable cost elements will vary with the facility, system, or item being analyzed. Most costs are self-explanatory, with the possible exception of the categories listed as "functional use costs," "loss of

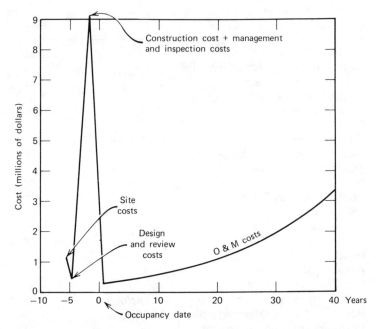

Figure 10.6 Life-cycle costs for a typical office building—dollars versus years.

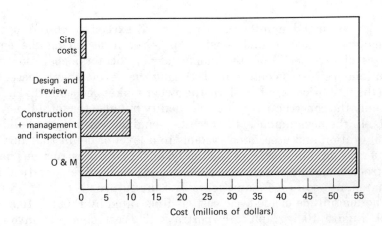

Figure 10.7 Life-cycle costs for a typical office building—categories of cost versus years. Note: 04M costs are escalated by 6% for a 40-year occupancy and do not include R&A costs.

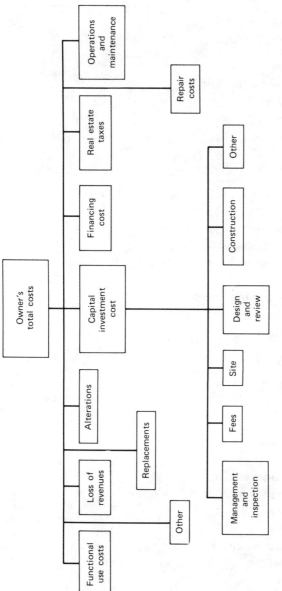

Figure 10.8 Life-cycle cost model.

- Site acquisition costs

  - Land
  - Legal fees
  - Surveys and filing fees
  - Appraisal fees
  - Relocation
  - Advertising

- Design and review costs

  - Personal services
  - A/E fees and services
  - Construction manager fee
  - Special consultants' services
  - Soil and preconstruction testing
  - Models
  - Invitation and reproduction
  - GSA engineering administration and travel
  - Data processing

- Construction costs

  - Foundations
  - Substructure
  - Superstructure
  - Exterior closure
  - Roofing
  - Interior construction
  - Conveying systems
  - Mechanical
  - Electrical
  - General conditions and profit
  - Equipment
  - Site work

- Management and inspection costs

  - Personal services
  - A/E fees and services

Figure 10.9 Life-cycle costs by category.

○ Construction manager fee
○ Special consultants' services
○ Materials testing
○ GSA engineering administration and travel
○ Data processing

• Operations and maintenance costs

○ Cleaning
○ Ground and roads maintenance
○ Elevators O&M
○ Utilities and fuel
○ Space changes
○ Electrical system O&M
○ Heating system O&M
○ Air-conditioning and ventilating system O&M
○ Plumbing and sewerage system O&M
○ Conveyor systems maintenance
○ Structural maintenance
○ Fire protection systems maintenance
○ Waste and trash removal services
○ Pest control services
○ Security services

Figure 10.9 (*Continued*)

revenues," and "other." Functional use costs are those costs associated with the functioning of the facility. For example, for a laboratory these costs would be those associated with running and staffing the facility, such as laboratory equipment and personnel. However, this should not be confused with operational and maintenance costs (see Figure 10.9), which include such items as utilities and cleaning. Loss of revenues is the income lost because the facility is totally or partially inoperative—for example, when a nuclear power plant is shut down for refueling or a factory assembly line is closed down for repairs. The "other" category includes the costs of unique systems, such as a security system for a bank or a special electrical grounding system for hospital electronic equipment.

The primary objective of a life-cycle cost analysis is to provide a tool that will aid top management in making resource management deci-

~~sions~~. Life-cycle costs are the major informational input to any life-cycle costing system. The result of any analysis is only as good as the information upon which the analysis is based. Therefore ~~the life-cycle costs considered in a life-cycle costing analysis must meet the following criteria~~.

Relevancy. The costs must be relevant to the resources that would be affected by the decision under consideration. Relevant costs include not only those of the specific systems being compared but also those of any associated systems that may be affected by the decision.

Importance. The costs must be of significant magnitude and relation to the total cost that they could change the rank of one alternative relative to another. Costs that are constant for all alternatives are excluded from comparison since their inclusion will not alter the rank of the alternatives.

Common Dollar Units. All costs must be expressed in dollars. It is recognized that dollar units vary over time. This condition is neutralized by the use of ~~present value techniques~~ and the ~~equivalent uniform annual costs concept~~, both of which are discussed in detail in ~~Section 10.3~~. ~~Normally, intangible factors (such as esthetics) that cannot be assigned a dollar value are excluded~~.

Predictability. Future costs must be predictable. Some costs will be predictable within a small error range while others may be subject to substantial error. For example, sometime during the life cycle of a facility it will be necessary to repair or replace the roof. The precise time of occurrence and the associated costs are difficult to predict, but a probable range of time and cost is determined by using statistical methods. In addition, a ~~sensitivity analysis~~ is performed to determine the cost consequences of variations in the range. This will be discussed in more detail in ~~Section 10.3~~.

As can be seen in Figure 10.7, operation and maintenance costs have a dramatic impact on total ownership costs. Yet in the past they were treated independently of initial costs. Further, prior to the adoption of life-cycle costing, the predominance of initial cost as a criterion for determining building design resulted in generally inadequate recognition of operation and maintenance costs during the development and design phases. There are three major reasons why initial acquisition costs received the greatest share of attention.

1. In the past, the initial cost aspect was initiated very early in the building process in the form of estimates and budgets. Operation and maintenance cost, if considered at all, normally did not receive any attention until the facility was designed and under construction.

2. Operation and maintenance costs are more complex and insufficiently understood.

3. Operation and maintenance cost information was difficult to generate. Designers, consultants, and major owners are just now development historical cost data banks.

Much of the operation and maintenance cost problem can be attributed to the lack of emphasis on the downstream operating costs of the building during the development and design phases. Yet historically there is a significant correlation between operation and maintenance cost and initial acquisition cost. Higher operation and maintenance costs generally result from building systems with higher initial acquisition costs. In the past, higher initial costs generally reflected higher performance. The increased system complexity resulting from higher performance requirements tended to result in increased operation and maintenance costs.

There is no question that design influences total ownership costs. The configuration chosen for a building has a major effect on the magnitude of its operation and maintenance costs. To reduce these costs the owner must insist on a simplified design that will affect both initial acquisition cost and downstream operation and maintenance costs. This will necessarily require tradeoffs to establish the best balance between acquisition and operation and maintenance costs to minimize life-cycle costs. The importance of this is just now becoming apparent to the design community.

Life-cycle costing is a systematic process for estimating the total costs associated with satisfying the space requirements of an owner. The need for top management awareness and visibility in the life-cycle costing area is well known. Yet there is a particular need to define what management objectives are being sought in this area and to provide the technical tools, such as definitions, concepts, and analysis procedures, to accomplish the specified tasks. These items are discussed in detail in the following three sections.

10.3 BASIC CONCEPTS

This section introduces the basic concepts associated with life-cycle costing and analysis. The following discussion treats those concepts that are considered the most pertinent and are usually the most difficult to define.

10.3.1   TRADEOFF ANALYSIS

Tradeoff analysis is the process of evaluating a number of alternatives in terms of their life-cycle costs. The analyses can range from evaluating alternatives for a specific building system, such as alternative HVAC systems, to evaluating alternatives for the total building configuration, such as high-rise versus low-rise. Most construction projects are complex and could involve an almost infinite number of tradeoff studies. Therefore, it is essential to identify the most critical areas for analysis. Obviously these are the areas that have the highest and most sensitive costs associated with them. It is a waste of effort to perform a tradeoff analysis for a system whose life-cycle cost is a very small percentage of the total life-cycle cost of the project. Also, it is fruitless to perform a tradeoff analysis for even a very high cost system if the system is not cost sensitive so that there would be no significant impact on total life-cycle costs.

Unfortunately the traditional tradeoff analysis normally involves only initial acquisition costs. From the owner's point of view, this is self-defeating with respect to minimizing the total ownership costs. As will be seen in the next two sections, the greatest payoff from tradeoff analysis results when total life-cycle costs are considered. For example, tradeoff analyses should be performed for systems that have the greatest impact on future ownership costs such as:

• Yearly operating and maintenance expenses.
• Annual utility and fuel costs.
• Future repair and alteration costs.
• Future replacement of major systems.

In performing a tradeoff analysis, it is not always necessary to include all the costs of all the alternatives. Those costs that are assumed to be the same for all alternatives can be excluded, thereby simplifying the evaluation. For example, if all building alternatives involve the same foundation system, then the acquisition cost of the foundation need not be included. Only costs that will affect the ranking of the alternatives being considered are included.

10.3.2 DESIGN TO COST

In the design-to-cost concept, cost is a design parameter in the same sense as the performance parameters such as occupiable area, elevator speed, air-conditioning capacity, and so forth. The cost parameter is equal in importance to technical requirements and schedules throughout the life-cycle phases of a building. The intent is to achieve the best balance between life-cycle cost, acceptable performance, and schedule. Decision makers must be aware of and control cost in all phases of the program and be prepared to consider the effects on cost before making each program decision.

Design to cost involves the establishment of cost elements that then become the goal within which management must accomplish the desired balance between performance, cost, and schedule. Figure 10.10 illustrates this concept. For every proposed facility there are certain minimum performance parameters that must be achieved, or the building will not satisfy the owner's requirements and therefore should not be constructed. There is also a maximum cost ceiling that must not be exceeded or the facility is not affordable economically. These limits fix an area within which fall a range of acceptable design solutions.

In this area there are performance and schedule values above the minimum established requirement that are useful and can be obtained within the cost ceiling. There are also performance and schedule values within the acceptable range that are unjustifiable in view of the utility versus cost of the added performance. The design-to-cost process combined with life-cycle cost analysis identifies the optimum cost-effective design solution within the acceptable range and develops a design that can be successfully built within the cost goal.

Cost ceiling

Range of acceptable solutions

Minimum performance baseline

Figure 10.10 Cost and performance limits in design to cost.

10.3.3 SUNK COST

Sunk costs represent previous expenditures that cannot be recovered. An important criterion for selecting costs to be used in a life-cycle cost analysis is that the costs must be relevant to the decision of choosing between alternatives. A sunk cost represents money that has been spent prior to the time of the analysis and cannot be recovered. Therefore it is irrelevant to future expenditures. For example, if funds have been expended on a preliminary design effort for one site plan and an alternative site plan is to be evaluated, the expended funds are sunk costs for the original site plan. The evaluation can include only those remaining design costs for the original site plan that have not been spent. However, sunk costs do not necessarily include the total amount of previous outlays. Any residual value of previous expenditures that may subsequently reduce future outlays for an alternative must be taken into account. In a life-cycle cost analysis, sunk costs are disregarded unless they can reduce the future expenditure of funds for any one alternative.

10.3.4 SALVAGE VALUE

Salvage value—sometimes referred to as residual value—is the estimated economic value of a facility, including land, at the end of its life cycle. Usually, salvage value has little impact in a life-cycle cost tradeoff analysis of design alternatives because the present worth of the salvage value is normally small relative to the present worth of total ownership costs. However, there are cases where the salvage value is substantial. This may occur, for example, where special equipment can be sold easily to other building owners. If the salvage value is significant it must be included in the analysis. Refer to Section 10.2 for the criteria for selecting costs that are to be used in life-cycle cost analyses.

10.3.5 PRESENT VALUE, DISCOUNT RATE, AND UNIFORM ANNUITY

Present value—sometimes referred to as present worth—is the value at the present time of a sum of money or cash flow that will be received or spent at some future time. The concept allows the investor to determine, for example, what $500 that will be received 10 years from now is worth today. Money has a time value, and the procedure presumes that a dollar is worth more today than it will be in the future because of the interest cost of money and the value of the current resources that can be put to alternative uses. Thus, the present value of a future cash flow is less than its undiscounted dollar value. In other words, referring to the above example, $500 that will be received 10 years from now is worth much less than $500 received today. Furthermore, because of the time value of money, the present value of $500 that will be received five years from now is less than $500, and so forth. It must be recognized at this time that the time value of money reflects the opportunity for investment or the cost of the use of money and is not inflation.

Mathematically, present value of a single cash expenditure or receipt is calculated by the following formula.

$$PV = x \left[\frac{1}{(1 + i)^n} \right]$$

where PV = present value
  x = an expenditure or receipt occurring in the future, n
  n = number of years
  i = discount rate

Tabular solutions for this formula are available in most engineering economics books for a range of values for n and i. Use of the tables can greatly simplify the mathematics. For purpose of illustration, tabulated values (known as present value factors or discount factors) for the present value formula are shown in Figure 10.11. By multiplying a

| Year | Interest rate (i) | | | |
(n)	3%	7%	10%	15%
1	0.9709	0.9346	0.9091	0.8696
2	0.9426	0.8734	0.8264	0.7561
3	0.9151	0.8163	0.7513	0.6575
4	0.8885	0.7629	0.6830	0.5718
5	0.8626	0.7130	0.6209	0.4972
6	0.8375	0.6663	0.5645	0.4323
7	0.8131	0.6227	0.5132	0.3759
8	0.7894	0.5820	0.4665	0.3269
9	0.7664	0.5439	0.4241	0.2843
10	0.7441	0.5083	0.3855	0.2472

Figure 10.11 Present value factors.

given dollar value by the appropriate present value factor for a selected time (n) and discount rate (i), the same solution is obtained as if it were calculated from the formula. For example, with a discount rate of 10%, the present value of a $500 cost to be incurred 10 years from now may be calculated in two ways.

1. By using the present value formula:

$$PV = 500 \left[\frac{1}{(1 + 0.10)^{10}} \right] = \$193$$

where $n = 10$ years
   $i = 10\%$
   $x = \$500$

2. By using present value factors:

$$PV = \$500 \ (0.3855) = \$193$$

where 0.3855 is the present value factor from Figure 10.11 for a 10% discount rate at a period of 10 years.

The present value of multiple cash flows is determined by summing the present values of the individual cash flows. This is expressed algebraically as follows.

$$PV = \sum_{a=1}^{n} PV_a$$

where PV = present value of cash flows
   PV_a = present value of any single cash flow
   $\sum_{a=1}^{n}$ = summation of the individual cash flows from the first to the final, F

This concept is illustrated by the following example. Assume an owner has the opportunity to make an investment that will yield him the following cash flows.

First year	$500
Second year	400
Third year	300
Fourth year	200
Fifth (final) year	100
Salvage value at end of fifth year	50

Assuming a 10% discount rate, what is the present value of these cash flows? Using the present value factors from Figure 10.11, the individual present values are determined as follows.

$$
\begin{aligned}
PV_1 &= 500(0.9091) = 454.55 \\
PV_2 &= 400(0.8264) = 330.56 \\
PV_3 &= 300(0.7513) = 225.39 \\
PV_4 &= 200(0.6830) = 136.60 \\
PV_F &= 100(0.6209) = 62.09 \\
PV_{\text{salvage}} &= 50(0.6209) = 31.05
\end{aligned}
$$

The present value for the cash flows is then determined from the formula as follows.

$$ PV = \sum_{a=1}^{F} PV_a $$

$$ PV = PV_1 + PV_2 + PV_3 + PV_4 + PV_F + PV_{\text{salvage}} $$
$$ PV = \$454.55 + \$330.56 + \$225.39 + \$136.60 + \$62.09 + \$31.05 $$
$$ PV = \$1240.24 $$

An important factor in determining the present value of a cash flow, whether one employs the formula or the tabular solution, is the discount rate (i). This is the interest rate used to discount or apply the time value of money to future cash flows for the purpose of adjusting them to their present value. In private industry the discount rate takes two forms. First, if the firm is borrowing funds, the discount rate is the current or expected interest the firm must pay for the use of the borrowed funds. Second, if the firm uses its own money it forgoes the opportunity of loaning out that money or putting it to work on some other project. In this second situation the discount rate is known as the opportunity cost and is either the minimum acceptable return or the average return for all the firm's investments. In the federal government, the Office of Management and Budget sets the discount rate, which represents an estimate of the average rate of return on private investments before taxes and after inflation and is currently 10%.

The capital recovery factor (also known as the uniform annuity factor) is another discounting concept that is important in life-cycle cost analysis. Mathematically it is expressed as follows.

$$ CR = \frac{i(1 + i)^n}{(1 + i)^n - 1} $$

where CR = capital recovery factor
     i = discount rate
     n = number of years

Year	Interest rate (*i*)			
(*n*)	3%	7%	10%	15%
1	1.03000	1.07000	1.10000	1.15000
2	0.52261	0.55309	0.57619	0.61512
3	0.35353	0.38105	0.40211	0.43798
4	0.26903	0.29523	0.31547	0.35027
5	0.21835	0.24389	0.26380	0.29832
6	0.18460	0.20980	0.22961	0.26424
7	0.16051	0.18555	0.20541	0.24036
8	0.12246	0.16747	0.18744	0.22285
9	0.12843	0.15349	0.17364	0.20957
10	0.11723	0.14238	0.16275	0.19925

Figure 10.12   Capital recovery factors.

As illustrated in Figure 10.12, tabular solutions also exist for the capital recovery factor. The purpose of this factor is to convert a one-time cost or investment into an equivalent uniform cash flow at a certain discount rate for a certain period of years. For example, assume an owner made an investment of $1000 in a project that has an expected life of 10 years and a salvage value of zero. Further assume that the owner has selected an opportunity cost (interest rate) of 10%. What is the average annual return that the owner must receive to recoup his investment?

Average annual return = $1000 (0.16275) = $162.75

where 0.16275 is the capital recovery factor from Figure 10.12 for 10% and 10 years.

The discounting concepts discussed above are utilized in this book as major factors in computing the equivalent uniform annual cost (EUAC). This in turn is the heart of life-cycle cost analysis. The equivalent uniform annual cost concept is developed in Section 10.3.7 and applied to life-cycle cost analysis in Section 10.4.

10.3.6   PRICE LEVEL CHANGES

Price level changes are those variations that occur in the value of the dollar from time to time. They can be separated into two basic categories—general and relative. General price level changes are those variations in the value of the dollar that occur through the overall economy, for example, as a result of inflation. Relative price level changes pertain to the projected dollar value of a particular resource relative to the dollar value of other resources, after removing the effect of general inflation. In other words, the future price of a particular resource may increase or decrease more rapidly than the general price level. This condition results from particular market conditions such as shortages in supplies because of industrial capacity or labor market skills or surges in demand for scarce commodities such as oil and petroleum products. Changes in relative prices of major resources are important in life-cycle cost analysis. They may alter the ranking of alternatives that utilize differing amounts of those resources. To simplify the life-cycle cost analysis and to avoid unnecessary computations, a customary practice is to assume, in the absence of strong evidence to the contrary, that all general price level changes inflate or deflate at the same rate and therefore need not be included in the analysis. However, significant relative price level changes of major resources that can be forecasted with some confidence must be included in the analysis.

10.3.7   EQUIVALENT UNIFORM ANNUAL COST

The equivalent uniform annual cost (EUAC) is a constant annual amount which, if paid throughout the assumed life cycle of the building or system, equals the discounted total life-cycle costs. EUAC converts an uneven stream of expenditures occurring over a number of years to a constant annual amount to simplify the comparison of alternatives. That is, for each alternative the total ownership costs discussed in Section 10.2 are adjusted mathematically to a constant annual amount for comparison purposes as illustrated in Figure 10.13.

Equivalent uniform annual cost is an economic analysis methodology used in tradeoff analysis for comparing the life-cycle costs of several alternatives. EUAC is an equation that computes a constant annual dollar value for each alternative. The dollar values for each alternative are compared, and the alternative with the lowest annual dollar figure is the most cost effective. Furthermore, the annual dollar value of the most cost-effective alternative is compared with the anticipated annualized present value rent. If the EUAC exceeds the anticipated rent, then design-to-cost studies must be performed to generate additional alternative designs that will yield EUACs within the anticipated annualized present value rent.

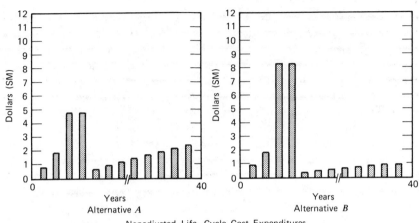

Nonadjusted Life—Cycle Cost Expenditures

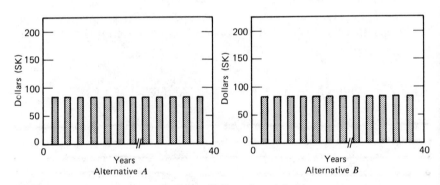

Equivalent Uniform Annual Costs

Figure 10.13 Computation of equivalent uniform annual cost.

Mathematically, EUAC is expressed as follows:

$$\text{EUAC} = CR \left[(I)(PV) + \sum_{a=1}^{n} (PV_a)\,(R + O_a E_a + M_a) + S(PV) \right]$$

where EUAC = equivalent uniform annual cost

CR = capital recovery factor (refer to Section 10.3.5)

PV = present value factor (refer to Section 10.3.5)

I = initial costs of development, design, and construction

$\displaystyle\sum_{a=1}^{n}$ = the sum as a varies from $a = 1$ to the end of the building life cycle, n

R = cost of replacing building components during the building's life cycle

O_a = annual operating cost for the ath year in base year dollars

E_a = differential escalator for the ath year to adjust utility costs for future rises in price greater than the general price level

M_a = annual maintenance cost for the ath year in base year dollars

S = salvage value of the building and land at the end of the assumed building life cycle

As can be seen by the equation, the EUAC is obtained by multiplying the costs of each year of ownership by the present value factor, summing these to reach the present value of the total life cycle costs, and then multiplying this value by the capital recovery factor. The formula can be calculated either manually or by computer. If several alternatives are involved, the calculations usually are computerized. The present value (PV) and capital recovery (CR) factors normally are taken from tabular solutions. The discount rate (i) and the life cycle (n) also are reflected in PV and CR as discussed in Section 10.3.5. Contained in the equation is an escalation factor to compensate for the projected rapid increases in fuel cost. Additional escalation factors can be added as necessary to take into consideration relative price changes of other resources as discussed in Section 10.3.6.

10.3.8 UNCERTAINTY AND SENSITIVITY ANALYSIS

As can be seen from the equation in the preceding section, evaluation results can be quite sensitive to both the estimates and assumptions employed in the analysis. That is, a significant change in any one factor of the equation, such as the discount rate or projected operation costs, could cause a significant change in the EUAC. Although there is a need to depend on historical cost data, statistical methods, and the forecasting of future costs, using such estimates and assumptions tends to generate a degree of uncertainty in the raw numerical results.

Uncertainty enters life-cycle costing in many ways. Examples of sources of uncertainty are:

• Differences between the actual and the expected performance of the system and subsystems could affect future operation and maintenance costs.

- Changes in operational assumptions arising from modifications in user activities (for example, going from an 8-hour, 5-day week to a 10-hour, 4-day week operation) can alter operating, maintenance, or repair costs.

- Uncertainty as to future technological advances that could provide lower-cost alternatives in the future can shorten the economic life of a proposed system.

- Changes in the price levels of a major resource (such as energy) relative to other resources can affect future alteration costs.

- Uncertainty develops in the estimating of initial costs due to errors in estimating relationships, price rates for specific resources, and the rate of inflation in overall building costs from the time the estimate is prepared until the building is ready for occupancy. This can result in actual acquisition costs that differ from the estimates.

A sensitivity analysis technique is available to reduce the degree of uncertainty. In essence, sensitivity simply means that the decision maker asks what will happen if an assumption is changed. A range of changes is developed for each assumption under question. The EUAC is recalculated for each change of one assumption while the other assumptions are held constant. This procedure is continued until recalculations are made for all assumptions being tested. Such a series of sensitivity tests provides the decision maker with the necessary information for appraising the impact of uncertainties on the ranking of alternatives. If the changes associated with the assumptions have an insignificant impact—that is, do not change the relative ranking of the alternatives—then the assumption can be used in the life-cycle cost analysis; otherwise, more valid assumptions must be found.

10.4 LIFE-CYCLE COST ANALYSIS

Life-cycle cost analysis considers total relevant costs over the life of a system, including costs of acquisition, maintenance, operation, alterations, and where applicable, disposal. It is a valuable tool for both the comparative analysis of design and ownership alternatives and the collection of data for future analyses. Life-cycle cost analysis can be applied during any stage of the building process: development, design, construction, and operation and maintenance. As shown in Figure 10.14, the process is composed of a number of key steps, normally performed sequentially.

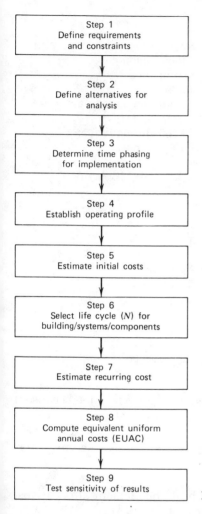

Step 1
Define requirements
and constraints

Step 2
Define alternatives for
analysis

Step 3
Determine time phasing
for implementation

Step 4
Establish operating profile

Step 5
Estimate initial costs

Step 6
Select life cycle (N) for
building/systems/components

Step 7
Estimate recurring cost

Step 8
Compute equivalent uniform
annual costs (EUAC)

Step 9
Test sensitivity of results

Figure 10.14 Life-cycle cost analysis process.

Define Requirements

The first step in life-cycle cost analysis is to define the requirements
that the building or system must meet. These requirements are developed from an analysis of the owner's needs. They must be expressed
quantitatively, as illustrated in Figure 10.15. Further, any special
constraints must be identified at this time.

Define Alternatives

A set of alternatives that satisfy the requirements are selected. The
intent here is to identify all practical design approaches for further

General Description

Building location	Anytown, Anystate
Building type	Office building
Occupancy date	March 1979
Number of occupants	1300
Special features/rooms	Auditorium, cafeteria
Budget	$13 million
Energy budget	50,000 Btu per square foot per year

Statistical Data

Gross square feet	360,000
Occupiable square feet	259,000
Parking spaces	
Interior	275
Exterior	110
Basements	2
Stories above grade	Maximum 10
Stories below grade	Maximum 3

Performance Criteria

Relative humidity	$> 30\% < 55\%$
Temperature	$> 65°F < 80°F$

Figure 10.15   Building requirements.

analysis. An alternative may be dropped from consideration because it offers little promise of meeting the requirements or because its cost is so great compared to other costs that in reality it does not provide a reasonable cost alternative. Essentially the process of selecting alternatives for further study is as follows:

- Identify feasible design, concept, and building element alternatives.
- Obtain performance requirements of each.
- Screen alternatives, eliminating those that do not meet defined performance requirements and constraints.
- Remaining alternatives are candidates for further analysis.

Determine Time Phasing

A crucial step is to determine when the life-cycle cost analysis will be accomplished. Figure 10.16 illustrates this concept. Selection of an implementation time is important because most costs incurred prior to the life-cycle cost analysis are sunk costs. In life-cycle cost analysis, sunk costs must be disregarded unless they can reduce the future

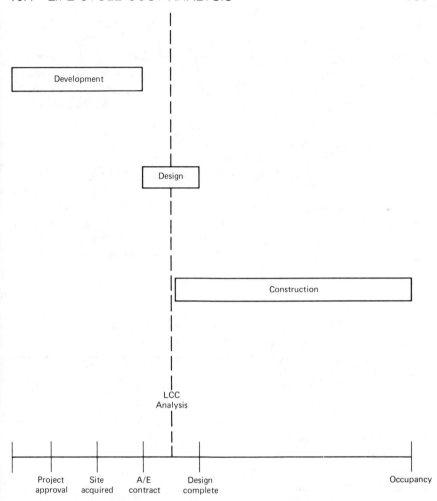

Figure 10.16 Time phasing of life-cycle cost analysis.

expenditure of funds for any one alternative. ~~The analysis must be accomplished as soon as reliable information is available.~~ Decisions concerning some alternatives must be made early, whereas decisions concerning other alternatives can be postponed to a later time. Therefore it is conceivable that several life-cycle cost analyses will be made throughout the life cycle of a project.

Establish Operating Profile

An operating profile is established for each alternative to be analyzed. That is, if two different building configurations are to be analyzed, an operating profile must be established for the entire building: the number of hours in use each day, the required energy, the number of janitorial help, and so forth. However, if the analysis compares elevators and escalators it is necessary to have only the operating profile for those two alternatives. The operating profile assists in defining and estimating recurring costs that are applicable to each alternative.

Estimate Initial Costs

The cost to acquire each alternative is estimated. To ensure consistency in cost estimating and the subsequent analysis of the alternatives, base year prices are used for each alternative. Base year prices are those of the current year in which the analysis is being performed. Cost estimates based upon historical and expected price levels are adjusted to base year values by industry-accepted escalation and de-escalation methods.

Select Life Cycle

The life cycle of each individual building element or system is estimated. The selection of a specific number of years for a life cycle establishes the duration of time over which operating costs are estimated. Whenever possible, a prediction of a life cycle is based upon actual historical data. However, in the absence of such data, estimates from engineers, technical and trade journals, trade associations, manufacturers, and operating personnel are used. In any case, the determined life cycle is applied consistently for all alternatives. That is, if it is determined that vertical transportation systems have a life cycle of 25 years, then this figure is employed in calculating all the vertical transportation system alternatives.

Estimate Recurring Costs

There are three types of recurring costs: the normal operation and maintenance costs that are incurred on a daily, weekly, or monthly basis; the annual costs for utilities and fuels; and the recurring costs of repair, alterations, and replacement of building elements or systems. Estimates of their occurrence and periodicity depend on the estimates of the life cycles derived in the previous step. Estimates of daily operation and maintenance costs are derived using the operating profile and are developed into a yearly lump sum cost. The computation of utility costs is based on the estimated consumption of energy for the determined operating profile. In the case of energy costs it may be necessary to adjust their future price levels. The differential escalation rate (E_a in the EUAC formula) is the predicted difference between the rise in the general price level and that of the specific utility or fuel. Estimates for repair, alteration, and replacement of building elements and systems are expressed in base year dollars without any adjustment for inflation.

Compute Equivalent Uniform Annual Costs

The computation of the EUAC is the actual analysis of the alternatives. The information generated in the previous steps is all that is needed to calculate the EUAC, with one exception—the discount rate, which is either the cost of borrowing money or the owner's opportunity cost. Once this is established, the present value and capital recovery factors are calculated or derived from tabular solutions as discussed in Section 10.3.5. The EUAC is calculated either manually or by computer. In many instances the analysis does not concern the design of the total building and its major elements but alternatives of much less significance, such as the installation of one type of floor covering versus another. The steps and procedures discussed in this section are equally as applicable to a tradeoff analysis of individual building elements or systems as to an analysis of total building cost. The only difference is in the depth of detail involved. The process of computing the EUAC is basically the same as discussed in Section 10.3.7, regardless of the significance of the alternatives being analyzed.

Test Sensitivity of Results

The results from the EUAC computation for each alternative automatically establish their ranking. The lowest EUAC is the preferred alternative, based on a total life-cycle cost approach. However, it is necessary to test the sensitivity of these results to ensure that the relative ranking of the alternatives does not shift. Those parameters (such as discount rate, differential escalation rate for adjustment of utility prices, length of life cycle, and so forth) for which a degree of uncertainty exists undergo further evaluation as explained in Section 10.3.8. Once these sensitivity tests are completed, the resulting lowest life-cycle cost alternative is recommended for implementation. Chapter 12 contains a life-cycle costing case study that illustrates the method of analysis.

CHAPTER 11

PROBLEM SOLVING
AND PROJECT VALUE

11.1 INTRODUCTION

Value management methodology provides a systematic approach to problem solving and decision making and can be applied to a wide variety of problem areas. For example, on an office building project a multistory structure was required. Because of the necessity of locating air conditioning ducts, conduits, telephone lines, and so forth between the ceiling and the floor above, the total height of the building would have exceeded the height limitation imposed by the zoning code. By using VM methodology and problem-solving techniques, a VM study team developed the solution shown in Figure 11.1. Illustrated is the underside of an inverted "pan" construction for a poured concrete floor with oblong holes left in the concrete beam portion of the floor. The holes perform the function of ducts through which pass conduits, cables, and so forth. The result was a savings in space that made possible the erection of the structure within the stipulated height limitation.

But the study team did not stop here. By employing potential problem analysis the team recognized and avoided two potential problems. First, was it possible to put holes in the concrete beam and still retain the required strength of the floor? The team took the new design to a concrete testing laboratory. Samples were built and tested. The new floor design was actually stronger than the similar design without holes. The second potential problem was one of fabrication. How could the holes be included at a reasonable cost? Several solutions were developed. The one selected consisted of wedging polyurethane foam between the pans (see Figure 11.1). The concrete was then poured around the foam and the blocks left in place. After the forms were

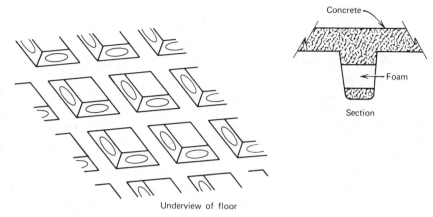

Figure 11.1 Problem solving—conduits through concrete floor.

removed it was a simple procedure to knock out the blocks at each location where a conduit was needed.

This simple example illustrates that value management is a valuable problem-solving tool. However, before applying VM techniques to problem solving, it is necessary to understand the nature of a problem and problem-solving concepts. These are treated in the following sections.

Problem solving and decision making are the most important tasks of a top manager. His success and the success of his project or organization virtually depend on doing these tasks well. Every manager, whether knowingly or not, uses some kind of system for making decisions and solving problems. Yet few recognize this fact, and even fewer follow a definite, prescribed methodology. As a result, quite frequently the best decision is not made or the best solution is not selected. Most managers claim they do not have sufficient time to apply a systematic method. They argue that they are forced by urgency to rely on intuition and to make quick decisions. They consider a systematic approach unsuited to the hectic demands of a modern project environment. Yet this is precisely where the manager desperately needs an efficient method for handling problems and decisions.

In a typical problem situation, the manager is frequently under pressure to do something. People are clamoring for action. Time may be short. The manager may not have all the information or resources he needs. Further, he needs to know what is wrong before he can make it right. He has to know specifically what the problem is and track down the cause before he can begin to decide on the best and most efficient corrective action. Doing this under pressure is not easy, but it can be done. A systematic way of doing something is always superior to a disorderly approach, which may require several attempts to reach the right answer. And the more systematic and logical the method, the faster and more efficiently it works.

More often than not, a top decision maker manages experts who know far more about the work details than he does. No manager can expect to keep up with all the technical information his subordinates deal with every day. The separation of the decision maker from the technical knowledge and skills of those he manages has always existed to a degree, but in recent years this separation has increased rapidly as projects become more complicated and sophisticated, as construction materials and methods proliferate and as laws and regulations multiply. His technical knowledge soon becomes antiquated and obsolete. The higher the decision maker is in management the further removed he is from the immediate problems of the project and the knowledge that might help in solving such problems. Without some method of analysis to tell him what his better informed subordinates should be doing about the problems, he cannot begin to monitor their operations or ask the penetrating questions that will improve the net result.

11.2 NATURE OF A PROBLEM

All problems basically are of a common nature. Figure 11.2 illustrates the essence of a problem. A problem has two essential characteristics. First, it is a deviation between what *should* be happening and what

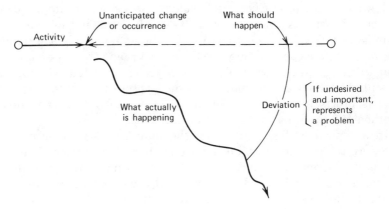

Figure 11.2 Nature of a problem.

actually is happening. Second, the deviation is undesired and important enough that the responsible manager thinks it should be corrected. The second characteristic is what makes the deviation a problem. For example, an undesired deviation is a schedule slippage which
if large and important could threaten the completion time of the project. Yet a desired deviation is an overall acceleration of the project
that could result in an early project completion date with the accompanying benefits of early occupancy and early generation of revenues
or savings of rent payments. Usually the deviation is brought about by
an unanticipated change or occurrence. Before the deviation the activity is proceeding as planned; afterwards it is off plan and possibly out of
control.

Problem solving is a procedure that necessarily involves a logical
sequence of activities. The process begins by identifying the problem, it
continues with an analysis to determine the cause of the problem, and
it concludes with the decision of what corrective action is to be taken.
The initial and obviously most important step is to precisely identify
and describe the problem.

A problem clearly stated is already half solved; conversely, a problem cannot be efficiently solved unless it is precisely described. How
can a decision maker correct a problem if he does not know exactly
what that problem is? In specifying a problem, the manager searches
for those facts that draw a boundary line around the problem. It is not a
blind hunt for "all the facts." Instead it is a careful investigation that
yields all the relevant and important information about the problem
and excludes everything that is superfluous and irrelevant. The specification procedure described in this section is the most valuable single
tool a manager can have for solving any kind of problem. The actual
specification process is simple and systematic, even to the extent of
being mechanical. However, the process does demand firm discipline of
the manager's thinking habits. He must restrain himself from the urge
to look for the cause of the problem and adhere to describing the
problem. The search for the cause comes later. The observant reader
will recognize the process as a modification of the early phases of the
VM methodology described in Chapter 8. As in any management undertaking, basic principles and concepts must be tailored to fit the
particular situations at hand.

Any problem can be precisely specified by systematically getting
answers to the following questions.

1. What is the deviation? What is the thing or activity in which the
deviation is observed?

2. Where is the deviation? Where is the thing when the deviation is observed, or where in the building process is the deviation observed?

3. When does the deviation appear?

4. How big or what is the extent of the deviation? How many different things or different activities are affected by the same deviation?

All that can be said about any problem is found in the answers to these questions. They provide the only relevant information needed to completely describe the problem. But there is one more factor to consider. What the problem *IS* must be sharply separated from what the problem *IS NOT*. In other words, the specification shows both the *IS* and the *IS NOT* for each question. The following example illustrates the entire technique for specifying a problem. On a high-rise building under construction, it is observed that at certain times particular window panes pop out of their frames and crash into the surrounding area below. Figure 11.3 shows how this problem is precisely specified by the information obtained from the questioning procedure described above. The reason for such precision in specification will be clear as soon as the search is begun to identify the cause of the problem.

	Is	Is not
What is deviation?	1. Window panes popping out of their frames	1. No other item is falling from the structure
Where is the deviation?	1. On upper floors of structure 2. On sides of structure not protected by other nearby high-rise buildings	1. Does not occur on other nearby structures 2. Does not occur on protected sides
When does deviation occur?	1. During high winds 2. During any time of the day when there are high winds	1. Does not occur at any other time
Extent (how big)?	1. All windows that are unprotected and subject to high winds	1. Is not a random occurrence

Figure 11.3 Specifying a problem.

As the example in Figure 11.3 shows, all the questions concern what, where, when, and how big. The question "why" is never asked. "Why" is answered only when the cause is known. Asking "why" at this time is an invitation to speculate as to causes. If speculation is allowed during the fact-finding phase, the tendency is to develop facts that "prove" a cause that the manager suspects or about which he has a hunch. This does not mean that hunches must be ignored. However, he must set them aside until he has specified the problem and is ready to analyze it for causes. Only after he has drawn a boundary line around the problem can he proceed to analyze the specifications for clues to the problem's cause.

11.3 SYSTEMS APPROACH TO PROBLEM ANALYSIS

Problem analysis is the logical process of narrowing down a body of information during the search for a solution. At each stage the procedure becomes more precise, as the process flows sequentially—from examining the overall situation, to recognizing the problem, to determining probable causes, and finally to deciding the most likely cause. Locating the cause makes it possible to take effective corrective action on the problem. However, if problem analysis is to be successful it must be executed in a systematic manner. Figure 11.4 illustrates the systems approach to problem solving. The sequential steps in this system are listed below.

1. Recognize the problem.
2. Specify the problem.
3. Develop possible causes.
4. Test and determine the true cause.
5. Develop solutions to the cause.
6. Test the solutions.
7. Decide on the best solution.

Steps 1 and 2 have been discussed in the previous two sections; step 7 is treated in Section 11.4. Steps 3 through 6 inclusive are the main concern of this section.

The search for the cause of any problem is a search for change. It is a search for that different and unplanned thing that has upset the course of an expected sequence of events. The plan identifies what should occur. Problems are identified by comparing actual to planned perfor-

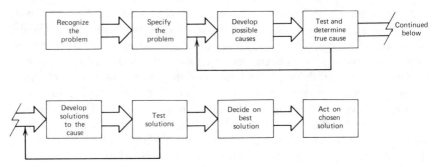

Figure 11.4   Systems approach to problem solving.

mance. To find the cause is to determine what produced the effect not identified in the plan. A manager who can precisely specify the problem can simplify the search by restricting it to those changes that could have produced the deviation and by ignoring others. What the manager wants is the one critical change that caused the problem. To find it he must confine himself to those changes that are related to the *IS* and the *IS NOT* of the problem specification. This concept greatly clarifies the determination of cause.

This concept is illustrated by further developing the example cited in the previous section. From Figure 11.3 it can be seen that there are three prominent items that could be related to the deviation: (1) the window frames, (2) the window panes, and (3) the high winds. To determine the changes associated with all or either of these items is a simple matter of comparing what actually exists with what was originally planned. This is done by asking the following questions:

1. Concerning the window frames.
   - Have they been built according to specification?
   - Was there any defect in the manufacturing process?
   - Are the frames at the upper levels different than those at the lower?
   - Are the frames on the unprotected sides of the structure different than those on the other sides?

2. Concerning the window panes, the same questions could be asked.
   - Are the panes different from those originally specified?
   - Was there any defect in the manufacturing process?
   - Are the panes on the upper levels different from those at the lower level?

  ○ Are the panes on the unprotected sides of the structure different from those on the other sides?

3. Concerning the high winds.
  ○ Are the high winds different than what was predicted?
  ○ Did the very act of erecting the structure change the configuration of the skyline to such an extent that it influenced the wind pattern?
  ○ Were proper frames and panes specified for the anticipated and actual winds?

In researching these questions the manager came up with negative answers for all the questions concerning both the frames and panes. However, he uncovered the following facts about the wind patterns.

1. The existing wind patterns were different from what was predicted.
2. Tests made before and after the structure was erected indicated that the structure itself was causing a chimney effect, resulting in higher wind velocities and greater wind pressures than was predicted on the unprotected sides of the upper level of the structure.

The manager then developed the hypothesis that the cause of the problem was extremely great wind force. To test this hypothesis a model was built and tested in a wind tunnel. Slow motion pictures made of the tests showed that the window panes, although meeting their original specifications, were too thin for the existing wind conditions. The wind force was sufficiently great to bend the panes just enough to pull the edges from the window frames.

Once the cause was known, the next step was to develop possible solutions. By using the techniques described in Chapters 8 and 9, the following solutions were generated.

1. Replace the existing window panes with thicker panes that will withstand the greater wind velocities and pressures. Also replace those parts of the window frame necessary to accept the thicker glass.
2. Substitute for the existing window frame a frame that will take several small panes instead of a single large one. Being smaller, the glass will be less flexible and therefore less likely to bend and pop out of its frame.

Two additional models were built, each representing a different solution. Both models were tested in the wind tunnel. Test results indicated that both designs were technically good solutions to the problem. Two things yet remained to be done. First it was necessary to decide which was the one best solution. Second, the selected solution had to be analyzed to be certain that it in itself did not present any potential problems. These final two activities are treated in Sections 11.4 and 11.5, respectively.

11.4   DECISION MAKING

Making a good decision is the toughest duty of a manager. A decision is a choice between alternative methods of achieving a desired end. Usually it is a compromise between what is wanted and what is actually available. However, the manager must select that alternative that comes the closest to obtaining the desired result while minimizing the costs and disadvantages. Day-to-day decision making is related mainly to problem solving, and many of the related difficulties are eliminated if the manager thoroughly understands the systematic approach to problem solving. As can be seen from Figure 11.4, decision making is an important factor in the systems approach.

A good decision evolves systematically when the following procedure is employed.

1. Set objectives against which to choose alternatives.
2. Prioritize the objectives.
3. Evaluate the alternatives against the objectives.
4. Choose an alternative as a tentative decision.
5. Determine any potential problems that might arise from implementing the tentative decision.
6. Implement the selected alternative and follow up on the decision.

Set Objectives

This is an extremely important step because it establishes the desired results. Furthermore, the objectives must be as specific as possible. For example, the objectives for the window-pane problem are as follows: eliminate the cause of the problem; must not exceed the available contingency funds; should not alter the appearance of the building; and must not lengthen the critical path of the overall project schedule.

Establish Priorities for the Objectives

All objectives influence the alternative that is selected. However, some are more important than others, and some are mandatory while others are just desirable. Therefore, it is critical to establish priorities for the objectives. Priorities are established in many ways; the owner may arbitrarily establish them, the state of the art of the technology of the proposed alternatives may determine them, the availability of resources or the manufacturers' capabilities to produce the alternatives may influence the ranking of the objectives, and so forth. In the example under study, the priorities were determined to be:

1. Must eliminate the cause of the problem.
2. Should not exceed the available contingency funds.
3. Should not lengthen the critical path of the project schedule.
4. Should not alter the appearance of the building.

Evaluate the Alternatives

To evaluate an alternative, the manager tests it against the objectives. This screens out the impossibilities and reduces the number of feasible alternatives to a relevant few. The easiest procedure for doing this is to use a numerical scoring system. For example, the top priority objective may be assigned a value of 10, the next a value of 9, and so forth. How well each alternative accomplishes the objective is scored over a range of, say, 1 to 10. This score is multiplied by the value of the objective to arrive at a total score of that alternative for that objective. The individual objective scores of each alternative are summed to arrive at the total score for that alternative. Figure 11.5 illustrates this procedure.

	Alternatives (score)	
Objectives (value)	1. Replace glass (1 to 10)	2. Substitute frames (1 to 10)
1. Eliminate cause (10)	$10 \times 10 = 100$	$10 \times 10 = 100$
2. Within available funds (9)	$9 \times 10 = 90$	$9 \times 9 = 81$
3. Effect on schedule (8)	$8 \times 7 = 56$	$8 \times 4 = 32$
4. Effect on appearance (7)	$7 \times 10 = 70$	$7 \times 2 = 14$
Total score	316	227

Figure 11.5 Evaluating alternatives.

Both alternatives would have eliminated the cause, so they were both given the maximum score. The costs of both would have been within the allowable funds. However, alternative 2 would have cost slightly more than alternative 1, so was given a lower score. Both would have caused a slippage in the critical path, with alternative 2 creating a greater slippage. Because alternative 1 would not have changed the appearance of the building, it was given a perfect score. However, alternative 2 scored very low on this objective because it would have affected the building's appearance.

Choose a Tentative Decision

The alternative that receives the highest total score is presumably the best selection. However, this is only a tentative decision and may not be the best choice when everything has been considered.

Determine Any Potential Problems

The manager at this point is looking for any hidden or obscure shortcomings. He investigates the tentatively chosen alternative as if it were already in operation. He wants to know how his decision will affect the project and how the other events of the project will affect his decision. What are the secondary effects, if any? The manager asks staff members to help poke holes in his decision, and one or more of the staff may play the devil's advocate. For simple decisions, questioning the side effects is sufficient; however, for major decisions the potential problem analysis technique discussed in the next section must be used.

Implement the Decision and Follow Up

This final step is crucial to the entire decision-making procedure. To ensure that the selected decision is properly implemented, the manager must follow a systematic implementation procedure as follows:

1. Set up controls and reporting procedures to monitor the implementation.

2. Follow up on directions and instructions to assure that they are executed in a timely and appropriate manner.

3. Determine areas of responsibility and make sure that everyone concerned knows who is responsible for what.

4. Set up specific milestones for each event that must be executed to carry out the decision.

5. Set up a warning system that flags potential problem areas as early as possible.

The decision-making methodology described herein does not guarantee success, but it does greatly reduce the uncertainty related to decision making.

11.5 POTENTIAL PROBLEM ANALYSIS

The most competent managers take action before any particular problem occurs. The analysis of potential problems is more of an art than a science and is still rare. Yet the philosophy is so well known that it has become an axiom: An ounce of prevention is worth a pound of cure. Potential problem analysis requires an approach different from problem analysis. In problem analysis the cause has happened, and the manager tries to identify it. But in potential problem analysis, both the deviations and causes are only possibilities, and the manager must take action to prevent them from occurring. Any potential problem can jeopardize or wreck a project. Therefore, the manager must consider all of them in an orderly fashion. Such a systematic approach is outlined below.

1. Identify what could go wrong.
2. Specifically describe each potential problem.
3. Determine problem priorities.
4. Identify the causes of each high priority problem.
5. Determine priorities of the causes.
6. Take preventive action against high priority causes.
7. Develop contingency plans.

The manager must scrutinize his master plan to identify anything that could go wrong. During this review he trusts only in Murphy's Law: If anything can go wrong, it will. Using this philosophy he will end up with a multitude of potential problems. He then proceeds to develop an accurate description of each one. This tells the manager exactly what the potential problem is, where it might occur, when it might happen, and to what degree. Since the manager cannot cope with every potential problem he must set priorities, culling out the small risks and concentrating on the greatest threats. He selects those high priority problems that require preventive action according to the criteria:

1. How serious will it be if it happens?
2. How probable is it that it might happen?

The manager must act on the problems he considers to be the

greatest risks, treating the others as calculated and accepted risks. For those that he has selected the manager lists all potential causes, drawing heavily on personal judgment and experience. Once again, the manager cannot cope with every cause. By going over each possible cause and estimating the probability of its occurring the manager selects those causes to which he will devote the most attention. He then takes preventive action that removes the possible cause completely or reduces the probability of its occurring. He must take preventive action against each high-risk possible cause, and each possible cause he prevents will reduce the probability of the problem's occurring. Whenever a potential problem is so serious that the manager cannot depend on preventive actions to eliminate the possible causes, he must prepare a contingency plan. This is essential when the stakes are very high and when there is great risk that a failure at any one point will jeopardize the entire project.

Potential problem analysis is the process of applying systematic forethought to the achievement of goals, while problem analysis is the process of applying systematic afterthought. Although the latter is a valuable process, it is far more costly and time consuming than the former. Potential problem analysis is the best means, not only of making past decisions succeed, but of making future decisions fewer and easier.

CHAPTER 12

CASE STUDIES

12.1 LIFE-CYCLE COST ANALYSIS: OFFICE BUILDING ENERGY SYSTEM

Illustrated in this study is the application of life-cycle cost analysis for deciding between two alternative heating systems—a conventional system and a solar system that consists of a solar heat collecting unit and a conventional auxiliary unit. It was chosen for two reasons. First, energy systems currently are foremost in the thoughts of both owners and designers. Second, an analysis of a building system is far simpler than an analysis of an entire building configuration, and the intent here is to employ the simplest and most understandable case which thoroughly illustrates the life-cycle costing technique.

Life-cycle costing is a tool for managing the total value of a project. The emphasis is on an economic analysis and an economically oriented decision. Therefore, to keep this case study as neat as possible, technical and design considerations of the alternatives are not discussed; they have been decided upon in earlier feasibility studies. It now is necessary only to make an economic decision as to which alternative will be utilized. This case study is based on an actual situation.

The structure consists of a two-story office building containing a total of 230,000 gross square feet of floor space. The energy budget for the building is 50,000 Btu per square foot per year, or a total annual load of 115×10^8 Btu.

Two alternative designs had been investigated and chosen for a life-cycle cost analysis—a conventional system and a solar system composed of a solar heat collecting unit and a conventional auxiliary unit. The performance requirements of each are listed below.

1. Conventional system:
   100% of load.
   Efficiency: 55%.
   Fuel: No. 2 heating oil.
2. Solar system:
   60% of load.
   Conventional auxiliary: 40% of load.
   Efficiency of auxiliary: 55%.
   Fuel for auxiliary: No. 2 heating oil.

The analysis was undertaken early in the conceptual design phase; therefore, no sunk costs were incurred. Since either alternative was to be used in the same building configuration, either had to supply energy to an identical operating profile. So in this specific instance the analysis was simplified because the established operating profile was determined to be a heating requirement of 115×10^8 Btu per year. It was further determined that the conventional systems for both alternatives would be of the same capacity since the solar heat collecting unit would not function properly during periods of overcast.

Additional initial costs for the solar heating unit subsystem are as follows:

Solar panels	$350,000
Storage tanks	110,000
Installation of panels and tanks	100,000
Pumps	
Circulation	2,000
Auxiliary circulation	1,000
Piping valves and fittings	37,000
Total	$600,000

It should be emphasized that the only initial costs involved in the analysis are the additional initial costs for the solar heating portion of the solar energy system. The conventional auxiliary heating subsystem of the solar system is identical to the heating unit for the conventional energy alternative and therefore is of equal cost. Furthermore, since both alternatives use the same distribution system, this cost also is identical for both alternatives. In life-cycle cost analysis, costs that are identical for alternatives are ignored. The only costs included in the analysis are the significant, different costs of the alternatives that could influence their ranking.

The life cycle of the solar heat collecting subsystem was estimated to be 20 years. Since there is practically no historical data for units of this size, this life cycle was determined after consultation with the manufacturer's design and production engineers and thus selected for use in the life-cycle cost analysis.

Recurring costs and savings of the solar heat collecting portion of the solar energy system are as follows:

Annual maintenance costs	$ 2,000
Major overhaul at 10th year	$ 4,000
Annual electricity costs	$ 500
Yearly loss of rent (space occupied by storage tanks)	$ 100
Annual savings in fuel oil (see Figure 12.1)	($35,850)

As in determining the initial costs, these costs and savings represent only the differences resulting from the addition of the solar heat collecting unit.

The equivalent uniform annual cost or savings is calculated from the following formula (refer to Section 10.3.7).

$$\text{EUAC} = (CR) \left[(I)(PV) + \sum_{a=1}^{n} (PV_a)(R + U_a + O_a + M_a + I_a) - S(PV) \right]$$

where EUAC = equivalent uniform annual cost (or savings).
  CR = capital recovery factor (refer to section 10.3.5).
  PV = present value factor (refer to Section 10.3.5).
  I = initial costs
  $\sum_{a=1}^{n}$ = the sum as a varies from a = 1 to the end of the system's life cycle, n
  R = cost of major overhauls during the system's life cycle.
  O_a = annual fuel costs or savings for the ath year in base-year dollars
  U_a = annual electric utility costs
  I_a = yearly loss of rent
  M_a = annual maintenance cost for the ath year in base-year dollars
  S = salvage value of the system at the end of the assumed life cycle

Alternative	Gallons of no. 2 fuel oil required per year	Cost (40 cents per gallon)

Solar	115×10^8 Btu $\times$ 40% = 46×10^8 Btu
	 46×10^8 Btu $\div$ 14×10^4 Btu per gallon
	     = 32,900 gallons
	 32,900 gallons $\div$ 0.55 Btu output per Btu input
	     = 59,750 gallons
		$23,900

Conventional	115×10^8 Btu $\div$ 14×10^4 Btu per gallon
	     = 82,250 gallons
	 82,250 gallons $\div$ 0.55 Btu output per Btu input
	     = 149,375 gallons
		$59,750

Annual savings in fuel oil, assuming fuel prices increase with the general price level		$35,850

Figure 12.1   Annual savings in fuel oil.

Only two final items must be covered before calculating the EUAC. First, it was determined that the salvage value of the solar collector and its associated equipment would be zero. Second, the owner of this building employed a discount rate of 10%. This was determined to be the owner's cost of capital. By inserting the figures developed above and from Figures 12.2 and 12.3, the EUAC formula now becomes:

$$EUAC = (0.11746) \{(600,000)(1) + (0.3855)(4000)$$
$$+ (8.514) \times (500 + [-35,850] + 2000 + 100)\}$$
$$= \$37,405.31$$

The capital recovery factor of 0.11746 is for 20 years at a 10% discount rate and is taken from figure 12.2. The present value factor for initial costs is 1 because the analysis was carried out during the projected construction year. Since it is a one-time occurrence, the major overhaul of $4000 is pulled from within the summation symbol. The present value factor for 10 years (the time at which the overhaul is predicted to occur) at 10% is taken from Figure 12.2. The mathematical operation remaining within the summation symbol then becomes a uniform series, and its present value factor of 8.514 is taken from Figure 12.3. It also is for 20 years at a 10% discount rate. The solution to the above equation yields a EUAC of $37,405.31.

This positive number represents an equivalent uniform annual cost. That is, by using a solar collector heating unit to provide 60% of the

Year	Interest rate (*i*)			
(*n*)	3%	7%	10%	15%

Capital recovery factors

Year	3%	7%	10%	15%
1	1.03000	1.07000	1.10000	1.15000
2	0.52261	0.55309	0.57619	0.61512
3	0.35353	0.38105	0.40211	0.43798
4	0.26903	0.29523	0.31547	0.35027
5	0.21835	0.24389	0.26380	0.29832
6	0.18460	0.20980	0.22961	0.26424
7	0.16051	0.18555	0.20541	0.24036
8	0.12246	0.16747	0.18744	0.22285
9	0.12843	0.15349	0.17364	0.20957
10	0.11723	0.14238	0.16275	0.19925
11	0.10808	0.13336	0.16396	0.19107
12	0.10046	0.12590	0.14676	0.18448
13	0.09403	0.11965	0.14078	0.17911
14	0.03853	0.11434	0.13575	0.17469
15	0.08377	0.10979	0.13147	0.17102
16	0.07961	0.10586	0.12782	0.16795
17	0.07595	0.10243	0.12466	0.16537
18	0.07271	0.09941	0.12193	0.16319
19	0.06981	0.09675	0.11977	0.16134
20	0.06722	0.09439	0.11746	0.15976

Present value factors

Year	3%	7%	10%	15%
1	0.9709	0.9346	0.9091	0.8696
2	0.9426	0.8734	0.8264	0.7561
3	0.9151	0.8162	0.7513	0.6575
4	0.8885	0.7629	0.6830	0.5718
5	0.8626	0.7130	0.6209	0.4972
6	0.8375	0.6663	0.5645	0.4323
7	0.8131	0.6227	0.5132	0.3759
8	0.7894	0.5820	0.4665	0.3269
9	0.7664	0.5439	0.4241	0.2843
10	0.7441	0.5083	0.3855	0.2472
11	0.7224	0.4751	0.3505	0.2149
12	0.7014	0.4440	0.3186	0.1869
13	0.6810	0.4150	0.2897	0.1625
14	0.6611	0.3878	0.2633	0.1413
15	0.6419	0.3624	0.2394	0.1229
16	0.6232	0.3387	0.2176	0.1069
17	0.6050	0.3166	0.1978	0.0929
18	0.5874	0.2959	0.1799	0.0808
19	0.5703	0.2765	0.1635	0.0703
20	0.5537	0.2584	0.1486	0.0611

Figure 12.2 Capital recovery and present value factors.

| Year | Interest rate (i) | | | |
(n)	3%	7%	10%	15%
1	0.971	0.935	0.090	0.870
2	1.913	1.808	1.736	1.626
3	2.829	2.624	2.487	2.283
4	3.717	3.387	3.170	2.855
5	4.580	4.100	3.791	3.352
6	5.417	4.767	4.355	3.784
7	6.230	5.389	4.868	4.160
8	7.020	5.971	5.335	4.487
9	7.786	6.515	5.759	4.772
10	8.530	7.024	6.144	5.019
11	9.253	7.499	6.495	5.234
12	9.954	7.943	6.814	5.421
13	10.635	8.358	7.103	5.583
14	11.296	8.745	7.367	5.724
15	11.938	9.108	7.606	5.847
16	12.561	9.447	7.824	5.954
17	13.166	9.763	8.022	6.047
18	13.754	10.059	8.201	6.128
19	14.324	10.336	8.365	6.198
20	14.877	10.594	8.514	6.259

Figure 12.3 Uniform series present value factors.

heat load of the building, the owner will realize an additional average annual cost in the total life-cycle cost of ownership of about $37,405. In other words the analysis indicates that from an economic viewpoint the conventional system must be selected over the solar system.

However, before the final decision can be made, a sensitivity analysis must be accomplished. This is to ensure that the ranking of the alternatives does not change. In this case it is assumed that the fuel oil costs will increase at a rate 5% per year greater than the general price level changes. The EUAC formula now becomes:

$$\left[EUAC = (CR) \left[(I)(PV) + \sum_{a=1}^{n} (PV_a)(R + U_a + E_a O_a + M_a + I_a) - S(PV) \right] \right.$$

The difference between this and the previous formula is the factor E_a. E_a is the differential escalator for the ath year to adjust fuel oil costs for future rises in prices greater than the general price level. E_a factors are illustrated in Figure 12.4.

Year	Escalation factors		
(n)	2%	5%	7%
1	1.020	1.050	1.070
2	1.040	1.103	1.145
3	1.061	1.158	1.225
4	1.082	1.216	1.311
5	1.104	1.276	1.403
6	1.126	1.340	1.501
7	1.149	1.407	1.606
8	1.172	1.477	1.718
9	1.195	1.551	1.838
10	1.219	1.629	1.967
11	1.243	1.710	2.105
12	1.268	1.796	2.252
13	1.294	1.886	2.410
14	1.319	1.980	2.579
15	1.346	2.079	2.759
16	1.373	2.183	2.952
17	1.400	2.292	3.159
18	1.428	2.407	3.380
19	1.457	2.527	3.617
20	1.486	2.653	3.870

Figure 12.4 Differential escalation factors.

This formula is now so complicated that it should be calculated by computer. However, for the purpose of this case study it is calculated manually in Figures 12.5 and 12.6.

The EUAC is now $19,702.78. This means that the owner will realize an additional average annual cost in the total life-cycle cost of ownership of about $19,702. This is less than the previous EUAC of $37,405. The difference is due to the fact that in the second calculation it was assumed that fuel oil costs will increase more rapidly than the general price levels, resulting in greater fuel savings from use of a solar heat collecting unit. However, the second calculation does confirm an increase (although a smaller one) in total ownership costs. Therefore, the ranking of alternatives does not change. That is, the conventional energy system remains the best economic choice.

Illustrated in this case study is the general concept and technique of life-cycle cost analysis. However, each actual case has its uniqueness. The EUAC formula must be tailored to the specific situation by deleting or adding elements as in the second calculation of this study.

$$EUAC = (CR)\left[(PV)(I) + \sum_{a=1}^{n}(PV_a)(R + U_a + E_aO_a + M_a + L_a) - S(PV)\right]$$

$$= (CR)\left[(PV)(I) + \sum_{a=1}^{n}(PV_a \times E_a \times O_a) + (PV_a)(R + U_a + M_a + L_a) - S(PV)\right]$$

$$= (0.11746)[(1)(600,000) + \sum_{a=1}^{20}[(PV_a) \times (E_a) \times (-35,850)] + 0.3855 \times 4000 + 8.514 \times (500 + 2000 + 100)]$$

$$= (0.11746)[(1)(600,000) + \sum_{a=1}^{20}[(PV_a) \times (E_a) \times (-35,850)] + 1,542 + 22,136.40]$$

From figure 12.6: $\sum_{a=1}^{20}[(PV_a) \times (E_a) \times (-35,850)] = -455,938.03$

$$EUAC = (0.11746)[600,000 - 455,938.03 + 1,542 + 22,136.40]$$

$$= 19,702.78$$

Figure 12.5 Manual calculation of EUAC.

n	PV_a	×	E_a	×	35,850	=	
1	0.9091		1.050		35,850		34,220.80
2	0.8264		1.103		35,850		32,677.96
3	0.7513		1.158		35,850		31,189.69
4	0.6830		1.216		35,850		29,774.43
5	0.6209		1.276		35,850		28,402.82
6	0.5645		1.340		35,850		27,118.02
7	0.5132		1.407		35,850		25,886.30
8	0.4665		1.477		35,850		24,701.38
9	0.4241		1.551		35,850		23,581.38
10	0.3855		1.629		35,850		22,513.06
11	0.3505		1.710		35,850		21,486.88
12	0.3186		1.796		35,850		20,513.57
13	0.2897		1.886		35,850		19,587.52
14	0.2633		1.980		35,850		18,689.82
15	0.2394		2.079		35,850		17,842.99
16	0.2176		2.183		35,850		17,029.50
17	0.1978		2.292		35,850		16,252.87
18	0.1799		2.407		35,850		15,523.74
19	0.1635		2.527		35,850		14,811.95
20	0.1486		2.653		35,850		14,133.35
Total							455,938.03

Figure 12.6 Tabular solution of escalated fuel oil savings.

12.2 VALUE MANAGEMENT ANALYSIS: SITE SELECTION

The National Oceanographic and Atmospheric Administration (NOAA) had acquired a surplus military site outside of Seattle, Washington upon which it was to build a research facility. The problem was to determine the optimum site layout.

12.2.1 EVALUATION OF SITE ORGANIZATION ALTERNATIVES

The three site organization alternatives were developed equitably. The facilities were sized on the basis of requirements with suitable adjustments to gain gross factors from net, considering standards where applicable. Figures 12.7, 12.8, and 12.9 illustrate the three site layout alternatives.

Basis, Methods, and Rationale for Costs

Costs were developed for each alternative by using a "planalysis" matrix on which facility characteristics were presented in the usual units of measure (square feet, kilowatts, square yards, etc.). For each unit of measure a cost figure was developed. The functions to be satisfied by the facility were listed along with the units of measure, as shown in Figure 12.10. Organizational occupants or users were aligned to each function. Units required were tabulated and then multiplied by unit costs, which were specifically in 1975 Seattle dollars.

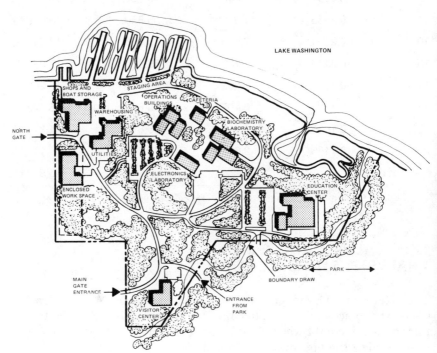

Figure 12.7 Site organization concept, alternative X.

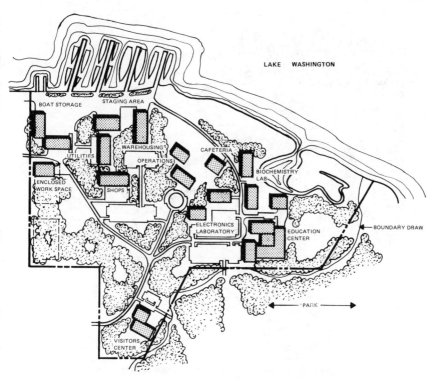

Figure 12.8 Site organization concept, alternative Y.

The matrixes, too large to be reproduced here in readily legible and referable form, are used for backup and also to evaluate impact of changes. A summary explanation of their use is also provided in Figure 12.10.

Since each site organization alternative concept has different characteristics, a series of overlays were used to identify quantitative requirements with respect to distribution of utilities, roads, and other characteristics that affect costs, including building size.

Comparisons and Evaluation

To perform evaluation on costs, the raw engineering estimates were used. Site organizational Alternatives X, Y, and Z are estimated on Tables 12.1, 12.2, and 12.3, respectively. Differences are apparent. Alternative X reflects the functional aggregation of structures. Y, reflective of the organizational array, has more structures; hence, an increased cost over alternative X for that cost element is exposed, as

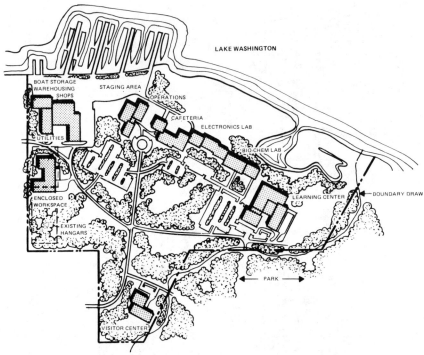

Figure 12.9 Site organization concept, alternative Z.

well as an increase in utilities. Alternative Z, a megastructure, has the lowest cost in both structures and utilities distributions. The differences increase as budget factors emerge as shown below:

	Alternative Costs in Millions		
	X	Y	Z
Engineering estimate of construction	$34.00	$35.38	$33.76
Contingency at 10%	3.40	3.54	3.37
Subtotal	$37.40	$38.82	$37.13
Design at 4%	1.49	1.55	1.48
SIES at 17.5% (design and supervision)	0.26	0.27	0.26
SIES at 6% (construction management)	2.24	2.33	2.23
Total	$41.39	$42.97	$41.10

	Site work	Utilities	Structures			Mechanical	Electrical	Occupancy			
				Piers	Hoists	Pumps			NOS	PMEL	NASO	Others

Functions					Units of measure							Personnel			
Warehousing				●	●		●				●	●	●	●
Ship support	●			●		●		●●	●		●	●		
Workshops		●●					●							●
Aquaculture	●		●		●			●	●●				●	
Number of units	1	1	1	1	2	2	1	1	2	2	1	1	2	1	1	2	1	1	2	1
Unit cost																
Construction costs																

Figure 12.10 Summary of planalysis methodology. Steps: (1) Based on requirements (input from NOS, PMEL, NASO, and others) apportionment is made to function (warehouse, ship support, etc.) by quantity, normalized to units of measure (square feet, kilowatts, etc.). Occupancy is entered on the right. (2) Quantities are added up vertically, as shown on the line marked "Number of units." (3) Numbers of units are multiplied by 1975 (Seattle) costs per unit. (4) Unit costs and quantities are aggregated by construction costs (site work, utilities, etc.).

The total cost differential between the highest alternative (Y) and the lowest (Z) is less than 10%, amounting to about $1.87 million. The difference between alternative Z, the lowest, and alternative X is only about 1%, amounting to about $0.29 million.

The closeness of the three alternatives in terms of capital costs should be sufficient to make the cost tradeoff without resorting to life-cycle cost analysis. Within the accuracy of the rough order of magnitude estimates used for this programmatic stage, a projection of 10 years of operation and maintenance, based on functions and population on site, would result in perpetuating the closeness.

Because costs alone are not the sole factor for recommendation of the optimum site organization concept alternative, a number of additional tests have been made for the benefit of the ultimate users. Users are represented on the building committee and these alternatives have been presented in drawing on a year-by-year basis, with traffic overlays and landscaping/view considerations. Based on esthetics, the

TABLE 12.1 Cost Summary, Site Organization Alternative X

	Engineering estimates				
Facility elements	Concept sensitive	Demolition on site	North gate access	Main gate modification	Total costs
Areas					
Paved aprons	311,590	6,078			
Roads	85,063		113,423	31,450	
Parking	52,325				
Walkways	63,888		36,663	21,020	
Landscaping	3,811,500		157,500	14,875	
Natural	191,664		10,500		
Shoreline/dredging	1,116,000				
Total areas	5,632,030	6,078	318,086	67,345	6,023,539
Utilities					
Power	125,000		60,000		
Water	357,675		70,800	14,750	
Communications	62,816		47,112	14,000	
Control center	790,000		17,520	11,640	
Utilidors	752,000				
Chilled water	74,496		4,656		
Sewage	65,000		31,200	3,900	
Storm drainage	195,720		16,800	14,700	
Liquid wastes	66,000				
Total utilities	2,488,707		248,088	58,990	2,795,785
Structures					
Piers	6,724,111				
Warehousing	1,860,650	15,585			
Electronics	2,299,050				
Operations	3,634,362		8,200		
Lab research	3,107,500				
Visitors	855,000				
Education center	4,163,755				
Shops	1,020,000				
Hangars	53,083				
Shelters	324,130			74,000	
Total structures	24,041,641	15,585	94,358	99,558	24,251,142
Total equipment	938,000				938,000
Grand total	33,100,378	21,663	660,532	225,893	34,008,466

TABLE 12.2 Cost Summary, Site Organization Alternative Y

	Engineering estimates				
Facility elements	Concept sensitive	Demolition on site	North gate access	Main gate modification	Total costs
Areas					
Paved aprons	311,590	6,078			
Roads	157,250		113,423	31,450	
Parking	52,325				
Walkways	49,863		36,663	21,020	
Landscaping	3,811,500		157,500	14,875	
Natural	191,664		10,500		
Shoreline/dredging	1,116,000				
Total areas	5,690,192	6,078	318,086	67,345	6,081,701
Utilities					
Power	150,000				
Water	265,930				
Communications	75,379				
Control center	790,000				
Utilidors	902,400				
Chilled water	89,395				
Sewage	71,500				
Storm drainage	206,850				
Liquid wastes	66,000				
Total utilities	2,617,454		248,088	58,990	2,924,532
Structures					
Piers	6,724,111				
Warehousing	2,075,150				
Electronics	2,528,955				
Operations/others[a]	3,942,707				
Lab research	3,542,550				
Visitors	855,000				
Education center	4,163,755				
Shops	1,020,000				
Hangars	53,083				
Shelters	324,130				
Total structures	25,229,441	15,585	94,358	99,558	25,438,942
Total equipment	938,000				938,000
Grand total	34,475,087	21,663	660,532	225,893	35,383,175

[a]Cafeteria and social services.

TABLE 12.3 Cost Summary, Site Organization Alternative Z

Facility elements	Concept sensitive	Demolition on site	North gate access	Main gate modification	Total costs
		Engineering estimates			
Areas					
Paved aprons	311,590	6,078			
Roads	175,133		113,423	31,450	
Parking	52,325				
Walkways	67,467		36,663	21,020	
Landscaping	3,811,500		157,500	14,875	
Natural	191,664		10,500		
Shoreline/dredging	1,116,000				
Total areas	5,725,679	6,078	318,086	67,345	6,117,188
Utilities					
Power	97,500				
Water	244,100				
Communications	51,038				
Control center	790,000				
Utilidors	611,000				
Chilled water	60,528				
Sewage	62,400				
Storm drainage	168,000				
Liquid wastes	66,000				
Total utilities	2,150,556		248,088	58,990	2,457,644
Structures					
Piers					
Warehousing					
Electronics					
Operations	Same as for				
Lab research	alternative X				
Visitors					
Education center					
Shops					
Hangars					
Shelters					
Total structures	24,041,641	15,585	94,358	99,558	24,251,142
Total equipment	938,000				938,000
Grand total	32,855,886	21,663	660,532	225,893	33,763,974

megastructure, concept Z, was unanimously rejected. Based on functionality (and in consideration), concept Y, formerly a viable concept, was also rejected. That Y turns out to have the highest cost of the three concepts is additional reason for the unanimous acceptance of alternative X, heretofore the most attractive on the basis of functionality alone.

Recommendation

The site organization concept, alternative X, has withstood the critical review of the site users. It offers a reasonable cost differential in comparison with the least cost alternative and can meet the general criteria for esthetics by avoiding mass and concentration of structure density.

It is also achievable with a constrained funding plan that completes construction at the end of 1980. Alternative X meets the spatial and functional requirements set forth by the major line components. Therefore, it is recommended that the project development planning and criteria use this concept as the basis for design.

12.2.2 BENEFITS AND ECONOMIC ANALYSES

At the outset of this analysis, the NOAA economic data furnished was based on the factors and figures incorporated in the *Draft Environmental Impact Statement* (DEIS), published in January 1975. The scenario in April 1975 had caused changes, and that data required updating. As a matter of record, the existence of the Sand Point development plan has required, and will continue to require, constant updating as priorities and major line component programs change. Thus, the *Draft Environmental Impact Statement* data, and even the updated (as of 1 May 1975) data, are subject to iteration and refinements.

Table 12.4 has been prepared to indicate the scope and circumstances of leased facilities for the organizations in Seattle, Bellevue (Northwestern Regional Calibration Center), and Kansas City, Missouri (Technical Training Center). It should be noted that the personnel figures are current and do not include projections to 1980, which Sand Point should accommodate. The average cost of lease space averages about $6 per square foot for 1975. What does not show is that the growth projections cannot be met by expanding facilities as they are now constituted and located. The projections have been met, in part, by the acquisition of hangars at Sand Point, one of which when renovated will accommodate groups from the leased facilities on U.S. Naval

TABLE 12.4 Comparison of Existing and Planned Space and Costs (1975 Dollars)

	Lake Union and storage annex 1 October 1977	Pacific Marine Center 1983 (20-year)	Montlake Owned	University of Washington 11 March 1977	Naval Support Activity N/A	Education Center (Kansas City) Unknown	NRCC, Bellevue 1977	Total
Location: / **Lease expiration:** / **Organization:**	NASO NMFS NWS	NOSO NAS USPH	PURC CZF&ES MF&SC NFCL	PMEL MSP	CMP MZF&E MDE&SL	Training Staff	Contractor	
1. Number of personnel (1975) / Total	59 44 33 / 136	572 2 / 574	*Existing* / 33 21 57 137 / 248	73 12 / 85	26 8 2 6 / 42	35	6	1,126
2. Occupied space, (square feet, 1975)	35,335	35,160	98,680	13,755	67,250	40,100	5,400	290,680
3. Capital costs of facilities and equipment (through 1975)	0	0	0	0	0	$ 225,000	0	$ 225,000
4. Recurring facilities lease costs (annual as of 1975) of utilities and leases	$ 238,700	$ 218,900	$ 225,000	$ 66,600	$ 42,570	$ 252,000	$ 14,290	$1,001,200
5. Lines 3 + 4 × number of years occupied	$ 656,425	$1,094,500	$ 675,000	$ 106,180	—	$ 477,000	$ 42,870	$3,051,975
6. Upgraded/improved space (square feet, 1975 through 1978)	0	0	*Upgrading* / 0	NOAA / 0	$ 118,000	—	—	$ 118,000
7. Cost of upgrading/improvements (1975 through 1978)	0	—	0	—	$ 500,000	—	—	$ 500,000
8. Recurring costs and upgraded/improved space (1976 through 1978)	$ 716,100	$ 656,700	*1978* / $ 675,000	$ 199,800	$ 753,000	$ 756,000	$ 42,870	$3,799,370
9. Total cost of facilities (through 1978), line 5 + line 8	$1,372,525	$1,751,200	$1,350,000	$ 305,980	$ 753,000	$1,233,000	$ 85,740	$6,851,345

Support Activity property, Montlake, and Pacific Marine Environmental Laboratory (PMEL) facilities. The perpetuation of existing circumstances with no capital investment at Sand Point, other than the renovation cost for Hangar 32, is calculated in 1975 through 1978 as shown.

Consideration of Other Sites for Collocation and Centralization

Recognizing the problems of growth and existing circumstances, NOAA made reconnaissance visits to potential sites in the Puget Sound region. With assistance from local government officials, representatives of the State's congressional delegation, and regional federal agency officials, the following prospective sites were identified: Manchester, Sand Point, Lake Union, Duwamish, Piers 90 and 91, and Fort Worden. The Fort Worden site was subsequently rejected because of its extreme distance from the Seattle metropolitan area and the emerging certainty of substantial development there by the State Parks and Recreation Commission.

As a test of the objectivity of selection of a consolidated site, a comparative site effectiveness study was commissioned. Consideration was also given to the possibility of consolidating NOAA facilities on two sites, such as building new administration and research facilities at Sand Point and using refurbished ship berthing facilities on Lake Union. Nearly half of the local NOAA personnel and key fisheries and oceanographic research activities are either ship-based or ship-related. Thus, such a split-site strategy would so dissipate the justification for consolidated facilities that no new facility could be rationalized economically or operationally.

Table 12.5 lists evaluation criteria and summarizes the pro and con features considered in selecting Sand Point as the optimum site which resulted in its selection.

Economic Evaluation of Existing Facilities versus Sand Point Development

The estimated costs for development of Sand Point for NOAA occupancy were produced for several purposes prior to the work documented herein. The planning and estimates used for site selection and set forth in the *Draft Environmental Impact Statement*, while prepared by a separate organization and using different cost techniques and factors, actually compare reasonably in range with the estimates developed and incorporated in the project development plan.

TABLE 12.5 Site Alternatives and Criteria Comparison

EFFECTIVENESS CRITERIA	SANDPOINT		MANCHESTER	
1. Proximity to Univ. of Wash. (Travel times from U.W.)	10 minutes	9	120 minutes	4
2. Site Features (Physical attributes of the site)	PRO Flat; no fill; easy drainage; land stability CON Remove runways; poor bearing soil; piling required; high de- gree of landscaping required; dredging required	8	PRO No demolition; good bearing soil; excellent landscaping potential CON Hilly topography; cut & fill needed; long piers required; scattered buildings required; shoreline dredging	9
3. Moorage Space (3,000 linear feet of vessel moorage required)	PRO Space adequate; wind protec- tion adequate; easy access from buildings to piers CON High demand shoreline	9	PRO Some wind protection CON Limited space for moorage; poor access from buildings to piers	9
4. Water Type (Fresh water is the most cost effective)	Fresh water	10	Salt water	7
5. Spatial Characteristics (On-shore building space and topography)	Easy expansion; ample space	10	Some difficulty in ex- pansion; scattered build- ing sites	8
6. Overall Environmental Amenity (Visual and sonic attributes of the site and vicinity)	Scenic views; desirable resi- dential context	9	Rural atmosphere; attractive scenery	10
7. Personnel Amenity (Resources available to employees making NOAA an attractive employer)	Housing and services readily available	9	Outdoor recreation oppor- tunities available; distant from commercial & cultural facilities; rural atmosphere	7
8. Housing (Housing choices for employees)	Little change from present employee circumstances	10	An expensive move re- quired for nearly all employees	5
9. Transportation (Public transportation & private vehicle access availability)	Bus service, public service & facility services reasonably available	9	Public transportation service difficult; facility services difficult	5
10. Utilities Availability (Water, sewage, storm drainage and electrical energy resources)	Previous Navy use estab- lished utility system re- sources which could be used if some adjustments are made	8	All utilities would have to be brought to the site	5
11. Facilities Services (Fire protection, library, technical services, ship provisioning & ship repair & maintenance services)	Necessary services easily available	10	Services largely remote or absent from the vicinity of site	6
12. Vessel Accessibility (Time & ease of vessel movement from Puget Sound)	Transit involves locks, four bridges & some contact with other waterway traffic	5	Minimum time, no obstruction	10
13. Site Availability (Land cost & ease of land consolidation)	City favors NOAA use of the site; congressional legislation mandates NOAA use	10	State plans major park development on the site in the next biennium; small por- tion used by State & Federal agencies	7
14. Environmental Resource Utilization (Least adverse primary or secon- dary environmental impact & State & local policies & priorities regard- ing environmental quality.)	NOAA use would upgrade present circumstances & be- come a valued community & park feature. Minimum adverse effects.	9	Proposed park probably of more environmental value than NOAA use which is of an urban character. High ad- verse impact on surrounding community.	6

Scale   1 = lowest effective
           10 = highest effective

Draft Environmental Impact Statement, January 1975

338

Since only a minor adjustment in total costs in 1975 was made between the submittal of the project development plan initially in early May 1975, and in the estimate submitted after minor revision to the project development plan, the conclusions remain the same and are therefore valid for presentation here.

An economic analysis was performed to determine the cost impact of Sand Point development. The objective was to identify the short- and/or long-term benefits of the Sand Point facility versus the alternative of continued leasing of dispersed facilities. The baseline 1975 Seattle dollars for the Sand Point alternative were compared to the 1975 Seattle dollars currently obligated through leases. The cost comparison is totally biased in that the leased spaces are not functionally comparable to the proposed facilities. For example, it is necessary to compare new facility costs with lease rates for laboratory research on the order of $8 per square foot when in fact the lease rate could be twice that amount for floor space functionally appropriate for such use.

The rental or lease costs to continue the present programs with the arrangement of dispersed facilities, compared to that planned for the collocated Sand Point facility, were estimated for the *Draft Environmental Impact Statement* of January 1975 (pp. 27 and 28). The estimated rental cost for 380,900 square feet of mixed types of facilities at the 1975 price level is $1,695,870. This area is equivalent to the square footage of planned structures for Sand Point, excluding the piers.

The present value of total rentals over an extended future period is calculated from standard present worth factors. The computations are shown in Table 12.6.

With the tabulation of present value of NOAA leases identified, a cost model of the capital investment in Sand Point facilities was prepared. The estimate in 1975 dollars was, at that time, just over $39

TABLE 12.6 Present Value of Future NOAA Lease Payments

Annual lease costs		Discount rate	Total lease costs	Present value
1975–1990	$1,695,870	5⅝%	$ 25,438,050	$16,881,900
1990–2000	$2,055,125	5⅝%	$ 20,551,250	$ 6,776,000
2000–2035	$2,245,000	5⅝%	$ 78,579,000	$ 8,664,200
Total			$124,564,300	$32,322,100

340   CASE STUDIES

million. It has since been increased to just over $41 million, which does not significantly affect the outcome of the conclusions in comparing the present value of leased versus Sand Point development, presented on Table 12.7. For the computations shown in Table 12.7, the following factors were considered.

Escalation of rentals in the Seattle area is averaging from over 3% up to 5% a year according to local real estate experts—over 3% attributed to operating expenses and over 1% to market forces. The present value of escalated rental, however, is counterbalanced by the discount rate of 7% used in determining the present value of future rental costs. Inflation of annual rental costs of 4% (3.88%, exactly), combined with a 7% discount rate, gives a net discount rate of 3%. An inflation rate of 4.39%, combined with a 7% discount rate, gives a net discount rate of 2.5%. The present value of total rentals over an extended future period can then be calculated from standard present worth factors.

Two periods are used for comparison: 60 years, which represents the standard life of the new structures, and 30 years, which is a more comprehensible real estate horizon. For the 60-year period, either discount rate results in a higher present value for rental costs than for Sand Point construction costs. In comparison with the 30-year period, the larger size and greater qualitative benefits of the Sand Point location are of more significance. Over a 60-year period it is more economical to build Sand Point, without regard to its greater size and qualitative values.

TABLE 12.7   Present Value of Cumulative Rental Costs for Dispersed Facilities at Planned 1980 Capacity (for 380,900 Square Feet)

Estimated rental 1975 prices[a]	Net discount rate	Total period years	Present worth factor	Present worth of cumulative rentals	Ratio to Sand Point development present value[b]
$1,695,070	2.5%	60	30.909	$52,418	1.16
$1,695,870	3.0%	60	27.676	$46,935	1.04
$1,695,870	2.5%	30	20.930	$35,495	0.79
$1,695,870	3.0%	30	19.600	$33,239	0.74

[a]Source: *Draft Environmental Impact Statement,* January 1975, p. 28. ". . . Comparisons assume a 60 year useful life (the time generally applied by GSA to new building construction). . . . the estimated rental was considered to be the average for 1975–1990."

[b]Alternative A, Sand Point Development, has a present value of $45,029,000.

Alternative Funding Levels

Accepting that the initial cost model of just over $39 million was a fairly accurate representation of NOAA Sand Point development project investment, a series of funding alternatives was postulated. These alternatives began with a totally unconstrained flow of authorization—limited only by the amount of normal or unaccelerated design and construction time that could be accomplished year by year. The lower end of the scale of funding levels was one with an annual ceiling of $10 million per year. The latter proved to have many cost penalties, and stretched the project out to 1984. Three alternatives were deemed competitive: the unconstrained became alternative A, a $20 million ceiling plan was designated B, and a $15 million scheme is identified as alternative C. The comparison of inflation and cost avoidance is shown on Table 12.8.

Following NOAA and Department of Commerce analysis, a slightly lesser funding level than alternative C at $15 million was seen to be the most attractive alternative. It combines the requirements for new obligational authority of $13 million per year to completion, with a current obligational authority of $1.16 for a total ceiling of $14.16 per year. This alternative provides the basis for the elements of the project plan resources and timing described in subsequent sections of this document.

12.3 VALUE MANAGEMENT STUDIES AT THE R. D. BAILEY LAKE PROJECT

The R. D. Bailey Lake Project is located in southern West Virginia near the Town of Justice. This project provides flood protection to the downstream area along the Guyandot River, which flows into the Ohio River at Huntington, West Virginia.

12.3.1 THE DAM

The dam was designed in the conventional manner with an impervious core and rock supporting shells on both the upstream and downstream sides. An internal drainage system was also necessary to carry off seepage through the core. (See Figure 12.11.) The dam design required borrowing 900,000 cubic yards of impervious material from areas which, even though reseeded, would be environmentally affected. Transportation of the material in the small loads required by bridge

TABLE 12.8 NOAA Sand Point Project—Capital Cost 1975 Dollars at 1 Percent Per Month from 1 July 1975,[a] Present Value at 7 Percent Discount Rate

Alternative	Calendar dates	Inflation factor	Capital cost 1975 dollars (000's)	Capital cost current dollars	Discount factor at 7 percent per year (1.0057 per month)	Present value of capital cost (dollars 1 July 1975)
A	7-01-75	—	—	—	—	—
	1-01-76	1.0615	998.6	1,160.0	0.9664	1,024.4
	8-15-76	1.1436	1,362.0	1,557.6	0.9261	1,442.5
	4-01-77	1.2324	16,111.1	19,860.3	0.8874	17,619.6
	4-01-78	1.3887	18,288.5	24,400.2	0.8289	21,051.7
	4-01-79	1.5648	3,211.3	5,025.0	0.7743	3,890.9
Totals			39,971.5	53,003.1		45,027.1
B	7-01-75	—	—	—	—	—
	1-01-76	1.0615	998.6	1,160.0	0.9664	1,024.4
	8-15-76	1.1436	1,362.0	1,557.6	0.9261	1,442.5
	4-01-77	1.2324	16,117.3	19,863.0	0.8874	17,626.4
	4-01-78	1.3887	13,907.7	19,313.6	0.8289	16,009.0
	4-01-79	1.5648	7,542.2	11,982.0	0.7743	9,138.3
	4-01-80	1.7633	50.0	88.2	0.7232	63.8
Totals		39	39,977.8	53,964.4		45,304.4

C

7-01-75	—	—	—	—	—
1-01-76	1.0615	998.6	1,160.0	0.9664	1,024.4
8-15-76	1.1436	1,350.7	1,544.7	0.9261	1,430.5
4-01-77	1.2324	12,019.5	14,812.8	0.8874	13,144.9
4-01-78	1.3887	10,897.9	14,733.9	0.8289	12,544.5
4-01-79	1.5648	8,746.6	13,686.7	0.7743	10,597.6
4-01-80	1.7633	5,903.1	10,408.9	0.7232	7,527.7
4-01-81	1.9869	50.0	99.3	0.6755	67.1
Totals		39,966.4	56,446.3		46,336.7

"Based on an earlier capital cost estimate of $39.26 million, 1975 dollars.

restrictions in the area would be extremely expensive. Estimators said this was impractical to consider. These problems were brought to the attention of the District's Value Engineering Committee, through the Value Engineering Officer, and a study was authorized.

A value management study team composed of representatives from Soils, Geology, Project Engineering, Structural, and Planning organizations was formed. During the functional analysis of the impervious core it was determined that its purpose was to retain water. Various alternatives were developed for performance of this function including among others the use of soil cement, a concrete cutoff wall and an asphalt wall. The design that was recommended by the study team and approved by higher authorities was the construction of a rock fill dam with a concrete facing on the upstream side (see Figure 12.12). The outer slopes of the dam embankment were steepened from 1 vertical on 2.5 horizontal to 1 vertical to 2 horizontal. Earth borrow areas were eliminated, thereby preserving timbered hillsides. The requirement for stockpiling of impervious earth core material was eliminated from the contract for construction of the outlet work which was underway at the completion of the VM study. Since the operations berm on the upstream side would no longer be necessary as it would have been for the original rock faced dam, it was deleted from the concrete face design.

The concrete facing is a safer design than the original earth core design because of reduced foundation piping problems and the increased ability of the structure to withstand the effects of piping in the foundation broken rock zone.

Environmental protection measures would have been more costly for the original design because of the borrow necessary for the earth core than for the concrete facing operation. Environmental degradation will also be less for the concrete face design.

The total time for construction of the rock fill concrete-faced dam will be considerably less, and a savings in the amount of $3,967,354 will result.

This is the first dam of its kind to be constructed by the Corps of Engineers. The team that developed this design has been given the Presidential Management Improvement Award. This award was presented by the Secretary of the Army on 14 October 1975.

12.3.2 THE ACCESS ROAD, SERVICE ROAD, RECREATION AREA, AND OPERATIONS FACILITIES

The original layout for the access road to the R. D. Bailey Dam provided for a 22-foot roadway from a point on U.S. Route 52 near the

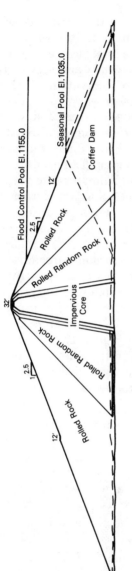

Figure 12.11 Dam profile before VM study.

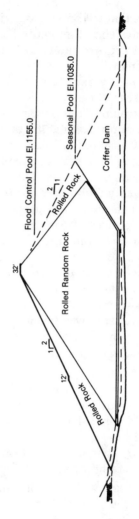

Figure 12.12 Dam profile after VM study.

south end of the bridge across Huff Creek along the north side of the hill to the top of the dam at the left abutment. A 16-foot service road continued on to the service bridge for the intake structure on the left abutment. The alignments for both the access road and service road required approximately 315,000 cubic yards of excavation which was predominantly rock. A 20-foot two-lane roadway was required across the top of the dam to service the damtender's quarters and maintenance area. These facilities were to be located on the right abutment just upstream of the center line of the dam and would require excavation of approximately 176,000 cubic yards of rock. The original plan provided very limited facilities for public use. An expensive deep cut would have been required to provide an overlook that would accommodate 20 cars and 2 buses. Due to its location, the cost of installing water and sanitary facilities was prohibitive. The maximum design dayload for this one public use area was 330 people.

The high cost of constructing the roadways through areas that required a large amount of rock excavation, the cost of preparing the area for the damtender's quarters and maintenance area, and problems that would be encountered during winter snows in maintaining the access road led the Value Engineering Committee to authorize a study. (The above roads and facilities are shown in Figure 12.13.)

A study team was formed which, after 3 months of dedicated work, developed the following plan for the access road, service road, recreation area, and operations facilities (see Figure 12.14).

1. The team proposed construction of a 22-foot wide two-lane roadway beginning at the same point as the original design, that, instead of using the north side of the hill, would continue up the south side of the hill over the general alignment of an existing haul road to the plateau created by strip mining operations. There are a number of advantages to this location over the original design, such as:

(a) The road will be more stable because the major portion of the construction will be along an established roadbed.

(b) Considerable less rock excavation will be required. The maximum height of excavation for this alignment is 30 feet as compared with 70 feet for the original design.

(c) The road will be exposed to the sun during the snowy winter months. This is of great value in keeping the access road open and should reduce maintenance considerably. It was entirely possible that the road as originally planned would be a maintenance headache throughout the winter months because of the continuing buildup of snow.

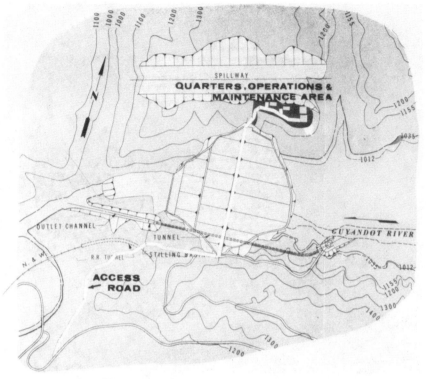

Figure 12.13 Site layout before VM study.

2. The service road was reduced in width from 16 feet to 12 feet. The road begins on the south side of the plateau created by the strip mine operation and proceeds down the hill to the top of the dam and on to the service bridge at the intake structure. This road will be for use of Operations personnel and will not be open to public vehicular traffic. It may, however, be used by pedestrian traffic for close viewing of the dam and outlet works.

3. With the access road providing entry to the plateau area at the strip mine, the following changes are possible:

(a) The damtender's quarters and operations and maintenance area were moved to the top of the strip mine area, thereby reducing the required excavation quantity by 176,000 cubic yards. There was also no necessity for the road across the top of the dam.

(b) The existing abandoned strip mine affords excellent viewing of the dam and the majestic mountain country that surrounds the lake. It provides much-needed flat lands for picnicking and nature trails as well as outstanding overlook areas. Inasmuch as the Operation's offices

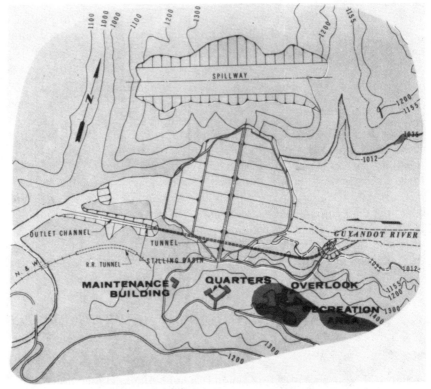

Figure 12.14   Site layout after VM study.

will be located on the strip area, the water and sanitary facilities
required for operation can be made available to the public by providing
a visitor center in the Operation's building. The hikers will have access
to nearly 2.5 miles of mountain top trail which presently exists because
of a coal plan exploration cut. This trail gives everyone views of the
lake and the surrounding flora and fauna that are normally limited to
the young and hardy. This reclaimed strip mine could accommodate a
maximum design dayload of 1290 people and give a conservative figure
of $100,000 in annual recreation benefits.

A net savings of $719,421 resulted from the efforts of this VM study
team.

12.3.3   THE INTAKE STRUCTURE

The original design for the intake structures provided for an operating
floor at elevation 1200 which would be reached by a 320-foot, two-span

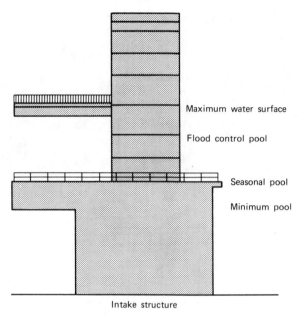

Maximum water surface

Flood control pool

Seasonal pool

Minimum pool

Intake structure

Figure 12.15   Intake structure before VM study.

service bridge. The structure was 350 feet high with seven intermediate floors located generally at the elevation when change in the wall thickness occurred. The operating floor was to house the reservoir water level recorder and controls, the elevator and appurtenant equipment for its operation, the service hoists, the standby generator, and the electrical control panel. (See Figure 12.15.)

The service hoists were to be located above the operating floor and used for making lifts during overhaul of the gates and standby generator and for other maintenance and operational requirements. A description of the procedures for placement of the bulkheads and removal of a selective withdrawal intake gate disc under the original design required three typewritten pages.

The problems that would be encountered in operating this structure were such that a VM study was initiated to find a better way.

The study team recommended eliminating that portion of the intake structure above elevation 1200, thus placing the top of the structure at the same elevation as the top of the bridge. A parapet wall with railing compatible to that used on the service bridge will be used for the safety of the visiting public and operating personnel. (See Figure 12.16.) The elevator equipment, reservoir water level recorder, and motor control panel were moved to the floor below. Access to the structure is provided

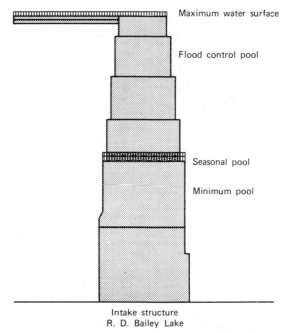

Figure 12.16   Intake structure after VM study.

by a stairwell in the top of the structure. The standby generator will be located in the maintenance building and will utilize the main power line to the intake structure for emergency service also.

It was necessary to modify the design of the service bridge to accommodate a 30-ton truck crane for use in placement and removal of bulkheads and selective withdrawal intake gate discs. A description of the procedures for placement of the bulkheads and removal of a selective withdrawal intake disc under the VM design requires one-half page. This change not only makes the project easier to operate and maintain but also reduced construction costs by $34,392.

12.4   A VM STUDY OF THE SOUTHEASTERN SIGNAL SCHOOL (PHASE III), FORT GORDON, GEORGIA

12.4.1   SITE LAYOUT

Before

The original design for the project consisted of five buildings with a combined square foot total of 219,461 square feet. In general, the five buildings were designed utilizing the same architectural motif as previous construction phases of the Signal School. All structures were designed around modular classrooms, except a hangar-type building, which was designed for actual training rather than a lecture-type classroom.

Action Taken

As a result of a value management study, the above buildings were redesigned combining the hangar-type structure and two of the classroom structures. Two buildings remained as basically designed, except that the crawl space beneath the first floor was eliminated and other adjustments made in the mechanical and electrical systems; that is, the installation of individual fan coil units in lieu of extensive duct work and central air conditioning units. In addition, electrical, mechanical, and structural changes further reduced construction cost for the project by combining the structures along with reduction of extensive site preparation and underground utilities. The above was accomplished while meeting all functional requirements and providing esthetic qualities and structures that will complement the existing buildings of the Signal School.

After

As a result of this in-house VM study conducted by the U.S. Army Engineer District, Savannah, savings in the amount of $1,208,400 were realized. This amount remains after all construction costs were included in the construction current working estimate and that cost subtracted from the programmed amount of $6,405,000. Additional advantages were that funds were available for the installation to award additional construction contracts, and a surplus will be returned to higher authority for use at other installations for critical items of construction (see p. 352).

12.4.2   TACTICAL EQUIPMENT SHOPS AND FACILITIES

Before

Design documents for construction of Tactical Equipment Shops & Facilities, Construction Contract DACA21-74-C-0090, Ft. Bragg, North Carolina, consisted of two major structures (Tactical Equipment Shops), eight grease racks, 20 washracks, two gasoline stations complete, two dispatch houses, with related facilities, services, and the

SAVINGS CALCULATIONS
SOUTHEASTERN SIGNAL SCHOOL
PHASE III
FORT GORDON, GEORGIA

Programmed amount		$6,405,000
Construction estimate		
Contract cost	$4,670,600	
Contingencies 2%	93,412	
Known changes	20,000	
VM cost	25,392	
Communications	75,000	
Subtotal	$4,884,404	
S&A, 5.8%	278,945	
As-built drawings	3,174	
E&D during construction	30,077	
Total Construction CWE		−5,196,600
Value management savings		$1,208,400

Value Management Team members:
    Captain: Robert L. McGraw, Sr.
    Recorder: Joseph Varon
    Members: Warren B. Bell
                Richard K. Little
                Robert E. Ramsey
                Wendell M. Houston
                William B. Verell

required paved areas. The two Tactical Equipment Shops consisted of four standard Tactical Equipment Shops for each building and were partitioned based on unit integrity for the respective using organizations. These Tactical Equipment Shops had a gross square foot area of 40,400 square feet with 20,200 square feet allotted for each building that made up the four unit Tactical Maintenance areas.

The siting arrangements upon which the final design was based located the eight grease racks approximately 200 feet from each of the four unit Tactical Equipment Shops. The nearest washrack was approximately 775 feet from the Tactical Equipment Shops; the effluent from the oil separators required for the washracks was designed to be wasted in the storm drainage system. The gasoline stations were located at the entrance drives at two separate locations near Gruber Road with the dispatch houses located along the front edge of the paved area at different entrances.

The entire site had been graded and paved by an Engineer Battalion prior to this design. Existing bituminous pavement consisted of a 8-inch stabilized base and aggregate surface treatment. The design pavement requirements consisted of a 2-inch bituminous overlay where existing pavements were to be retained and removal and replacement of existing pavement with 8-inch reinforced concrete pavement around the Tactical Equipment Shops and gasoline dispensing stations. Concrete pavement was placed over an area of approximately two-fifths of the motor pool area.

Action Taken

As a result of a joint VM study performed by personnel of the U. S. Army Engineer District, Savannah, and the Director of Facilities Engineering, Ft. Bragg, North Carolina, the design documents were modified resulting in the following:

1. Elimination of four grease racks.

2. Relocation of four grease racks.

3. Twenty washracks were relocated and combined into three multiunit washracks, i.e., a 10-unit washrack and two 8-unit washracks. This eliminated extensive water distribution piping and storm drainage requirements.

4. The gasoline stations, storage tanks, and dispensers were combined and relocated at the center of the motor pool near the entrance.

5. Existing bituminous pavement removal was reduced along with the requirement for replacement of new 8-inch reinforced concrete pavement. This existing paved area was surfaced with a 2-inch bituminous topping.

6. The new stabilized aggregate base course was reduced from 9 inches to 8 inches.

7. An 18-inch storm drainage pipe was added across the entrances to the motor pool, which eliminated an open ditch.

8. Dispatch offices were relocated for better operational traffic flow and organizational configuration.

9. Requirements for a forced sanitary main, lift station, and collec-

tion system for washrack effluent was avoided by relocation of the washracks.

In addition, a motor pool safety violation was eliminated. The environmental requirements for the State of North Carolina were complied with since the effluent for the washracks will be placed in the sanitary lines rather than being wasted in the surrounding area thru the storm drainage system and the Using Agency will receive a superior facility which operationally will be more functional.

After

As a result of this Value Engineering study the government realized estimated savings in the amount of $226,735.

Estimate of savings

(based on prices from abstract of bids and government bid estimate)

1. Delete grease racks		$ 34,000.00
2. Delete concrete pavement & surface with 2 in. bituminous overlay		
Pavement removal 8633 sq yd @ $.25	$ 2,158	
Delete concrete pavement 8633 sq yd @ $15.16	130,876	
Curb to remain 853 linear feet @ $.60	512	
Add 2 in. bituminous surface 7477 sq yd @ $1.52	(11,365)	
	$122,181	$122,181.00
3. Washrack water lines (delete)		
3 in. — 645 ft @ $4.00	$ 2,580	
2½ in. — 280 ft @ $3.60	1,008	
2 in. — 320 ft @ $3.35	1,072	
1½ in. — 260 ft @ $3.10	806	
1 in. — 610 ft @ $2.60	1,586	
1 in. — 22 valves & boxes @ $60	1,320	
1 in. — post hydrants 9 @ $110	990	
	$ 9,362	$9,362

Washrack water lines (add)

2 in. — 425 ft @ $3.35	($ 1,424)	
1½ in. — 310 ft @ $3.10	(961)	
1 in. — 165 ft @ $2.60	(429)	
1 in. — 11 valves & boxes @ $60	(660)	
	($ 3,474) ($3,474)	$ 5,888.00

4. Effluent line from oil
   separators
   (Storm) delete 6 in.
   drain

810 ft @ $7.00	$ 5,670	
(San) Add 6 in. drain		
410 ft @ $6.50	(2,665)	
(San) add 8 in. drain		
280 ft @ $7.50	(2,100)	
	$ 905	$ 905.00

5. Delete pavement removal

Washracks 3450 sq yd @ $.25	$ 863	
Other 5200 sq yd @ $.25	1,300	
	$ 2,163	$ 2,163.00

6. Additional 8 in. concrete
   pavement

115 sq yd @ $15.16	($ 1,743)	($ 1,743.00)
7. Combining washracks	$ 5,000	$ 5,000.00
8. Curbing @ washracks	$ 1,697	$ 1,697.00

9. Delete retaining wall

(grease rack)	$ 5,000	$ 5,000.00

10. Add 140 ft of 18 in. storm
    drainage at entrance &

regrade	($ 3,000)	($ 3,000.00)

11. Delete concrete pavement

under grease racks (4 in.)	$ 4,500	$ 4,500.00

12. Reduce bituminous stabilizer
    base by 1 in.

10,200 sq yd @ $.30	$ 3,060	$ 3,060.00

13. Avoidance of modification
    to install lift station,
    collection system & force
    main for effluent from

washracks	$ 25,000	$ 25,000.00

14. Guy wire tank anchors in lieu
     of reinforced concrete

Delete 4 @ $1,260	$ 5,040		
Delete 2 @ $850	1,700		
	$ 6,740	$6,740	
Add 30 guy anchors @ $40		($1,200)	
		$5,540	$ 5,540.00
Subtotal			$210,191.00
5% contingency			10,509.00
Subtotal			$220,700.00
5% S&A			11,035.00
Subtotal			$231,735.00
Implementation costs			(5,000.00)
Savings			$226,735.00

Team Members
Lewis T. Strickland
Reppard D. Thomas
Joe E. Greer
Robert L. McGraw, Sr.

CHAPTER 13

OUTLOOK FOR
VALUE MANAGEMENT

13.1 BACKGROUND

To be able to assess the outlook for value management, we need to examine where the techniques and processes are today.

Value management is not simply a skill, nor is it expertise that is only accumulated through experience. It is not learned solely from case histories; it is not necessarily acquired through participation on projects that have value incentives. Primarily, it is a philosophy or a policy that top managers should mandate as a practical approach to meet effective performance and economics for every stage in the life cycle of a program including the operations and maintenance and ultimate phaseout.

Currently, we have standardized procedures for the contractual aspects, "how to" guidance, and even a technical society for the advancement of value precepts dedicated as shown on Figure 13.1. The education of managers, engineers, designers, buyers, and technicians is still left to chance. When value and effectiveness are combined, it is still treated as a happy circumstance, or recognition for a meritorious contribution is given to the originating individual.

What remains to be done is to disseminate value management as a necessary tool for optimization. This obviously requires publicity and acceptance.

13.2 INCENTIVES AND FACILITIES PROJECTS

The goals of value management with respect to the products are obvious—effectiveness and economy. While these may be incentives for

As a representative of value engineering, I pledge myself to:

Uphold the high ideals and level of personal knowledge attested by Society membership or certification, and to participate in none but honest enterprises

Serve the interests of my employer and clients loyally, diligently, and honestly through worthy performance and fidelity

Maintain a broad and balanced outlook and recognize merit in the ideas and opinions of others

Refrain from any conduct or act which is discreditable to the reputation or integrity of the VE/VA profession, and be guided in all my activities by truth, accuracy, fair dealing, and good taste

Promote at every opportunity the public understanding of VE/VA, and apply my specialized skill and knowledge for public good

Keep informed on the latest developments in value techniques and applications; recommend or initiate improvements to increase the effectiveness of VE/VA

Pledge to all fellow value specialists, integrity and fair dealing, tolerance and respect, devotion to the standards and dignity of our profession

Support efforts to strengthen the profession through training and education, to help others reach personal and professional fulfillment

Earn and carefully guard my reputation for good moral character and good citizenship, recognizing that leadership is a call to service

Recognize that Society membership or certification as a value specialist is not the sole claim to professional competence

Figure 13.1   Standards of conduct.

the financial sponsors of acquisition programs as well as the owners, they are not, in our current acquisition process, incentives for the contractors and suppliers who participate in every aspect of the program.

The point may be dramatically illustrated by analyzing how contractors and contracting organizations arrive at the basis for their negotiations and contracts.

Architect-engineers estimate their level of effort and profit by a percentage of constructed value. From their point of view, this practice is most effective; it has a long history. American Institute of Architects (AIA) and American Society of Civil Engineers (ASCE) have given cost curves and factors for guidelines in scoping the costs of services. Experience has shown this to be the norm, and the practice is acceptable to both client and contractor. Sometimes a lot of profit is made; sometimes there is a loss. The latter is usually held to be because of complexity and changes or poor productivity.

It follows that the architect-engineer can be placed under contract for a firm fixed price, particularly for a building that at the time may only be defined by single line drawings or concepts with rough-order-of-magnitude (ROM) cost estimates, provided that the structure is not unique—an office, hotel, warehouse, or the like. Research facilities or first-of-a-kind chemical or manufacturing processes are another "ball-game" entirely.

Since architect-engineers provide *professional* services, the selection process, while it may be equally competitive, is not supposed to be carried out on the basis of price. It can be seen that selection of a Seattle, Washington architect-engineer for a Miami, Florida project might not be economical unless the project is so specialized that an experienced person may not be available locally.

Normally, selection of an architect-engineer begins with an initial screening of qualifications and experience. This is followed by notification to the short-listed architect-engineers that an interview is desired. A list of questions or topics to be discussed is provided with the interview notification. These may include:

- The project organization that will be responsive to the buyer's technical and management organization.
- The names of the key personnel, their individual experience, qualifications, and the period of time they will devote to the project.
- The amount of work that is current in the architect-engineer's office along with the capability and commitment to accomplish the project.
- The approach that will be used to start up and assure that schedules are met.
- Advantageous alternatives or special techniques that will be of benefit to the owner/buyer.
- References in the form of a listing of contracts of current or past work, of people who will provide statements of financial responsibility, or successful projects to evidence the validity of claims in qualifications/experience letters, brochures, and other materials submitted for favorable consideration.

The interview provides the opportunity for both buyer and seller to exchange viewpoints and hypothesize problems and solutions. The interview is both qualitative and quantitative to produce scores and adjectival ratings of competitors.

Often, and for selected projects, a concept will be used to judge equally qualified architects. Since an investment of time and cost is involved, the understanding of its value in the selection process should be made clear to proposers. Basically, this approach is very nearly a contest.

Following the interview (the ratings provide the buyer with his precedence), the number one choice is called in to negotiate. Only if there is no agreement on the contract costs, schedules, or scope will the number two candidate be called in for a negotiation.

Summarily, the architect-engineer's incentive is the reverse desired by the financing agency—the greater the cost, the greater the fee.

The construction contractor's incentive is to get the job. Knowledge that he will be selected by low bid provides the incentive at the proposal stage to find as many ways to keep the cost down as possible and yet meet the schedule set forth by the contracting agent. Often, the construction contractor's approach in the bidding stages has the most creativity since he wishes to save labor and time in getting the job done. There is little time to negotiate with material and equipment suppliers, so cost experience must be up to date, not only for the craft labor but also for the potential subcontracts. It can be seen that the bid will have to be extremely close with respect to the profit margin, since the contractor must estimate who his competitors are and what they are likely to propose. His experience also shows that there is likely to be a large number of changes, which the owner or construction agent must negotiate with him as "sole source" once the construction work is started. Often a construction contractor will anticipate that changes will have to provide the profit margin and therefore he will bid the job at close to the anticipated cost. The construction contractor's incentive then is anticipatory changes which will increase the scope of his effort; often a downscale change proposal in the structure results in an upscale of the construction contractor's original bid.

Suppliers of equipment—whether the owner does the buying and furnishes it to the construction contractor for installation or the construction contractor purchases and installs it under the provisions of construction documents—have a different incentive. They want to sell as much as possible, for as much as possible. Again, the lowest price offered will normally result in supplier selection, although other factors, such as quality and delivery schedules may also be considered.

Whether an acquisition program is for government or industry, there is little under today's ground rules that provides incentives for reducing the owner's cost. The incentive opportunities for the owner, scanty at best at the outset of the program, steadily decrease as contractors begin their efforts and the designs and engineering efforts become more and more definitive.

This is one of the reasons that value management has gathered attention. Its successes have been for the most part to "retrofit" design and engineering solutions. A strong movement toward value management by potential spenders would provide more impetus for the activity—a different approach to contracting would make it mandatory.

Savings, as an incentive, has prompted various government agencies to incorporate certain precepts of value analysis, value engineering, and/or value management. However, the restrictions as to percentage of construction cost that can be allocated to architect-engineers and the types of contracts for both architect-engineers and constructors has remained firm.

13.3   INCENTIVE SYSTEMS

Typically, industrial employees on unmeasured day work have been found to produce no more than 50 to 70% of what measurements would show to be a fair day's work. This has prompted management to provide incentive plans for increasing productivity. The plans can be divided into two categories: nonfinancial and financial. The value manager or engineer of any facilities project should have an understanding of incentive systems and productivity in order to make comparisons between activities that are realistically achievable and those that can be optimized.

13.3.1   NONFINANCIAL INCENTIVES

This category of incentive generally has appeal to emotions. If we are speaking of an individual, the favorable emotions consist of such things as pride in workmanship, recognition of achievement, patriotism, feelings of inclusion, gratitude, pride in superior performance, spirit of competition, and a host of other factors that tend to stimulate good performance. Factors that, although not considered favorable, nevertheless stimulate productivity include shame of poor productivity, not keeping up with others, insecurity, and the threat of termination or demotion whether expressed or implied.

For contractors or suppliers, nonfinancial incentives are related generally to prestige or future gains. Often an engineering consultant will perform work "at cost" to gain a business advantage. "At cost" efforts are usually related to short-term projects, with only out-of-pocket costs billed, without fee-for-profit and sometimes without inclusion of overhead expense.

Nonfinancial incentives cannot by themselves create the motivation of financial incentives but they can help to make them more effective.

13.3.2 FINANCIAL INCENTIVES

Financial incentives can be either indirect or direct. Indirect incentives include provisions for equitable pay structures, merit increases, pensions, profit-sharing, and stock-option plans. Other indirect incentives, generally referred to as "fringe benefits," include such items as hospitalization and insurance. While indirect incentives are definitely financial in nature, they are applied on an organization-wide basis and are not directly dependent on the productive contribution of an individual or group.

The direct financial incentive provides the opportunity for higher pay through increased productivity or effectiveness. It is based on the straightforward concept of *plus* pay for *plus* performance.

Under present-day circumstances, the net effect of financial reward as an incentive requires special consideration. It is obvious that there are ever-increasing costs and that this upward trend has predictable effects on productivity. Figure 13.2 provides a tabulation of the impact of a salary increase with the corresponding increase in deduction to

Salary Elements	Senior Engineer's Rate (80 Hour Pay Period)		
	"Was" Rate ($)	"Is" Rate ($)	Difference (%)
Gross	1,000.70	1,099.83	9.96
Federal withholding	164.85	196.37	19.12
F.I.C.A.	58.51	64.34	9.96
U.C.D.	10.00	11.00	10.00
State (California) withholding	36.01	44.60	23.85
Salary continuance	4.70	5.16	9.79
Net	699.48	752.07	7.52

Figure 13.2 Effect of an approximate 10% merit increase.

illustrate the net effect. It shows that what would otherwise be considered as a substantial increase as an incentive or good performance actually results in a moderate increase. Some of the "reward" aspects of the incentive disappear when the net increase of a 10% annual raise turns out to be 7.5% and the cost of living has increased 6% or more during the prior year.

For contractors, the financial incentive is more complex, and there are differences in incentive approach between the professionals (engineers, architects, planners, and consultants) and nonprofessionals (suppliers, manufacturers, and constructors). Nonprofessionals have more opportunity to implement group incentive plans. The premise is that productivity gains (over some experience "norm") are not necessarily due to overall employee effort but rather to improvements in methods or technology.

Professionals, on the other hand, whose product is mainly services, must rely on day-to-day employee participation in meeting management objectives to effect cost reductions and improve profits. This requires more emphasis on individual incentives.

In summary, very often the incentive for contractors is to keep the work force operative. A construction contractor will accept small projects with a small profit margin to maintain his forces and equipment between larger jobs; firms that provide professional services will often accept smaller profits for larger jobs; manufacturers and suppliers will often reduce the markup on goods to maintain volume of sales. Each of the concessions that professional and nonprofessional contractors will make is, conversely, an incentive to value management—to take advantage of in a facilities acquisition project.

13.4 INCENTIVIZATION

The future, with the economic constraints that will be imposed by escalation and energy situations, deserves the attention of value specialists. Achieving the optimum product for the minimum cost is likely to require innovative approaches and methods. We have discussed how government obtains both professional and nonprofessional services and materials under the rather rigid and restrictive procurement regulations. Today, changes to those practices are gradually incorporating incentive provisions. Perhaps it is a reaffirmation of the principles of free enterprise; perhaps it is recognition of the penalties of administrative delays. In any case, award and incentive contract structures are gaining impetus in government procurement practices. One weakness in the system of award and incentive contracting is that the remunerations do not flow down to the actual contributors. In most cases, the awards and fees are put into profits for stockholders rather than into direct benefits to those responsible for cost reductions and increased effectiveness. This is a refinement that can be expected to come about as new approaches to management are developed.

The analysis of incentives should lead the value specialist to the development of a facilities acquisition incentives plan. As described in Chapter 3, the systems approach provides for a contract work breakdown structure (CWBS), which depicts the work and cost elements that comprise a program. Certain of these elements, which are normally broken down into work package plans (WPP), can be considered as candidates for incentivization.

To illustrate, a programmatic construction cost of $2 million invites an estimate for professional services to prepare construction documents (final design) for $120,000, using a 6% factor. Assuming firm concepts and criteria are in hand and that all funding for both design and construction is available, work package plans for design and construction are prepared coincidentally. The design and engineering work is performed to lead the construction contractor's forces by packages. In this manner, the civil and structural work is initiated at the site, although the mechanical, electrical, and architectural detailing is not completed. It is the "fast-track" approach—an accepted technique that can result in time and cost savings to the owner/investor. The potential risk is that the design organization could be delayed or that some item of material that has long lead time might not be recognized at the proper time.

The usual contract structure for the acquisition process to get a lump sum bid from a construction contractor is foregone with the "fast-track" approach. With a construction manager, a large number of bids may be solicited for smaller increments of "packaged" work—an advantage. However, what is not obvious is that the designer should receive incentives to assure his commitment of forces to meet the schedules. In this respect, his fee should be structured for the awards and/or incentives that result in savings to a plan structured on conventional lines.

A value specialist should be prepared to identify the anticipated program cost for both the conventional and "fast-track" approach to contracting and to advocate the most appropriate approach before the contractor selection process. He must, however, consider the technical risk for the particular work package elements. For example, there is less risk, and therefore less contingency and room for savings, in earth-moving work than in making mechanical and electrical installations in a process plant. An analytical approach in identifying these aspects early in the program will provide valuable insights to incentivization.

13.5 VALUE MANAGEMENT IN AN OPERATING ENVIRONMENT

We have already explored the role of value management and value engineering in acquisition programs and projects. It remains to provide a framework for ongoing techniques to be applied during the life of the system and facilities.

To accommodate the application of VM/VE and provide the perception necessary to effect savings requires maintaining the cost structures established during the planning, design, construction, installation, and startup incident to acquisition. The operating and support cost estimates used in planning can be updated as the actual budgetary experience is gained. An overview of cost phasing is provided on Figure 13.3.

In many federal government projects, operating and support costs are exceeding the initial acquisition costs for facilities and production equipment. The primary reasons for the problem are increased costs of labor and, indirectly, energy. On a recent study of facilities for ammunition and explosives, for example, selected structures with on-going production processing were very nearly determined uneconomical for modernization. It was only through reductions in labor-dense activities that the addition of structural insulation and modern heating and ventilating systems were shown to be cost-effective solutions for the investment in old structures.

Under the current design-to-cost concept, potential cost performance tradeoffs (such as refurbishment versus replacement) and engineering changes must be evaluated in terms of their impact on the overall cost of ownership. The costs of refurbishment or replacement are considered to be acceptable provided the additional investment will be amortized within a reasonable period through lower operating and/or support costs.

To achieve a better balance between facility refurbishment and equipment repair or replacement, current operating and support costs are analyzed with reference to projections of the imminent and successive budgets. Included elements of the operating and support costs could be (as accounts payable identifies them):

- Labor costs (all types—administrative through janitorial)
- Materials (production and maintenance supplies, parts, and tools)
- Utilities (power, water, telephones, sewerage, etc.)
- Consumables (soft goods, stationery)
- Leases (reproduction equipment, vehicular equipment)
- Services (janitorial, gardening, security, trash haulout)

The overall life-cycle costs and phases depicted in Figure 13.3 are generally common to major programs. All costs to the owner are included regardless of how such costs are funded (assets, grants, loans, profits, etc.). This provides a common framework (Figure 13.4) for cost communications that will meet the following criteria:

1. It is compatible with both top-down and bottoms-up cost-estimating approaches. The framework (Figure 13.4) should not, by its composition, preclude use of either approach.
2. It must capture 100% of costs, not necessarily in every detail, but it must be comprehensive. While cost analysis detail is essential, the framework must still be manageable.

Within this cost structure, simplified in the example, the VM function must still be able to cope with other factors, which are discussed in the following pages.

13.5.1 STATIC AND TIME-PHASED COSTS

In Figure 13.4, the cost estimates and support phases are presented in 1975 dollars without regard to the time dimension. This is a normal practice in the planning stages of a program involving one or more major alternatives. The alternatives can be compared on a life-cycle basis in constant dollars; where differences exist in time taken to arrive at specific milestones, the economics of the time dimension are added. The constant-dollar cost estimates are usually displayed in budget year dollars of the fiscal year following the calendar year in which the cost estimate is made (base year dollars). For example, if the estimates were made in calendar year 1975, constant fiscal year 1976 (budget) dollars will be used. Costs can be shown in constant and current inflated dollars, time-phased by fiscal year and by the major appropriation made (rather than a breakdown of payments for every element).

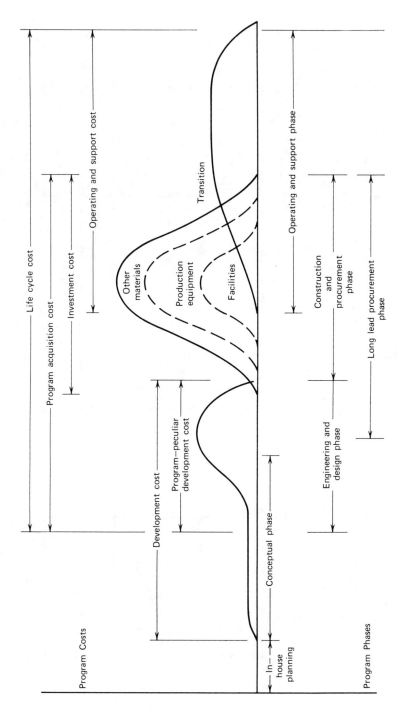

Figure 13.3 Program cost and phase structure.

Phased Costs / System Elements	Facilities				Equipment			Other material		
	House	Garage	Barn		Fridge	Washer	Drier	Beds	Tables	Rugs
Planning	0.1									
Concepts	0.2	0.1	0.2							
Engineering and design	6.0	0.6	3.0							
Long lead procurement					0.5	0.5	0.5			
Construction and procurement	100.0	10.0	50.0					0.5	0.5	5.0
Operating and support cost (transitional)	1.0	0.1	0.5							
Ten–year operating and support costs including tax (unescalated)	60.0	6.0	30.0		0.05	0.05	0.05	0.01	0.01	0.5
Element life–cycle costs	167.3	16.8	83.7		0.55	0.55	0.55	0.51	0.51	0.55
Life–cycle cost in constant year dollars = $271.02	267.8				1.65			1.57		

Figure 13.4 Work breakdown structure. Costs in thousands of 1975 dollars.

368

13.5.2   ASSETS AND SUNK COSTS

In the breakdown of costs (Figure 13.4) for the acquisition of house, barn, and garage, the costs of equipment and other materials were shown. Although these items are shown to be funded separately (i.e., not a part of the design and construction costs), they are nevertheless a part of the "system." They are identifiable as part of sunk costs in that repair or replacement cost is not included in the system cost if it is an "inherited asset" that will not be replaced. In government programs, each inherited asset is evaluated on its own merit and in terms of whether its use in connection with the system being costed will cause some future expense to the government. The terms are:

1. If there will be a future expense to the government, that expense must be included in some cost element in the system's life-cycle cost estimate.
2. If there will be no future expense such as a drawdown of inventory that will not be replaced, the cost of the item will be included in the total life-cycle cost but it will be highlighted as a sunk cost.

To illustrate, the cost of radio equipment that has been funded separately from an original acquisition (a facility or a vehicle) in which it will be used is included in the overall life-cycle estimate. If the radio equipment came to the program from stock that will not be replaced (i.e., it is obsolescent), the equipment cost will be identified as sunk cost. When it comes from stocks that will be replaced, it will be treated as any other cost of the system.

13.5.3   RANGE VERSUS POINT ESTIMATES

A point estimate does not reflect the uncertainty associated with it. It implies a precise cost for a specific point (in the phasing). The point estimate is normally used when the details of cost are rather exact, such as the midpoint of conventional construction projects that have been estimated by the architect-engineer and the successful construction contractor.

A range of costs should be provided to reflect any cost-estimating uncertainty. The level at which the ranges can be provided depends on the level of detail at which the costs are estimated. Within the data base and the cost-estimating approach employed, ranges should be presented at the highest aggregate level.

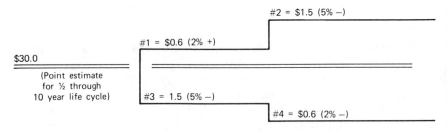

High and Low Estimate Assumptions

High

  #1. Increase utilities costs per by 50% from $44 to $66 per
      averaged per month over a year.

  #2. Increase on annual property tax and/or an assessment
      is imminent.

Low

  #3. Decrease number of occupants of house and barn by
      one half.

  #4. Extend interval between exterior and interior painting
      to 5 years.

Figure 13.5 Estimated operating and support cost sensitivity for facilities.

The energy crisis played havoc with operating and support cost estimates. The contingency against sudden future impact increases in fuel costs is now apportioned by utility companies as part of the users' billing. Experience, then, tells budgeters that there are both predictables and unpredictables in operating and support cost projections. The sensitivity of projected costs must be analyzed for all critical assumptions. This should include factors such as the impact of changes in performance characteristics, changes in configuration to meet performance requirements, schedule alterations, and an alternative operational or production process (as appropriate).

Cost sensitivity analysis is illustrated in Figure 13.5. It gives a point estimate halfway through the 10-year life expectancy period of $30,000 projected for the remaining 5 years. Two items are shown as assumed increases and estimates. Two low estimate assumptions are given to show an offsetting effect, although this may only occur where a ceiling is imposed on annual expenditures and offsets must be made.

13.5.4 ESTIMATING THE OPERATING AND SUPPORT EXPENSE

Too often a facility and its equipment fall into a state of disrepair because of a directed budget for its upkeep. In business, the gross profit must allow sufficient funds to assure that the investment can be wholly amortized over the life of the system and still remain an asset. Older structures and equipment can pose a problem for the value manager since an estimate for operating and support may have to include the additional expense of bringing them up to current codes and standards, preferably without loss of production or occupancy time.

It is also correct to assume that older buildings and machinery require more labor and material expense than newer ones. When older facilities are being dealt with, the value manager should not rely on past budgets and records to project new expenses. The true condition of the facility must be established and the costs of refurbishment and code compliance identified.

It will be beneficial to the value management function to consider use of the estimates and statistics that are prepared by the Building Owners and Managers Association (BOMA). Their information provides accurate assessments of operating and support expenses in tabular format for:

• Types of facilities by function and material.
• Age of facilities.
• Localities.

The revised cost of maintenance and the upgrade cost may provide information that will aid in establishing the correct life cycle for the total facility.

13.6 LIFE-CYCLE COST MANAGEMENT

Life-cycle costing concepts are having a major impact on the real estate and construction industry. A development or building project no longer can be treated as a series of fragmented activities such as planning, design, construction, and operation. Instead, the entire process from conception to disposal must be thought of as a system for procuring value; that is, an owner is committing and expending resources in return for which he expects something of value. That value may be a monetary return on total investment, a public service, an increase in the quality of life, and so forth. Furthermore, that value is affected considerably throughout the life cycle of the project by a myriad of circumstances, some within and some beyond the control of the owner, designer, builder, and operator.

Construction is a basic industry in a rapidly changing world. In the past, structures were erected to last for centuries, as evidenced by the pyramids of Egypt and Mexico and the medieval churches of Europe. Even in the United States within the past century, government, insurance, and bank buildings were built of monumental style to last for generations. But this is no longer so. Changing technology, the energy situation, unpredictable future conditions, and other factors certainly affect the life cycle of a modern project. As a result, today's structures are erected for a much shorter economic life cycle. For example, a building envelope may be constructed to last 50 to 60 years, but the interior may be constructed initially as luxury apartments with an expected economic life cycle of only 10 years. During that period the area may change or the space requirements in that area may change. At the end of the 10-year period, the interior may be recycled to whatever use is desirable—apartments, stores, offices, warehouses, or whatever.

Therefore a more precise system is needed to manage the life cycle of a development or building project. This is where life-cycle costing concepts become a valuable management and decision-making tool. Life-cycle costing and procurement concepts are merging into an overall systems approach for managing total project value.

13.6.1 PROPOSED LIFE-CYCLE COST SYSTEM

This section discusses a proposed life-cycle cost system that will meet the requirements stated above. The proposed system consists of four basic subsystems:

- Cost estimating subsystem.
- Cost monitoring and control subsystem.
- Project scheduling subsystem.
- Data bank/historical records system.

A basic requirement for all subsystems is the application of computer technology. The large amount of data to be accumulated, manipulated, and updated necessitates the use of an automated data processing system.

Cost Estimating Subsystem

The cost estimating subsystem is based on a standard methodology of cost categories, elements, and components. This methodology is tailored to the owner's or construction manager's operating procedures but must be standardized over all projects if it is to be of optimum value.

The methodology provides a common cost language that is used throughout the proposed life-cycle cost system. The cost estimating subsystem has the following capabilities:

- Perform economic analyses and studies.
- Prepare development cost estimate.
- Prepare design cost estimate.
- Prepare construction cost estimate.
- Project operation and maintenance costs for the building's estimated life.
- Project repair and alteration schedules and costs for the building's estimated life.
- Prepare a life-cycle cost estimate.
- Prepare equivalent uniform annual costs:
  —for target cost.
  —for each alternative.
- Estimate/evaluate building systems and components at any level of detail.
- Perform life-cycle cost tradeoff analyses:
  —for total building configuration.
  —for individual systems and components.
- Perform sensitivity analyses on variable parameters such as:
  —present value discount rate.
  —building life cycle.
  —depreciation rate.
  —appreciation rate.
  —capital recovery factor.
  —differential escalation factors.

The derivation of these interrelationships is of great value throughout the building's life cycle, especially during the planning and designing phases. The cost estimating subsystem provides the owner and his engineers the capability to design and trade off specific building systems while meeting basic function and cost requirements. It substantially enhances the ability to produce within the given cost constraints a facility that meets the owner's needs.

Cost Monitoring and Control Subsystem

The cost monitoring and control subsystem is applied at the level of detail necessary to adequately track costs during each phase of the building process. It must be capable of tracking all in-house and contract costs from project conception to user occupancy to final disposal.

Such a subsystem provides two major benefits. First, it facilitates the control and evaluation of construction progress payments. Second, it provides trends and forecasts for operation, maintenance, repair, and alterations costs throughout the life of the facility. This information is valuable in the decision-making process with respect to both the existing building and proposed projects.

Project Scheduling Subsystem

A major cause of poor project control is the lack of a standard scheduling system. For example, each contractor may have a unique scheduling technique. This represents a burden to the owner or his scheduling consultant, who must evaluate and monitor a variety of different reporting systems. A standard schedule reporting system helps ensure commonality in systems reporting. It also aids in comparing historical experience on other projects with the one under consideration. Thus lessons learned from one effort are more easily applied to future efforts. Furthermore, it facilitates schedule versus cost tradeoffs during the design phase. In the industry today there are many critical path method/scheduling systems. Therefore, the implementation of the project scheduling subsystem is not expected to be as difficult as the cost estimating or cost control subsystems.

Data Bank/Historical Records Subsystem

This subsystem is a dynamic feedback system that allows the owner to keep track of all costs related to the entire building process. It provides for the updating of estimates to actual costs; the removal of earlier costs to be supplanted by current costs; and the revision of projected rates of interest, discount, inflation, materials, and labor to reflect changing economic conditions. The data subsystem ties together the entire life-cycle cost system. It is the key to making the life-cycle cost system a valuable decision-making tool.

The concepts that have been discussed are necessary to the creation of a viable life-cycle cost system. However, the specific requirements of the mechanics of the system must be tailored to the individual user's needs. These in turn are influenced by the type of building in which the user is engaged and how much use will be made of the system.

13.6.2 CONTRACTING APPROACH TO LIFE-CYCLE COST MANAGEMENT

Expansion of the life-cycle cost concept requires a review of traditional contracting procedures. Traditionally, low initial cost was a major factor in awarding a contract. Under life-cycle costing, the major factor is total cost. It is important that the owner inform potential project participants that life-cycle costing is of major importance and that it is one of the primary considerations in selecting project contractors. Contracts must contain clauses specifically addressing life-cycle costing.

Contract provisions must require that the contractor submit ownership cost estimates along with the price bid for production or construction, regardless of whether the estimate is for the total facility design, for a building system, or for a major system component. To simplify matters, emphasis must be placed on total facility design and those systems or components constituting the bulk of the project cost. The contractor is required to perform continuous tradeoff analysis to minimize cost of ownership consistent with the overall needs of the owner. His contract contains a data item requiring a semiannual report on his continuing life-cycle cost analysis. Since changes made during actual construction can have a significant impact on costs, the contract must require that all change proposals contain an assessment of life-cycle cost impact.

Ideally the contract contains incentive provisions—both positive and negative—for reducing total ownership costs. The objective is to provide an incentive for the designers, constructors, and manufacturers to emphasize operation and maintenance costs during design and construction. For this to work, there must be followup procedures to validate initial contractor estimates. A target cost for operation and maintenance is established at the time of contract award. This cost can be in dollars, units of energy consumption, or factors of reliability such as mean time between failures. During early operation a followup measurement program is conducted to determine actual performance. The positive or negative provision of the contract is triggered by comparing actual costs to target costs.

13.6.3 WARRANTIES AS A LIFE-CYCLE COST MANAGEMENT TOOL

An additional contracting technique for encouraging designers and constructors to develop and build facilities with optimal minimum life-cycle cost is the warranty. Where their use is suitable, warranties provide significant benefits. Perhaps the major difference between some standard approaches and the warranty approach to life-cycle cost management is that in the normal approach the owner attempts to control operation and maintenance costs by closely prescribing system factors that influence them. In reality, however, these costs depend largely on the designer and contractors' efforts during planning, design, and construction. They alone can direct their efforts to minimizing total ownership costs, yet have little economic motivation to do so.

Consider how the use of a warranty provision might affect this situation. The contract warranty is a provision in which the contractor:

• Is provided with a monetary incentive to develop and construct a design that will exceed, in a way favorable to the owner, certain operation and maintenance target costs.

• Agrees that, during a specified or measured period of use, he will repair or replace, within a specified turnaround time, all systems that fail. If the contract is definitive in requiring that virtually all malfunctions be corrected by the contractor, there is no problem in defining failure.

Such a provision can be placed in the designer or construction manager's contract. In this situation the designer or construction manager is responsible for the overall design. Although more complicated, warranty provisions can be placed in individual contracts. Here individual contractors are then responsible only for their own contract work.

A fixed or variable incentive price is agreed upon during negotiation of the contract, preferably in competition. The objective of the warranty is to motivate and provide an incentive to contractors to design and construct facilities whose systems have low failure rates as well as low operation and maintenance costs. This warranty concept can be introduced at any point during the building cycle, but the maximum benefit is realized if it is introduced as early as possible.

13.7 OUTLOOK

The steady growth of value analysis, value engineering, and value management on a national basis has had dramatic results. Case histories have been brought to the notice of highly industrialized nations abroad. It is not inconceivable that the next decade will see the precepts of both the systems approach and value management incorporated into engineering curriculums. From the viewpoint of the experienced engineer-manager, "systems" and "value" work are practical, real-world applications rather than theoretical. At the present time, technology, science, and economics are taught as separate disciplines. The same is true of the business aspects that are inherent in procurement and contracting. Today's engineer-manager must have a first-hand working knowledge of administrative processes. Since it is gained through "real world" experience rather than formal academic processes, it is not likely to be either progressive or innovative because it is cursory rather than in-depth. The blend of technical and administrative skills needed by the value specialist cannot be gained by chance. Value analysis needs to be performed by full-time, dedicated specialists who are chartered organizationally.

Value management is likely to gain inroads into startup, training, operations, and maintenance. There is a distinct overlap between value analysis and the objectives of industrial engineering. Whereas the latter is concerned primarily with time and motion factors and human engineering in *producing* the product, the former is interested in the function and cost of the materials and the product as well as possible materials sources and disposition of the product.

BIBLIOGRAPHY

Books

Drucker, Peter F., *Management: Tasks, Responsibilities, Practices,* Harper & Row, New York, 1974.

Falcon, William D. (Ed.), *Value Analysis/Value Engineering,* American Management Association, New York, 1964.

General Services Administration, *Value Engineering Handbook* PBS-P80101.1., General Services Administration, Washington, D.C.

Grossman, Lee, *The Change Agent,* American Management Association, New York, 1974.

Heyel, Carl (Ed.), *The Encyclopedia of Management,* Second Edition, Van Nostrand Reinhold, New York, 1974.

Kepner, Charles H. and Tregoe, Benjamin B., *The Rational Manager,* McGraw-Hill, New York, 1965.

Macedo, M. C., Goldhaber, S., and Jha, C. K., *Construction Management: Principles and Practices,* Wiley-Interscience, New York, 1977.

Meller, E. D., *Value Management: Value Engineering and Cost Reduction,* Addison-Wesley, Reading, Mass., 1971.

Miles, L. D., *Techniques of Value Analysis and Engineering,* McGraw-Hill, New York, 1961.

Morgan, John S., *Managing Change,* McGraw-Hill, New York, 1972.

Mudge, A. E., *Value Engineering: A System Approach,* McGraw-Hill, New York, 1971.

Parnes, S. J. and Harding, H. F., *A Source Book for Creative Thinking.* Chas. Scribner & Sons, New York, 1962.

Articles

Anderson, Richard H. and Dixon, Thomas E., "Design To Cost Models: Helping Program Managers Manage Programs." *Defense Management Journal,* January 1976.

Arnold, John E., "The Creative Engineer," *The Yale Scientific Magazine,* March 1956.

Bennett, John J., "Comment," *Defense Management Journal,* January 1976.

Bennett, John J., "Design To Cost," *Commanders Digest,* August 12, 1976.

Boden, William H., "Designing for Life-Cycle Cost," *Defense Management Journal,* January 1976.

Boileau, O. C., "I Dreamed We Went Nowhere In Our Solid Gold Airplane," *Defense Management Journal,* January 1976.

Bradtmiller, P., O'Rourke, J. J., et al., "Energy: The New Planning Parameter," *Navy Civil Engineer*, Fall 1974.

Collins, Dwight E., "Models: A Key To Air Force Life Cycle Cost Implementation," *Defense Management Journal*, January 1976.

Earles, Don, "Techniques for a Multifaceted Discipline," *Defense Management Journal*, January 1976.

Goldman, A. S., "Problems in Life Cycle Support Cost Estimation," *Naval Research Logistics Quarterly*, March 1969.

Macedo, M. C., "Value Engineering, A New Tool in Construction," *Baltimore Engineer*, September 1974.

Raudsepp, Eugene, "The Creative Engineer," *Machine Design*, May 28, June 11, June 25, 1959.

Shorey, Russell R., "Managing Downstream Weapons Acquisition Costs," *Defense Management Journal*, January 1976.

Stansberry, J. W., "Source Selection and Contracting Approach to Life Cycle Cost Management," *Defense Management Journal*, January 1976.

Wojciechowski, F. X., "FAST diagram—Its Many Uses," *Proceedings, SAVE Regional Conference, Detroit*, October, 1972.

Reports

Comptroller General of the United States, *Report to Congress: Greater Emphasis on Competition Is Needed in Selecting Architects and Engineers for Federal Projects*, U.S. General Accounting Office, Washington, D.C., 1976.

Comptroller General of the United States, *Report to Congress: Need for Increased Use of Value Engineering, A Proven Cost Saving Technique, in Federal Construction*. U.S. General Accounting Office, Washington, D.C., 1974.

Department of Defense, *Reduce Costs and Improve Equipment*, U.S. Government Printing Office, Washington, D.C., 1967.

Federal Construction Council, *Value Engineering in Federal Construction Agencies*, National Academy of Sciences, Washington, D.C., 1969.

General Services Administration, *A Report on the Life Cycle Planning and Budgeting Model*, General Services Administration, Washington, D.C., 1976.

General Services Administration, *Life Cycle Costing in the Public Buildings Service*, General Service Administration, Washington, D.C., 1976.

Hearings (Value Engineering) before the Subcommittee on Buildings and Grounds of the Committee on Public Works, United States Senate, U.S. Government Printing Office, Washington, D.C., 1973.

Operating and Support Cost Guide, Department of the Army Pamphlet No. 11-4, April 1976.

O'Rourke, J. J., *Preliminary Program of Facility Requirements for National Oceanic and Atmospheric Administration (NOAA)*, The Ralph M. Parsons Co., Pasadena, CA, June 1975.

O'Rourke, J. J., Whitman, K. E., et al., *STS Ground Support System*, USAF Technical Report AF-SAMSO-TR-72-145, March 1972.

SAVE, *Proceedings of the 1976 International Conference, Society of American Value Engineers, Southfield, Michigan, 1976*.

SAVE, *Proceedings, Eleventh National Meeting, Society of American Value Engineers, May 1971.*

SAVE, *Proceedings, Regional Conference, Detroit, Society of American Value Engineers, October 1972.*

SAVE, *Proceedings, Eighth National Meeting, Society of American Value Engineers, April 1968.*

SAVE, *Proceedings, Fifth National Meeting, Society of American Value Engineers, April 1965.*

INDEX

Adjacency analysis, 87-89
  measure of effectiveness, 87-88
Adjacency chart, 81
  relationship ratings, 85
Advertised procurement, 215
  ASPR requirements for, 216
AE contract: pricing structures, 132
  services and organizations, 133
Algorithm: bond energy, 77-91
  suboptimal, 88
Analysis phase: checklist, 247
  key questions, 246
  objective, 246
  techniques used, 246-247
Architect-engineer, 358
  selection of, 359
Armed Services Procurement Regulations, 216-219
  incentive provisions of, 8
Arnold, John E., 255
Audit system, 26, 28-29

Baseline, 149, 277
  performance requirements, 276
Base year: dollars, 305
  prices, 304
  values, 304
Bond energy algorithm, 77-91
  activity division of, 81
  adjacency analysis, 87
  adjacency chart, 81
  chart production methods, 84-85
  developing facility requirements, 80-87
  development planning, 89-91
  flow analysis, 84
Brainstorming, 269

definition of, 264
rules for, 265
Building systems concept, 110-111
Building systems and costs, 134
Bytheway, Charles W., 231, 238

Capital recovery factor, 295-296, 299, 305
Case studies: life-cycle cost analysis, 319-327
  R. D. Bailey lake project, 341-350
  signal school, 350-356
  site selection, 327-341
Cash flow: annual, 277
  equivalent uniform, 296
  future, 292
  individual, 294
  multiple, 294
Changes clause, 217-219
  provisions of, 218
Compensation, 107, 216
  incentive basis, 108
  sharing, 108
Conference technique: brainstorming, 264-265
  Gordon technique, 265-266
Configuration, 370
  affect on procurement, 126, 131
  building, 283, 289, 290, 303
  build-to, 149, 200
  management, 148, 149, 200, 203
Constant-dollar cost estimate, 366
Construction and value management, 107-111
  construction manager, 107, 207
  contractor participation, 108
  incentive program, 108

subcontractor participation, 108
Construction contractor, 360
Construction management, 133-135
    approaches to, 133
    creative thinking in, 254
    methods of compensation, 134
Consultants, 230
    services, 226
    use of, 104
Contract: activity reward, 134
    award, 363, 364
    cost-plus-fixed-fee, 135, 137
    cost reimbursement, 216-219
    firm-fixed price, 136, 137, 141,
        216-219, 220, 359
    fixed-price-with-escalation, 141
    government, modification of, 217
    and life-cycle cost management,
        374
    selection process, 128
Contract clauses, 215-225, 226
    changes, 217-219
    program requirement, 219, 220
    supplemental agreement, 217, 219
    value incentive, 219-220
Contractor data requirements list, 206
Contractor participation, 219
Contractor's cost/schedule manage-
        ment system, 144
Contractor's management control
        system, 141
    objectives of, 141-142
Contract work breakdown structure,
        142, 364
Cost: acquisition, 64, 69, 71, 75, 99,
        101, 107, 112, 273-277, 283,
        288-290, 304
    analysis, 275
    analysis, factor, 126
    annual, 304
    anticipated, 360
    apportionment of, 203
    consequences, 277
    constant-dollar estimate, 366
    construction, 283
    control, 94
    C/SPC, 111, 113-114
    design to, 76, 111, 112
    discretionary treatment of, 126
    effectiveness, 116-117

efficiencies, 277
energy, 273, 304
external, 148
facilities construction, 67
first, 101
functional use, 283, 287
historical, 289, 299
internal, 148
involuntary treatment of, 126
labor, 70
life-cycle, 59, 64, 101, 107, 111-
    113, 273, 277
loss of revenue, 283, 287
maintenance, 69, 276, 283, 287,
    288, 304
material, 70
operating, 64, 273, 276, 283, 287,
    288, 289, 299, 304
operating and support, 365, 370
ownership, 273-276, 288, 290, 297
point estimate, 369
programmatic estimate, 64
range of, 369
recurring, 277, 304
relative, 70, 101
relevant, 288
rough order of magnitude, 67
sensitivity analysis, 370
sunk, 292, 302, 369
target, 61, 64
unit, 67, 90
unnecessary, 3, 24, 40-43, 117
utility, 304
Cost advantages, 137, 140
Cost awareness program: cost effec-
        tiveness, 116
    cost reduction, 116
    maintainability, 117
    quality assurance, 117
    reliability, 117
    standardization, 117
    trade-off analysis, 118
    zero defects, 117
Cost effectiveness study, 116
Cost estimating, 247
    capabilities of subsystem, 373
    rough-order-of-magnitude, 359
Cost monitoring and control sub-
        system: benefits of, 374
    components of, 374

Cost of capital, 274
Cost reduction, 140, 363
    candidate concept, 62
    estimating, 134-135
    functional approach to, 1
    goal method, 210
    identification of unnecessary cost, 3
    program, 116
    proposal, 121
    targets, 215
    twofold approach to, 62
    value specialist, 62
    widespread techniques of, 4
Cost reimbursement contract, 216-219
    types of, 217
Cost responsibility: degree of, 135
Cost savings goals, 215
Cost/Schedule Control Systems Criteria, 140-145
    implementation, 142-145
    overview, 141-142
Cost/scheduling systems, 148
Cost sensitivity analysis, 370
Cost visibility worksheet, 235
Cost techniques, 111-114, 235
Cost-volume relationship curve, 127
CPM scheduling systems, 113
Crawford, R.P., 267
Creative atmosphere, 259
    development of, 260-261
Creative engineer: attributes of, 255-257
Creative idea generation, 264
Creative process: steps in, 263-264
Creativity, 254-272
    checklist, 266, 270-272
    creative process, 263
    definition of, 255
    in value management, 261-263
    negative factors affecting, 257-260
    positive factors affecting, 260-261
    problem solving, 264-269
    summary, 269
Critical path, 314, 316
Critical path method, 144, 145
C/SPC, 111
    advantages of, 113-114

Data: bank, 139, 289

historical, 304
    requirements for collection, 140-141
Data item description, 206
Data management, 148, 203, 206
Decision making, 306, 314-318
    alternatives, 315-316
    follow-up, 316-317
    implementation, 316-317
    objectives, 314
    potential problems, 316
    priorities, 315
    procedure, 314
    tentative decision, 316
De-escalation methods, 304
Design, 100-107
    concept formulation, 103
    effort, 99
    final, 104
    present methods of, 101-102
    review, 61, 104
    task team, 104
    team approach, 102
    tentative, 103-104
    workshop concept, 105-107
Design to cost, 365
    and life-cycle cost, 74-77
    approach, 74
    as cost control, 75
    aspects of, 111-112
    cost parameter, 291
    implementation of, 112
    technical requirements, 291
Developmental phase: checklist, 249-250
    key question, 247
    objective, 247
    techniques used, 248-249
Deviation, 308-309, 312
Differential escalation rate, 305
Discount factors, 293
Discount rate, 292-296, 299, 305
    forms of, 295
Dollars: base year, 366
    budget year, 366
DTC/LCC analysis, 112

Economic life: definition of, 279
    factors affecting, 279, 282
Edison, Thomas, A., 6

Einstein, Albert, 256
End item, 149
Energy
    crisis, 60, 277, 282, 370
    impact on value management, 71
    planning parameter, 71-74
Environmental protection regulations,
    60
Equivalent uniform annual cost, 296,
    297-299, 305
Erlicher, Harry, 1
Escalation: factor, 299
    methods, 304

Facilities acquisition program, 122,
    131, 133, 135, 140, 142,
    147, 148, 360, 365
    candidate quantity procurement
        items, 126
    contract and statement of work
        preparation, 123-124
    market research, 124-127
    specialized aspects of, 123
Facility: characteristics, 65
    developing requirements of, 80-87
    functions of, 65, 67
FAST, 231-239
    characteristics of, 233
    definition of, 233
FAST diagram: brainstorming,
        238-239
    definition of, 233
    use of, 235-238
Fast-track approach, 364
Feasibility systems, 149
Federal procurement regulations,
    132
    limit set by, 128
Financial incentives: direct, 362
    indirect, 362
Fixed-price contracts, 216-219, 220
    types of, 217
Flow analysis, 84
Follow-up and implementation phase:
        objectives, 251-252
Forced relationship technique, 268
Free association techniques: brain-
        storming, 264-265
    Gordon technique, 265-266
Function: block, 235

definition of, 233
determination of, 242-243
evaluation of, 243
types of, 234
value analysis technique, 2
Functional analysis, 233, 239
Functional Analysis System Technique,
    231-239
    characteristics of, 233
    definition of, 233
Functional description, 243
Functional use cost, 283
    definition of, 287

Gilbreth, Frank and Lillian, 3
Gordon, William J. J., 265
Gordon technique, 265-266
Government contracts: modification
        of, 217, 219
Grant, Eugene L., 3
Guidance documents, 127

Human factors, 38
    and unnecessary costs, 40-42
    motivation and incentives, 43
    personnel, 45
    principles of, 38-40
    resisting innovation, 43
Human relations, 38
    principles of, 38-40
HVAC systems, 282, 290

Incentive: AE, 359
    and productivity, 361
    construction contractor, 359
    individual, 363
    owner, 360
    savings, 361
    value, 357
Incentive clause, 121
    government, 108
    in subcontract, 108
    sharing arrangements, 108
Incentive contract, 25, 363, 364
Incentive plans: financial, 362-363
    group, 363
    nonfinancial, 361-362
Incentive price: fixed or variable, 376
Incentivization, 363-365
    facilities acquisition incentives plan,
        364

Index code system, 203
Information phase: checklist, 243
  key questions, 241
  objectives, 240-241
  techniques used, 241
Inherited asset, 369
Innovation, 254, 259, 260
  management of, 21-22
  resistance, to, 43
Input-output technique, 268-269
  steps in use of, 268
Interface, 203, 209
  and cost, 126, 131

Job plan: functional analysis effort
    of, 231
  key features of, 240
  phases of, 240-252
  purpose of, 252
  sequence of, 253
  summary of, 252-253

Life cycle, 98, 207, 220
  analysis of cost, 278, 282
  and system complexity, 289
  cost, 273, 277, 290
  cost estimate, 277, 278
  costing, 15, 273-305
  definition of, 278
  definition of cost, 282
  estimate, 304
  expenditure of smallest cost, 100
  magnitude of cost, 283
  ownership savings, 121
  phases of, 278-279
  savings, 19
  total cost, 283, 290
  values, 282
  versus economic life, 279
Life-cycle cost, 59, 64, 101, 107,
    111-113, 140
  analysis, areas of activity, 112
  and design to cost, 74-77
  estimate, 304
Life-cycle cost analysis, 290-292,
    295-297, 375
  alternatives, 301-302
  criteria, 288
  EUAC, 305

  initial cost, 304
  newness to industry, 282
  objective of, 287
  operating profile, 303-304
  recurring cost, 304-305
  requirements, 301
  sensitivity test, 305
  time phasing, 302-303
Life cycle costing, 273-305
  application to economic analysis,
    277
  basic concepts, 289-300
  definition of, 273, 289
  problem areas, 275-276
  technique, 273
  visibility in, 289
Life-cycle cost management, 371-376
  capabilities, 373
  contracting approach to, 374-375
  proposed system, 372
  warranty approach to, 375-376
Localization of services, 125
Loss of revenue, 283
  definition, 287

Macroscopic data structure, 77
Maintainability, 117
Major line component, 81, 87, 89
Market research, 124-127
  approaches to, 126
Master equipment list, 200, 203
Matrix: analytical, 65
  clumpy, 77
  data, 77, 87-88
  facility characteristics, 65
  symmetric, 88
Matrix planning: acquisition tabula-
    tions, 67-69
  functions and characteristics, 65-67
  maintenance tabulations, 69-71
  operations tabulations, 69-71
  unit costs, 67
Maximum cost ceiling, 291
McCormick, Dr. William T., Jr., 87
McMorrow, Brig. Gen. F. J., 7
Measure of effectiveness, 87-88
  unnormalized, 87
Miles, Lawrence D., 1-3, 12-13
Morphological analysis, 266-267
  steps in, 267

Murther, Richard, 81

Negotiated procurement, 215-216

Operating function: responsibilities of, 31
Operations and maintenance planning, 131
Opportunity cost, 295, 296, 305
Optimization, 357
Organization, 15, 29-37
    factors influencing value management, 24
    in procuring activity, 36
    in producing activity, 34
    line, 62
    staff, 62
    of value management functions, 31

Percent profit improvement, 211
Personnel: categories of, 45
    motivative and incentive forces, 45-47
    training of, 47-57
Phased construction, 278
Point estimate, 369, 370
Potential problem analysis, 117, 306
    and risks, 318
    procedure, 317
Predicted expenses guidelines, 127
    formulation of, 128
Preliminary cost estimates, 128
Preliminary engineering reports, 128
Presentation phase: checklist, 251
    objective, 250
    techniques used, 250-251
Present value, 292-296, 305
    definition, 292
    factors, 293, 299
    formula, 293-295
Present worth, 292
Price level: changes, 296-297, 305
    expected, 304
    historical, 304
Problem: characteristics of, 308
    specification, 312
Problem analysis, 317, 318
    definition, 311
    determination of cause, 312
    problem specification, 312

systems approach to, 311-314
Problem solving, 261, 306-318
    approaches to, 262-263
    characteristics of, 115
    concepts, 307
    rules for, 263
    techniques, 254, 264-269, 306
Procedural review points, 36
Procurement, 122-139
    alternatives, in facilities acquisition program, 125-126
    function, 122
    two-step, 131
    types of, 215
Procurement planning, 114, 135
Productivity: gains, 134-135
    reward, 134
Profit margin, 360
Programmatic estimate: of cost, 149
    reliability of, 135, 136
Project: management controls, 147
    requirements, 220
    responsibility, 23-24
    value specialist, 35
Purchase order, 126
Purchasing, 138

Quality assurance, 117

Randolph, Senator Jennings, 10, 11-12
Range of cost, 369
Raudsepp, Eugene, 255
Relationship ratings: means of establishing, 85
Reliability, 117
Reporting system, 26, 27-28
    by exception, 27
    definition of, 27
Residual value: definition of, 292
Requests for proposals, 206, 213
Roadblocks: definition of, 4
    quotations, 5
    recognition of, 5
Rogers, Dr. Carl, 261

Salvage value, 292
S.A.V.E., 211, 212, 239
Savings: sharing of, 108, 121
    targets, 26-27

to cost ratio, 215
Scheduling techniques, 111-114
Senate Resolution 172, 10-11
Sensitivity analysis, 129, 288, 299-300, 305
Sharing of savings, 121
  collateral, 108
  incentive, 219, 220
  instant, 108
Specification: analysis, 61
  hierarchy, 149
  procedure, 309
Speculation phase: checklist, 245-246
  key questions, 244
  objective, 243-244
  techniques used, 244-245
Standardization, 117, 131
Subcontract: incentive clause, 108
Suboptimization, 101
Sunk cost, 292, 302, 369
Supplemental agreement, 217, 219
Surveillancce, 129, 133, 203
  initial, 125
  subsequent, 125
Systems approach, 110
  application of value management through, 63-74
  bond energy algorithm, 80
  evolution of, 59, 60
  matrix planning, 65
Systems/value management: objective, 93
  philosophy, 91-93

Target cost, 64, 210, 375, 376
Task team, 104
Taylor, Frederic W., 3
Towne, Henry R., 3
Tradeoff, 125, 213, 289
  alternatives, 139
  analysis, 118, 290, 292, 297, 375
  definition of analysis, 290
  preconcept, 64
  studies, 61, 290
Training, 104
  indoctrination lecture, 51, 54
  workshop seminar, 48
Uncertainty, 299-300, 305
Uniform annual cost, 274, 288
Uniform annuity factor, 295

Value analysis, 1, 63, 98, 138, 145, 206, 376, 377
  definition of, 13
  function, 2
  priority selection system, 27
  progress of, 6-8
  scope of, 3
Value clauses: governing, 207
Value engineering, 1, 3, 4, 13, 138, 361, 376
  comprehensive treatment of, 8
  establishment of, 7
  incentive provisions, 8
  progress of, 6-8
  roadblocks, 4, 5
  Senate Resolution 172, 10-12
Value improvement, 103, 104
Value incentive clause, 219-220
Value management, 13, 254, 255, 269
  activities, 63
  application of, 99, 207-230
  benefits of, 15, 16-20
  and building systems concept, 110-111
  categories of resistance to, 15
  changes, circulation of, 118-119
    sources of, 95-96
  compensation for services, 107
  and cost awareness program, 116-118
  creativity in, 261-263
  definition of, 14
  degree of visibility, 92
  design reviews, 61
  effort, 37, 208-209, 211-214
  evolution of, 60
  federal agency program, 119-121
  function, 135, 213, 366, 371
  goals, 208, 357
  human factors of, 38-47
  incentive clause, 62
  influential factors, 24
  internal effort, 109
  job plan, 240-253
  management control of, 26-29
  management participation, 15, 20-29
  methodology, 105, 208, 209, 227, 228, 230

objectives, 208
and organization, 31-34
outlook for, 357-377
philosophy, 57, 91
procedural review points, 36
and procurement planning, 122
program implementation, 24-26
project value specialist, 35
resources, 98, 100
specification analysis, 61
study team, 35, 216, 246, 306
and systems approach, 63-74
target costs, 61
techniques, 207, 274, 307
Value management opportunities:
      construction, 107-111
   costing, 111-114
   design, 100-107
   high potential areas, 95-98
   operations and maintenance, 111
   problem solving, 115-116
   procurement planning, 114
   scheduling, 111-114
   timing of, 98-100
   various programs, 119-121
Value management organization, 15,
      29-37
   co-ordinating function, 30
   definition of, 29
   key variables, 31-34
   operating function, 31
Value management program, 219, 226
   achievements of, 215
   activities of, 214
   control of, 26
   effectiveness of, 210-215
   evaluating, 211
   implementation of, 24-26
   in-house, 208, 210, 211, 230
   management support, 212-214
   organizational support, 212-214
   purpose of, 207
Value management training, 209, 213,
      214, 226, 227
   implementation of, 56
   indoctrination lectures, 51-54
   informal approaches, 55-56
   in-house, 56, 57
   on-the-job, 55
   rotational job assignments, 55
   selection criteria, 54-55
   sources of, 57
   workshop seminar, 48-51

Value management workshops, 207,
      227-230
Value manager, 89, 211, 213, 214,
      226, 227, 229, 241, 250,
      371
   responsibilities of, 209-210
   selection of, 208-209
Value proposal, 213, 250, 252
   disseminating information of, 110
   elements of, 109-110
Value specialist, 3, 62, 148, 203, 206,
      214, 364, 377
Value studies, 109, 208, 210, 214,
      215, 220, 226, 227-228,
      230, 239, 251, 265, 269
   advantages of, 111
   data required, 242
   functional analysis, 233
   fundamentals of, 231
   in-house, 120
   scope of, 234
   team, 209, 227, 230, 241, 243,
      244, 248, 252, 253
VA/VE program: establishment of, 6
   progress of, 6-8
Vendor/supplier evaluations, 138-139
Visibility: of unit cost, 67
   of value management, 92

Warranty, 375
   contract, 376
   provision, 376
Whiting, Charles S., 268
Winn, Congressman Larry, 10, 16
Work breakdown structure, 142
Work package plans, 364
Workshop seminar, 227
   characteristics of, 48-51
   concept, 105-107
   curriculum, 51
   duration and session schedule, 49
   number of participants, 49
   objectives of, 48
   priority of attendance, 49
   project features, 50
   purpose of, 48
   seminar leadership, 50
   team, 230
   team organization, 49-50
   team responsibility, 49-50
   vendor participation, 51

Zero defects program, 117